Dedicated to
Alexis, Madeleine, and Katherine,
who teach me as they learn (AJC)
and to
Tracy (HBK)

TABLE OF CONTENTS

PARKIN ◆ BADE

MICROECONOMICS
CANADA IN THE GLOBAL ENVIRONMENT

STUDY GUIDE
THIRD EDITION

AVI J. COHEN
York University

HARVEY B. KING
University of Regina

Addison-Wesley Publishers Limited

Don Mills, Ontario • Reading, Massachusetts • Menlo Park, California
New York • Wokingham, England • Amsterdam • Bonn
Sydney • Singapore • Tokyo • Madrid • San Juan • Paris • Seoul
Milan • Mexico City • Taipei

ISBN 0-201-42959-4

Printed and bound in Canada.

C D E -MP- 01 00 99 98

Executive Editor:	**Joseph Gladstone**
Managing Editor:	**Linda Scott**
Acquisitions Editor:	**Dawn Lee**
Copy Editor:	**Pamela Erlichman**
Production Coordinator:	**Melanie van Rensburg**
Manufacturing Coordinator:	**Sharon Latta Paterson**
Cover Design:	**Anthony Leung**
Desktop:	**Nelson Gonzalez**

INTRODUCTION

Before You Begin...

Our experience has taught us that what first-year economics students want most from a study guide is help in mastering course material in order to do well on examinations. We have developed this *Study Guide* to respond specifically to that demand. Using this *Study Guide* alone, however, is not enough to guarantee that you will do well in your course. In order to help you overcome the problems and difficulties that most first-year students encounter, we have some general advice on how to study, as well as some specific advice on how to best use this *Study Guide*.

Some Friendly Advice

The study of economics requires a different style of thinking than what you may encounter in other courses. Economists make extensive use of assumptions to break down complex problems into simple, analytically manageable parts. This analytical style, while not ultimately more demanding than the styles of thinking in other disciplines, feels unfamiliar to most students and requires practice. As a result, it is not as easy to do well in economics simply on the basis of your raw intelligence and high school knowledge as it is in many other first-year courses. Many students who come to our offices are frustrated and puzzled by the fact that they are getting A's and B's in their other courses but only a C or worse in economics. They have not recognized that the study of economics is different and requires practice. In order to avoid a frustrating visit to your instructor after your first test, we suggest you do the following.

Don't rely solely on your high school economics. If you took high school economics, you will have seen the material on supply and demand which your instructor will lecture on in the first few weeks. Don't be lulled into feeling that the course will be easy. Your high school knowledge of economic concepts will be very useful, but it will not be enough to guarantee high marks on exams. Your college or university instructors will demand much more detailed knowledge of concepts and ask you to apply them in new circumstances.

Keep up with the course material on a weekly basis. Read the appropriate chapter in the textbook before your instructor lectures on it. In this initial reading, don't worry about details or arguments you can't quite follow—just try to get a general understanding of the basic concepts and issues. You may be amazed at how your instructor's ability to teach improves when you come to class prepared. As soon as your instructor has finished covering a chapter, complete the corresponding *Study Guide* chapter. Avoid cramming the day before or even just the week before an exam. Because economics requires practice, cramming is an almost certain recipe for failure.

Keep a good set of lecture notes. Good lecture notes are vital for focusing your studying. Your instructor will only lecture on a subset of topics from the textbook. The topics your instructor covers in a lecture should usually be given priority when studying. Also give priority to studying the figures and graphs covered in the lecture. If you use the *Notetaker* (see description below) to insert key figures and graphs in your notes, you will have a clear and concise study aid.

Instructors do differ in their emphasis on lecture notes or the textbook, so ask early on in the course which is more important in reviewing for exams— lecture notes or the textbook. If your instructor answers that both are important, then ask the following, typically economic question: at the margin, which will be more beneficial—spending an extra hour re-reading your lecture notes or an extra hour re-reading the textbook? This question assumes that you have read each textbook chapter twice (once before lecture for a general understanding, and then later for a thorough understanding); that you have prepared a good set of lecture notes; and that you have worked through all of the problems in the appropriate *Study Guide* chapters. By applying this style of analysis to the problem of efficiently allocating your study time, you are already beginning to think like an economist!

Use your instructor and/or teaching assistants for help. When you have questions or problems with course material, come to the office to ask questions. Remember, you are paying for your education and instructors are there to help you learn. We are often amazed at how few students come to see us during office hours. Don't be shy. The personal contact that comes from one-on-one tutoring is professionally gratifying for us as well as (hopefully) beneficial for you.

Form a study group. A very useful way to motivate your studying and to learn economics is to discuss the course material and problems with other students. Explaining the answer to a question out loud is a very effective way of discovering how well you understand the question. When you answer a question only in your head, you often skip steps in the chain of reasoning without realizing it. When you are forced to explain your reasoning aloud, gaps and mistakes quickly appear, and you (with your fellow group members) can quickly correct your reasoning. The True/False/Uncertain questions in the *Study Guide* and the Review and Critical Thinking questions at the end of each textbook chapter are good study group material. You might also get together after having worked the *Study Guide* problems, but before looking at the answers, and help each other solve unsolved problems.

Work old exams. One of the most effective ways of studying is to work through exams your instructor has given in previous years. Old exams give you a feel for the style of question your instructor may ask, and give you the opportunity to get used to time pressure if you force yourself to do the exam in the allotted time. Studying from old exams is not cheating, as long as you have obtained a copy of the exam legally. Some institutions keep old exams in the library, others in the department or at the student union. Upper-year students who have previously taken the course are usually a good source as well. Remember, though, that old exams are a useful study aid only if you use them to understand the reasoning behind each question. If you simply memorize answers in the hopes that your instructor will repeat the identical question, you are likely to fail. From year to year, instructors routinely change the questions or change the numerical values for similar questions.

Use the other study aids. In addition to the *Study Guide*, there are two other study aids that we believe are worth purchasing for the help they will provide in mastering course material and doing well on examinations. However, don't just take our word for it— ask students who have used these aids for their opinions.

The *NoteTaker* (previously called *Graphpad*) contains all of the graphs from the textbook that your instructor is likely to use in class. This means that you do not have to spend time in class copying the graphs. Instead, just tear off the appropriate graph from the *NoteTaker* and insert it into your notebook. The graphs are printed on notebook-sized pages with three-ring binder holes already punched for convenience. In addition to the graphs, the pages are covered with grids for drawing additional graphs or taking notes. By eliminating tedious copying, the *NoteTaker* allows you to concentrate on understanding what your instructor is saying. And better understanding translates into better grades.

Economics in Action is a state-of-the-art interactive software for IBM-compatible computers. It is an integrated tutorial, graphing, demonstration, and testing program that covers all the main themes in the textbook using three modes. The tutorial mode places you in an economics-related job situation and leads you through assignments that reveal and explore

economic concepts and principles. The free mode allows you to interact with economic models by changing parameters and observing the effects on graphs. The quiz mode gives you graphical or data-related multiple-choice questions. When you select an answer, you are given a detailed explanation (and graphical illustration) of why your answer is right or wrong. All software modes are closely integrated with the textbook.

Using the Study Guide

You should only attempt to complete a chapter in the *Study Guide* after you have read the corresponding textbook chapter and listened to your instructor lecture on the material. Each *Study Guide* chapter contains the following sections.

Key Concepts   This first section is a one- to two-page summary, in point form, of all key definitions, concepts, and material from the textbook chapter. The summary is organized using the same major section headings from the textbook chapter. Key terms from the textbook appear in bold. This section is designed to focus you quickly and precisely on the core material that you must master. It is an excellent study aid for the night before an exam. Think of it as crib notes that will serve as a final check of the key concepts you have studied.

Helpful Hints   When you encounter difficulty in mastering concepts or techniques, you will not be alone. Many students find certain concepts difficult and often make the same kinds of mistakes. We have seen these common mistakes often enough to have learned how to help students avoid them. The hints point out these mistakes and offer tips to avoid them. The hints focus on the most important concepts, equations, and techniques for problem solving. They also review crucial graphs that appear on every instructor's exams. We hope that this section will be very useful, since instructors always ask exam questions designed to test these possible mistakes in your understanding.

This section sometimes includes extra material that your instructor may add to the course, but is not in textbook chapters. Examples of extra material include the mathematical solutions to demand and supply equations in the mathematical note to textbook Chapter 4 and the website appendix to textbook Chapter 19 on "Ideas About Fairness." This extra material is marked with the symbol ⊕ for extra, and may be skipped if your instructor does not cover it.

The symbol ⊕ is used in the *Study Guide* to identify questions and answers based on extra material.

Self-Test   This will be one of the most useful sections of the *Study Guide*. The questions are designed to give you practice and to test skills and techniques you must master to do well on exams. There are plenty of the multiple-choice questions (25 for each chapter) that you are most likely to encounter on course tests and exams. There are other types of questions, described below, each with a specific pedagogical purpose. Questions (and answers) based on extra material covered in the Helpful Hints are marked with an ⊚ so that you can easily skip them if your instructor does not assign the extra material. Before we describe the three parts of the Self-Test section, here are some general tips that apply to all parts.

Use a pencil to write your answers in the *Study Guide*. This will allow you to erase your mistakes and have neat, completed pages from which to study. Draw graphs wherever they are applicable. Some questions will ask explicitly for graphs; many others will not but will require a chain of reasoning that involves shifts of curves on a graph. *Always draw the graph.* Don't try to work through the reasoning in your head—you are much more likely to make mistakes that way. Whenever you draw a graph, even in the margins of the *Study Guide*, label the axes. You may think that you can keep the labels in your head, but you will be confronting many different graphs with many different variables on the axes. Avoid confusion and label. As an added incentive, remember that on exams where graphs are required, instructors will deduct marks for unlabelled axes.

Do the Self-Test questions as if they were real exam questions, which means do them *without looking at the answers*. This is the single most important tip we can give you about effectively using the *Study Guide* to improve your test and exam performance. Struggling for the answers to questions that you find difficult is one of the most effective ways to learn. The athletic adage—no pain, no gain—applies equally well to studying. You will learn the most from right answers you had to struggle for and from your wrong answers and mistakes. Only after you have attempted all the questions should you look at the answers. When you finally do check the answers, be sure to understand where you went wrong and why the right answer is correct.

If you want to impose time pressure on yourself to simulate the conditions of a real exam, allow two minutes for each True/False/Uncertain and Multiple-Choice question. The Short Answer Problems vary considerably in their time requirements, so it is difficult to give time estimates for them. However, we believe that such time pressure is probably not a good idea for *Study Guide* questions. A state of mind of relaxed concentration is best for work in the *Study Guide*. Use old exams if you want practice with time pressure, or use the Part Overview Midterm Examinations (see description on page viii).

There are many questions in each chapter, and it will take you somewhere between two and five hours to answer all of them. If you get tired (or bored), don't burn yourself out by trying to work through all of the questions in one sitting. Consider breaking up your Self-Test over two (or more) study sessions.

The three parts of the Self-Test section are:

True/False/Uncertain and Explain   These questions test basic knowledge of chapter concepts and your ability to apply the concepts. Some of the questions challenge your understanding, to see if you can identify mistakes in statements using basic concepts. These questions will quickly identify gaps in your knowledge and are useful to answer out loud in a study group.

When answering, identify each statement as *true*, *false*, or whether you are *uncertain* because the statement may be true or false depending on circumstances or assumptions. Explain your answer in one sentence. The space underneath each question is sufficient for writing your answer.

Multiple-Choice   These more difficult questions test your analytical abilities by asking you to apply concepts to new situations, manipulate information, and solve numerical and graphical problems.

This is the most frequently used type of test and exam question, and the Self-Test contains 25 of them in a scrambled order to reflect a real exam situation. The *Test Bank* that your instructor will likely use to make up exams contains all of the *Study Guide* multiple-choice questions, numerous questions that closely "parallel" the *Study Guide* questions, plus many similar questions.

Read each question and all five choices carefully before you answer. Many of the choices will be plausible and will differ only slightly. You must choose the one best answer. A useful strategy in working these questions is first to eliminate any obviously wrong choices and then to focus on the remaining alternatives. Be aware that sometimes the correct answer will be "none of the above choices is correct." Don't get frustrated or think that you are dim if you can't immediately see the correct answer. These questions are designed to make you work to find the correct choice.

Short Answer Problems   The best way to learn to do economics is to do problems. Problems are also the second-most popular type of test and exam question—practice them as much as possible! Each Self-Test concludes with ten short answer, numerical or graphical problems, often based on economic policy issues. In many chapters, this is the most challenging part of the Self-Test. It is also likely to be the most helpful for deepening your understanding of the chapter material. We have, however, designed the questions to teach as much as to test. We have purposely arranged the parts of each multipart question to lead you through the problem-solving analysis in a gradual and sequential fashion, from easier to more difficult parts.

Difficult problems are marked with the symbol ◑ for difficult, to alert you to the need for extra time and effort. These ◑ symbols give you the same indication you would have on a test or exam from the number of marks or minutes allocated to a problem.

Answers The Self-Test is followed by answers to all questions. But do not look at an answer until you have attempted a question. When you do finally look, use the answers to understand where you went wrong and why the right answer is correct.

Each True/False/Uncertain and Multiple-Choice answer includes a brief, point-form explanation to suggest where you might have gone wrong and the economic reasoning behind the answer. At the end of each answer are page numbers in the textbook where you can go to find a more complete explanation. Answers to difficult questions are marked with a ◔ to indicate why you might have struggled with that question! [We purposely did not mark which True/False/Uncertain and Multiple-Choice questions were difficult, to stay as close as possible to a real test or exam format. In an exam, all Multiple-Choice questions, for example, are worth the same number of marks, and you have no idea which questions are the difficult ones.]

The detailed answers to the Short Answer Problems should be especially useful in clarifying and illustrating typical chains of reasoning involved in economic analysis. Answers to difficult problems are marked with a ◔. If the answers alone do not clear up your confusion, go back to the appropriate sections of the textbook. If that still does not suffice, go to your instructor's or teaching assistants' office, or to your study group members, to get help and clarification.

Part Overview Problem and Midterm Examination Every few chapters, at the end of each of the nine parts of the textbook, you will find a special problem (and answer). These multipart problems draw on material from all chapters in the part, and emphasize policy and real-world questions (for example, the impact of cigarette smuggling on tax revenues). These Overview Problems will help you integrate concepts from different chapters that may seem unconnected, but that are actually related. We often design exam questions similar to these problems.

Each Part Overview also contains a Midterm Examination, consisting of four multiple-choice questions from each chapter in the textbook part. The Midterm is set up like a real examination or test, with a time limit for working the questions. Like the other multiple-choice questions in the *Study Guide*, there are answers with point-form explanations as well as page numbers in the textbook where you can go to find more complete explanations.

If you effectively combine the use of the textbook, the *Study Guide*, the *NoteTaker*, *Economics in Action*, and all other course resources, you will be well prepared for exams. Equally importantly, you will also have developed analytical skills and powers of

reasoning that will benefit you throughout your life and in whatever career you choose.

Do You Have Any Friendly Advice For Us?

We have attempted to make this *Study Guide* as clear and as useful as possible, and to avoid errors. No doubt, we have not succeeded entirely, and you are the only judges who count in evaluating our attempt. If you discover errors, or if you have other suggestions for improving the *Study Guide*, please write to us. In future editions, we will try to acknowledge the names of all students whose suggestions help us improve the *Study Guide*. Send your correspondence or e-mail to either of us:

Professor Avi J. Cohen
Department of Economics
Vari Hall, York University
Toronto, Ontario M3J 1P3
avicohen@yorku.ca

Professor Harvey B. King
Department of Economics
University of Regina
Regina, Saskatchewan S4S 0A2
Harvey.King@uregina.ca

Acknowledgments

This third edition of the *Study Guide* has benefited from help and advice from many sources. We have adopted some ideas from the Australian *Study Guide* by Teresita Bentick, and from our co-author of the U.S. *Study Guide*, Mark Rush. Many colleagues have helped raise the quality of our questions with suggestions and corrections—we would especially like to thank Robin Bade, Gordon Church, Keith MacKinnon, Michael Parkin, Michael Rushton, and John Stewart. Various students have pointed out mistakes and ambiguities they found in using the *Study Guide*. Thanks to Rupert Baudais, Mark Burton, Henry Chan, Men Kim Chu, Aaron Dantowitz, Sachin Davé, Anna DeSantis, Lanna Fisher, Debra George (for explaining just what currency drain means), Stephen Kertzman, Filippo Lucchese, Shelly Sheets, and Edie Slugoski for helping us in this area. Thanks also to Joseph Gladstone, Pamela Erlichman, Dawn Lee, and Linda Scott for excellent editorial guidance. HK would like to thank Tracy, Harrison, and Morgan for being so patient and supportive while he hid away in his study all those nights and weekends, and Harrison for giving up his computer time. AJC would like to thank Susan for accommodation, encouragement, support, understanding, and for keeping him laughing.

Harvey King
Avi Cohen
January 1997

Chapter 1

What Is Economics?

How Economists Think

The fundamental economic problem is **scarcity**.

◆ Because wants exceed the resources available to satisfy them, we cannot have everything we want and must make choices. This problem leads to economizing behaviour—choosing the best or optimal use of available resources.

◆ **Economics** is the study of how people make choices to cope with scarcity.

Opportunity cost is the single most important concept for making optimizing choices. The **opportunity cost** of any action is the best alternative forgone.

◆ The real opportunity cost of an action is measured in goods and services forgone, not in money cost.

◆ Opportunity cost includes time cost and external cost.

Economic choices are made at the margin, by comparing the *additional* cost—**marginal cost**—and *additional* benefit—**marginal benefit** of a small increase in an activity. If marginal benefit exceeds marginal cost, you choose to increase the activity.

The **principle of substitution** states that when the opportunity cost of an activity increases, people substitute other activities in its place.

◆ Changes in marginal costs (opportunity costs) and marginal benefits change the **incentives** people face and change their actions.

◆ Competition creates ripples along the chain of substitution—second round effects—that dominate first round effects.

What Economists Do

Economists study

◆ **Microeconomics**—decisions of individual households and firms.

◆ **Macroeconomics**—the national and global economy and how economic aggregates grow and fluctuate.

Economics, as a social science, distinguishes between

◆ *Positive statements*—statements about what *is,* that can be tested by checking them against the facts.

◆ *Normative statements*—statements about what *ought* to be, that depend on values and cannot be tested.

Economic science attempts to *understand* the economic world and is only concerned with positive statements. Economists try to discover positive statements that are consistent with observed facts by

◆ Observation and measurement.

◆ Building **economic models**—abstract, simplified representations of the real world with two components

- *Assumptions* about what is essential versus inessential detail.
- *Implications* or *predictions* that can be tested by comparison with observed facts.

◆ Developing **economic theories**—generalizations for understanding economic choices developed by building and testing economic models (Text Fig. 1.1).

Useful economic models and theories isolate important economic forces and disentangle cause and effect. This requires

◆ *Ceteris paribus* assumptions to hold other things equal to isolate the effects of one force at a time.

◆ Avoiding errors of reasoning including the

- • Fallacy of composition—the false statement that what is true of the parts is true of the whole, or what is true of the whole is true of the parts.
- • *Post hoc* fallacy—the false claim that event *a* caused event *b* just because event *a* occurred first.

Economic policy attempts to *improve* the economic world by achieving the objectives of

◆ **Economic efficiency**—efficient production, consumption, and exchange.

◆ **Equity**—economic justice or fairness.

◆ **Economic growth**—increase in incomes and production per person.

◆ **Economic stability**—minimizing fluctuations in growth, employment, and average prices.

The Economy: An Overview

The economy is a mechanism that allocates scarce resources among competing uses. It determines *what, how, when,* and *where* to produce and *who* consumes what is produced. The economy consists of

◆ Decision makers—households, firms, and governments.

◆ **Markets**—coordinate buying and selling plans of decision makers through prices. There are two kinds of markets.

- • *Goods markets*—for goods and services.
- • *Factor markets*—for **factors of production (labour, land, capital, entrepreneurial ability)**.

The Canadian economy is a(n)

◆ *mixed economy* that operates mainly on the market mechanism, but also on command mechanisms.

◆ *open economy* with economic links to other economies through exports and imports and through international borrowing and lending. A closed economy has no links with any other economy.

HELPFUL HINTS

1 The definition of economics (how people use limited resources to try to satisfy unlimited wants) leads us directly to three important economic concepts—choice, opportunity cost, and competition. If wants exceed resources, we cannot have everything we want and therefore must make *choices* among alternatives. In making a choice, we forgo other alternatives, and the *opportunity cost* of any choice is the value of the best alternative forgone. Also, if wants exceed resources, then wants and individuals must *compete* against each other for the scarce resources.

2 Marginal analysis is a fundamental tool economists use to predict people's choices. The key to understanding marginal analysis is to focus on *additional*, rather than total, costs and benefits. For example, to predict whether or not Taejong will eat a fourth Big Mac, the economist compares Taejong's *additional* benefit or satisfaction from the fourth Big Mac with its *additional* cost. The total benefits and costs of all four Big Macs are not relevant. Only if the marginal benefit exceeds the marginal cost, will Taejong eat a fourth Big Mac.

3 In attempting to understand how and why something works (for example, an airplane, a falling object, an economy), we can try to use description or theory. A description is a list of facts about something. But it does not tell us which facts are essential for understanding how an airplane works (the shape of the wings) and which facts are less important (the colour of the paint).

Scientists use theory to abstract from the complex descriptive facts of the real world and focus only on those elements essential for understanding. Those essential elements are fashioned into models—highly simplified representations of the real world.

In physics and some other natural sciences, if we want to understand the essential force (gravity) that causes objects to fall, we use theory to construct a simple model, then test it by performing a controlled experiment. We create a vacuum to eliminate less important forces like air resistance.

Economic models are also attempts to focus on the essential forces (competition, self-interest) operating in the economy, while abstracting from less important forces (whims, advertising, altruism). Unlike physicists, economists cannot perform controlled experiments to test their models. As a result, it is difficult to conclusively prove or disprove a theory and its models.

4 Models are like maps, which are useful precisely because they abstract from real-world detail. A map that reproduced all of the details of the real world (streetlamps, fireplugs, electric wires)

would be useless. A useful map offers a simplified view, which is carefully selected according to the purpose of the map. Remember that economic models are not claims that the real world is as simple as the model. Models claim to capture the simplified effect of some real force operating in the economy. Before drawing conclusions about the real economy from a model, we must be careful to consider whether, when we reinsert all of the real-world complexities the model abstracted from, the conclusions will be the same as in the model.

5   The most important purpose of studying economics is not to learn what to think about economics but rather *how* to think about economics. The "what"—the facts and descriptions of the economy—can always be found in books. The value of an economics education is the ability to think critically about economic problems and *to understand how* an economy works. This understanding of the essential forces governing how an economy works comes through the mastery of economic theory and model-building.

SELF-TEST

True/False/Uncertain and Explain

1   Economics is the study of how to use unlimited resources to satisfy limited wants.

    F

2   If Fred slept in instead of either going to lecture or jogging, the missed lecture is his opportunity cost of sleep.

    T

3   When the opportunity cost of an activity increases, people substitute it for other activities.

    T

4   In an economy in which economic activity is coordinated by a command mechanism, the decisions of *what, how, when,* and *who* are the result of price adjustment.

    T

5   In economics, a closed economy is one in which there is very limited economic freedom.

    T

6   Economics is not a science since it deals with the study of wilful human beings and not inanimate objects in nature.

    F

7   A positive statement is about what *is*, while a normative statement is about what *will* be.

    F

8   Macroeconomics includes the study of the causes of inflation.

    T

9   Testing an economic model requires comparing its predictions against real-world events.

    T

10 When the predictions of a model conflict with the relevant facts, a theory must be discarded or modified.

    T

Multiple-Choice

1   The fact that human wants cannot be fully satisfied with available resources is called the problem of
    a   opportunity cost.
    b   scarcity.
    c   normative economics.
    d   what to produce.
    e   who will consume.

2   The problem of scarcity exists
    a   only in economies that rely on the market mechanism.
    b   only in economies that rely on the command mechanism.
    c   in all economies.
    d   only when people have not optimized.
    e   now but will be eliminated with economic growth.

3 When the government chooses to use resources to build a dam, those resources are no longer available to build a highway. This illustrates the concept of

a a market mechanism.
b macroeconomics.
c opportunity cost.
d a closed economy.
e cooperation.

4 A positive statement is

a about what ought to be.
b about what is.
c always true.
d capable of evaluation as true or false by observation and measurement.
e b and d.

5 A mixed economy has both

a internal and international trade.
b open and closed industries.
c positive and normative mechanisms.
d command and market mechanisms.
e wealth and poverty.

6 Renata has the chance either to attend an economics lecture or play tennis. If she chooses to attend the lecture, the value of playing tennis is

a greater than the value of the lecture.
b not comparable to the value of the lecture.
c equal to the value of the lecture.
d the opportunity cost of attending the lecture.
e zero.

7 The opportunity cost to a customer of getting a $10 haircut is the

a customer's best alternative use of the $10.
b customer's best alternative use of the time it takes to get a haircut.
c customer's best alternative use of both the $10 and the time it takes to get a haircut.
d value to the barber of $10.
e value to the barber of the time it takes to give a haircut.

8 All of the following are policy objectives *except*

a equity.
b efficiency.
c entrepreneurship.
d stability.
e growth.

9 Which of the following is an example of capital as a factor of production?

a money held by General Motors
b a General Motors bond
c an automobile factory owned by General Motors
d all of the above
e none of the above

10 An economic model is tested by

a examining the realism of its assumptions.
b comparing its predictions with the facts.
c comparing its descriptions with the facts.
d the Testing Committee of the Canadian Economic Association.
e all of the above.

11 All of the following are factors of production *except*

a natural resources.
b tools.
c entrepreneurship.
d government.
e land.

12 A closed economy is one that has

a more exports than imports.
b more imports than exports.
c strict government control of production.
d no economic links between households and government.
e no economic links with other economies.

13 The branch of economics that studies the decisions of individual households and firms is called

a macroeconomics.
b microeconomics.
c positive economics.
d normative economics.
e home economics.

14 Scarcity can be eliminated through

a cooperation.
b competition.
c market mechanisms.
d command mechanisms.
e none of the above.

15 The Canadian economy is best described as a

a closed economy.
b market economy.
c command economy.
d mixed economy.
e wealthy economy that avoids the problem of scarcity.

16 A normative statement is a statement regarding

a what is usually the case.
b the assumptions of an economic model.
c what ought to be.
d the predictions of an economic model.
e what is.

17 "The rich face higher income tax rates than the poor" is an example of

a a normative statement.
b a positive statement.
c a descriptive statement.
d a theoretical statement.
e b and c.

18 Other things being equal, which of the following statements is correct?

1 If unemployment increases, the opportunity cost of attending university decreases.
2 If men generally earn more than women in the labour market, the opportunity cost of attending university is higher for men than for women.

a 1 only
b 2 only
c 1 and 2
d neither 1 nor 2
e impossible to judge without additional information

19 Which of the following is *not* a capital resource?

a money
b a carpenter's hammer
c a shoe factory
d a bread-slicing machine
e the SkyDome

20 Which of the following is a positive statement?

a Low rents will restrict the supply of housing.
b High interest rates are bad for the economy.
c Housing costs too much.
d Owners of apartment buildings ought to be free to charge whatever rent they want.
e Government should control the rents that apartment owners charge.

21 All of the following are microeconomic questions *except*

a technological change.
b wages and earnings.
c national differences in wealth.
d production.
e consumption.

22 Which of the following is *not* part of the opportunity cost of attending university?

a cost of tuition
b cost of textbooks
c cost of meals
d income that could have been earned by working
e all of the above

23 Opportunity cost does *not* include

a external cost.
b the best alternative forgone.
c all alternatives forgone.
d time cost.
e real cost.

24 Which of the following statements is/are normative?

a Scientists should not make normative statements.
b Warts are caused by handling toads.
c As compact disc prices fall, people will buy more of them.
d If income increases, sales of luxury goods will fall.
e c and d.

25 Which of the following would *not* be considered a macroeconomic topic?

a the reasons for a decline in the price of orange juice
b the reasons for a decline in average prices
c the cause of recessions
d the effect of the government budget deficit on inflation
e the determination of aggregate income

Short Answer Problems

1 What is meant by scarcity, and why does the existence of scarcity mean that we must make choices?

2 If all people would only economize, the problem of scarcity would be solved. Agree or disagree and explain why.

3 Ashley, Doug, and Mei-Lin are planning to travel from Halifax to Sydney. The trip takes one hour by airplane and five hours by train. The air fare is $100 and train fare is $60. They all have to take time off from work while travelling. Ashley earns $5 per hour in her job, Doug $10 per hour, and Mei-Lin $12 per hour.

Calculate the opportunity cost of air and train travel for each person. Assuming they are all optimizers, how should each of them travel to Sydney?

4 Explain the interdependence that exists between households and firms in Text Fig. 1.2 on page 18 (ignore governments for this question).

5 Suppose the government builds and staffs a hospital in order to provide "free" medical care.
   a What is the opportunity cost of the free medical care?
   b Is it free from the perspective of society as a whole?

6 Indicate whether each of the following statements is positive or normative. If it is normative (positive), rewrite it so that it becomes positive (normative).
   a The government ought to reduce the size of the deficit in order to lower interest rates.
   b Government imposition of a tax on tobacco products will reduce their consumption.

7 Suppose we examine a model of plant growth that predicts that, given the amount of water and sunlight, the application of fertilizer stimulates plant growth.
   a How might you test the model?
   b How is the test different from what an economist could do to test an economic model?

8 When asked in a television interview what she felt she was missing out on because she spent most of her time training for the last Olympics, a rower answered, "A normal social life." She also revealed that she had given up a job that paid $20,000 per year in order to train full-time. She was fortunate to receive a grant from Sport Canada of $10,000 per year, but this was not enough to cover all of her expenses. Her food and rent were $5,000 per year and training expenses (coach's fee, equipment costs, etc.) were $16,000 per year.
   a What is the annual opportunity cost of "going for Gold" for this rower?
   b What is the annual opportunity cost to Canada of training this rower?
   c In general, what is the annual opportunity cost to Canada of sending this rower and other athletes to the Olympics?

9 Why is the Canadian economy considered to be mixed?

10 Suppose your friend, who is a history major, claims that economic theories are useless because the models on which they are based are so unrealistic. He claims that since the models leave out so many descriptive details about the real world, they can't possibly be useful for understanding how the economy works. How would you defend your decision to study economic theory?

ANSWERS

True/False/Uncertain and Explain

1 F Limited resources and unlimited wants. (8–9)
2 U Opportunity cost is the *best* forgone alternative; don't know whether lecture or jogging more valuable to Fred. (8–9)
3 F People substitute other activities in place of the more expensive activity. (9–10)
4 F Price adjustments are the hallmarks of market mechanism. (19–20)
5 F Closed economy has no links with other economies. (20–21)
6 F Science not defined by subject, but by method of observation, measurement, and testing of theoretical models. (12–13)
7 F Normative statements are about what *ought* to be. (12–13)
8 T Inflation involves price level as a whole. (11–12)
9 T Test predictions, not assumptions. (12–13)
10 T A model's predictions must be consistent with the facts to become part of accepted theory. (12–13)

Multiple-Choice

1 b Definition. (1–2)
2 c With infinite wants and finite resources, scarcity will never be eliminated. (1–2)
3 c Highway is forgone alternative. (1–2)
4 e Definition. (12–13)
5 d Definition. (20–21)
6 d Choosing lecture means its value > tennis. Tennis = (best) forgone alternative to lecture. (8–9)
7 c Opportunity cost includes the real goods the $10 could buy and time costs. (8–9)
8 c Entrepreneurship is a factor of production. (15)
9 c Capital defined as manufactured goods used in production. (18–19)

10 b Assumptions not realistic descriptions; are simplified representations of world. (12–13)

11 d Government is decision maker. (18–19)

12 e Definition. (20–21)

13 b Definition. (11–12)

14 e Scarcity is inescapable fact of life. (8–9)

15 d Mixed economy relies on market and command mechanisms. (20–21)

16 c Key word for normative statements is *ought*. (12–13)

17 e Positive statements describe facts about what is. (12–13)

18 c Unemployment decreases expected average income from working. Higher opportunity cost for men may not be fair, but is a fact. (8–9)

19 a Money not a manufactured good used in production. (18–19)

20 a While **a** may be evaluated as true or false, other statements are matters of opinion. (12–13)

21 c c is a macroeconomic question. (11)

22 c Meals must be paid for whether or not one attends university, so are not forgone costs. (8–9)

23 c You do not forgo all alternatives. If you went to lecture, you could not have stayed in bed *and* gone jogging. (8–9)

24 a Key word is *should*. Even statement **b** is positive. (12–13)

25 a Price of individual good is a microeconomic topic. (11)

Short Answer Problems

1 Scarcity is the universal condition that human wants always exceed the resources available to satisfy them. The fact that goods and services are scarce means that individuals cannot have all of everything they want. It is therefore necessary to choose among alternatives.

2 Disagree. If everyone economized, then we would be making the best possible use of our resources and would be achieving the greatest benefits or satisfaction possible, given the limited quantity of resources. But this does not mean that we would be satisfying all of our limitless needs. The problem of scarcity can never be "solved" as long as people have infinite needs and finite resources for satisfying those needs.

3 The main point is that the total opportunity cost of travel includes the best alternative value of travel time as well as the train or air fare. The total costs of train and air travel for Ashley, Doug, and Mei-Lin are calculated in Table 1.1.

TABLE **1.1**

Traveller	Train	Plane
Ashley		
(a) Fare	$ 60	$100
(b) Opportunity cost of travel time at $5/hr	$ 25	$ 5
Total cost	**$ 85**	**$105**
Doug		
(a) Fare	$ 60	$100
(b) Opportunity cost of travel time at $10/hr	$ 50	$ 10
Total cost	**$110**	**$110**
Mei-Lin		
(a) Fare	$ 60	$100
(b) Opportunity cost of travel time at $12/hr	$ 60	$ 12
Total cost	**$120**	**$112**

Based on the cost calculation in Table 1.1, Ashley should take the train, Mei-Lin should take the plane, and Doug could take either.

4 Firms depend on households for the supply of factors of production. In exchange, households depend on firms for income. Households use that income to buy goods and services from firms, while firms depend on the money they get from household purchases to purchase more factors of production in the next period and renew the circular flow.

5 a Even though medical care may be offered without charge ("free"), there are still opportunity costs. The opportunity cost of providing such health care is the best alternative use of the resources used in the construction of the hospital, and the best alternative use of the resources (including human resources) used in the operation of the hospital.

  b These resources are no longer available for other activities and therefore represent a cost to society.

6 a The given statement is normative. The following is positive: If the government reduces the size of the deficit, interest rates will fall.

  b The given statement is positive. The following is normative: The government ought to impose a tax on tobacco products.

7 a The prediction of the model can be tested by conducting the following controlled experiment and carefully observing the outcome. Select a number of plots of ground of the same size that have similar characteristics and are subject to the same amount of water and sunlight. Plant equal quantities of seeds in all the plots. In some of the plots apply no fertilizer and in some of the plots apply (perhaps varying amounts of) fertilizer. When the plants have grown, measure the growth of the plants and compare the growth of the fertilized plots and the unfertilized plots. If plant growth is greater in fertilized plots, we provisionally accept the model and the theory on which it is based. If plant growth is not greater in fertilized plots, we discard the theory (model), or modify its assumptions. Perhaps the effective use of fertilizer requires more water.

Then construct a new model that predicts that given more water (and the same amount of sunlight), fertilized plants will grow larger than equivalently watered unfertilized plants. Test that model and continue modifying assumptions until predictions are consistent with the facts.

b Economists cannot perform such controlled experiments and instead must change one assumption at a time in alternative models and compare the results. Then differences in outcomes can only be tested against variations in data that occur naturally in the economy. This is a more difficult and less precise model-building and testing procedure than exists for the controlled fertilizer experiment.

8 a The point here is to realize which costs are specific to training for the Olympics. First, there is the value to the athlete of a forgone "normal social life." Second, because she is training for the Olympics, this rower forgoes her $20,000 salary. Third, her training expenses total $16,000, which are partially covered by her $10,000 government grant. She thus forgoes $6,000 worth of goods and services by training. Fourth, her ordinary living expenses are not part of the opportunity cost of training, since she incurs these whether or not she trains.

The total annual opportunity cost of training to this rower is $26,000 plus the value to her of a normal social life (a subjective cost that is difficult for others to measure).

b The annual opportunity cost to Canada of training this rower is $20,000 (opportunity cost of the rower's time) plus $16,000 training expenses (which are probably a good measure of the opportunity cost of the coach's services and equipment), plus the value to the rower of a forgone social life—a total cost of $36,000, plus

the value of the forgone social life. Had this rower not trained for the Olympics, the Canadian economy could have produced *alternative* goods and services worth $36,000.

c The annual opportunity cost to Canada of sending a team of athletes to the Olympics is the annual value of the goods and services that could have been produced with the resources devoted to training athletes.

9 The Canadian economy is a mixed economy because it relies on both the market and command mechanisms. Most coordination is carried out through the market mechanism, but governments and large firms also use command mechanisms.

10 A brief answer to your friend's challenge appears in Helpful Hint **3**. Models are like maps, which are useful precisely because they abstract from real-world detail. A useful map offers a simplified view, which is carefully selected according to the purpose of the map. No map maker would claim that the world is as simple as her map, and economists do not claim that the real economy is as simple as their models. What economists claim is that their models isolate the simplified effect of some real forces (like optimizing behaviour) operating in the economy, and yield predictions that can be tested against real-world data.

Another way to answer your friend would be to challenge him to identify what a more realistic model or theory would look like. You would do well to quote Milton Friedman (a Nobel Prize winner in Economics) on this topic: "A theory or its 'assumptions' cannot possibly be thoroughly 'realistic' in the immediate descriptive sense. ... A completely 'realistic' theory of the wheat market would have to include not only the conditions directly underlying the supply and demand for wheat but also the kind of coins or credit instruments used to make exchanges; the personal characteristics of wheat-traders such as the color of each trader's hair and eyes, ... the number of members of his family, their characteristics, ... the kind of soil on which the wheat was grown, ... the weather prevailing during the growing season; ... and so on indefinitely. Any attempt to move very far in achieving this kind of 'realism' is certain to render a theory utterly useless."

From Milton Friedman, "The Methodology of Positive Economics," in *Essays in Positive Economics* (Chicago: University of Chicago Press, 1953), p. 32.

Chapter 2

Making and Using Graphs

Graphing Data

Graphs represent quantity as a distance. On a two-dimensional graph

- horizontal line is *x-axis*.
- vertical line is *y-axis*.
- intersection (0) is the *origin*.

Main types of economic graphs

- **Scatter diagram**—shows relationship between two variables, one measured on *x-axis*, the other measured on *y-axis*.
- **Time-series graph**—shows relationship between time (measured on *x-axis*) and other variable(s) (measured on *y-axis*). Reveals variable's level, direction of change, speed of change, and **trend** (general tendency to rise or fall).
- **Cross-section graph**—shows level of a variable across different groups at a point in time.

Misleading graphs often omit origin or stretch/squeeze measurement scale to exaggerate or understate variation. Always look closely at the values and labels on axes before interpreting a graph.

Graphs Used in Economic Models

Graphs showing relationships between variables fall into four categories

- **Positive (direct) relationship**—variables move together in same direction: upward sloping.
- **Negative (inverse) relationship**—variables move in opposite directions: downward sloping.

- Relationships with a maximum/minimum
  - Relationship slopes upward, reaches a maximum (zero slope), and then slopes downward.
  - Relationship slopes downward, reaches a minimum (zero slope), and then slopes upward.
- Unrelated (independent) variables—one variable changes while the other remains constant; graph is vertical or horizontal straight line.

The Slope of a Relationship

Slope of a relationship is change in value of variable on *y-axis* divided by change in value of variable on *x-axis*.

- Δ means "change in."
- Formula for slope is $\Delta y / \Delta x$ = rise/run.
- Straight line (**linear relationship**) has constant slope.
  - A positive, upward-sloping relationship has a positive slope.
  - A negative, downward-sloping relationship has a negative slope.
- Curved line has varying slope, which can be calculated
  - *at a point*—by drawing straight line tangent to the curve at that point and calculating slope of the line.
  - *across an arc*—by drawing straight line across two points on the curve and calculating slope of the line.

Graphing Relationships Among More Than Two Variables

Relationships among more than two variables can be graphed by holding constant the values of all variables except two. This is done by making a *ceteris paribus* assumption—"other things remaining the same."

H E L P F U L   H I N T S

1 Throughout the text, relationships among economic variables will almost invariably be represented and analysed graphically. An early, complete understanding of graphs will greatly facilitate your mastery of the economic analysis of later chapters. Avoid the common mistake of assuming that a superficial understanding of graphs will be sufficient.

2 If your experience with graphical analysis is limited, this chapter is crucial to your ability to readily understand later economic analysis. You will likely find significant rewards in occasionally returning to this chapter for review. If you are experienced in constructing and using graphs, this chapter may be "old hat." Even so, you should skim the chapter and work through the Self-Test in this *Study Guide*.

3 Slope is a *linear* concept since it is a property of a straight line. For this reason, the slope is constant along a straight line but is different at different points on a curved (nonlinear) line. For the slope of a curved line, we actually calculate the slope of a straight line. The text presents two alternatives for calculating the slope of a curved line: (1) slope at a point, and (2) slope across an arc. The first of these calculates the slope of the *straight line* that just touches (is tangent to) the curve at a point. The second calculates the slope of the *straight line* formed by the arc between two points on the curved line.

© **4** A straight line on a graph can also be described by a simple equation. The general form for the equation of a straight line is:

$$y = a + bx$$

If you are given such an equation, you can graph the line by finding the y-intercept (where the line intersects the vertical y-axis), finding the x-intercept (where the line intersects the horizontal x-axis), and then connecting those two points with a straight line:
To find the y-intercept, set $x = 0$.

$$y = a + b\,(0)$$
$$y = a$$

To find the x-intercept, set $y = 0$.

$$0 = a + bx$$
$$x = -a/b$$

Connecting these two points $((x = 0, y = a)$ and $(x = -a/b, y = 0))$ or $(0, a)$ and $(-a/b, 0)$ yields the line in Fig. 2.1.

FIGURE **2.1**

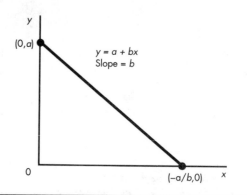

For any straight line with the equation of the form $y = a + bx$, the slope of the line is b. To see how to apply this general equation, consider this example:

$$y = 6 - 2x$$

To find the y-intercept, set $x = 0$.

$$y = 6 - 2(0)$$
$$y = 6$$

To find the x-intercept, set $y = 0$.

$$0 = 6 - 2x$$
$$x = 3$$

Connecting these two points, $(0, 6)$ and $(3, 0)$, yields the line in Fig. 2.2.

FIGURE **2.2**

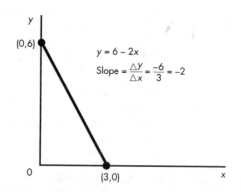

The slope of this line is -2. Since the slope is negative, there is a negative relationship between the variables x and y.

S E L F - T E S T

True/False/Uncertain and Explain

1 A graph that omits the origin is misleading.

2 If the graph of the relationship between two variables slopes upward (to the right), the graph has a positive slope.

3 The graph of the relationship between two variables that are in fact unrelated is vertical.

4 The slope of a straight line is calculated by dividing the change in the value of the variable measured on the horizontal axis by the change in the value of the variable measured on the vertical axis.

5 In Fig. 2.3, the relationship between y and x is first negative, reaches a minimum, and then becomes positive as x increases.

FIGURE **2.3**

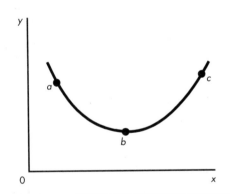

6 In Fig.2.3, the slope of the curve is increasing as we move from point b to point c.

7 In Fig. 2.3, the slope of the curve is approaching zero as we move from point a to point b.

8 In Fig. 2.3, the value of x is a minimum at point b.

9 For a straight line, if a small change in y is associated with a large change in x, the slope is large.

10 For a straight line, if a large change in y is associated with a small change in x, the line is steep.

Multiple-Choice

1 Figure 2.4 is
  a a one-variable time-series graph.
  b a two-variable time-series graph.
  c a scatter diagram.
  d b and c.
  e none of the above.

FIGURE **2.4**

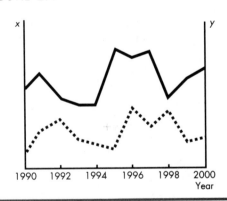

2 The dotted line in Fig. 2.4 represents variable *y*. Which of the following statements best describes the relationship between *x* and *y* in Fig. 2.4?

a *x* and *y* tend to move in opposite directions over time.

b *y* tends to move in the opposite direction from *x*, but one year later.

c *x* and *y* tend to move together over time.

d *x* tends to move in the same direction as *y*, but one year later.

e *y* tends to move in the same direction as *x*, but one year later.

3 From the data in Table 2.1, it appears that

a *x* and *y* have a negative relationship.

b *x* and *y* have a positive relationship.

c there is no relationship between *x* and *y*.

d there is first a negative and then a positive relationship between *x* and *y*.

e there is first a positive and then a negative relationship between *x* and *y*.

TABLE **2.1**

Year	x	y
1990	6.2	143
1991	5.7	156
1992	5.3	162

4 If variables *x* and *y* move up and down together, they are said to be

a positively related.

b negatively related.

c conversely related.

d unrelated.

e trendy.

5 The relationship between two variables that move in opposite directions is shown graphically by a line that is

a positively sloped.

b relatively steep.

c relatively flat.

d negatively sloped.

e curved.

6 To graph a relationship among more than two variables, what kind of assumption is necessary?

a normative

b positive

c linear

d independence of variables

e *ceteris paribus*

7 The tendency for a variable to rise or fall over time is called its

a slope.

b trend.

c *y*-coordinate.

d level.

e correlation.

8 In Fig. 2.5 the relationship between *x* and *y* as *x* increases is

a positive with slope decreasing.

b negative with slope decreasing.

c negative with slope increasing.

d positive with slope increasing.

e positive with slope first increasing then decreasing.

FIGURE **2.5**

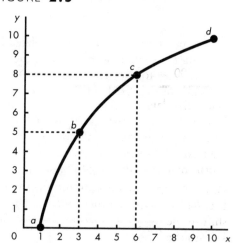

9 What is the slope across the arc between *b* and *c* in Fig. 2.5?

a 1/2

b 2/3

c 1

d 2

e 3

10 In Fig. 2.5, consider the slopes of arc *ab* and arc *bc*. The slope at point *b* is difficult to determine exactly, but it must be

a greater than 5/2.

b about 5/2.

c between 5/2 and 1.

d about 1.

e less than 1.

11 Given the data in Table 2.2, holding income constant, the graph relating the price of strawberries (vertical axis) to the purchases of strawberries (horizontal axis)

a is a vertical line.
b is a horizontal line.
c is a positively sloped line.
d is a negatively sloped line.
e reaches a minimum.

TABLE **2.2**

Weekly Family Income ($)	Price per Box of Strawberries ($)	Number of Boxes Purchased per Week
300	$1.00	5
300	$1.25	3
300	$1.50	2
400	$1.00	7
400	$1.25	5
400	$1.50	4

12 Given the data in Table 2.2, suppose family income decreases from $400 to $300 per week. Then the graph relating the price of strawberries (vertical axis) to the purchases of strawberries (horizontal axis) will

a become negatively sloped.
b become positively sloped.
c shift to the right.
d shift to the left.
e no longer exist.

13 Given the data in Table 2.2, holding price constant, the graph relating family income (vertical axis) to the purchases of strawberries (horizontal axis) is a

a vertical line.
b horizontal line.
c positively sloped line.
d negatively sloped line.
e positively or negatively sloped line, depending on the price that is held constant.

14 In Fig. 2.6, x is

a positively related to y and negatively related to z.
b positively related to both y and z.
c negatively related to y and positively related to z.
d negatively related to both y and z.
e greater than z.

FIGURE **2.6**

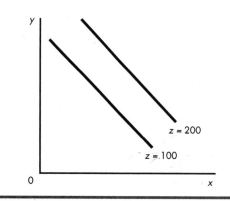

15 In Fig. 2.6, a decrease in the value of z will cause, *ceteris paribus*,

a a decrease in the value of x.
b an increase in the value of x.
c an increase in the value of y.
d no change in the value of y.
e a and d.

16 In Table 2.3, suppose that w is the independent variable measured along the horizontal axis. The slope of the line relating w and u is

a positive with a decreasing slope.
b negative with a decreasing slope.
c positive with an increasing slope.
d negative with a constant slope.
e positive with a constant slope.

TABLE **2.3**

w	2	4	6	8	10
u	15	12	9	6	3

17 Refer to Table 2.3. Suppose that w is the independent variable measured along the horizontal axis. The slope of the line relating w and u is

a +3.
b −3.
c −2/3.
d +3/2.
e −3/2.

18 In Fig. 2.7, if household income increases by $1,000, household expenditure will

a increase by $1,333.
b decrease by $1,333.
c remain unchanged.
d increase by $1,000.
e increase by $750.

FIGURE **2.7**

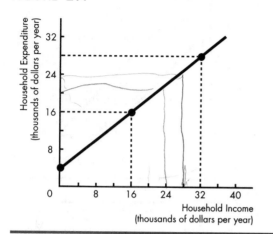

FIGURE **2.8**

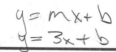

$y = mx + b$
$y = 3x + b$

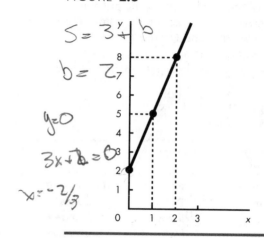

$5 = 3 + b$

$b = 2$

$y = 0$

$3x + b = 0$

$x = -2/3$

19 In Fig. 2.7, if household income is zero, household expenditure is

a 0.
b –$4,000.
c $4,000.
d $8,000.
e impossible to determine from the graph.

20 In Fig. 2.7, if household expenditure is $28,000, household income is

a $36,000.
b $32,000.
c $28,000.
d $25,000.
e none of the above.

21 At all points along a straight line, slope is

a positive.
b negative.
c constant.
d zero.
e none of the above.

22 What is the slope of the line in Fig. 2.8?

a 2
b 1/2
c 3
d 1/3
e –3

23 If the line in Fig. 2.8 were to continue down to the x-axis, what would the value of x be when y is zero?

a 0
b 2
c 2/3
d –2/3
e –3/2

24 If the equation of a straight line is $y = 6 + 3x$, then the slope is

a –3 and the y-intercept is 6.
b –3 and the y-intercept is –2.
c 3 and the y-intercept is 6.
d 3 and the y-intercept is –2.
e 3 and the y-intercept is –6.

25 If the equation of a straight line is $y = 8 - 2x$, then the slope is

a –2 and the x-intercept is –4.
b –2 and the x-intercept is 4.
c –2 and the x-intercept is 8.
d 2 and the x-intercept is –4.
e 2 and the x-intercept is 4.

Short Answer Problems

1 Draw a graph of variables x and y that illustrates each of the following relationships:

a x and y move up and down together.
b x and y move in opposite directions.
c as x increases y reaches a maximum.
d as x increases y reaches a minimum.
e x and y move in opposite directions, but as x increases y decreases by larger and larger increments for each unit increase in x.
f y is unrelated to the value of x.
g x is unrelated to the value of y.

2 What does it mean to say that the slope of a line is –2/3?

3 Explain two ways to measure the slope of a curved line.

4 How do we graph a relationship among more than two variables using a two-dimensional graph?

5 Consider the data in Table 2.4.
  a Draw a time-series graph for the interest rate.
  b Draw a two-variable time-series graph for both the inflation rate and the interest rate.
  c Draw a scatter diagram for the inflation rate (horizontal axis) and the interest rate (vertical axis).
  d Would you describe the general relationship between the inflation rate and the interest rate as positive, negative, or unrelated?

TABLE **2.4**

Year	Inflation Rate (%)	Interest Rate (%)
1970	5.4	6.4
1971	3.2	4.3
1972	3.4	4.1
1973	8.3	7.0
1974	11.8	7.9
1975	6.7	5.8
1976	4.9	5.0
1977	6.5	5.3
1978	8.6	7.2
1979	12.3	10.0

6 Compute the slopes of the lines in Fig. 2.9(a) and (b).

FIGURE **2.9**

(a)

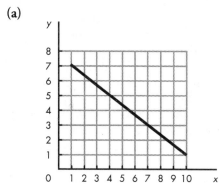

(b)

7 Draw each of the following:
  a a straight line with slope –10 and passing through the point (2, 80).
  b a straight line with slope 2 and passing through the point (6, 10).

8 The equation for a straight line is $y = 4 - 2x$.
  a Calculate: the y-intercept; the x-intercept; the slope.
  b Draw the graph of the line.

9 Use the graph in Fig. 2.10 to compute the slope
  a across the arc between points a and b.
  b at point b.
  c at point c, and explain your answer.

FIGURE **2.10**

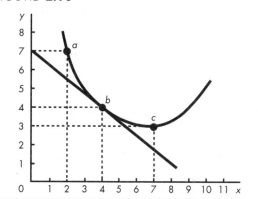

10 In Table 2.5, x represents the number of umbrellas sold per month, y represents the price of an umbrella, and z represents the average number of rainy days per month.
  a On the same diagram, graph the relationship between x (horizontal axis) and y (vertical axis) when $z = 4$, when $z = 5$, and when $z = 6$. On average, it rains 6 days per month. This implies a certain average relationship between monthly umbrella sales and umbrella price. Suppose that the "greenhouse effect" reduces the average monthly rainfall to 4 days per month. What happens to the graph of the relationship between umbrella sales and umbrella prices?
  b On a diagram, graph the relationship between x (horizontal axis) and z (vertical axis) when $y = \$10$ and when $y = \$12$. Is the relationship between x and z positive or negative?
  c On a diagram, graph the relationship between y (horizontal axis) and z (vertical axis) when $x = 120$ and when $x = 140$. Is the relationship between y and z positive or negative?

TABLE **2.5**

Umbrellas Sold per Month (x)	Price per Umbrella (y)	Average Number of Rainy Days per Month (z)
120	$10	4
140	$10	5
160	$10	6
100	$12	4
120	$12	5
140	$12	6
80	$14	4
100	$14	5
120	$14	6

A N S W E R S

True/False/Uncertain and Explain

1 U Sometimes it's misleading, sometimes omitting origin enables graph to reveal its information. (28–29, 32)

2 T Upward-sloping curves/lines have positive slopes. (32–33)

3 U Graph of unrelated variables may be vertical or horizontal. (34–35)

4 F Slope = (Δ variable on vertical (y) axis)/ (Δ variable on horizontal (x) axis). (36–37)

5 T Arc ab would have negative slope, arc bc positive slope. (33–35)

6 T Curve becomes steeper, meaning Δy increasing faster than Δx, so slope increasing. (32–33)

7 T At b, tangent has slope = 0, since Δy = 0 along horizontal line through b. (33–35)

8 F Value of y is minimum at point b. (34–35)

9 F Large slope means large Δy associated with small Δx. (36–37)

10 T Steep line has large slope, meaning large Δy associated with small Δx. (36–37)

Multiple-Choice

1 b Two variables are x and y. Scatter diagrams don't have time on an axis. (30–31)

2 e For example, x begins falling in 1991, y begins falling in 1992. (30–31)

3 a Higher values x (6.2) associated with lower values y (143). (32–34)

4 a Definition. (32–33)

5 d Graph may be steep, flat, or curved, but must have negative slope. (33–34)

6 e Must hold constant other variables to isolate relationship between two variables. (38–39)

7 b Definition. (30–31)

8 a Slope of arc ab = +2.5. Slope of arc bc = +1. (32–33)

9 c Δy = 3 (8 – 5); Δx = 3 (6 – 3). (37–38)

10 c 5/2 is slope of ab, while 1 is slope of bc. (37–38)

11 d Look *either* at data in top 3 rows (income = 300) *or* data in bottom 3 rows (income = 400). Higher price associated with lower purchases. (38–39)

12 d At each price, fewer boxes will be purchased. (32–34)

13 c For $P = 1$, two points on line are (5 boxes, $300) and (7 boxes, $400). Same relationship for other prices. (32–34)

14 c $\uparrow y \rightarrow \downarrow x$ holding z constant. $\uparrow z \rightarrow \uparrow x$ holding y constant. (38–39)

15 a $\downarrow z \rightarrow \downarrow x$ holding y constant. $\downarrow z \rightarrow \downarrow y$ holding x constant. (38–39)

16 d As $w\uparrow$, $u\uparrow$. $\Delta u / \Delta w$ is constant. (36–37)

17 e Between any two points, $\Delta u = 3$, $\Delta w = -2$. (36–37)

18 e Slope $(\Delta y/\Delta x) = 3/4$. If Δx (Δ household income) = $1,000, then Δy (Δ household expenditure) = $750. (36–37)

19 c Where the line intersects the household expenditure (y)-axis. (27–28)

20 b From $28,000 on *vertical* (expenditure) axis, move across to line, then down to $32,000 on *horizontal* (income) axis. (27–28)

21 c Along straight line, slope may or may not be a, b, or d. (36–37)

22 c Between any two points, $\Delta y = 3$ and $\Delta x = 1$. (36–37)

23 d Equation of line is $y = 2 + 3x$. Solve for x-intercept (set y = 0). (27–28)

24 c Use formula $y = a + bx$. Slope = b, y-intercept = a. (36–37)

25 b Use formula $y = a + bx$. Slope = b, x-intercept = –a/b. (36–37)

Short Answer Problems

1 Figure 2.11(a) through (g) illustrates the desired graphs.

2 The negative sign in the slope of –2/3 means that there is a negative relationship between the two variables. The value of 2/3 means that when the variable measured on the vertical axis decreases by 2 units (the *rise* or Δy), the variable measured on the horizontal axis increases by 3 units (the *run* or Δx).

2 The negative sign in the slope of –2/3 means that there is a negative relationship between the two variables. The value of 2/3 means that when the variable measured on the vertical axis decreases by 2 units (the *rise* or Δy), the variable measured on the horizontal axis increases by 3 units (the *run* or Δx).

3 The slope of a straight line can be measured at a point or across an arc. The slope at a point is measured by calculating the slope of the straight line that is tangent to (just touches) the curved line at the point. The slope across an arc is measured by calculating the slope of the straight line that forms the arc.

4 To graph a relationship among more than two variables, we hold all of the variables but two constant, and graph the relationship between the remaining two. Thus, we can graph the relationship between any pair of variables, given the constant values of the other variables.

5 a A time-series graph for the interest rate is given in Fig. 2.12(a).

b Figure 2.12(b) is a two-variable time-series graph for both the inflation rate and the interest rate. The inflation rate is the dotted line; the interest rate is the solid line.

c The scatter diagram for the inflation rate and the interest rate is given in Fig. 2.12(c).

d From the graphs in Fig. 2.12(b) and (c), we see that the relationship between the inflation rate and the interest rate is generally positive.

6 To find the slope, pick any two points on a line and compute $\Delta y/\Delta x$. The slope of the line in Fig. 2.9(a) is –2/3, and the slope of the line in Fig. 2.9(b) is 1/2.

7 a The requested straight line is graphed in Fig. 2.13(a). First plot the point (2, 80). Then pick a second point whose *y*-coordinate decreases by 10 for every 1 unit increase in the *x*-coordinate, e.g., (5, 50). The slope between the two points is –30/3 = –10.

b The requested straight line is graphed in Fig. 2.13(b). First plot the point (6, 10). Then pick a second point whose *y*-coordinate decreases by 2 for every 1 unit decrease in the *x*-coordinate, e.g., (5, 8). The slope between the two points is –2/–1 = 2.

FIGURE **2.11**

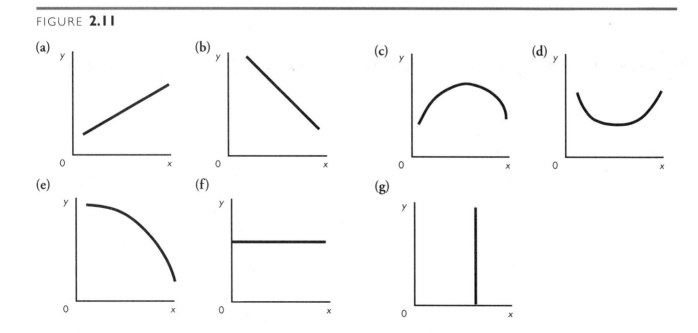

FIGURE **2.12**

(a)

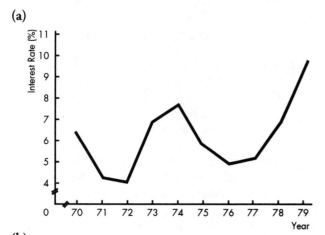

(b)

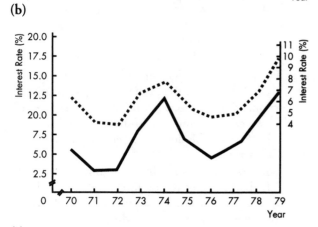

(c)

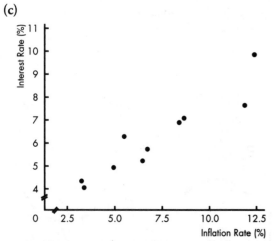

FIGURE **2.13**

(a)

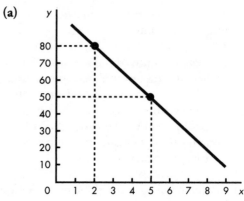

(b)

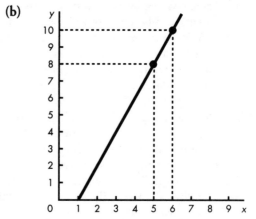

8 a To find the y-intercept, set $x = 0$.

$$y = 4 - 2(0)$$
$$y = 2$$

To find the x-intercept, set $y = 0$.

$$0 = 4 - 2x$$
$$x = 2$$

The slope of the line is -2, the value of the "b" coefficient on x.

b The graph of the line is shown in Fig. 2.14.

FIGURE **2.14**

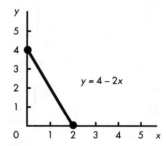

9 a The slope across the arc between points a and b is $-3/2$.
  b The slope at point b is $-3/4$.
  c The slope at point c is zero because it is a minimum point. Nearby a minimum point the slope changes from negative to positive and must pass through zero, or no slope, to do so.

10 a The relationships between x and y for $z = 4$, 5, and 6 are graphed in Fig. 2.15(a). If the average monthly rainfall drops from 6 days to 4 days, the curve representing the relationship between umbrella sales and umbrella prices will shift from the curve labelled $z = 6$ to $z = 4$.
  b The relationships between x and z when y is \$10 and when y is \$12 are graphed in Fig. 2.15(b). The relationship between x and z is positive.
  c The relationships between y and z when $x = 120$ and when $x = 140$ are graphed in Fig. 2.15(c). The relationship between y and z is positive.

FIGURE **2.15**

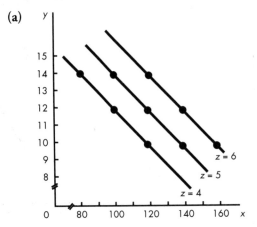

(a)

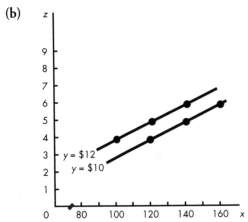

(b)

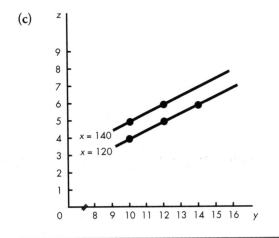

(c)

Production, Growth, and Trade

The Production Possibility Frontier

Production converts factors of production into goods and services.

♦ The four factors of production are labour, land, capital (including **human capital**—skill and knowledge arising from education and training), and entrepreneurial ability.

♦ Goods are tangible and services are intangible.

♦ Goods are classified as capital goods (used to produce other goods) and consumption goods.

The **production possibility frontier** (*PPF*)

♦ is the boundary between unattainable and attainable production possibilities.

♦ shows maximum combinations of outputs (goods and services) that can be produced with given resources and technology.

PPF characteristics

♦ Points on *PPF* represent **production efficiency**—more of one good cannot be produced without producing less of another good.

♦ Points inside *PPF* are inefficient—attainable, but not maximum combinations of outputs; they represent unemployed or misallocated resources.

♦ Points on *PPF* are preferred to points inside *PPF*.

♦ Points outside *PPF* are unattainable.

Choosing among efficient points on *PPF* involves an opportunity cost and a **tradeoff**. For a linear (straight line) *PPF*

♦ resources are homogeneous—equally productive in all activities.

♦ opportunity costs are constant for tradeoffs anywhere along the *PPF*.

Increasing Opportunity Cost

*PPF*s are generally bowed outward (concave), reflecting increasing opportunity costs as more of a good is produced.

♦ *PPF* is bowed outward because resources are nonhomogeneous—resources are *not* equally productive in all activities. Resources most suitable for a given activity are the first to be used.

♦ Bowed-out shape *PPF* represents increasing opportunity cost—opportunity cost of good ↑ as its quantity produced ↑.

♦ In moving between two points on *PPF*, more good *X* can be obtained only by producing less good *Y*. Opportunity cost on *PPF* of additional *X* is amount of *Y* forgone.

♦ No opportunity cost in moving from point inside *PPF* to point on *PPF*.

Economic Growth

Economic growth is the expansion of production possibilities—an outward shift of *PPF*.

♦ *PPF* shifts from changes in resources or technology.

♦ **Capital accumulation** and **technological progress** shift *PPF* outward—economic growth.

♦ Opportunity cost of ↑ goods and services in future (economic growth through capital accumulation and technological progress) is ↓ consumption today.

Gains from Trade

Production increases if people specialize in the activity in which they have a comparative advantage.

◆ Person has **comparative advantage** in producing a good if she can produce at lower opportunity cost than anyone else.

◆ When each person specializes in producing a good at which she has comparative advantage and exchanges for other goods, there are gains from trade.

◆ Specialization and exchange allow consumption (not production) at points outside *PPF*.

◆ Person has **absolute advantage** in producing all goods if, using the same quantity of inputs, she can produce more of all goods than anyone else.

  • Absolute advantage is *irrelevant* for specialization and gains from trade.
  • Even a person with an absolute advantage gains by specializing in activity in which she has a comparative advantage and trading.

◆ **Dynamic comparative advantage** results from specializing in an activity, **learning-by-doing**, and over time becoming the producer with the lowest opportunity cost.

The Evolution of Trading Arrangements

Social arrangements that have evolved to help organize trade are

◆ Markets

◆ **Property rights**—governing ownership, use, and disposal of factors of production and goods and services.

◆ Money—monetary exchange overcomes **barter** problem of double coincidence of wants.

H E L P F U L   H I N T S

I This chapter reviews the absolutely critical concept of *opportunity cost*—the best alternative forgone—that was introduced in Chapter 1. A very helpful formula for opportunity cost, which works well in solving problems, especially problems that involve moving up or down a production possibility frontier (*PPF*) is:

$$\text{Opportunity Cost} = \frac{\text{Give Up}}{\text{Get}}$$

Opportunity cost equals the quantity of goods you must give up divided by the quantity of goods you will get. This formula applies to all *PPF*s, whether they are linear as in Text Fig. 3.1 or bowed out as in Text Fig. 3.2. To illustrate, look again at the bowed-out *PPF*.

FIGURE **3.1**

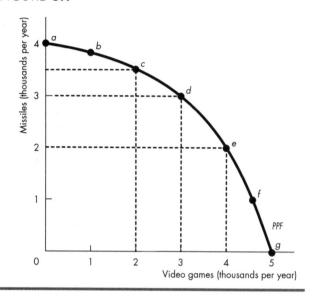

First, consider an example of moving down the *PPF*. In moving from *c* to *d*, what is the opportunity cost of an additional video game? This economy must *give up* 500 missiles (3,500 − 3,000) to *get* 1,000 video games (3,000 − 2,000). Substituting into the formula, the opportunity cost is:

$$\frac{500 \text{ missiles}}{1,000 \text{ video games}} = \frac{1}{2} \text{ missile per video game}$$

Next, consider an example of moving up the *PPF*. In moving from *d* to *c*, what is the opportunity cost of an additional missile? We must *give up* 1,000 video games (3,000 − 2,000) to *get* 500 missiles (3,500 − 3,000). Substituting into the formula, the opportunity cost is:

$$\frac{1,000 \text{ video games}}{500 \text{ missiles}} = 2 \text{ video games per missile}$$

Opportunity cost is always measured in the units of the *forgone good*.

2 Opportunity cost can also be related to the slope of the *PPF*. As we move down between any two points on the *PPF*, the opportunity cost of an additional unit of the good on the *horizontal* axis is:

$$|\text{ slope of } PPF|$$

The slope of the *PPF* is negative, but economists like to describe opportunity cost in terms of a positive quantity of forgone goods. Therefore, we must use the *absolute value* of the slope to calculate the desired positive number.

As we move up between any two points on the *PPF*, the opportunity cost of an additional unit of the good on the *vertical* axis is:

$$\left| \frac{1}{\text{slope of } PPF} \right|$$

This is the reciprocal relation we saw between possibilities *c* and *d*. The opportunity cost of an additional video game (on the horizontal axis) between *c* and *d* is 1/2 missile. The opportunity cost of an additional missile (on the vertical axis) between *d* and *c* is 2 video games.

3 The missile/video games production possibility frontier assumes nonhomogeneous resources, that is, resources that are *not* equally useful in all activities. As a result of this assumption, opportunity cost increases as we increase the production of either good. In moving from possibility *c* to *d*, the opportunity cost per video game is 1/2 missile. But in increasing video game production from *d* to *e*, the opportunity cost per video game increases to 1 missile. In producing the first 1,000 video games, we use the resources best suited to video game production. As we increase video game production, however, we must use resources that are less well suited to video game production— hence increasing opportunity cost. A parallel argument accounts for the increasing opportunity cost of increasing missile production.

It is also possible to construct an even simpler model of a *PPF* that assumes homogeneous resources, resources that are *equally* useful in all activities. As a result of this assumption, opportunity cost is *constant* as we increase production of either good. Constant opportunity cost means that the *PPF* will be a straight line (rather than bowed out). As you will see in some of the following exercises, such a simple model is useful for illustrating the principle of comparative advantage, without having to deal with the complications of increasing opportunity cost.

4 The text defines absolute advantage as a situation where one person has greater productivity than another in the production of all goods. We can also define *absolute advantage in the production of one good*. In comparing the productivity of two persons, this narrower concept of absolute advantage can be defined either in terms of greater output of the good per unit of inputs, or fewer inputs per unit of output. It is useful to understand these definitions of absolute advantage only to demonstrate that absolute advantage has *no role* in explaining specialization and trade. The gains from trade depend only on differing comparative advantages. People have a comparative advantage in producing a good if they can produce it at lower opportunity cost than others.

5 This chapter gives us our first chance to develop and use economic models. It is useful to think about the nature of these models in the context of the general discussion of models in Chapter 1. For example, one model in this chapter is a representation of the production possibilities in the two-person and two-good world of Mark and Marjorie. The model abstracts greatly from the complexity of the real world in which there are billions of people and numerous different kinds of goods and services. The model allows us to explain a number of phenomena that we observe in the world such as specialization and exchange. The model also has some implications or predictions. For example, countries that devote a larger proportion of their resources to capital accumulation will have more rapidly expanding production possibilities. The model can be subjected to "test" by comparing these predictions to the facts we observe in the real world.

SELF-TEST

True/False/Uncertain and Explain

Refer to the production possibility frontier (*PPF*) in Fig. 3.2 for Questions 1 to 4 .

FIGURE **3.2**

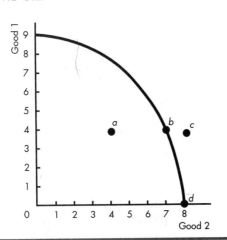

I Point *a* is not attainable.

F

2 The opportunity cost of increasing the production of good 2 from 7 to 8 units is 4 units of good 1.

T

3 Point *c* is not attainable.

T

4 In moving from point *b* to point *d*, the opportunity cost of increasing the production of good 2 equals the absolute value of the slope of the *PPF* between *b* and *d*.

T

5 Economic growth, by shifting out the *PPF*, eliminates the problem of scarcity.

F

6 In a model where capital resources can grow, points on the *PPF* that have more consumption goods yield faster growth.

F

7 The incentives for specialization and exchange do not depend on property rights but only on differing opportunity costs.

F

8 With specialization and trade, a country can produce at a point outside its *PPF*.

T

9 Canada has no incentive to trade with a cheap-labour country like Mexico.

F

10 A monetary exchange system requires a double coincidence of wants.

F

Multiple-Choice

1 If Harold can increase production of good *X* without decreasing the production of any other good, then Harold

a is producing on his *PPF*.
b is producing outside his *PPF*.
c is producing inside his *PPF*.
d must have a linear *PPF*.
e must prefer good *X* to any other good.

2 The bowed-out (concave) shape of a *PPF*

a is due to the equal usefulness of resources in all activities.
b is due to capital accumulation.
c is due to technological improvement.
d reflects the existence of increasing opportunity cost.
e reflects the existence of decreasing opportunity cost.

3 The economy is at point *b* on the *PPF* in Fig. 3.3. The opportunity cost of producing one more unit of *X* is

a 1 unit of *Y*.
b 20 units of *Y*.
c 1 unit of *X*.
d 8 units of *X*.
e 20 units of *X*.

FIGURE **3.3**

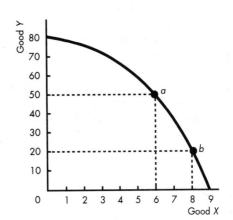

4 The economy is at point *b* on the *PPF* in Fig. 3.3. The opportunity cost of increasing the production of *Y* to 50 units is

a 2 units of *X.*
b 6 units of *X.*
c 8 units of *X.*
d 20 units of *Y.*
e 30 units of *Y.*

5 Refer to the *PPF* in Fig. 3.3. Which of the following statements is *false*?

a Resources are nonhomogeneous.
b Points inside the frontier represent unemployed resources.
c Starting at point *a*, an increase in the production of good *Y* will shift the frontier out.
d The opportunity cost of producing good *Y* increases as production of *Y* increases.
e Shifts in preferences for good *X* or good *Y* will not shift the frontier.

6 Because productive resources are scarce, we must give up some of one good in order to acquire more of another. This is the essence of the concept of

a specialization.
b monetary exchange.
c comparative advantage.
d absolute advantage.
e opportunity cost.

7 A movement *along* a given *PPF* will result from

a technological change.
b change in the stock of capital.
c change in the labour force.
d all of the above.
e none of the above.

8 The opportunity cost of pushing the *PPF* outward is

a capital accumulation.
b technological change.
c reduced current consumption.
d the gain in future consumption.
e all of the above.

In an eight-hour day, Andy can produce either 24 loaves of bread or 8 kilograms of butter. In an eight-hour day, Rolfe can produce either 8 loaves of bread or 8 kilograms of butter. Use this information to answer Questions 9 and 10.

9 Which of the following statements is *true*?

a Andy has an absolute advantage in butter production.
b Rolfe has an absolute advantage in butter production.
c Andy has an absolute advantage in bread production.
d Andy has a comparative advantage in butter production.
e Rolfe has a comparative advantage in bread production.

10 Andy and Rolfe

a can gain from exchange if Andy specializes in butter production and Rolfe specializes in bread production.
b can gain from exchange if Andy specializes in bread production and Rolfe specializes in butter production.
c cannot gain from exchange.
d can exchange, but only Rolfe will gain.
e can exchange, but only Andy will gain.

11 There are two goods—*X* and *Y.* If the opportunity cost of producing good *X* is lower for Pam than for Gino, then

a Pam has an absolute advantage in the production of *X.*
b Gino has an absolute advantage in the production of *Y.*
c Pam has a comparative advantage in the production of *X.*
d Gino has a comparative advantage in the production of *Y.*
e c and d are true.

12 In general, the higher the proportion of resources devoted to technological research in an economy the

a greater will be current consumption.
b faster the *PPF* will shift outward.
c faster the *PPF* will shift inward.
d closer it will come to having a comparative advantage in the production of all goods.
e more bowed out will be the shape of the *PPF.*

13 Anything that is generally acceptable in exchange for goods and services is

a a commodity.
b a medium of exchange.
c private property.
d a barter good.
e called an exchange resource.

14 Mexico and Canada produce both oil and apples using labour only. A barrel of oil can be produced with 4 hours of labour in Mexico and 8 hours of labour in Canada. A bushel of apples can be produced with 8 hours of labour in Mexico and 12 hours of labour in Canada. Canada has

a an absolute advantage in oil production.
b an absolute advantage in apple production.
c a comparative advantage in oil production.
d a comparative advantage in apple production.
e none of the above.

15 In Portugal, the opportunity cost of a bale of wool is 3 bottles of wine. In England, the opportunity cost of 1 bottle of wine is 3 bales of wool. Given this information,

a England has an absolute advantage in wine production.
b England has an absolute advantage in wool production.
c Portugal has a comparative advantage in wine production.
d Portugal has a comparative advantage in wool production.
e no trade will occur.

16 The scarcity of resources implies that the *PPF* is
a bowed inward (convex).
b bowed outward (concave).
c positively sloped.
d negatively sloped.
e linear.

17 If additional units of any good can be produced at a constant opportunity cost, the *PPF* is
a bowed inward (convex).
b bowed outward (concave).
c positively sloped.
d perfectly horizontal.
e linear.

18 Refer to Fig. 3.4, which shows the *PPF* for an economy without discrimination operating at maximum efficiency. If discrimination against women workers is currently occurring in this economy, the elimination of discrimination would result in a(n)
a movement from *a* to *b*.
b movement from *b* to *c*.
c movement from *a* to *c*.
d outward shift of the *PPF*.
e inward shift of the *PPF*.

FIGURE **3.4**

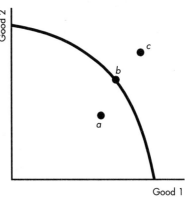

Suppose a society produces only two goods—hockey sticks and maple leaves. Three alternative combinations on its *PPF* are given in Table 3.1. Use the information in Table 3.1 to answer Questions 19 and 20.

TABLE **3.1** PRODUCTION POSSIBILITIES

Possibility	Units of Hockey Sticks	Units of Maple Leaves
a	3	0
b	2	3
c	0	9

19 In moving from combination *c* to combination *b*, the opportunity cost of producing *one* additional hockey stick is
a 2 maple leaves.
b 1/2 maple leaves.
c 6 maple leaves.
d 1/6 maple leaves.
e 3 maple leaves.

20 According to this *PPF*
a resources are homogeneous.
b a combination of 3 hockey sticks and 9 maple leaves is attainable.
c a combination of 3 hockey sticks and 9 maple leaves would not employ all resources.
d the opportunity cost of producing hockey sticks increases as more hockey sticks are produced.
e the opportunity cost of producing hockey sticks decreases as more hockey sticks are produced.

21 The *PPF* for wine and wool will shift if there is a change in
a the price of resources.
b the unemployment rate.
c the quantity of resources.
d preferences for wine and wool.
e all of the above.

22 Refer to the *PPF* in Fig. 3.5. A politician who argues that "if our children are to be better off, we must invest now for the future" is recommending a current point like

- **a** *a.*
- **b** *b.*
- **c** *c.*
- **d** *d.*
- **e** *e.*

FIGURE **3.5**

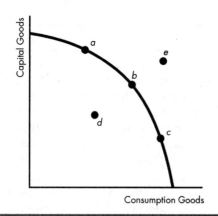

23 Refer to the *PPF* in Fig. 3.5. The statement that "unemployment is a terrible waste of human resources" refers to a point like

- **a** *a.*
- **b** *b.*
- **c** *c.*
- **d** *d.*
- **e** *e.*

24 Which of the following is an advantage of a monetary exchange system over barter?

- **a** A monetary exchange system eliminates the basis for comparative advantage.
- **b** A monetary exchange system does not require a medium of exchange.
- **c** Only in a monetary exchange system can gains from trade be realized.
- **d** A monetary exchange system does not require a double coincidence of wants.
- **e** All of the above are advantages of a monetary exchange system over barter.

25 Learning-by-doing is the basis of

- **a** absolute comparative advantage.
- **b** dynamic comparative advantage.
- **c** intellectual property rights.
- **d** monetary exchange.
- **e** none of the above.

Short Answer Problems

1 Why is a *PPF* negatively sloped? Why is it bowed out?

2 Consider two economies, one with no tool-making possibilities and one with tool-making.
- **a** With no tool-making possibilities (constant capital goods), what is the opportunity cost of moving from a point inside the economy's *PPF* to a point on the *PPF*? Explain.
- **b** In a tool-making economy, what is the opportunity cost of current consumption?

3 Lawyers earn $200 per hour while secretaries earn $15 per hour. Use the concepts of absolute and comparative advantage to explain why a lawyer who is a better typist than her secretary will still *specialize* in doing only legal work and will *trade* with the secretary for typing services.

4 Explain, using a specific example of exchange, why a monetary exchange system is more efficient than barter.

5 Suppose that an economy with unchanged capital goods has the *PPF* shown in Table 3.2.

TABLE **3.2** PRODUCTION POSSIBILITIES

Possibility	Maximum Units of Butter per Week	Maximum Units of Guns per Week
a	200	0
b	180	60
c	160	100
d	100	160
e	40	200
f	0	220

- **a** On graph paper, plot these possibilities, label the points, and draw the *PPF*. (Put guns on the *x*-axis.)
- **b** If the economy moves from possibility *c* to possibility *d*, the opportunity cost *per unit of guns* will be how many units of butter?
- **c** If the economy moves from possibility *d* to possibility *e*, the opportunity cost *per unit of guns* will be how many units of butter?
- **d** In general terms, what happens to the opportunity cost of guns as the output of guns increases?
- **e** In general terms, what happens to the opportunity cost of butter as the output of butter increases? What do the results in parts **d** and **e** imply about resources?

f If (instead of the possibilities given) the *PPF* were a straight line joining points *a* and *f,* what would that imply about opportunity costs and resources?

g Given the original *PPF* you have plotted, is a combination of 140 units of butter and 130 units of guns per week attainable? Would you regard this combination as an efficient one? Explain.

h Given the original *PPF,* is a combination of 70 units of butter and 170 units of guns per week attainable? Is this an efficient combination? Explain.

6 If the following events occurred (each is a separate event, unaccompanied by any other event), what would happen to the *PPF* in Short Answer Problem 5?

a A new, easily exploited, energy source is discovered.

b A large number of skilled workers immigrate into the country.

c The output of butter increases.

d A new invention increases output per person in the butter industry but not in the guns industry.

e A new law is passed compelling workers, who could previously work as long as they wanted, to retire at age sixty.

7 France and Germany each produce both wine and beer, using a single homogeneous input—labour. Their production possibilities are:

France has 100 units of labour and can produce a maximum of 200 bottles of wine *or* 400 bottles of beer.

Germany has 50 units of labour and can produce a maximum of 250 bottles of wine *or* 200 bottles of beer.

a Complete Table 3.3.

TABLE **3.3**

	Bottles Produced by 1 Unit of Labour		Opportunity Cost of 1 Additional Bottle	
	Wine	Beer	Wine	Beer
France				
Germany				

Use the information in part **a** to answer the following questions.

b Which country has an absolute advantage in wine production?

c Which country has an absolute advantage in beer production?

d Which country has a comparative advantage in wine production?

e Which country has a comparative advantage in beer production?

f If trade is allowed, describe what specialization, if any, will occur.

8 Suppose the country of Quark has historically devoted 10 percent of its resources to the production of new capital goods. Use *PPF* diagrams like Text Fig. 3.5 on page 52 to compare the consequences (costs and benefits) of each of the following:

a Quark continues to devote 10 percent of its resources to the production of capital goods.

b Quark begins now to permanently devote 20 percent of its resources to the production of capital goods.

9 Tova and Ron are the only two remaining inhabitants of the planet Melmac. They spend their 30-hour days producing widgets and woggles, the only two goods needed for happiness on Melmac. It takes Tova 1 hour to produce a widget and 2 hours to produce a woggle, while Ron takes 3 hours to produce a widget and 3 hours to produce a woggle.

a For a 30-hour day, draw an individual *PPF* for Tova, for Ron.

b What does the shape of the *PPFs* tell us about opportunity costs? about resources?

c Assume initially that Tova and Ron are each self-sufficient. Define self-sufficiency. Explain what the individual consumption possibilities are for Tova, for Ron.

d Who has an absolute advantage in the production of widgets? of woggles?

e Who has a comparative advantage in the production of widgets? of woggles?

f Suppose Tova and Ron each specialize in producing only the good in which she/he has a comparative advantage (one spends 30 hours producing widgets, the other spends 30 hours producing woggles). What will be the total production of widgets and woggles?

g Suppose Tova and Ron exchange 7 widgets for 5 woggles. On your *PPF* diagrams, plot the new point of Tova's consumption, of Ron's consumption. Explain how these points illustrate the gains from trade.

10 The Netsilik and Oonark families live on the arctic coast, west of Hudson Bay. They often go fishing and hunting for caribou together. During an average working day, the Netsiliks can, at most, catch *either* 6 kilograms of fish or kill 6 caribou. The Oonarks can catch *either* 4 kilograms of fish or kill 4 caribou.

a Assuming linear *PPF*s, draw each family's *PPF* on the same diagram. Put fish on the horizontal axis and caribou on the vertical axis.

b Complete Table 3.4.

TABLE **3.4**

	Opportunity Cost of 1 Additional	
	Fish (kg)	Caribou
Netsiliks		
Oonarks		

c Which family has a comparative advantage in catching fish? in hunting caribou?

d Can specialization and trade increase the total output of fish and caribou produced by the two families? Explain.

A N S W E R S

True/False/Uncertain and Explain

1 F Attainable but not a maximum. (44–45)

2 T Moving from *b* to *d*, production good 1 ↓ by 4 units. (48–49)

3 T Outside *PPF*. (44–45)

4 T See Helpful Hint 2. (48–49)

5 F Cost of growth is forgone current consumption. (50–52)

6 F Points with capital goods yield faster growth. (51–53)

7 F Property rights prerequisite for specialization and exchange. (57–58)

8 F Can *consume* at point outside *PPF*. (53–55)

9 F Mutually beneficial trade depends on comparative advantage, not absolute advantage. (55–56)

10 F Monetary exchange eliminates problem of double coincidence wants. (58)

Multiple-Choice

1 c For 0 opportunity cost, must be unemployed resources. (44–45)

2 d a would be true if *un*equal resources; **b** and **c** shift *PPF*. (47–48)

3 b To ↑ quantity *X* to 9, must ↓ quantity *Y* from 20 to 0. (48–49)

4 a To move from *b* to *a*, quantity *X* ↓ from 8 to 6. (48–49)

5 c ↑ production *Y* moves up *along PPF*. (44–48)

6 e Definition. (45–46)

7 e a, b, and c all shift *PPF*. (50–52)

8 c a and b cause outward shift *PPF*, not opportunity cost; d effect of outward shift *PPF*. (50–52)

9 c Andy produces 3 loaves bread per hour; Rolfe produces 1 loaf per hour. (53–56)

10 b Andy has comparative advantage (lower opportunity cost) bread, Rolfe has comparative advantage butter production. (53–56)

11 e c by definition comparative advantage; d because opportunity cost *Y* reciprocal of opportunity cost *X*. (53–56)

12 b Technological progress shifts *PPF* outward at cost of current consumption. (51–53)

13 b Definition. (58)

14 d Opportunity cost oil in bushels of apples — Canada 2/3, Mexico 1/2. Opportunity cost apples in barrels of oil — Canada 3/2, Mexico 2. (53–54)

15 c Opportunity cost wine in bales of wool— Portugal 1/3, England 3. Opportunity cost wool in bottles of wine—Portugal 3, England 1/3. (53–54)

16 d Scarcity → opportunity cost → negative relationship—to get more of *X* you must give up *Y*. (45–46)

17 e Constant opportunity cost → constant slope *PPF*. (44–46)

18 a Discrimination causes underemployment of resources. Women not allowed to produce up to full abilities. (44–45)

19 e Give up 6 maple leaves to get 2 hockey sticks: 6/2 = 3 maple leaves per hockey stick. (44–46)

20 a Constant opportunity cost → resources equally useful for producing all goods. (44–47)

21 c Only changes in resources or technology shift *PPF*. (50–51)

22 a Producing more capital goods now, shifts *PPF* outward in future. (51–52)

23 d Points inside *PPF* represent unemployed resources, whether labour, capital, or land. (44–45)

24 d Money irrelevant to comparative advantage (**a**) and gains from trade (**c**); monetary exchange requires medium exchange (**b**). (58)

25 b Definition. (56)

Short Answer Problems

1 The negative slope of the *PPF* reflects opportunity cost: in order to have more of one good, some of the other must be forgone.

It is bowed out because the existence of nonhomogeneous resources creates increasing opportunity cost as we increase the production of either good.

2 a In an economy with no tool-making possibilities, a point inside the *PPF* represents unemployed or underutilized resources. By moving to a point on the frontier, more output can be produced from the same resources, simply by utilizing the resources more efficiently. Since resources do not have to be withdrawn from the production of any other good, the opportunity cost of moving to a point on the frontier is zero. This is the closest we get to a "free lunch" in the discipline of economics.

b In a tool-making economy, we can forgo current consumption to produce capital goods, which subsequently increase future production and consumption. By consuming all that is currently produced, we forgo tool making and, ultimately, increased future consumption.

3 The lawyer has an absolute advantage in producing both legal and typing services relative to the secretary. Nevertheless, she has a comparative advantage in legal services, and the secretary has a comparative advantage in typing. To demonstrate these comparative advantages, we can construct Table 3.5 of opportunity costs.

TABLE **3.5**

	Opportunity Cost of 1 Additional Hour ($)	
	Legal Services	**Typing**
Lawyer	200	200
Secretary	>200	15

Consider first the lawyer's opportunity costs. The lawyer's best forgone alternative to providing 1 hour of legal services is the $200 she could earn by providing another hour of legal services. If she provides 1 hour of typing, she is also forgoing $200 (1 hour) of legal services. What would the secretary have to forgo to provide 1 hour of legal

services? He would have to spend 3 years in law school, forgoing 3 years of income in addition to the tuition he must pay. His opportunity cost is a very large number, certainly greater than $200. If he provides 1 hour of typing, his best forgone alternative is the $15 he could have earned at another secretarial job.

Thus Table 3.5 shows that the lawyer has a lower opportunity cost (comparative advantage) of providing legal services, and the secretary has a lower opportunity cost (comparative advantage) of providing typing services. It is on the basis of comparative advantage (not absolute advantage) that trade will take place from which both parties gain.

4 The principal reason for the efficiency of a monetary exchange system relative to barter is that the monetary system does not require a double coincidence of wants to complete a successful exchange. For example, suppose you specialize in the production of apples but like to eat bananas. In a barter economy, you would likely not be able to complete an exchange with the first person you found who had bananas to trade. It would be necessary for that person to also want to trade the bananas for apples and not for carrots or some other good. In a monetary economy, you would always be able to make a successful exchange with the first person you found with bananas to trade since that person would be willing to accept money in exchange. Similarly, in a money exchange system, you would be able to sell your apples for money to the first person you found who wanted apples (even if that person did not have bananas to sell).

5 a The graph of the *PPF* is given in Fig. 3.6.

FIGURE **3.6**

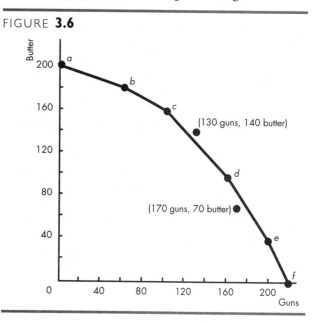

(130 guns, 140 butter)

(170 guns, 70 butter)

b In moving from *c* to *d*, in order to gain 60 units of guns, we must give up 160 − 100 = 60 units of butter. The opportunity cost per unit of guns is

$$\frac{60 \text{ units butter}}{60 \text{ units guns}} = 1 \text{ unit butter per unit of guns}$$

c In moving from *d* to *e*, in order to gain 40 units of guns, we must give up 100 − 40 = 60 units of butter. The opportunity cost per unit of guns is:

$$\frac{60 \text{ units butter}}{40 \text{ units guns}} = \begin{array}{l}1.5 \text{ unit butter per unit} \\ \text{of guns}\end{array}$$

d The opportunity cost of producing more guns increases as the output of guns increases.

e Likewise, the opportunity cost of producing more butter increases as the output of butter increases. Increasing opportunity costs imply that resources are nonhomogeneous; that is, they are not equally useful in gun and butter production.

f Opportunity costs would always be constant, regardless of the output of guns or butter. The opportunity cost per unit of guns would be

200/220 = 10/11 units of butter

The opportunity cost per unit of butter would be

220/200 = 1.1 units of guns

Constant opportunity costs imply that resources are homogeneous; that is, they are equally useful in gun and butter production.

g This combination is outside the *PPF* and therefore is not attainable. Since the economy cannot produce this combination, the question of efficiency is irrelevant.

h This combination is inside the *PPF* and is attainable. It is inefficient because the economy could produce more of either or both goods. Therefore some resources are not fully utilized.

6 a Assuming that both goods require energy for their production, the entire *PPF* shifts out to the northeast as in Fig. 3.7(a).

b Assuming that both goods use skilled labour in their production, the entire *PPF* shifts out to the northeast.

c The *PPF* does not shift. An increase in the output of butter implies a movement *along* the *PPF* to the left, not a shift of the *PPF* itself.

d The new invention implies that for every level of output of guns, the economy can now produce more butter. The *PPF* swings to the right, but remains anchored at point *f* as in Fig. 3.7(b).

e The entire *PPF* shifts in towards the origin.

FIGURE **3.7**

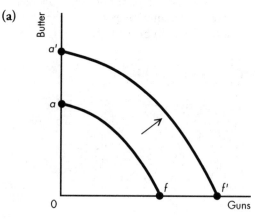

(a)

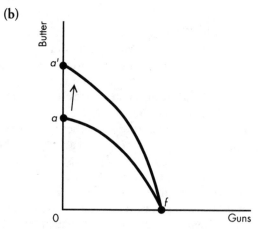

(b)

7 a The completed table is shown here as Table 3.3 Solution.

TABLE **3.3** SOLUTION

	Bottles Produced by 1 Unit of Labour		Opportunity Cost of 1 Additional Bottle	
	Wine	**Beer**	**Wine**	**Beer**
France	2	4	2.0 beer	0.50 wine
Germany	5	4	0.8 beer	1.25 wine

b Germany, which can produce more wine (5 bottles) per unit of input, has an absolute advantage in wine production.

c Neither country has an absolute advantage in beer production, since beer output (4 bottles) per unit of input is the same for both countries.

d Germany, with the lower opportunity cost (0.8 beer), has a comparative advantage in wine production.

e France, with the lower opportunity cost (0.5 wine), has a comparative advantage in beer production.

f The incentive for trade depends only on differences in comparative advantage. Germany will specialize in wine production and France will specialize in beer production.

8 a The situation for Quark is depicted by Fig. 3.8. Suppose Quark starts on *PPF* 1. If it continues to devote only 10 percent of its resources to the production of new capital goods, then it is choosing to produce at a point like *a*. This will shift the *PPF* out in the next period, but only to the curve labelled 2 (where, presumably, Quark will choose to produce at point *b*).

FIGURE **3.8**

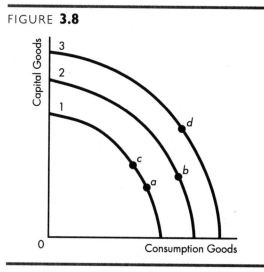

b Starting from the same initial *PPF*, if Quark now decides to increase the resources devoted to the production of new capital to 20 percent, it will be choosing to produce at a point like *c*. In this case, next period's *PPF* will shift further—to curve 3, and a point like *d*, for example.

Thus in comparing points *a* and *c*, we find the following costs and benefits: point *a* has the benefit of greater present consumption but at a cost of lower future consumption; point *c* has the cost of lower present consumption, but with the benefit of greater future consumption.

9 a The individual *PPF*s for Tova and Ron are given by Fig. 3.9(a) and (b), respectively.

FIGURE **3.9**

(a) Tova

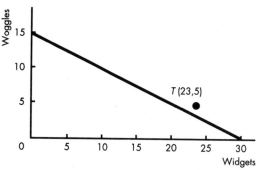

(b) Ron

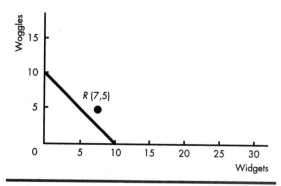

b The linear shape of the *PPF*s tells us that opportunity costs are constant along each frontier and that resources are homogeneous.

These linear *PPF*s with constant opportunity costs abstract from the complexity of the real world. The world generally has increasing opportunity costs, but that fact is not essential for understanding the gains from trade, which is the objective of this problem. Making the model more complex by including increasing opportunity costs would not change our results, but it would make it more difficult to see them.

c Individuals are self-sufficient if they consume only what they produce. This means there is no trade. Without trade, Tova's (maximum) consumption possibilities are exactly the same as her production possibilities—points along her *PPF*. Ron's (maximum) consumption possibilities are likewise the points along his *PPF*.

d Tova has an absolute advantage in the production of both widgets and woggles. Her absolute advantage can be defined either in terms of greater output per unit of inputs or fewer inputs per unit of output. A comparison of the *PPF*s in Fig. 3.9 shows that, for given inputs of 30 hours, Tova produces a greater output of widgets than Ron (30 versus 10) and a greater output of woggles than Ron (15 versus

10). The statement of the problem tells us equivalently that, per unit of output, Tova uses fewer inputs than Ron for both widgets (1 hour versus 3 hours) and woggles (2 hours versus 3 hours). Since Tova has greater productivity than Ron in the production of all goods (widgets and woggles), we say that overall she has an absolute advantage.

e Tova has a comparative advantage in the production of widgets, since she can produce them at lower opportunity cost than Ron (1/2 woggle versus 1 woggle). On the other hand, Ron has a comparative advantage in the production of woggles since he can produce them at a lower opportunity cost than Tova (1 widget versus 2 widgets).

f Tova will produce widgets and Ron will produce woggles, yielding a total production between them of 30 widgets and 10 woggles.

g After the exchange, Tova will have 23 widgets and 5 woggles (point *T*). Ron will have 7 widgets and 5 woggles (point *R*). These new post-trade consumption possibility points lie outside Tova's and Ron's respective pre-trade consumption (and production) possibilities. Hence trade has yielded gains that allow the traders to improve their consumption possibilities beyond those available with self-sufficiency.

10 a The *PPF*s of the Netsiliks and Oonarks are shown in Fig. 3.10.

FIGURE **3.10**

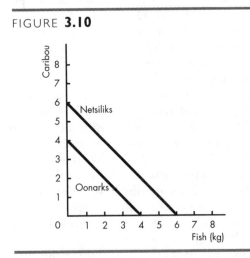

b The completed table is shown here as Table 3.4 Solution.

TABLE **3.4** SOLUTION

	Opportunity Cost of 1 Additional	
	Fish (kg)	Caribou
Netsiliks	1 caribou	1 kg fish
Oonarks	1 caribou	1 kg fish

c Neither family has a comparative advantage in catching fish since the opportunity cost of fish is the same (1 caribou) for each family. Similarly, neither family has a comparative advantage in hunting caribou since the opportunity cost of a caribou is the same (1 kg fish) for each family.

d Gains from specialization and trade are due to the existence of comparative advantage. In this case, no family has a comparative advantage in either fishing or hunting, so there are no gains from specialization and trade.

To illustrate the absence of gains, suppose that initially each family devoted half of its time to each activity. Then suppose that the Netsiliks specialized completely in catching fish and the Oonarks specialized completely in hunting caribou. Production before and after specialization is shown in Table 3.6.

TABLE **3.6**

	Before Specialization		After Specialization	
	Fish (kg)	Caribou	Fish (kg)	Caribou
Netsiliks	3	3	6	0
Oonarks	2	2	0	4
Total Production	5	5	6	4

Compare the total production of both commodities before and after specialization. Specialization has increased the total production of fish by 1 kilogram, but it has also led to a decrease in the total production of caribou by 1. There are no clear gains in consumption from specialization and trade.

Chapter 4

Demand and Supply

Opportunity Cost and Price

The **relative price** of a good is the ratio of its money price to the money price of another good. Relative price measures the opportunity cost of buying a good—the other goods that must be forgone. The theory of demand and supply explains relative prices and makes predictions about whether the price of a good will rise or fall *relative to* the average price of other goods and services.

Demand

The **quantity demanded** of a good is the amount consumers plan to buy at a particular price during a given time period. The law of **demand** states: "Other things remaining the same, the higher the price of a good, the smaller is the quantity demanded." ↑ price → ↓ quantity demanded for two reasons:

◆ *substitution effect* —with an ↑ in the relative price of a good, people buy less of it and more of substitutes for the good.

◆ *income effect* —with an ↑ in the relative price of a good and unchanged incomes, people have less money to spend on all goods, including the good whose price ↑.

The **demand curve** represents the inverse relationship between quantity demanded and price, *ceteris paribus*.

◆ A change in price causes movement along the demand curve. This is called a **change in quantity demanded**. The higher the price of a good, the lower is the quantity demanded.

◆ A shift of the demand curve is called a **change in demand**. The demand curve shifts from changes in

- prices of related goods.
- income.
- expected future prices.
- population.
- preferences.

◆ Increase in demand—demand curve shifts right. Decrease in demand—demand curve shifts left.

◆ For an increase in

- price of a **substitute**—demand shifts right.
- price of a **complement**—demand shifts left.
- income (**normal good**)—demand shifts right.
- income (**inferior good**)—demand shifts left.
- expected future prices—demand shifts right.
- population—demand shifts right.
- preferences—demand shifts right.

Supply

The **quantity supplied** of a good is the amount producers plan to sell at a particular price during a given time period. The law of **supply** states: "Other things remaining the same, the higher the price of a good, the greater is the quantity supplied." Because opportunity costs increase with increases in quantity produced, producers require an ↑ price to be willing to ↑ quantity supplied.

The **supply curve** represents the positive relationship between quantity supplied and price, *ceteris paribus*.

◆ A change in price causes movement along the supply curve. This is called a **change in quantity supplied**. The higher the price of a good, the greater is the quantity supplied.

◆ A shift of the supply curve is called a **change in supply**. The supply curve shifts from changes in

- prices of factors of production.
- prices of other goods produced.
- expected future prices.

- number of suppliers.
- technology.

◆ Increase in supply—supply curve shifts right. Decrease in supply—supply curve shifts left.

◆ For an increase in
  - price of factors of production—supply shifts left.
  - price of a substitute in production—supply shifts left.
  - price of a complement in production—supply shifts right.
  - expected future prices—supply shifts left.
  - number of suppliers—supply shifts right.
  - technology—supply shifts right.

Price Determination

The **equilibrium price** is where the demand and supply curves intersect, where quantity demanded equals quantity supplied.

◆ Above the equilibrium price, there is a surplus (quantity supplied > quantity demanded), and price will fall.

◆ Below the equilibrium price, there is a shortage (quantity demanded > quantity supplied), and price will rise.

◆ Only in equilibrium is there no tendency for the price to change. The **equilibrium quantity** is the quantity bought and sold at the equilibrium price.

Predicting Changes in Price and Quantity

When there is a single change *either* in demand *or* in supply, *ceteris paribus*, an

◆ increase in demand → $\uparrow P$ and $\uparrow Q$.

◆ decrease in demand → $\downarrow P$ and $\downarrow Q$.

◆ increase in supply → $\downarrow P$ and $\uparrow Q$.

◆ decrease in supply → $\uparrow P$ and $\downarrow Q$.

When there is a simultaneous change *both* in demand *and* supply, we can determine the effect on either price or quantity. But without information about the relative size of the shifts of the demand and supply curves, the effect on the other variable is ambiguous. *Ceteris paribus*, an

◆ increase in both demand and supply → $\uparrow, \downarrow$, or constant P and $\uparrow Q$.

◆ decrease in both demand and supply → $\uparrow, \downarrow$, or constant P and $\downarrow Q$.

◆ increase in demand and decrease in supply → $\uparrow P$ and $\uparrow, \downarrow$, or constant Q.

◆ decrease in demand and increase in supply → $\downarrow P$ and $\uparrow, \downarrow$, or constant Q.

HELPFUL HINTS

1 When you are first learning about demand and supply it is useful to think in terms of concrete examples to help build an intuitive understanding. Have some favourite examples in the back of your mind. For example, in analysing complementary goods, think about hamburgers and french fries; in analysing substitute goods, think of hamburgers and hot dogs. This will help reduce the "abstractness" of the economic theory.

2 The statement that "price is determined by demand and supply" is a shorthand way of saying that price is determined by all of the factors affecting demand (prices of related goods, income, expected future prices, population, preferences) and all of the factors affecting supply (prices of other goods produced, prices of factors of production, expected future prices, number of suppliers, technology). The benefit of using demand and supply curves is that they allow us to sort out the influences on price of each of these separate factors systematically. Changes in the factors affecting demand shift the demand curve and move us up or down the given supply curve. Changes in the factors affecting supply shift the supply curve and move us up or down the given demand curve.

Any demand and supply problem requires you to sort out these influences carefully. In so doing, *always draw a graph*, even if it is just a small graph in the margin of a true/false/uncertain or multiple-choice problem. Graphical representation is a very efficient way to "see" what happens. As you become comfortable with graphs, you will find that they are effective and powerful tools for systematically organizing your thinking.

Do not make the common mistake of thinking that a problem is so easy that you can do it in your head, without drawing a graph. This mistake will cost you dearly on examinations. Also, when you do draw a graph, be sure to label the axes. As the course progresses, you will encounter many graphs with different variables on the axes. It is very easy to become confused if you do not develop the habit of labelling the axes.

3 Another very common mistake among students is failing to *distinguish* correctly *between a shift in a curve* and *a movement along a curve*. This distinction applies both to demand and supply curves. Many questions in the self-test are designed to test your understanding of this distinction, and you can be sure that your instructor will test you heavily on this. The distinction between "shifts in" versus "movements along" a curve is crucial for systematic thinking about the factors influencing demand and supply, and for understanding the determination of equilibrium price and quantity.

Consider the example of the demand curve. The quantity of a good demanded depends on its own price, the prices of related goods, income, expected future prices, population, and preferences. The term "demand" refers to the relationship between the price of a good and the quantity demanded, holding constant all of the other factors on which the quantity demanded depends. This demand relationship is represented graphically by the demand curve. Thus, the effect of a change in price on quantity demanded is already reflected in the slope of the demand curve; the effect of a change in the price of the good itself is given by a movement along the demand curve. This is referred to as a **change in quantity demanded**.

On the other hand, if one of the other factors affecting the quantity demanded changes, the demand curve itself will shift; the quantity demanded at each price will change. This shift of the demand curve is referred to as a **change in demand**. The critical thing to remember is that a change in the price of a good will not shift the demand curve, it will only cause a movement along the demand curve. Similarly, it is just as important to distinguish between shifts in the supply curve and movements along the supply curve.

To confirm your understanding, consider the effect (draw a graph!) of an increase in household income on the market for compact discs (CDs). First note that an increase in income affects the demand for CDs and not supply. Next we want to determine whether the increase in income causes a shift in the demand curve or a movement along the demand curve. Will the increase in income increase the quantity of CDs demanded even if the price of CDs does not change? Since the answer to this question is yes, we know that the demand curve will shift to the right. Note further that the increase in the demand for CDs will cause the equilibrium price to rise. This price increase will be indicated by a movement along the supply curve (an increase in the quantity supplied) and will not shift the supply curve itself.

Remember: It is shifts in demand and supply curves that cause the market price to change, not changes in the price that cause demand and supply curves to shift.

4 When analysing the shifts of demand and supply curves in related markets (for substitute goods like beer and wine), it often seems as though the feedback effects from one market to the other can go on endlessly. To avoid confusion, stick to the rule that each curve (demand and supply) for a given market can shift a maximum of *once*. (See Short Answer Problems 4 and 6 on page 40 for further explanation and examples.)

@ **5** The relationships between price and quantity demanded and supplied can be represented in three equivalent forms: demand and supply schedules, curves, and equations. Textbook Chapter 4 illustrates schedules and curves, but demand and supply equations are also powerful tools of economic analysis. The mathematical note to Chapter 4 provides the general form of these equations. The purpose of this helpful hint and the next is to further explain the equations and how they can be used to determine the equilibrium values of price and quantity.

Figure 4.1 presents a simple demand and supply example in three equivalent forms: (a) schedules, (b) curves, and (c) equations. The demand and supply schedules in (a) are in the same format as Text Fig. 4.8. The price—quantity combinations from the schedules are plotted on the graph in (b), yielding linear demand and supply curves. What is new about this example is the representation of those curves by the equations in (c).

If you recall (Chapter 2) the formula for the equation of a straight line ($y = a + bx$), you can see that the demand equation is the equation of a straight line. Instead of y, P is the dependent variable on the vertical axis, and, instead of x, Q_D is the independent variable on the horizontal axis. The intercept on the vertical axis a is +5, and the slope b is −1. The supply equation is also linear and graphed in the same way, but with Q_S as the independent variable. The supply curve intercept on the vertical axis is +1, and the slope is +1. The negative slope of the demand curve reflects the law of demand, and the positive slope of the supply curve reflects the law of supply.

You can demonstrate the equivalence of the demand schedule, curve, and equation by substituting various values of Q_D from the schedule into the demand equation, and calculating the associated prices. These combinations of quantity demanded and price are the coordinates (Q_D, P) of the points on the demand curve. You can similarly demonstrate the equivalence of the supply schedule, curve, and equation.

FIGURE **4.1**

(a) **Demand and Supply Schedules**

Price ($)	Q_D	Q_S	Shortage (–)/ Surplus (+)
1	4	0	–4
2	3	1	–2
3	2	2	0
4	1	3	+2
5	0	4	+4

(b) **Demand and Supply Curves**

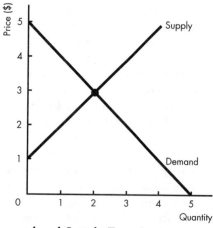

(c) **Demand and Supply Equations**

Demand: $P = 5 - 1Q_D$
Supply: $P = 1 + 1Q_S$

The demand and supply equations are very useful for calculating the equilibrium values of price and quantity. As the schedules and curves both show, two things are true in equilibrium: (1) the price is the same for consumers (the highest price they are willing to pay for the last unit) and producers (the lowest price they are willing to accept for the last unit), and (2) the quantity demanded equals the quantity supplied, so that there are no surpluses or shortages. In terms of the demand and supply equations, this means that *in equilibrium*: (1) the price in both equations is the same. We will denote the equilibrium price as P^*. (2) $Q_D = Q_S =$ the

equilibrium quantity bought and sold. We will denote the equilibrium quantity as Q^*. This means that, in equilibrium, the equations become

Demand: $P^* = 5 - 1Q^*$
Supply: $P^* = 1 + 1Q^*$

These equilibrium equations constitute a simple set of simultaneous equations. Since there are two equations (demand and supply) and two unknowns (P^* and Q^*), we can solve for the unknowns.

Begin the solution by setting demand equal to supply:

$$5 - 1Q^* = 1 + 1Q^*$$

Collecting like terms, we find

$$4 = 2Q^*$$
$$2 = Q^*$$

Once we have Q^* (equilibrium quantity), we can solve for the equilibrium price using *either* the demand or supply equations. Look first at demand:

$$P^* = 5 - 1Q^*$$
$$P^* = 5 - 1(2)$$
$$P^* = 5 - 2$$
$$P^* = 3$$

Alternatively, substituting Q^* into the supply equation yields the same result:

$$P^* = 1 + 1Q^*$$
$$P^* = 1 + 1(2)$$
$$P^* = 1 + 2$$
$$P^* = 3$$

Once you have solved for Q^*, the fact that substituting it into either the demand or supply equation yields the correct P^* provides a valuable check on your calculations. If you make a mistake in your calculations, when you substitute Q^* into the demand and supply equations, you will get two *different* prices. If that happens, you know to recheck your calculations. If you get the same price when you substitute Q^* into the demand and supply equations then you know your calculations are correct.

℮ **6**   Economists have developed the convention of graphing quantity as the independent variable and price as the dependent variable, and the forgoing equations reflect this. Despite this convention, economists actually consider real-world prices to be the independent variables and quantities as the dependent variables. In that case, the equations would take the form

Demand: $Q_D = 5 - 1P$
Supply: $Q_S = -1 + 1P$

You can solve these equations for yourself to see that they yield exactly the same values for P^* and Q^*. [*Hint*: First solve for P^* and then for Q^*.] Whichever form of the equations your instructor may use, the technique for solving the equations will be similar and the results identical.

SELF-TEST

True/False/Uncertain and Explain

1 The law of demand tells us that as the price of a good rises, demand decreases.

2 A decrease in income will shift the demand curve to the left.

3 A supply curve shows the maximum price at which the last unit will be supplied.

4 If A and B are substitutes, an increase in the price of A will shift the supply curve of B to the left.

5 When a cow is slaughtered for beef, its hide becomes available to make leather. Thus beef and leather are substitutes in production.

6 If the price of beef rises, there will be an increase in both the supply of leather and the quantity of beef supplied.

7 If the expected future price of a good increases, there will be an increase in equilibrium price and a decrease in equilibrium quantity.

8 Suppose new firms enter the steel market. The equilibrium price of steel will fall and the quantity will rise.

9 Suppose the demand for personal computers increases while the cost of producing them decreases. The equilibrium quantity of personal computers will rise and the price will fall.

10 When the actual price is above the equilibrium price, a shortage occurs.

Multiple-Choice

1 If an increase in the price of good A causes the demand curve for good B to shift to the left, then
a A and B are substitutes in consumption.
b A and B are complements in consumption.
c A and B are complements in production.
d B is an inferior good.
e B is a normal good.

2 Which of the following could *not* cause an increase in demand for a commodity?
a an increase in income
b a decrease in income
c a decrease in the price of a substitute
d a decrease in the price of a complement
e an increase in preferences for the commodity

3 The fact that a decline in the price of a good causes producers to reduce the quantity of the good supplied illustrates
a the law of supply.
b the law of demand.
c a change in supply.
d the nature of an inferior good.
e technological improvement.

4 A shift of the supply curve for rutabagas will be caused by
a a change in preferences for rutabagas.
b a change in the price of a related good that is a substitute in consumption for rutabagas.
c a change in income.
d a change in the price of rutabagas.
e none of the above.

5   If a resource can be used to produce either good *A* or good *B*, then *A* and *B* are

a   substitutes in production.
b   complements in production.
c   substitutes in consumption.
d   complements in consumption.
e   normal goods.

6   If the market for twinkies is in equilibrium, then

a   twinkies must be a normal good.
b   producers would like to sell more at the current price.
c   consumers would like to buy more at the current price.
d   there will be a surplus.
e   equilibrium quantity equals quantity demanded.

7   Some sales managers are talking shop. Which of the following quotations refers to a movement along the demand curve?

a   "Since our competitors raised their prices our sales have doubled."
b   "It has been an unusually mild winter; our sales of wool scarves are down from last year."
c   "We decided to cut our prices, and the increase in our sales has been remarkable."
d   "The Green movement has sparked an increase in our sales of biodegradable products."
e   none of the above

8   Which of the following will definitely cause an increase in the equilibrium price?

a   an increase in both demand and supply
b   a decrease in both demand and supply
c   an increase in demand combined with a decrease in supply
d   a decrease in demand combined with an increase in supply
e   none of the above

9   The price of a good will tend to fall if

a   there is a surplus at the current price.
b   the current price is above equilibrium.
c   the quantity supplied exceeds the quantity demanded at the current price.
d   all of the above are true.
e   none of the above is true.

The market for coffee is initially in equilibrium with supply and demand curves of the usual shape. Pepsi is a substitute for coffee; cream is a complement for coffee. Questions **10** to **12** concern the market for *coffee*.

Assume that all *ceteris paribus* assumptions continue to hold *except* for the event(s) listed. Answer each question without considering the others.

10   Coffee is a normal good. A decrease in income will

a   increase the price of coffee and increase the quantity demanded of coffee.
b   increase the price of coffee and increase the quantity supplied of coffee.
c   decrease the price of coffee and decrease the quantity demanded of coffee.
d   decrease the price of coffee and decrease the quantity supplied of coffee.
e   cause none of the above.

11   An increase in the price of Pepsi will

a   increase the price of coffee and increase the quantity demanded of coffee.
b   increase the price of coffee and increase the quantity supplied of coffee.
c   decrease the price of coffee and decrease the quantity demanded of coffee.
d   decrease the price of coffee and decrease the quantity supplied of coffee.
e   cause none of the above.

12   A technological improvement lowers the cost of producing coffee. At the same time, preferences for coffee decrease. The *equilibrium quantity* of coffee will

a   rise.
b   fall.
c   remain the same.
d   rise or fall depending on whether the price of coffee falls or rises.
e   rise or fall depending on the relative shifts of demand and supply curves.

13   Since 1960, there has been a dramatic increase in the number of working mothers. Based on this information alone, we can predict that the market for child-care services has experienced a(n)

a   increase in demand.
b   decrease in demand.
c   increase in quantity demanded.
d   decrease in quantity supplied.
e   increase in supply.

14 If Hamburger Helper is an inferior good, then, *ceteris paribus*, a decrease in income will cause a

a leftward shift of the demand curve for Hamburger Helper.

b rightward shift of the demand curve for Hamburger Helper.

c movement up along the demand curve for Hamburger Helper.

d movement down along the demand curve for Hamburger Helper.

e none of the above.

15 A surplus can be eliminated by

a increasing supply.

b government raising the price.

c decreasing the quantity demanded.

d allowing the price to fall.

e allowing the quantity bought and sold to fall.

16 A decrease in quantity demanded is represented by a

a rightward shift of the supply curve.

b rightward shift of the demand curve.

c leftward shift of the demand curve.

d movement upward and to the left along the demand curve.

e movement downward and to the right along the demand curve.

17 If A and B are complementary goods (in consumption) and the cost of a resource used in the production of A decreases, then the price of

a both A and B will rise.

b both A and B will fall.

c A will fall and the price of B will rise.

d A will rise and the price of B will fall.

e A will fall and the price of B will remain unchanged.

18 All of the following "other things" are held constant along a demand curve *except*

a income.

b prices of related goods.

c the price of the good itself.

d preferences.

e all of the above.

19 Which of the following will shift the supply curve for good X leftward?

a a decrease in the wages of workers employed to produce X

b an increase in the cost of machinery used to produce X

c a technological improvement in the production of X

d a situation where quantity demanded exceeds quantity supplied

e all of the above

20 A shortage is the amount by which quantity

a demanded exceeds quantity supplied.

b supplied exceeds quantity demanded.

c demanded increases when the price rises.

d demanded exceeds the equilibrium quantity.

e supplied exceeds the equilibrium quantity.

21 Some producers are chatting over a beer. Which of the following quotations refers to a movement along the supply curve?

a "Wage increases have forced us to raise our prices."

b "Our new, sophisticated equipment will enable us to undercut our competitors."

c "Raw material prices have skyrocketed; we will have to pass this on to our customers."

d "We anticipate a big increase in demand. Our product price should rise, so we are planning for an increase in output."

e "New competitors in the industry are causing prices to fall."

22 If an increase in the price of good A causes the supply curve for good B to shift to the right, then

a A and B are substitutes in consumption.

b A and B are complements in consumption.

c A and B are substitutes in production.

d A and B are complements in production.

e A is a factor of production for making B.

23 "As domestic car prices have increased, consumers have found foreign cars to be a better bargain. Consequently, domestic car sales have fallen and foreign car sales have risen." Based on this information alone, there has been a

a   shift in the demand curves for both domestic and foreign cars.

b   shift in the supply curves for both domestic and foreign cars.

c   movement along the demand curves for both domestic and foreign cars.

d   movement along the demand curve for domestic cars and a shift of the demand curve for foreign cars.

e   shift of the demand curve for domestic cars and a movement along the demand curve for foreign cars.

ⓔ 24 The demand curve for whatnots is $P = 75 - 6Q_D$ and the supply curve for whatnots is $P = 35 + 2Q_S$. What is the equilibrium price of a whatnot?

a $5

b $10

c $40

d $45

e   none of the above

ⓔ 25 The demand curve for tribbles is $P = 300 - 6Q_D$. The supply curve for tribbles is $P = 20 + 8Q_S$. If the price of a tribble was set at $120, the tribble market would experience

a   equilibrium.

b   excess demand causing a rise in price.

c   excess demand causing a fall in price.

d   excess supply causing a rise in price.

e   excess supply causing a fall in price.

Short Answer Problems

1   Explain the difference between wants and demands.

2   The price of personal computers has continued to fall even in the face of increasing demand. Explain.

3   A tax on crude oil would raise the cost of the primary resource used in the production of gasoline. A proponent of such a tax has claimed that it will not raise the price of gasoline using the following argument. While the price of gasoline may rise initially, that price increase will cause the demand for gasoline to decrease, which will push the price back down. What is wrong with this argument?

4   Brussel sprouts and carrots are substitutes in consumption and, since they can both be grown on the same type of land, substitutes in production too. Suppose there is an increase in the demand for brussel sprouts. Trace through the effects on price and quantity traded in both the brussel sprout and carrot markets. (Keep in mind Helpful Hint 4.)

5   The information given in Table 4.1 is about the behaviour of buyers and sellers of fish at the market on a particular Saturday.

TABLE **4.1**   DEMAND AND SUPPLY SCHEDULES FOR FISH

Price (per fish)	Quantity Demanded	Quantity Supplied
$0.50	280	40
$1.00	260	135
$1.50	225	225
$2.00	170	265
$2.50	105	290
$3.00	60	310
$3.50	35	320

a   On graph paper, draw the demand curve and the supply curve. Be sure to label the axes. What is the equilibrium price?

b   We will make the usual *ceteris paribus* assumptions about the demand curve so that it does not shift. List five factors that we are assuming do not change.

c   We will also hold the supply curve constant by assuming that five factors do not change. List them.

d   Explain briefly what would happen if the price was initially set at $3.00.

e   Explain briefly what would happen if the price was initially set at $1.00.

f   Explain briefly what would happen if the price was initially set at $1.50.

6   The market for wine in Canada is initially in equilibrium with supply and demand curves of the usual shape. Beer is a close substitute for wine; cheese and wine are complements. Use demand and supply diagrams to analyse the effect of each of the following (separate) events on the equilibrium price and quantity in the Canadian wine market. Assume that all of the *ceteris paribus* assumptions continue to hold except for the event listed. For both equilibrium price and quantity you should indicate in each case whether the variable rises, falls, remains the same, or moves ambiguously (may rise or fall).

a The income of consumers falls (wine is a normal good).

b Early frost destroys a large part of the world grape crop.

c A new churning invention reduces the cost of producing cheese.

d A new fermentation technique is invented that reduces the cost of producing wine.

e A government study is published that links wine drinking and heart disease.

f Costs of producing both beer and wine increase dramatically.

7 A newspaper reported that "despite a bumper crop of cherries this year, the price drop for cherries won't be as much as expected because of short supplies of plums and peaches."

a Use a demand and supply graph for the cherry market to explain the effect of the bumper crop alone.

b On the same graph, explain the impact on the cherry market of the short supplies of plums and peaches.

8 Table 4.2 lists the demand and supply schedules for cases of grape jam.

TABLE **4.2** DEMAND AND SUPPLY SCHEDULES FOR GRAPE JAM PER WEEK

Price (per case)	Quantity Demanded (cases)	Quantity Supplied (cases)
$70	20	140
$60	60	120
$50	100	100
$40	140	80
$30	180	60

a On the graph in Fig. 4.2, draw the demand and supply curves for grape jam. Be sure to properly label the axes. Label the demand and supply curves D_0 and S_0, respectively.

FIGURE **4.2**

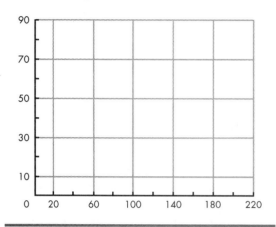

b What are the equilibrium price and quantity in the grape jam market? On your diagram, label the equilibrium point a.

c Is there a surplus or shortage at a price of $40? How much?

@ d The demand and supply schedules can also be represented by the following demand and supply equations:

Demand: $P = 75 - 0.25Q_D$
Supply: $P = 0.5Q_S$

Use these equations to solve for the equilibrium quantity (Q^*); equilibrium price (P^*). [*Hint:* Your answers should be the same as those in **8b**.]

e Suppose the population grows sufficiently that the demand for grape jam increases by 60 cases per week at every price.

i Construct a table (price, quantity demanded) of the new demand schedule.

ii Draw the new demand curve on your original graph and label it D_1.

iii Label the new equilibrium point b. What are the new equilibrium price and quantity?

@ iv What is the new demand equation? [*Hints:* What is the new slope? What is the new price-axis intercept?]

@ **9** The demand equation for dweedles is

$$P = 8 - 1Q_D.$$

The supply equation for dweedles is

$$P = 2 + 1Q_S,$$

where P is the price of a dweedle in dollars, Q_D is the quantity of dweedles demanded, and Q_S is the quantity of dweedles supplied. The dweedle market is initially in equilibrium and income is $300.

a What is the equilibrium quantity (Q^*) of dweedles?

b What is the equilibrium price (P^*) of a dweedle?

c As a result of an increase in income to $500, the demand curve for dweedles shifts (the supply curve remains the same). The new demand equation is

$$P = 4 - 1Q_D$$

Use this information to calculate the new equilibrium quantity of dweedles; calculate the new equilibrium price of a dweedle.

d On the graph in Fig. 4.3, draw and label: (1) the supply curve, (2) the initial demand curve, (3) the new demand curve.

e Are dweedles a normal or inferior good? How do you know?

FIGURE **4.3**

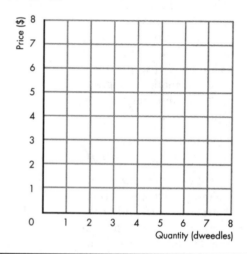

Quantity (dweedles)

@ **10**   The demand equation for flubits is

$$P = 80 - 2Q_D.$$

The supply equation for flubits is

$$P = 50 + 1Q_S,$$

where P is the price of a flubit in dollars, Q_D is the quantity of flubits demanded, and Q_S is the quantity of flubits supplied. Assume that there are no changes in *ceteris paribus* assumptions.

a If the price of flubits was set at $56, calculate the exact surplus or shortage of flubits.

b Explain the adjustment process that will bring the situation above to equilibrium.

c What is the equilibrium quantity (Q^*) of flubits?

d What is the equilibrium price (P^*) of a flubit?

e Now assume that as a result of technological advance, the supply curve for flubits shifts (the demand curve remains the same). The new supply equation is

$$P = 20 + 1Q_S$$

Use this information to calculate the new equilibrium quantity of flubits; calculate the new equilibrium price of a flubit.

A N S W E R S

True/False/Uncertain and Explain

1 **F** As price rises, quantity demanded decreases. (69–70)

@ **2** **U** Leftward shift for normal good, rightward shift for inferior good. (71–72)

3 **F** Supply curve shows minimum price at which last unit supplied. (74–75)

@ **4** **U** True if A and B substitutes in production, but false if substitutes in consumption. (74–76)

@ **5** **F** Beef and leather complements in production because produced together of necessity. (74–76)

6 **T** For complements in production, ↑ price for one good → ↑ quantity supplied and ↑ supply other good. (74–76)

7 **U** ↑ expected future prices → rightward shift demand and leftward shift supply. Price ↑ but Δ quantity depends on relative magnitude shifts. (71–72, 75–76)

8 **T** ↑ number firms → rightward shift supply → ↓ price and ↑ quantity. (75–77)

9 **U** Quantity will ↑ but Δ price depends on relative magnitude shifts in demand and supply. (82–83)

10 **F** At $P >$ equilibrium P, there is surplus (quantity supplied > quantity demanded). (78–79)

Multiple-Choice

1 **b** For example, ↑ price french fries → ↓ demand hamburgers. (71–72)

@ **2** **c** Both income answers could be correct if commodity were normal (**a**) or inferior (**b**). (71–72)

3 **a** Question describes movement down along supply curve. (74–75)

4 **e** Answers **a**, **b**, and **c** shift demand, while **d** causes movement along supply curve. (74–75)

5 **a** Definition of substitute in production. (75)

6 **e** At equilibrium price, plans producers and consumers match; quantity demanded = quantity supplied. (78–79)

7 c Other answers describe shifts of demand curve. (71–73)

8 c Answers **a** and **b** have indeterminate effect on price, while **d** → ↓ price. (82–84)

9 d All answers describe price above equilibrium price. (78–79)

10 d Demand shifts left. (80–81)

11 b Demand shifts right. (80–81)

12 e Supply shifts right, and demand shifts left. (82–84)

13 a ↑ working mothers → ↑ preferences for child care → ↑ demand child-care services. (71–73)

14 b Changes in income shift demand curve rather than causing movement along demand curve. (71–72)

15 d Other answers make surplus (excess quantity supplied) larger. (78–79)

16 d ↓ Quantity demanded is movement up along demand curve. Could also be caused by leftward shift supply. (72–73)

◑ 17 c Supply *A* shifts right → ↓ price *A* This → ↑ demand for *B* → ↑ price *B*. (71–73)

18 c "Other things" shift demand curve. Only price can change along fixed demand curve. (71–73)

19 b ↑ price factor of production shifts supply left. (75–77)

20 a Shortage is horizontal distance between demand and supply curves at price below equilibrium price. (78–79)

21 d Other answers describe shifts of supply curve. (76–77)

22 d Definition complements in production. Price changes related goods in consumption shift demand. (75–76)

23 d ↑ price domestic cars due to leftward shift supply. Domestic and foreign cars substitutes → rightward shift demand foreign cars. (71–72, 75–76)

◎◑ 24 d Set demand equal to supply, solve for $Q^* = 5$. Substitute $Q^* = 5$ into either demand or supply equation to solve for P^*. (96)

◎◑ 25 b At $P = \$120$, $Q_D = 30$, and $Q_S = 12.5$. Excess demand so price will ↑. (78–79, 96)

Short Answer Problems

1 Wants reflect our unlimited desires for goods and services without regard to our ability or willingness to make the sacrifices necessary to obtain them. The existence of scarcity means that many of those wants will not be satisfied. On the other hand, demands refer to plans to buy and, therefore, reflect decisions about which wants to satisfy.

2 Due to the tremendous pace of technological advance, not only has the demand for personal computers been increasing, but the supply has been increasing as well. Indeed, supply has been increasing much more rapidly than demand, which has resulted in falling prices. Thus *much* (but not all) of the increase in sales of personal computers reflects a movement down along a demand curve rather than a shift in demand.

3 This argument confuses a movement along an unchanging demand curve with a shift in the demand curve. The proper analysis is as follows. The increase in the price of oil (the primary resource in the production of gasoline) will shift the supply curve of gasoline leftward. This will cause the equilibrium price of gasoline to increase and thus the quantity demanded of gasoline will decrease. Demand itself will not decrease, that is, the demand curve will not shift. The decrease in supply causes a movement along an unchanged demand curve.

4 The answer to this question requires us to trace through the effects on the two graphs in Fig. 4.4—(a) for the brussel sprout market and (b) for the carrot market. The sequence of effects occurs in order of the numbers on the graphs.

Look first at the market for brussel sprouts. The increase in demand shifts the demand curve rightward from D_0 to D_1 (1), and the price of brussel sprouts rises. This price rise has two effects (2) on the carrot market. Since brussel sprouts and carrots are substitutes in consumption, the demand curve for carrots shifts rightward from D_0 to D_1. And, since brussel sprouts and carrots are substitutes in production, the supply curve of carrots shifts leftward from S_0 to S_1. Both of these shifts in the carrot market raise the price of carrots, causing feedback effects on the brussel sprout market. But remember the rule (Helpful Hint 4) that each curve (demand and supply) for a given market can shift a maximum of *once*. Since the demand curve for brussel sprouts has already shifted, we can only shift the supply curve from S_0 to S_1 (3) because of the substitutes in production relationship. Each curve in each market has now shifted once and the analysis must stop. We can predict that the net effects are increases in the equilibrium prices of both brussel sprouts and carrots, and indeterminate changes in the equilibrium quantities in both markets.

FIGURE **4.4**

(a) Brussel Sprout Market

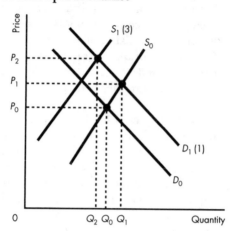

(b) Carrot Market

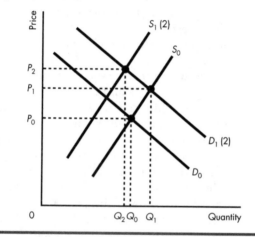

5 a The demand and supply curves are shown in Fig. 4.5. The equilibrium price is $1.50 per fish.

FIGURE **4.5**

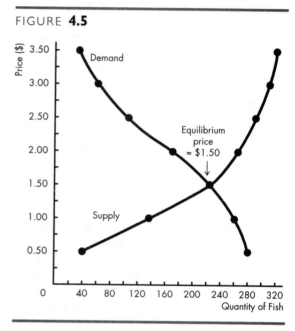

b Prices of related goods; income; expected future prices; population; preferences.

c Prices of factors of production; prices of other goods produced; expected future prices; number of suppliers; technology.

d At a price of $3.00, quantity supplied (310) exceeds quantity demanded (60). Fish sellers find themselves with surplus fish. Rather than be stuck with unsold fish (which yields no revenue), some sellers cut their price in an attempt to increase the quantity of fish demanded. Competition forces other sellers to follow suit, and the price falls until it reaches the equilibrium price of $1.50, while quantity demanded increases until it reaches the equilibrium quantity of 225 units.

e At a price of $1.00, the quantity demanded (260) exceeds the quantity supplied (135)—there is a shortage. Unrequited fish buyers bid up the price in an attempt to get the "scarce" fish. As prices continue to be bid up as long as there is excess demand, quantity supplied increases in response to higher prices. Price and quantity supplied both rise until they reach the equilibrium price ($1.50) and quantity (225 units).

f At a price of $1.50, the quantity supplied exactly equals the quantity demanded (225). There is no excess demand (shortage) or excess supply (surplus), and therefore no tendency for the price or quantity to change.

6 The demand and supply diagrams for parts **a** to **e** are shown in Fig. 4.6.

FIGURE **4.6**

(a)

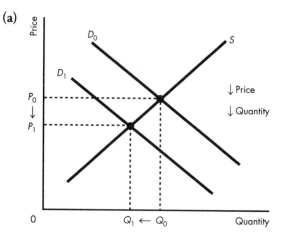

↓ Price

↓ Quantity

(b)

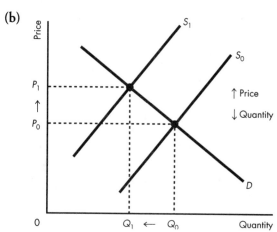

↑ Price

↓ Quantity

(c)

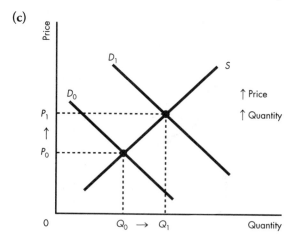

↑ Price

↑ Quantity

(d)

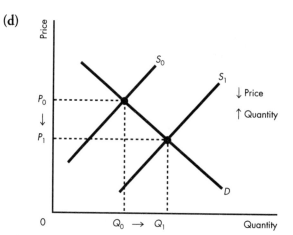

↓ Price

↑ Quantity

(e)

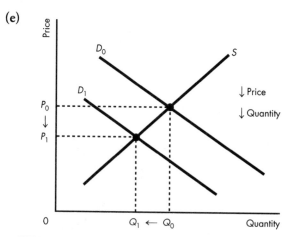

↓ Price

↓ Quantity

f Questions like this require the examination of two separate but related markets—the beer and wine markets. Since this kind of question often causes confusion for students, Fig. 4.7 gives a more detailed explanation of the answer.

Look first at the beer market. The increase in the cost of beer production shifts the supply curve of beer leftward from S_0 to S_1. The resulting rise in the price of beer affects the wine market since beer and wine are substitutes (in consumption).

Turning to the wine market, there are two shifts to examine. The increase in beer prices causes the demand for wine to shift rightward from D_0 to D_1. The increase in the cost of wine production shifts the supply curve of wine leftward from S_0 to S_1. This is the end of the analysis, since the question only asks about the wine market. The final result is a rise in the equilibrium price of wine and an ambiguous change in the quantity of wine. Although the diagram shows $Q_1 = Q_0$, Q_1 may be $\geq$ or $\leq Q_0$.

FIGURE **4.7**

(a) **Beer Market**

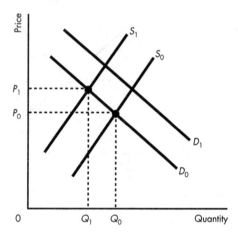

(b) **Wine Market**

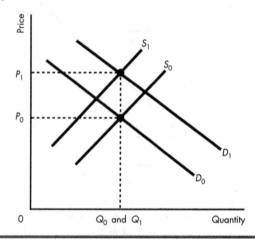

Many students rightfully ask, "But doesn't the rise in wine prices then shift the demand curve for beer rightward, causing a rise in beer prices and an additional increase in the demand for wine?" This question, which is correct in principle, is about the dynamics of adjustment, and these graphs are only capable of analysing once-over shifts of demand or supply. We could shift the demand for beer rightward, but the resulting rise in beer prices would lead us to shift the demand for wine a *second time.* In practice, stick to the rule that each curve (demand and supply) for a given market can shift a maximum of *once.*

7 a The demand and supply curves for the cherry market are shown in Fig. 4.8.

FIGURE **4.8**

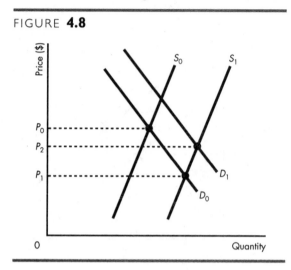

Suppose D_0 and S_0 represent the demand and supply curves for cherries last year. This year's bumper crop increases supply to S_1. Other things being equal, the price of cherries would fall from P_0 to P_1.

b But other things are not equal. Short supplies of plums and peaches (their supply curves have shifted left) drive up their prices. The increase in the prices of plums and peaches, which are substitutes in consumption for cherries, increases the demand for cherries to D_1. The net result is that the price of cherries only falls to P_2 instead of all the way to P_1.

8 a The demand and supply curves for grape jam are shown in Fig. 4.2 Solution.

FIGURE **4.2**   SOLUTION

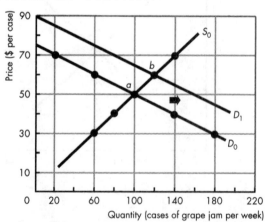

b The equilibrium is given at the intersection of the demand and supply curves (labelled point *a*). The equilibrium price is $50 per case and the equilibrium quantity is 100 cases per week.

c At a price of $40 there is a shortage of 60 cases per week.

◉ d In equilibrium, the equations become:

Demand: $P^* = 75 - 0.25Q^*$
Supply: $P^* = 0.5Q^*$

To solve for Q^*, set demand equal to supply:

$$75 - 0.25Q^* = 0.5Q^*$$
$$75 = 0.75Q^*$$
$$100 = Q^*.$$

To solve for P^*, we can substitute Q^* into either the demand or supply equations. Look at demand first:

$$P^* = 75 - 0.25Q^*$$
$$P^* = 75 - 0.25(100)$$
$$P^* = 75 - 25$$
$$P^* = 50$$

Alternatively, substituting Q^* into the supply equation yields the same result:

$$P^* = 0.5Q^*$$
$$P^* = 0.5(100)$$
$$P^* = 50$$

e i Table 4.3 also contains the (unchanged) quantity supplied, for reference purposes.

TABLE **4.3** DEMAND AND SUPPLY SCHEDULES FOR GRAPE JAM PER WEEK

Price (per case)	Quantity Demanded (cases)	Quantity Supplied (cases)
$70	80	140
$60	120	120
$50	160	100
$40	200	80
$30	240	60

ii The graph of the new demand curve, D_1, is shown in Fig. 4.2 Solution.

iii The new equilibrium price is $60 per case and the quantity is 120 cases of grape jam per week.

◉ iv The new demand equation is $P = 90 - 0.25Q_D$. Notice that the slope of the new demand equation is the same as the slope of the original demand equation. An increase in demand of 60 cases at every price results in a rightward *parallel* shift of the demand curve. Since the two curves are parallel, they have the same slope. The figure of 90 is the price-axis intercept of the new demand curve, which you can see on your graph. *Remember* that the

demand equation is the equation of a straight line ($y = a + bx$); in this case, $a = 90$.

If you want additional practice in the use of demand and supply equations for calculating equilibrium values of price and quantity, you can use the new demand curve equation together with the supply curve equation to calculate the answers you found in e iii.

◉ **9** In equilibrium, the equations become

Demand: $P^* = 8 - 1Q^*$
Supply: $P^* = 2 + 1Q^*$

a To solve for Q^*, set demand equal to supply:

$$8 - 1Q^* = 2 + 1Q^*$$
$$6 = 2Q^*$$
$$3 = Q^*$$

b To solve for P^*, we can substitute Q^* into either the demand or supply equations. Look first at demand:

$$P^* = 8 - 1Q^*$$
$$P^* = 8 - 1(3)$$
$$P^* = 8 - 3$$
$$P^* = 5$$

Alternatively, substituting Q^* into the supply equation yields the same result:

$$P^* = 2 + 1Q^*$$
$$P^* = 2 + 1(3)$$
$$P^* = 2 + 3$$
$$P^* = 5$$

c In equilibrium, the equations are

Demand: $P^* = 4 - 1Q^*$
Supply: $P^* = 2 + 1Q^*$

To solve for Q^*, set demand equal to supply:

$$4 - 1Q^* = 2 + 1Q^*$$
$$2 = 2Q^*$$
$$1 = Q^*$$

To solve for P^*, we can substitute Q^* into either the demand or supply equations. Look first at demand:

$$P^* = 4 - 1Q^*$$
$$P^* = 4 - 1(1)$$
$$P^* = 4 - 1$$
$$P^* = 3$$

Alternatively, substituting Q^* into the supply equation yields the same result:

$$P^* = 2 + 1Q^*$$
$$P^* = 2 + 1(1)$$
$$P^* = 2 + 1$$
$$P^* = 3$$

d The supply curve, initial demand curve, and new demand curve for dweedles are shown in Fig. 4.3 Solution.

FIGURE **4.3** SOLUTION

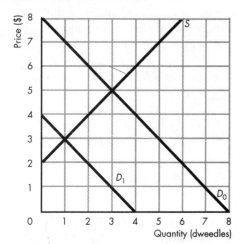

e Dweedles are an inferior good. An increase in income (from $300 to $500) caused a decrease in demand—the demand curve for dweedles shifted leftward.

10 a Substitute the price of $56 into the demand and supply equations to calculate the quantities demanded and supplied at that price. This is the mathematical equivalent of what you do on a graph when you identify a price on the vertical axis, move your eye across to the demand (or supply) curve, and then move your eye down to read the quantity on the horizontal axis.

Substituting into the demand equation we find

$$P = 80 - 2Q_D$$
$$56 = 80 - 2Q_D$$
$$2Q_D = 24$$
$$Q_D = 12.$$

Substituting into the supply equation

$$P = 50 + 1Q_S$$
$$56 = 50 + 1Q_S$$
$$6 = Q_S$$

Quantity demanded exceeds quantity supplied by 6 (12 – 6), so there is a shortage of 6 flubits.

b A shortage means the price was set below the equilibrium price. Competition between consumers for the limited number of flubits will bid up the price and increase the quantity supplied until we reach the equilibrium price and quantity.

c In equilibrium, the equations are

Demand: $P^* = 80 - 2Q^*$
Supply: $P^* = 50 + 1Q^*$

To solve for Q^*, set demand equal to supply:

$$80 - 2Q^* = 50 + 1Q^*$$
$$30 = 3Q^*$$
$$10 = Q^*$$

d To solve for P^*, substitute Q^* into the demand equation:

$$P^* = 80 - 2Q^*$$
$$P^* = 80 - 2(10)$$
$$P^* = 80 - 20$$
$$P^* = 60$$

You can check this answer yourself by substituting Q^* into the supply equation.

e The new equilibrium equations are

Demand: $P^* = 80 - 2Q^*$
Supply: $P^* = 20 + 1Q^*$

To solve for Q^*, set demand equal to supply:

$$80 - 2Q^* = 20 + 1Q^*$$
$$60 = 3Q^*$$
$$20 = Q^*$$

To solve for P^*, substitute Q^* into the supply equations:

$$P^* = 20 + 1Q^*$$
$$P^* = 20 + 1(20)$$
$$P^* = 20 + 20$$
$$P^* = 40$$

You can check this answer yourself by substituting Q^* into the demand equation.

C h a p t e r

5

Elasticity

KEY CONCEPTS

Elasticity of Demand

Price elasticity of demand (η) measures *responsiveness* of quantity demanded to change in price.

◆ η is units-free measure of responsiveness.

◆ $\eta = \left| \dfrac{\% \, \Delta \text{ quantity demanded}}{\% \, \Delta \text{ in price}} \right| = \left| \dfrac{(\Delta Q / Q_{ave})}{(\Delta P / P_{ave})} \right|$

◆ Elasticity is *not* equal to slope. Moving down along a linear demand curve, slope ($\Delta P / \Delta Q$) is constant but elasticity $\downarrow$ as $P_{ave} \downarrow$ and $Q_{ave} \uparrow$.

◆ <u>*When*</u>   <u>Demand is</u>
  $\eta = \infty$ **perfectly elastic** (horizontal)
  $1 < \eta < \infty$ **elastic**
  $\eta = 1$ **unit elastic**
  $0 < \eta < 1$ **inelastic**
  $\eta = 0$ **perfectly inelastic** (vertical)

Elasticity of demand depends on

◆ *closeness of substitutes*—closer substitutes for a good $\rightarrow \uparrow$ elasticity.

  • Necessities generally have poor substitutes and inelastic demands.
  • Luxuries generally have many substitutes and elastic demands.

◆ *proportion of income spent on good*—higher proportion of income spent on a good $\rightarrow \uparrow$ elasticity.

◆ *time elapsed since price change*—longer time elapsed $\rightarrow \uparrow$ elasticity.

• Short-run demand describes responsiveness to a change in price *before* sufficient time for all substitutions to be made.
• Long-run demand describes responsiveness to a change in price *after* sufficient time for all substitutions to be made.
• Short-run demand is usually less elastic than long-run demand.

Elasticity and **total revenue** ($P \times Q$)—the **total revenue test**

◆ <u>*When demand is*</u>   <u>$\uparrow$ *Price causes*</u>
  inelastic ($\eta < 1$) $\uparrow$ total revenue
  unit elastic ($\eta = 1$) no change total revenue
  elastic ($\eta > 1$) $\downarrow$ total revenue

More Elasticities of Demand

Cross elasticity of demand (η_x) measures the *responsiveness* of quantity demanded of good A to a change in price of good B.

◆ $\eta_x = \dfrac{\% \, \Delta \text{ quantity demanded good } A}{\% \, \Delta \text{ price good } B}$

◆ $\eta_x > 1$ Goods are substitutes
  $\eta_x < 0$ Goods are complements

Income elasticity of demand (η_y) measures *responsiveness* of demand to change in income.

◆ $\eta_y = \dfrac{\% \, \Delta \text{ quantity demanded}}{\% \, \Delta \text{ income}}$

◆ <u>*When*</u>   <u>*Demand is*</u>
  $\eta_y > 1$ income elastic (normal good)
  $0 < \eta_y < 1$ income inelastic (normal good)
  $\eta_y < 0$ negative income elasticity (inferior good)

Elasticity of Supply

Elasticity of supply (η_s) measures *responsiveness* of quantity supplied to change in price.

◆ $\eta_s = \dfrac{\% \,\Delta \text{ quantity supplied}}{\% \,\Delta \text{ price}}$

Elasticity of supply depends on

◆ factor substitution possibilities—the more common the factors of production used → ↑ η_s.

◆ time frame for supply decision—η_s ↑ with ↑ time from momentary to short-run to long-run supply.

- Momentary supply describes responsiveness of quantity supplied immediately following a price change.
- Short-run supply describes responsiveness of quantity supplied to a price change when *some* technologically possible adjustments to production have been made.
- Long-run supply describes responsiveness of quantity supplied to a price change when *all* technologically possible adjustments to production have been made.

H E L P F U L   H I N T S

1   There are many elasticity formulae in this chapter, but they are all based on the same simple, intuitive principle—*responsiveness*. All of the demand and supply elasticity formulae measure the *responsiveness* (sensitivity) *of quantity* (demanded or supplied) to changes in something else. Thus percentage change in quantity is always in the numerator of the relevant formula. As you come to understand how quantity responds to changes in price, income, and prices of related goods, you will be able to work out each elasticity formula, even if you have temporarily forgotten it.

2   The complete formula (see Text Fig. 5.2, page 101) for calculating the price elasticity of demand between two points on the demand curve is

$$\eta = \frac{\% \,\Delta \text{ quantity demanded}}{\% \,\Delta \text{ in price}}$$

$$= \left| \left(\frac{\Delta Q}{Q_{ave}} \right) \Big/ \left(\frac{\Delta P}{P_{ave}} \right) \right|$$

The law of demand assures us that price and quantity demanded always move in opposite

directions along any demand curve. Thus without the absolute value sign, the formula for the price elasticity of demand would yield a negative number. Because our main interest is in the *magnitude* of the response in quantity demanded to a change in price, for simplicity, we take the absolute value to guarantee a positive number. Whenever you see the often-used shorthand term, *elasticity* of demand, remember that it means the absolute value of the *price* elasticity of demand.

3   Elasticity is *not* the same as slope (although they are related). Along a straight-line demand curve the slope is constant, but the elasticity varies from infinity to zero as we move down the demand curve. To see why, look at the formula below, which is just a rearrangement of the elasticity formula in Helpful Hint 2.

$$\eta = \left| \left(\frac{\Delta Q}{\Delta P} \right) \times \left(\frac{P_{ave}}{Q_{ave}} \right) \right|$$

The term in the first parentheses is simply the inverse of the slope. Since the slope is constant everywhere along a straight-line demand curve, so is the inverse of the slope. Consider, however, what happens to the term in the second parentheses as we move down the demand curve. At the "top" of the demand curve, P_{ave} is very large, Q_{ave} is very small, so the term in the second parentheses is large. As we move down the demand curve, P_{ave} becomes smaller and Q_{ave} becomes larger, so the term in the second parentheses falls in value. The net result is that the absolute value of the price elasticity of demand falls as we move down the demand curve.

4   One of the most practical and important uses of the concept of elasticity of demand is that it allows us to predict the effect on total revenue of a change in price. A fall in price will increase total revenue if demand is elastic, leave total revenue unchanged if demand is unit elastic, and decrease total revenue if demand is inelastic. Because price and quantity demanded always move in opposite directions along a demand curve, a fall in price will cause an increase in quantity demanded. Since total revenue equals price times quantity, the fall in price will tend to decrease total revenue, while the increase in quantity demanded will increase total revenue. The net effect depends on which of these individual effects is larger.

The concept of elasticity of demand conveniently summarizes the net effect. For example, if demand is elastic, the percentage change in quantity demanded is greater than the percentage change in price. Hence, with a fall in price, the quantity effect dominates and total revenue will increase. If, however, demand is inelastic, the percentage change in quantity demanded is less than the percentage change in price. Hence, with a fall in price, the price effect dominates and total revenue will decrease.

5 Two other important elasticity concepts are the income elasticity of demand and the cross elasticity of demand

Income elasticity of demand

$$\eta_y = \frac{\% \Delta \text{ quantity demanded}}{\% \Delta \text{ income}}$$

$$= \left(\frac{\Delta Q}{Q_{ave}}\right) \Big/ \left(\frac{\Delta Y}{Y_{ave}}\right)$$

Cross elasticity of demand

$$\eta_x = \frac{\% \Delta \text{ quantity demanded of good } A}{\% \Delta \text{ in price of good } B}$$

$$= \left(\frac{\Delta Q^A}{Q^A_{ave}}\right) \Big/ \left(\frac{\Delta P^B}{P^B_{ave}}\right)$$

Notice that these two elasticity formulae do *not* have absolute value signs and can take on either positive or negative values. While these formulae measure responsiveness, both the magnitude *and the direction* of the response are important. In the case of income elasticity of demand, the response of quantity demanded to an increase in income will be positive for a normal good and negative for an inferior good. In the case of cross elasticity of demand, the response of the quantity demanded of good *A* to an increase in the price of good *B* will be positive if the goods are substitutes and negative if the goods are complements.

In calculating an income elasticity or a cross elasticity, be alert to the fact that the *price of the good in the numerator* of the formula *is assumed constant*. Income elasticity measures the quantity response to a change in income, *ceteris paribus*. Cross elasticity measures the quantity response of good *A* to a change in the price of good *B*, *ceteris paribus*. This means that we cannot simply read numerical values for calculating these elasticities from the equilibrium positions of a set of demand and supply curves. For example, when income increases, demand shifts right (for a normal good), and the new equilibrium quantity will also have a higher equilibrium

price. To calculate income elasticity correctly, we compare the income and quantity demanded of the initial equilibrium with the new income and quantity demanded. To obtain the correct new quantity demanded, we must use the new demand curve, but must calculate the quantity demanded that would have prevailed at the *initial*, unchanged price. (See Short Answer Problems **9** and **10** for examples.)

SELF-TEST

True/False/Uncertain and Explain

1 The price elasticity of demand measures how responsive prices are to changes in demand.

2 The demand for gasoline is likely to become more inelastic with the passage of time after a price increase.

3 Price elasticity of demand is constant along a linear demand curve.

4 If you like Pepsi Cola and Coca-Cola about the same, your demand for Pepsi is likely to be elastic.

5 If your expenditures on toothpaste are a small proportion of your total income, your demand for toothpaste is likely to be inelastic.

6 The more narrowly we define a good, the more elastic is its demand.

7 An inferior good will have a negative cross elasticity of demand.

8 If a 10 percent increase in the price of widgets causes a 6 percent increase in the quantity of woozles demanded, then widgets and woozles must be complements.

9 If a decrease in supply causes revenue to increase, then demand must be inelastic.

10 If a 9 percent increase in price leads to a 5 percent decrease in quantity demanded, total revenue has decreased.

Multiple-Choice

1 If price elasticity of demand is zero, then as the price falls

a total revenue does not change.
b quantity demanded does not change.
c quantity demanded falls to zero.
d total revenue increases from zero.
e none of the above occurs.

2 There are two points on the demand curve for volleyballs, as shown in Table 5.1.

TABLE **5.1**

Price per Volleyball	Quantity Demanded
$19	55
$21	45

What is the elasticity of demand between these two points?

a 2.5
b 2.0
c 0.5
d 0.4
e none of the above

3 The fact that butter has margarine as a close substitute in consumption

a makes the supply of butter more elastic.
b makes the supply of butter less elastic.
c makes the demand for butter more elastic.
d makes the demand for butter less elastic.
e does not affect butter's elasticity of supply or demand.

4 A sudden end-of-summer heat wave increases the demand for air conditioners and catches suppliers with no reserve inventories. The momentary supply curve for air conditioners is

a perfectly elastic.
b perfectly inelastic.
c elastic.
d upward sloping.
e horizontal.

5 A technological breakthrough lowers the cost of photocopiers. If the demand for photocopiers is price inelastic, we predict that photocopier sales will

a fall and total revenue will rise.
b fall and total revenue will fall.
c rise and total revenue will rise.
d rise and total revenue will fall.
e rise but changes in total revenue will depend on elasticity of supply.

6 A perfectly vertical demand curve has a price elasticity of

a zero.
b greater than zero but less than one.
c one.
d greater than one.
e infinity.

7 If a 10 percent increase in income causes a 5 percent increase in quantity demanded (at a constant price), what is the income elasticity of demand?

a 0.5
b −0.5
c 2.0
d −2.0
e none of the above

8 If the price elasticity of demand is 2, then a 1 percent decrease in price will

a double the quantity demanded.
b reduce the quantity demanded by half.
c increase the quantity demanded by 2 percent.
d reduce the quantity demanded by 2 percent.
e increase the quantity demanded by 0.5 percent.

9 A given percentage increase in the price of a good is likely to cause a larger percentage decline in quantity demanded

a the shorter the passage of time.
b the larger the proportion of income spent on it.
c the harder it is to obtain good substitutes.
d all of the above.
e none of the above.

10 A negative value for

a price elasticity of supply implies an upward-sloping supply curve.

b cross elasticity of demand implies complementary goods.

c price elasticity of demand implies an inferior good.

d income elasticity of demand implies a normal good.

e income elasticity of demand implies an error in your calculation.

11 A decrease in tuition fees will decrease the university's total revenue if the price elasticity of demand for university education is

a negative.

b greater than zero but less than one.

c equal to one.

d greater than one.

e less than the price elasticity of supply.

12 When price goes from $1.50 to $2.50, quantity supplied increases from 9,000 to 11,000 units. What is the price elasticity of supply?

a 0.4

b 0.8

c 2.5

d 4.0

e none of the above

13 If the demand for frozen orange juice is price elastic, then a severe frost that destroys large quantities of oranges will likely

a reduce the equilibrium price of juice, but increase total consumer spending on it.

b reduce the equilibrium quantity of juice as well as total consumer spending on it.

c reduce both the equilibrium quantity and the price of juice.

d increase the equilibrium price of juice as well as total consumer spending on it.

e increase the equilibrium price of juice, but leave total consumer spending on it constant.

14 If a 4 percent rise in the price of peanut butter causes total revenue to fall by 8 percent, then demand for peanut butter

a is elastic.

b is inelastic.

c is unit elastic.

d has an elasticity of 1/2.

e has an elasticity of 2.

15 Tina and Brian work for the same recording company. Tina claims that they would be better off by increasing the price of their CDs while Brian claims that they would be better off by decreasing the price. We can conclude that

a Tina thinks the demand for CDs has price elasticity of zero, and Brian thinks price elasticity equals one.

b Tina thinks the demand for CDs has price elasticity equal to one, and Brian thinks price elasticity equals zero.

c Tina thinks the demand for CDs is price elastic, and Brian thinks it is price inelastic.

d Tina thinks the demand for CDs is price inelastic and Brian thinks it is price elastic.

e Tina and Brian should stick to singing and forget about economics.

16 The cross elasticity of the demand for white tennis balls with respect to the price of yellow tennis balls is probably

a negative and high.

b negative and low.

c positive and high.

d positive and low.

e zero.

17 Preferences for brussel sprouts increase. The price of brussel sprouts will not change if the price elasticity of

a demand is 0.

b demand is 1.

c supply is 0.

d supply is 1.

e supply is infinity.

18 A union leader who claims that "higher wages increase living standards without causing unemployment" believes that the demand for labour is

a income elastic.

b income inelastic.

c perfectly elastic.

d perfectly inelastic.

e unit elastic.

19 Luxury goods tend to have income elasticities of demand that are

a greater than one.

b greater than zero but less than one.

c positive.

d negative.

e first positive and then negative as income increases.

20 Given the relationship shown in Fig. 5.1 between total revenue from the sale of a good and the quantity of the good sold, then

a this is an inferior good.
b this is a normal good.
c the elasticity of demand is zero.
d the elasticity of demand is infinity.
e the elasticity of demand is one.

FIGURE **5.1**

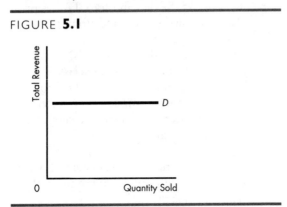

21 If a 4 percent decrease in income (at a constant price) causes a 2 percent decrease in the consumption of dweedles, then

a the income elasticity of demand for dweedles is negative.
b dweedles are a necessity and a normal good.
c dweedles are a luxury and a normal good.
d dweedles are an inferior good.
e a and d are true.

22 The long-run supply curve is likely to be

a more elastic than momentary supply, but less elastic than short-run supply.
b less elastic than momentary supply, but more elastic than short-run supply.
c less elastic than both momentary and short-run supply curves.
d more elastic than both momentary and short-run supply curves.
e vertical.

23 Business people speak about price elasticity of demand without using the actual term. Which of the following statements reflect elastic demand for a product?

a "A price cut won't help me. It won't increase sales, and I'll just get less money for each unit that I was selling before."
b "I don't think a price cut will make any difference to my bottom line. What I may gain from selling more I would lose on the lower price."
c "My customers are real bargain hunters. Since I set my prices just a few cents below my competitors, customers have flocked to the store and sales are booming."
d "With the recent economic recovery, people have more income to spend and sales are booming, even at the same prices as before."
e None of the above.

24 If the Jets decrease ticket prices and find that total revenue does not change, then the price elasticity of demand for tickets is

a zero.
b greater than zero, but less than one.
c equal to one.
d greater than one.
e inferior.

25 Long-run elasticity of supply of a good is greater than short-run elasticity of supply because

a more substitutes in consumption for the good can be found.
b more complements in consumption for the good can be found.
c more technological ways of adjusting supply can be exploited.
d income rises with more elapsed time.
e the long-run supply curve is steeper.

Short Answer Problems

I Why is elasticity superior to slope as a measure of the responsiveness of quantity demanded to changes in price?

2 In each of the following, compare the price elasticity of demand for each pair of goods and explain why the demand for one of the goods is more elastic than demand for the other.

  a IBM personal computers before the development of other "clone" personal computers versus IBM personal computers after the production of such clones

  b television sets versus matches

  c electricity just after an increase in its price versus electricity two years after the price increase

  d acetaminophen versus Tylenol-brand acetaminophen

3 Why does supply tend to be more elastic in the long run?

4 In Fig. 5.2, which demand curve (D_A or D_B) is more elastic in the price range P_1 to P_2? Explain why. [*Hint*: Use the formula for price elasticity of demand.]

FIGURE **5.2**

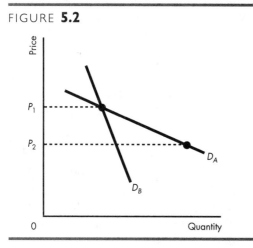

5 Consider the demand curve in Fig. 5.3(a). A portion of the demand curve is also described by the demand schedule in Table 5.2.

FIGURE **5.3**

(a)

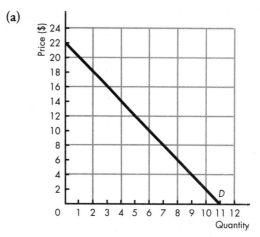

(b)

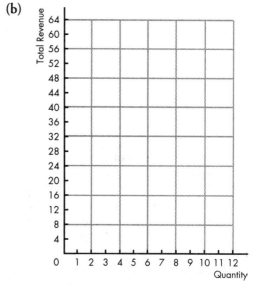

TABLE **5.2**

Price ($)	Quantity Demanded	Total Revenue
22	0	
20	1	
18	2	
16	3	
14	4	
12	5	
10	6	
8	7	
6	8	

Fill in the numbers for total revenue in the last column of Table 5.2, and graph your results on Fig. 5.3(b). Describe the shape of the total revenue curve as quantity increases (price decreases).

6   Using the same information for the demand curve in Short Answer Problem 5:
a   Complete the second and third columns of Table 5.3: η (the price elasticity of demand) and ΔTR (the change in total revenue) as the price falls from the higher price to the lower price. Describe the relationship between elasticity and change in total revenue as price falls (moving down the demand curve).

TABLE **5.3**

ΔP (\$)	η	ΔTR (\$)	η′	$\Delta TR′$ (\$)
16 — 14				
14 — 12				
12 — 10				
10 — 8				
8 — 6				

b   Suppose income increases from \$10,000 to \$14,000, causing an increase in demand: at every price, quantity demanded increases by 2 units. Draw the new demand curve on Fig. 5.3(a) and label it $D′$. Use this new demand curve to complete the last two columns of Table 5.3 for η′ (the new price elasticity of demand) and $\Delta TR′$ (the new change in total revenue).
c   Using the price range between \$16 and \$14, explain why $D′$ is more inelastic than D.
d   Calculate the income elasticity of demand, assuming the price remains constant at \$12. Is this a normal or inferior good? Explain why you could have answered the question even without calculating the income elasticity of demand.

7   The demand equation for woozles is $P = 60 - 2Q_D$. The supply equation for woozles is $P = 32 + 5Q_S$, where P is the price of a woozle in dollars, Q_D is the quantity of woozles demanded, and Q_S is the quantity of woozles supplied.
a   Calculate the price elasticity of demand for woozles between $Q_D = 4$ and $Q_D = 6$.
b   Initially, the woozle market is in equilibrium with $P^* = 52$ and $Q^* = 4$. Then, the supply curve shifts (the demand curve remains

constant) yielding a new equilibrium price of $P^* = 48$.
   Using all of the relevant information above, show *two separate methods* for determining whether total revenue increases, decreases, or remains constant in moving from the initial equilibrium to the new equilibrium.

8   Suppose Jean loses his present job and his monthly income falls from \$10,000 to \$6,000, while his monthly purchases of grits increase from 200 to 400.
a   Calculate his income elasticity of demand for grits.
b   Are grits a normal or inferior good? Explain why.

9   The demand equation for tribbles is $P = 50 - 1Q_D$. The supply equation for tribbles is $P = 20 + 0.5Q_S$, where P is the price of a tribble in dollars, Q_D is the quantity of tribbles demanded, and Q_S is the quantity of tribbles supplied. The tribble market is initially in equilibrium, and income is \$180.
a   What is the equilibrium quantity (Q^*) of tribbles?
b   What is the equilibrium price (P^*) of a tribble?
c   As a result of a decrease in income to \$120, the demand curve for tribbles shifts (the supply curve remains the same). The new demand equation is:

$$P = 110 - 1Q_D$$

   Use this information to calculate the new equilibrium quantity of tribbles; calculate the new equilibrium price of a tribble.
d   Calculate the income elasticity of demand for tribbles. Are tribbles a normal or inferior good? [*Hint:* In your calculation be sure to: (1) use the information about the *initial* equilibrium conditions (price, quantity, and income), and (2) keep in mind that price is assumed *constant* in calculating income elasticity. Only income and quantity change.]

10   Table 5.4 gives the demand schedules for good A when the price of good B (P_B) is \$8 and \$12. Complete the last column of the table by computing the cross elasticity of demand between goods A and B for each of the three prices of A. Are A and B complements or substitutes?

	$P_B = \$8$	$P_B = \$12$	
P_A	Q_A	Q'_A	η_x
$8	2,000	4,000	
$7	4,000	6,000	
$6	6,000	8,000	

TABLE **5.4** DEMAND SCHEDULES FOR GOOD A

A N S W E R S

True/False/Uncertain and Explain

1 F Responsiveness quantity demanded to ΔP. (99–100)

2 F Elasticity $\uparrow$ with elapsed time. (104–105)

3 F Slope constant; $\eta \downarrow$ as move down demand curve. (102–103)

4 T Colas are substitutes for you. (103)

5 T $\downarrow$ proportion income spent on good, more inelastic demand. (104)

6 T Narrower definition $\rightarrow$ more substitutes. (103)

⊘ 7 U Inferior good has negative income elasticity; cross elasticity sign depends on whether substitute or complement. (107–108)

⊘ 8 F η_x positive so goods are substitutes. (107)

9 T $\downarrow S \rightarrow \uparrow P \rightarrow \uparrow$ total revenue, so demand inelastic. (105–106)

10 F (% $\uparrow P$) > (% $\downarrow Q$), so total revenue ($P \times Q$) $\uparrow$. (105–106)

Multiple-Choice

1 b Demand curve vertical so $\downarrow P \rightarrow$ no Δ quantity demanded. (101–102)

2 b $|(-10/50)/(2/20)| = 2$. (100–101)

3 c Closer substitutes $\rightarrow \uparrow$ elasticity demand. (103–104)

4 b Definition. (110–111)

⊘ 5 d Rightward shift supply $\rightarrow \uparrow$ quantity sold and $\downarrow P$, with inelastic demand $\rightarrow \downarrow$ total revenue. (105–106)

6 a Definition. (101–102)

7 a $\eta_y = (\% \Delta Q_D)/(\% \Delta \text{income}) = 5/10 = 0.5$. (107–108)

8 c $\eta = |(\% \Delta Q_D)/(\% \Delta P)|$. $2 = |2/-1|$. Q_D and P always inversely related on demand curve. (100–101)

9 b $\eta \uparrow$ with $\uparrow$ proportion income spent on good. $\eta \uparrow$ when longer time passage and easier to obtain substitutes. (103–105)

10 b η_s and η never negative. η_y negative for inferior good. (107–108)

11 b $\downarrow P \rightarrow \downarrow$ total revenue when $\eta < 1$. η never negative. (105–106)

12 a $\eta_s = (\% \Delta Q_S)/(\% \Delta P) = (2,000/10,000)/(1/2) = 0.4$. (110–111)

13 b $\downarrow S \rightarrow \downarrow Q_D$ and $\uparrow P$. Since $\eta > 1$, $\uparrow P \rightarrow \downarrow$ expenditure. (105–106)

⊘ 14 a If $\uparrow P \rightarrow \downarrow$ total revenue, then η must be > 1. Must know (% ΔQ_D) to precisely calculate η. (105–106)

15 d Better off means $\uparrow$ total revenue. By definition relation $\uparrow P$, η, and total revenue. (105–106)

16 c Close substitutes so η_x positive and very elastic (high). (107)

17 e $\uparrow D \rightarrow$ no ΔP if supply curve horizontal (η_s = infinity). (110–111)

18 d Labour demand curve would be vertical. (101–102)

19 a See answer to 25 below. **c** correct, but **a** best answer. (107–109)

⊘ 20 e Note total revenue (*TR*) on *y*–axis. Since *TR* constant as $\uparrow Q$ (and presumably $\downarrow P$), $\eta = 1$. **a**, **b** depend on η_y. (105–106)

⊘ 21 b $\eta_y > 0$ so normal good. Necessities tend to have $\eta_y < 1$, while luxuries tend to have $\eta_y > 1$. (107–109)

22 d Definition. Momentary supply curve most vertical. (110–111)

23 c Small $\downarrow P \rightarrow$ large $\uparrow$ quantity demanded. **a** inelastic, **b** unit elastic, **d** on income elasticity. (101–102)

24 c Total revenue test. (105–106)

25 c Definition. **a**, **b**, **d** affect demand, not supply. Long-run supply curve flatter than short-run. (110–111)

Short Answer Problems

1 The slope of a demand curve tells us how much quantity demanded changes when price changes. However, the numerical value of the slope depends on the units we use to measure price and quantity and will change if the unit of measure is changed even though demand is unchanged. For example, if we change the unit of measure for quantity from tonnes to kilograms, the new slope of the (same) demand curve will be 1,000 times the old slope. On the other hand, elasticity gives a unit-free measure of the responsiveness of quantity demanded to price changes.

2 a The demand for IBM personal computers will be more elastic after the production of clone personal computers since there would then be more readily available substitutes.

b The demand for television sets will be more elastic since they will generally take a larger proportion of consumer income.

c The demand for electricity after the passage of two years will be more elastic since consumers will have more time to find substitutes for electricity, for example, a gas stove.

d The demand for Tylenol is more elastic. There are far more substitutes for Tylenol (other brands of acetaminophen) than for acetaminophen in general.

3 Supply is more elastic in the long run because the passage of time allows producers to find better (more efficient) ways of producing that are not available in the short run. The responsiveness of production to an increase in price will increase as firms have time to discover and implement new technologies or to increase the scale of operation.

4 D_A is more elastic than D_B. To see why, look at the formula for price elasticity of demand:

$$\eta = \left| \frac{\% \, \Delta \text{ quantity demanded}}{\% \, \Delta \text{ price}} \right|$$

The percentage change in price is the same for the two demand curves. But the percentage change in quantity is greater for D_A. At P_1, the initial quantity demanded is the same for both demand curves (Q_1). With the fall in price to P_2, the increase in quantity demanded is greater for D_A (to Q_{2A}) than for D_B (to Q_{2B}). Therefore D_A is more elastic than D_B.

FIGURE **5.2** SOLUTION

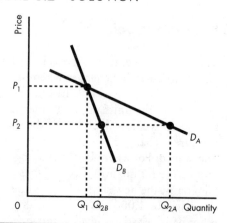

5 The numbers for total revenue are shown in Table 5.2 Solution. The total revenue curve is shown in Fig. 5.3(b) Solution. The total revenue curve first increases (at a diminishing rate—its slope is decreasing as we move up the curve), then reaches a maximum between $Q = 5$ and $Q = 6$, and then decreases. We will encounter this pattern of changing total revenue again in studying monopoly in Chapter 12.

TABLE **5.2** SOLUTION

Price ($)	Quantity Demanded	Total Revenue
22	0	0
20	1	20
18	2	36
16	3	48
14	4	56
12	5	60
10	6	60
8	7	56
6	8	48

FIGURE **5.3**(b) SOLUTION

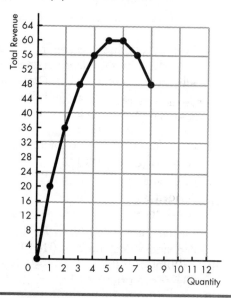

6 a The completed columns of Table 5.3 are shown here. The second and third columns of the table show that as price falls, total revenue increases when demand is elastic; total revenue remains constant when demand is unit elastic; total revenue falls when demand is inelastic.

TABLE **5.3**   SOLUTION

ΔP ($)	η	ΔTR($)	η′	ΔTR′ ($)
16 — 14	2.14	+8	1.36	+4
14 — 12	1.44	+4	1.00	0
12 — 10	1.00	0	0.73	−4
10 — 8	0.69	−4	0.53	−8
8 — 6	0.47	−8	0.37	−12

b The new demand curve is labelled D' in Fig 5.3(a) Solution. The last two columns of the table have been completed on the basis of the new demand curve.

FIGURE **5.3** (a)   SOLUTION

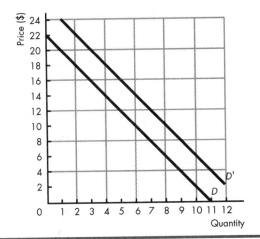

c Since they are parallel, D' and D have exactly the same slope. Thus we know that for a given change in price, the change in quantity demanded will be the same for the two curves. However, elasticity is determined by *percentage* changes, and the percentage change in quantity demanded is different for the two curves, although the percentage change in price will be the same. For a given percentage change in price, the percentage change in quantity demanded will always be less for D'. For example, as the price falls from $16 to $14 (a 13 percent change), the quantity demanded increases from 5 to 6 units along D', but from 3 to 4 along D. The percentage change in quantity demanded is only 18 percent along D' and 29 percent along D. Since the percentage change in price is the same for both curves, D' is more inelastic than D.

d Income increases from $10,000 to $14,000. At a constant price of $12, the increase in income, which shifts out the demand curve to D', increases the quantity consumers will demand from 5 units to 7 units. Substituting these numbers into the formula for the income elasticity of demand yields

$$\eta_y = \left(\frac{\Delta Q}{Q_{ave}}\right) \Big/ \left(\frac{\Delta Y}{Y_{ave}}\right)$$

$$= \left(\frac{2}{6}\right) \Big/ \left(\frac{4,000}{12,000}\right) = +1$$

The income elasticity of demand is a positive number, since both ΔQ and ΔY are positive. Therefore, this is a normal good. We already knew that from the information in part **b**, which stated that the demand curve shifted rightward with an increase in income. If this were an inferior good, the increase in income would have shifted the demand curve leftward and the income elasticity of demand would have been negative.

7 a In order to calculate price elasticity of demand, we need to know two points (each point a combination of price and quantity demanded) on the demand curve. We only are given the quantity demanded coordinate of each point. By substituting $Q_D = 4$ and $Q_D = 6$ into the demand equation, we can solve for the two price coordinates:

At $Q_D = 4$; $P = 60 − 2(4) = 52$
At $Q_D = 6$; $P = 60 − 2(6) = 48$

These price and quantity demanded coordinates can now be substituted into the formula for the price elasticity of demand:

$$\eta = \left| \left(\frac{\Delta Q}{Q_{ave}}\right) \Big/ \left(\frac{\Delta P}{P_{ave}}\right) \right|$$

$$= \left| \left(\frac{-2}{5}\right) \Big/ \left(\frac{4}{50}\right) \right| = 5$$

b One method is simply to compare total revenue ($P \times Q$) at each equilibrium.

Initial equilibrium:
Total revenue = ($P \times Q$) = (52×4) = 208.

New equilibrium:
If $P^* = 48$, Q^* can be calculated by substituting P^* into the demand equation:

$$48 = 60 − 2 Q^*$$
$$2Q^* = 12$$
$$Q^* = 6$$

So total revenue = ($P \times Q$) = (48×6) = 288.

In moving from the initial to the new equilibrium, total revenue has increased.

A second method is to use the information from part **a** on the price elasticity of demand. We know that between $Q_D = 4$ and $Q_D = 6$

on the demand curve, demand is elastic. These two points correspond to the initial equilibrium and, after the shift of the supply curve, the new equilibrium. Since demand here is elastic, we know that the fall in price from $P = 52$ to $P = 48$ will increase total revenue.

8 a Using the formula for income elasticity of demand

$$\eta_y = \left(\frac{\Delta Q}{Q_{ave}}\right) \bigg/ \left(\frac{\Delta Y}{Y_{ave}}\right)$$

$$= \left(\frac{200 - 400}{\frac{1}{2}(200 + 400)}\right) \bigg/ \left(\frac{10,000 - 6,000}{\frac{1}{2}(10,000 + 6,000)}\right)$$

$$= \left(\frac{-200}{300}\right) \bigg/ \left(\frac{4,000}{8,000}\right) = -\frac{4}{3}$$

b Grits are an inferior good because the income elasticity of demand is negative.

9 a The initial equilibrium quantity (Q^*) of tribbles is 20. [Refer to *Study Guide* Chapter 4 if you need help in solving demand and supply equations.]

b The initial equilibrium price (P^*) of a tribble is $30. [Refer to *Study Guide* Chapter 4 if you need help in solving demand and supply equations.]

c The new equilibrium quantity of tribbles is 60. The new equilibrium price of a tribble is $50.

d At the initial income of $180 and price of $30, the quantity of tribbles demanded is 20. In order to find the new quantity demanded at income of $120, we have to use the new demand equation. But since *price* is assumed constant in calculating income elasticity, we have to substitute $P = 30$ into the new demand equation to get the appropriate new quantity. It would be *incorrect* to use the new equilibrium quantity, because that quantity corresponds to a *different price* ($50).

$$P = 110 - 1Q_D$$
$$30 = 110 - 1Q_D$$
$$Q_D = 80$$

We now have appropriate information about the initial quantity demanded (20) and income ($180), and about the new quantity demanded (80) and income ($120). Substituting this information into the formula for income elasticity of demand yields

$$\eta_y = \left(\frac{\Delta Q}{Q_{ave}}\right) \bigg/ \left(\frac{\Delta Y}{Y_{ave}}\right)$$

$$= \left(\frac{-60}{50}\right) \bigg/ \left(\frac{60}{150}\right) = -3$$

Since the income elasticity of demand for tribbles is negative, tribbles are an inferior good.

10 The cross elasticities of demand between A and B are listed in Table 5.4 Solution. Since the cross elasticities are positive, we know that A and B are substitutes.

TABLE **5.4** SOLUTION DEMAND SCHEDULES FOR GOOD A

	P_B = $8	P_B = $12	
P_A	Q_A	Q'_A	η_x
$8	2,000	4,000	1.67
$7	4,000	6,000	1.00
$6	6,000	8,000	0.71

Markets in Action

KEY CONCEPTS

Housing Markets and Rent Ceilings

In an unregulated housing market

- Shortage → ↑ rents → economizing on space, ↑ quantity supplied (short run), and building activity shifts supply rightward (long run).

- Rents ↓ and the housing stock ↑.

In a regulated housing market

- A **rent ceiling** (a **price ceiling** applied to rents) makes it illegal to ↑ rents.

- Housing stocks are lower than in an unregulated market both in short and long run. No incentive to economize on space or build new housing.

- Shortage → excess demand →

  - **search activity** (time spent looking for someone with whom to do business) and
  - **black markets** (illegal trading arrangements at prices in excess of ceilings).

- Total housing cost in regulated market, including cost of search activity, may be > cost in unregulated market.

The Labour Market and Minimum Wages

Minimum wage laws make it illegal to hire labour below a specified wage.

- Minimum wages create excess supply of labour and lower the quantity of labour demanded and hired.

- Unemployed workers willing to work at a lower wage spend more time searching for work.

- Minimum wage laws contribute to high unemployment among unskilled and younger workers.

Taxes

Sales tax shifts up supply curve by vertical distance equal to amount of tax. Who pays tax depends on elasticities of supply and demand.

Supply elasticity and tax division

- Perfectly inelastic supply—sellers pay all.

- More inelastic supply—more sellers pay.

- More elastic supply—more buyers pay.

- Perfectly elastic supply—buyers pay all.

Demand elasticity and tax division

- Perfectly inelastic demand—buyers pay all.

- More inelastic demand—more buyers pay.

- More elastic demand—more sellers pay.

- Perfectly elastic demand—sellers pay all.

Markets for Prohibited Goods

Penalizing dealers for selling illegal goods → ↑ cost selling goods and ↓ supply. Penalizing buyers for consuming illegal goods → ↓ willingness to pay and ↓ demand.

- (Sellers' penalties > buyers' penalties) → ↓ Q, ↑ P.

- (Sellers' penalties < buyers' penalties) → ↓ Q, ↓ P.

- Taxing (decriminalized) goods can achieve the same consumption levels as prohibition.

Stabilizing Farm Revenue

Demand for most farm products is inelastic → large variations farm revenue.

- Poor harvest ($\downarrow S$) → $\uparrow P$, $\uparrow$ total revenue.
- Bumper harvest ($\uparrow S$) → $\downarrow P$, $\downarrow$ total revenue.

Farm revenue is stabilized through speculation by inventory holders, who buy at low prices and sell at high prices, reducing price fluctuations.

Farm stabilization agencies (**farm marketing boards**) also limit price fluctuations by setting

- price floors → $\uparrow$ market price and surpluses.
- **quotas** (quantity restrictions on production) → $\uparrow P$ and $\downarrow Q$ grown.
- **subsidies** (payments to producers by governments) → $\uparrow$ supply and $\downarrow$ market price (but farmers receive market price + subsidy).

HELPFUL HINTS

1 In the real world we frequently observe market regulation by governments in the form of price constraints of one form or another. It is thus important to study the effects of such regulation. Another benefit of studying government regulation is to obtain an understanding of how markets work when, by contrast, the government does *not* affect the normal operation of markets.

Whenever something disturbs an equilibrium in an unregulated (free) market, the desires of buyers and sellers are brought back into balance by price movements. If prices are controlled by government regulation, however, the price mechanism can no longer serve this purpose. Thus, *balance* must be restored in some other way. In the case of price ceilings, black markets are likely to arise. If black markets cannot develop because of strict enforcement of price ceilings, then demanders will be forced to bear the costs of increased search activity, waiting in line, or something else.

2 This chapter discusses government price constraints in three specific markets: rental housing, labour, and farm products. The principles raised in those discussions, however, can be generalized to other markets.

In any market with a legal price ceiling set below the market-clearing price, we will observe excess quantity demanded, because the price cannot increase to eliminate it. As a consequence, the value of the last unit of the good available will exceed the controlled price. Demanders are willing to engage in costly activities up to the value of that last unit (search activity, waiting lines, and black market activity) in order to obtain the good.

Furthermore, if price is allowed to increase in response to a decrease in supply or an increase in demand, there are incentive effects for suppliers to produce more and demanders to purchase less (movements along the supply and demand curves). Indeed, it is the response to these incentives that restores equilibrium in markets with freely adjusting prices. If, however, the price cannot adjust, these price-induced incentive effects do not have a chance to operate. Specifically, in the case of rent ceilings, the inability of rents (price) to rise means that: (1) there is no inducement to use the current stock of housing more intensively in the short run and (2) there is no incentive to construct new housing in the long run. Similarly, the effects on any market in which a minimum price (price floor) is set above the market-clearing (equilibrium) price will be similar to those discussed in the text for the labour market under a minimum wage or price floors in agricultural markets.

3 The division of the burden of a tax is also called tax incidence. Who pays a sales tax imposed on producers depends on the elasticities of demand and supply. The general principles of tax incidence are

- The more inelastic the demand, the more consumers pay.
- The more elastic the demand, the more producers pay.
- The more inelastic the supply, the more producers pay.
- The more elastic the supply, the more consumers pay.

SELF-TEST

True/False/Uncertain and Explain

1 When rents in an unregulated housing market rise due to a decrease in supply, people who are unable to pay the higher rents will not get housing.

2 The more elastic demand is for a product, the larger is the fraction of a sales tax paid by consumers.

3 If a rent ceiling exceeds people's willingness to pay, search activity and black markets will increase.

4 The statement "if we legalize and tax drugs, tax revenues could be used to finance more drug education programs" is normative.

5 An increase in the minimum wage will reduce the number of workers employed.

6 The impact of minimum wage laws on unemployment among young workers tends to be about the same as it is for older workers.

7 Suppose the supply curve for corn fluctuates widely but the demand curve is stable. The price of corn will fluctuate more if demand is elastic rather than inelastic.

8 If the price is higher than an inventory holder's expected future price, she sells goods from inventory.

9 If penalties are imposed on both sellers and buyers in a market for prohibited goods, the price remains constant and the quantity bought decreases.

10 A subsidy shifts the demand curve for a good rightward.

Multiple-Choice

1 The short-run supply curve for rental housing is positively sloped because
a the supply of housing is fixed in the short run.
b the current stock of buildings will be used more intensively as rents rise.
c the cost of constructing new buildings increases as the number of buildings increases.
d the cost of constructing new buildings is about the same regardless of the number of buildings in existence.
e new buildings will be constructed as rents rise.

2 Rent ceilings imposed by governments
a keep rental prices below the unregulated market price.
b keep rental prices above the unregulated market price.
c keep rental prices equal to the unregulated market price.
d increase the stock of rental housing.
e increase the intensity of use of the current stock of rental housing.

3 Figure 6.1 shows the market for frisbees before and after a sales tax is imposed. The sales tax on each frisbee is
a $0.40.
b $0.60.
c $1.00.
d $5.60.
e $6.60.

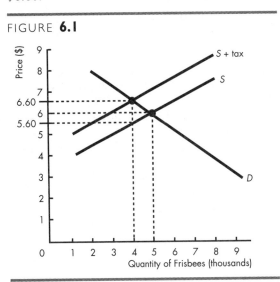

FIGURE **6.1**

4 Refer to Fig. 6.1. For each frisbee, the sellers' share of the tax burden is

a $0.40.
b $0.60.
c $1.00.
d $5.60.
e $6.60.

5 Refer to Fig. 6.1. For each frisbee, the buyers' share of the tax burden is

a $0.40.
b $0.60.
c $1.00.
d $5.60.
e $6.60.

6 Refer to Fig. 6.1. Government revenue from the tax is

a $4,000.
b $5,000.
c $22,400.
d $26,400.
e $30,000.

7 From Fig. 6.1 we can deduce that between 4,000 and 5,000 units, the demand for frisbees is

a inelastic.
b unit elastic.
c elastic.
d more elastic than the supply (S) of frisbees.
e soaring.

8 European Union (EU) countries have been accumulating butter and cheese mountains and wine lakes. These surpluses are consistent with

a floor prices for agricultural products that are below market prices.
b floor prices for agricultural products that are above market prices.
c ceiling prices for agricultural products that are below market prices.
d ceiling prices for agricultural products that are above market prices.
e quotas for agricultural products.

9 A momentary supply curve is

a elastic since price is fixed.
b relatively more elastic than a short-run supply curve.
c relatively inelastic since yields are known, but sales are not.
d inelastic since output is fixed.
e as ephemeral as gossamer wings.

10 A price ceiling set below the equilibrium price will result in

a excess supply.
b excess demand.
c the equilibrium price.
d an increase in supply.
e a decrease in demand.

11 If the minimum wage is set at $2 per hour in Fig. 6.2, what is the level of unemployment in millions of hours?

a 50
b 40
c 20
d 10
e 0

FIGURE **6.2**

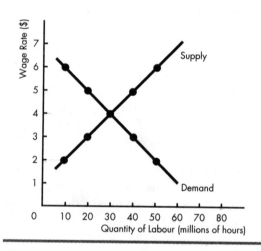

12 With inventory speculation, a bumper crop of barley will

a decrease farm revenue, while a poor harvest will increase farm revenue.
b increase farm revenue, while a poor harvest will decrease farm revenue.
c decrease farm revenue as will a poor harvest.
d increase farm revenue as will a poor harvest.
e do none of the above.

13 If enforcement is aimed at sellers of a prohibited good,

a price and quantity bought will decrease.
b price and quantity bought will increase.
c price will increase and quantity bought will decrease.
d price will decrease and quantity bought will increase.
e price change will be uncertain and quantity bought will decrease.

14 If the price of a good is not affected by a sales tax, then

   a   supply is perfectly elastic.
   b   demand is perfectly elastic.
   c   elasticity of supply is greater than elasticity of demand.
   d   elasticity of demand is greater than elasticity of supply.
   e   none of the above.

15 Which of the following statements is *false*?

   a   Buying goods to put into inventory is equivalent to decreasing quantity supplied.
   b   Selling goods from inventory is equivalent to increasing quantity supplied.
   c   In a market with inventories, producers' supply differs from market supply.
   d   Producers' supply is the sum of market supply and inventory supply.
   e   Inventory holders must forecast future prices.

16 Which of the following is *not* a likely outcome of rent ceilings?

   a   a black market for rent-controlled housing
   b   long waiting lists of potential renters of rent-controlled housing
   c   a short-run shortage of housing
   d   black market prices below the rent ceiling prices
   e   increased search activity for rent-controlled housing

17 Figure 6.3 illustrates the short-run demand and supply curves in the wheat bran market. If the Wheat Marketing Board sets a quota of 50 million bushels, then the market-clearing price of a bushel of wheat bran is

   a $1.00.
   b $3.00.
   c $5.00.
   d   two scoops of raisins.
   e   none of the above.

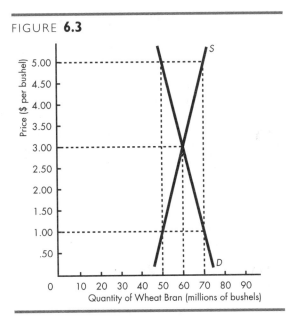

FIGURE **6.3**

18 Refer to Fig. 6.3. With the quota of 50 million bushels, farmers have an incentive to

   a   decrease output because the market-clearing price is below cost of production.
   b   decrease output because there is a surplus at the market-clearing price.
   c   increase output because the market-clearing price is above cost of production.
   d   increase output because there is a shortage at the market-clearing price.
   e   stick to the quota.

19 Refer to Fig. 6.3. Suppose the marketing board develops a new kind of subsidy called a direct payment plan. Farmers are told, "We will guarantee you $5.00 per bushel, but everything you produce at this price must be sold on the market for whatever buyers will pay; then we will give you (at taxpayers' expense) the difference between the market price and $5.00 per bushel." How many bushels of wheat bran will be sold?

   a   20 million
   b   50 million
   c   60 million
   d   70 million
   e   none of the above

20 Refer to Fig. 6.3. The amount of taxpayers' money that the marketing board pays to farmers in Question **19** is

   a   zero.
   b $70 million.
   c $250 million.
   d $280 million.
   e $350 million.

21 Which of the following statements about prohibited goods is *true*?

a Taxes are more effective in changing preferences than prohibition.

b Prohibition is more effective in generating revenue than an equivalent tax.

c Taxes and penalties cannot be set so as to yield equivalent outcomes.

d Taxes generate revenues, while prohibition generates more enforcement expenses.

e None of the above is true.

22 Which of the following types of labour would be most significantly affected by an increase in the legal minimum wage?

a professional athletes

b young, unskilled labour

c skilled union workers

d university professors

e self-employed labour

23 Which of the following combinations would generally yield the greatest price fluctuation?

a large supply shifts and inelastic demand

b large supply shifts and elastic demand

c large supply shifts and perfectly elastic demand

d small supply shifts and inelastic demand

e small supply shifts and elastic demand

24 With inventory speculation

a prices stabilize but farm revenue does not.

b prices do not stabilize but farm revenue does.

c bumper crops bring decreased total revenue.

d poor harvests bring increased total revenue.

e c and d.

25 An agricultural subsidy

a shifts the supply curve rightward.

b benefits consumers by lowering product prices.

c benefits farmers by raising the price they receive.

d imposes major costs on taxpayers.

e does all of the above.

Short Answer Problems

1 Suppose there is a significant reduction in the supply of gasoline. Explain how an unregulated market adjusts. What is it that induces consumers to reduce their consumption of gasoline willingly?

2 Governments tend to place high sales taxes (often called "sin" taxes) on liquor and cigarettes. Aside from moral and health reasons, why are these goods chosen as a source of tax revenue?

3 The supply of fruit is subject to unpredictable fluctuations. Why does the price of fresh fruit fluctuate much more than the price of canned fruit?

4 Suppose the Nudist Party wins the next federal election because all the clothed citizens forgot to vote. The Nudists pass a law making clothes illegal. Unfortunately for the Nudists, the police don't take the law seriously (where would officers pin their badges?) and put almost no effort into enforcement. Use a diagram to explain why the black market price of now illegal clothes will be close to the unregulated market equilibrium price.

5 Suppose that the market for rental housing is initially in long-run equilibrium. Use graphs to answer the following:

a Explain how an unregulated market for rental housing would adjust, if there is a sudden significant increase in demand. What will happen to rent and the quantity of units rented in the short run and in the long run? Be sure to discuss the effect on incentives (in both the short run and the long run) as the market-determined price (rent) changes.

b Now explain how the market would adjust to the increase in demand, if rent ceilings are established at the level of the initial equilibrium rent. What has happened to supplier incentives in this case?

6 The demand for and supply of gasoline are given in Table 6.1.

a What are the equilibrium price and quantity of gasoline?

TABLE **6.1**

Price ($ per litre)	Quantity Demanded	Quantity Supplied
	(millions of litres per day)	
1.40	8	24
1.30	10	22
1.20	12	20
1.10	14	18
1.00	16	16
0.90	18	14

b Suppose that the quantity of gasoline supplied suddenly declines by 8 million litres per day at every price. Construct a new table of price, quantity demanded, and quantity supplied, and draw a graph of the demand curve and the initial and new supply curves. Assuming that the market for gasoline is unregulated, use either your table or graph to find the new equilibrium price and quantity of gasoline.

c How has the change in price affected the behaviour of demanders? the behaviour of suppliers?

7 Suppose that the government imposes a price ceiling of $1 per litre of gasoline at the same time as the decrease in supply reported in Short Answer Problem **6b**.

a What is the quantity of gasoline demanded? quantity supplied?

b What is the quantity of gasoline actually sold?

c What is the excess quantity of gasoline demanded?

d What is the highest price demanders are willing to pay for the last litre of gasoline available?

e Geordi values gasoline as in **d**. How long would Geordi be willing to sit in line to buy 10 litres of gasoline if the best alternative was to work at a wage rate of $8 per hour?

8 The Ministry of Treasury has been authorized to levy a 15¢ per unit excise (sales) tax on one of two goods—comic books or dog biscuits. As a summer student at the Ministry, you are given an assignment by the Director of Taxes, Dr. More. You must choose the good that meets two objectives: (1) it will yield the greatest tax revenue, and (2) the major burden of the tax will fall on consumers. Ministry researchers have estimated the supply and demand curves (without the tax) for each market. The comic book market is shown in Fig. 6.4 and the dog biscuit market in Fig. 6.5. The following questions will help you complete your assignment.

FIGURE **6.4**

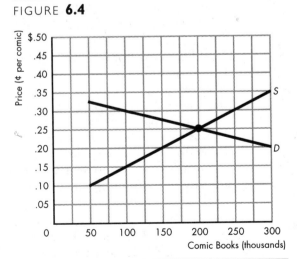

Comic Books (thousands)

a For the comic book market, shift the appropriate curve to reflect the tax and draw it on Fig. 6.4. Label the curve either *S + tax* or *D + tax*. Identify the new equilibrium price and quantity. Compare the total expenditure in the original and new equilibria.

b Calculate the total tax revenue collected, and indicate it as an area on Fig. 6.4.

c How much of the tax is paid by consumers? by producers?

FIGURE **6.5**

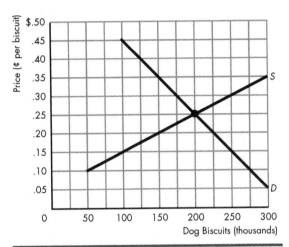

Dog Biscuits (thousands)

d Now perform the same analysis on the dog biscuit market. Shift the appropriate curve to reflect the tax and draw it on Fig. 6.5. Label the curve either *S + tax* or *D + tax*. Identify the new equilibrium price and quantity. Compare the total expenditure in the original and new equilibria.

e Calculate the total tax revenue collected, and indicate it as an area on Fig. 6.5.

f How much of the tax is paid by consumers? by producers?

g What is your recommendation to Dr. More? Explain.

9 Dr. More was pleased with your excise tax recommendation in Short Answer Problem **8**, but you can't stop wondering about his comment, "Hmm, I thought you would do it the other way." If you haven't already figured out to what he was referring, the following questions will help.

a For the comic book market, calculate the elasticity of demand between the original and new equilibrium points. Is demand elastic or inelastic?

b Perform the same calculation for the dog biscuit market. Is demand elastic or inelastic?

c What do you know about demand elasticities that would have allowed you to complete your assignment "the other way" and predict which market would yield maximum tax revenue, and which market would place most of the tax burden on consumers?

⊘ 10 Figure 6.6 shows the demand curve in the market for grinola seeds. Grinola is difficult to grow—simply a frown from a farmer in the field causes the seeds to develop split ends which makes them worthless. As a result, grinola harvests fluctuate widely.

FIGURE **6.6**

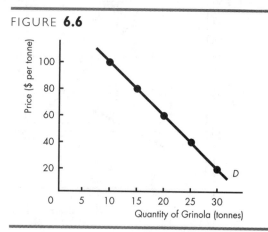

a If there are no inventory speculators in the grinola market, what will the market price be when momentary supply is 25 tonnes? 20 tonnes? 15 tonnes?

b Suppose inventory speculators discover that grinola can be stored easily and enter the market looking for a profit. They forecast an expected price of $60 per tonne. Explain what happens when the momentary supply is 25 tonnes. Identify the amount the inventory speculators buy or sell, the quantity bought by consumers, and the market price.

c Repeat the analysis in part **b** for a momentary supply of 20 tonnes.

d Repeat the analysis in part **b** for a momentary supply of 15 tonnes.

e What has happened to price fluctuations in the grinola market?

f Inventory speculators don't operate out of the goodness of their hearts. Have they made a profit in grinola? Explain your calculation.

ANSWERS

True/False/Uncertain and Explain

1 **T** At equilibrium rent, all who can afford housing get it, but not necessarily those who need housing. (120–121)

2 **F** More elastic demand → more substitutes → better able to escape tax by not buying. (127–128)

3 **F** Ceiling is above market price so search activity won't ↑ and black markets won't arise. (122–123)

⊘ 4 **F** Positive statement; can be verified by observation. (130–132)

5 **T** ↑ minimum wage → ↓ quantity labour demanded. (125–126)

6 **F** Greater impact on young workers since they have lower wages. (125–126)

7 **F** Fluctuate more if demand inelastic. (133–134)

8 **T** Buy low, sell high. (134–135)

⊘ 9 **U** Effect on P depends on relative magnitude of penalties. (130–132)

10 **F** Shifts supply rightward. (137)

Multiple-Choice

1 **b** c, d, and e refer to long run. (120–121)

2 **a** Definition. **d** and **e** result of ↑ rent in unregulated market. (122–123)

3 **c** Equals the vertical distance between the two supply curves. (126–127)

4 **a** Original $P = \$6$, new $P = \$6.60$. Sellers pay $1 tax and get $0.60 more from buyers, so sellers pay $0.40. (126–127)

5 **b** See previous answer. (126–127)

6 **a** $1 per frisbee × 1,000 units sold. (126–127)

⊘ 7 **c** ↑ P ($6 to $6.60) → ↓ total revenue ($30,000 to $26,400). **d** wrong—$\eta = 2.3$ and $\eta_s = 3.2$. (126–130)

8 **b** Floor above market P → excess supply. (135–137)

9 **d** Definition. (133–134)

10 **b** Draw graph. No Δ *ceteris paribus* assumptions → no shift supply or demand. (122–123)

⊘ 11 **e** Floor below equilibrium P doesn't prevent market from reaching equilibrium. (124–126)

12 **b** Price remains constant so total revenue is positively correlated with output. (134–135)

13 **c** Supply shifts leftward as penalties are added to other costs. (130–132)

14 **b** **a** would ↑ P by full amount tax. **c** and **d** affect P but amounts uncertain. (127–128)

15 **d** Market supply = producers' supply + inventory supply. (134–135)

16 d Black market prices will be above ceiling. (122–123)

17 c Where momentary supply curve at 50 million bushels intersects demand. (135–137)

18 c Farmers receiving $5 but willing to supply this quantity at (their cost of) $1. (135–137)

19 d Quantity supplied at $P = \$5$. (135–137)

20 d 70 million bushels sell for $1 per bushel. Taxpayers make up difference of $4 per bushel × 70 million. (135–137)

21 d Reverse taxes and prohibition to make **a** and **b** true. (130–132)

22 b Lowest wage labour. (124–126)

23 a Draw graphs to see. (133–134)

24 a Quantities (and revenues) still fluctuate. **c** and **d** true if reverse decrease and increase. (134–135)

25 e Definition. (137)

Short Answer Problems

1 If the market for gasoline is initially in equilibrium and there is a significant reduction in supply, there will be excess quantity demanded at the existing price. As a result, the price of gasoline will rise, which will cause movements along the new supply curve and the demand curve. As the price rises there will be a price-induced increase in quantity supplied and a price-induced decrease in quantity demanded. The price continues to rise until the excess quantity demanded is eliminated. The price increase causes consumers to reduce their desired consumption of gasoline.

2 Because alcohol and nicotine are addictive, the demands for liquor and cigarettes are relatively inelastic. When liquor and cigarette prices are increased by "sin" taxes, the percentage fall in quantity demanded is less than the percentage increase in price. Thus total revenue increases as does tax revenue. To raise a fixed amount of revenue, it takes a much smaller per unit tax on goods with inelastic demand than on goods with elastic demand. Inelastic demand also means, *ceteris paribus*, that a greater portion of the tax is borne by consumers rather than producers.

3 The key difference between the two goods is that most fresh fruit cannot be stored effectively while canned fruit is stored easily. Without storage, inventory speculation is difficult, and fresh fruit prices fluctuate widely with variations in the momentary supply curve. Since canned fruit can be stored, inventory holders operate to make the supply of canned fruit perfectly elastic

at the inventory holders' expected price. Thus supply-induced price fluctuations for canned fruit are eliminated. Canned fruit prices can still fluctuate if the inventory holders' expected price changes.

4 The clothing market is illustrated in Fig. 6.7. The demand curve is D and the supply curve is S. The equilibrium price is P_c and the quantity is Q_c. Since police enforcement is lax, the cost of breaking the law (CBL) is very small for both buyers and sellers. Thus the curves that incorporate CBL are very close to the original demand and supply curves. The intersection of $D - CBL$ and $S + CBL$ yields a new equilibrium price identical to the original price (the price may be slightly higher or lower depending on the relative magnitude of the shifts of demand and supply) and a new equilibrium quantity (Q_p) only slightly less than the original quantity.

FIGURE **6.7**

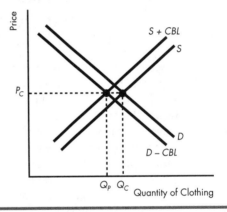

5 a Figure 6.8 corresponds to an unregulated market for rental housing. The initial demand, short-run supply, and long-run supply curves are D_0, SS_0, and LS respectively. The market is initially in long-run equilibrium at point a corresponding to rent R_0 and quantity of rental units Q_0. Demand then increases to D_1, creating excess quantity demanded of $Q_2 - Q_0$ at the initial rent. In the short run, in an unregulated market, rent will rise to R_1 to clear the markets and the equilibrium quantity of housing rented is Q_1 (point b). Note that as the rent rises, the quantity of rental housing supplied increases (a movement from point a to point b along supply curve SS_0) as the existing stock of housing is used more intensively. Also the quantity of housing demanded decreases (a movement from point c to point b along demand curve D_1). Together, these movements eliminate the excess quantity demanded. The higher rent also

provides an incentive to construct new housing in the long run. This is illustrated by the shift in the supply curve from SS_0 to SS_1. Finally, a new long-run equilibrium is achieved at point c, with rent restored to its original level and the number of units rented equal to Q_2.

FIGURE **6.8**

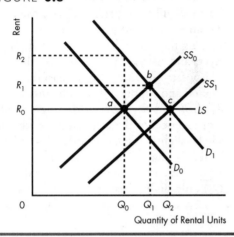

Quantity of Rental Units

b We can also use Fig. 6.8 to discuss the behaviour of a market with a rent ceiling set at R_0. Start in the same long-run equilibrium at point a. Once again we observe an increase in demand from D_0 to D_1. In this case, however, the rent cannot rise to restore equilibrium. There will be no incentive to use the existing stock of housing more intensively in the short run or to construct new housing in the long run. The quantity of rental housing supplied will remain at Q_0. Since the last unit of rental housing is valued at R_2, but rent is fixed at R_0, demanders of rental housing will be willing to bear additional costs up to $R_2 - R_0$ (in the form of additional search activity or illegal payments) in order to obtain rental housing.

6 a The equilibrium price of gasoline is $1.00 per litre since, at that price, the quantity of gasoline demanded is equal to the quantity supplied (16 million litres per day). The equilibrium quantity of gasoline is 16 million litres per day.
   b The new table and graph are shown in Table 6.2 and Fig. 6.9.

TABLE **6.2**

Price	Quantity Demanded (millions of litres per day)	Quantity Supplied (millions of litres per day)
1.40	8	16
1.30	10	14
1.20	12	12
1.10	14	10
1.00	16	8
0.90	18	6

FIGURE **6.9**

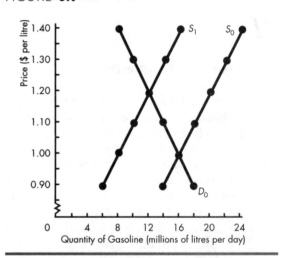

Quantity of Gasoline (millions of litres per day)

The new equilibrium price is $1.20 per litre since, at that price, the quantity of gasoline demanded equals the new quantity supplied (12 million litres per day). The new equilibrium quantity is 12 million litres of gasoline per day.
   c The increase in price has caused the quantity of gasoline demanded to decrease by 4 million litres per day (from 16 to 12 million). Given the new supply curve S_1, the increase in price from $1.00 to $1.20 per litre increases the quantity of gasoline supplied by 4 million litres per day (from 8 to 12 million).

7 a At the ceiling price of $1.00, quantity demanded is 16 million litres per day, quantity supplied is 8 million litres per day.
   b The quantity of gasoline actually sold is 8 million litres per day. When, at a given price, quantity demanded and quantity supplied differ, whichever quantity is *less* determines the quantity actually sold.
   c The excess quantity of gasoline demanded is 8 million litres per day.

d The highest price consumers are willing to pay for the last unit of gasoline supplied (the 8-millionth litre per day) is $1.40. You can obtain this answer from your graph by imagining a vertical line from the quantity 8 million litres up to where it intersects the demand curve at $1.40. The demand curve shows the highest price consumers are willing to pay for that last litre supplied.

e The regulated price of gasoline is $1.00 per litre but the value to Geordi of the last litre is $1.40, so he would be willing to bear costs of $4.00 above the regulated price of gasoline to obtain 10 litres ($0.40 × 10 litres). If the best alternative is to earn $8.00 per hour, Geordi would be willing to spend up to half an hour sitting in line to buy 10 litres.

8 a See Fig. 6.4 Solution. In the comic book market, the supply curve shifts up vertically by an amount equal to the tax (15¢). The original equilibrium price is 25¢ and quantity is 200,000. The new equilibrium price is 30¢ and quantity is 100,000. Total expenditure has decreased, from $50,000 (25¢ × 200,000) to $30,000 (30¢ × 100,000).

FIGURE **6.4** SOLUTION

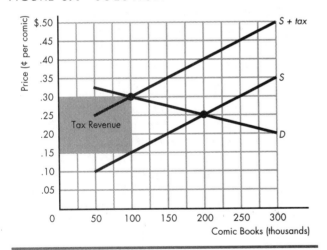

b Total tax revenue is 15¢ per comic book × 100,000 units sold = $15,000 and is indicated by the shaded area on Fig. 6.4 Solution.

c As a result of the tax, the price to consumers has gone up by 5¢ (from 25¢ to 30¢). Consumers' share of the tax burden is $5,000 (5¢ × 100,000). Producers pay the 15¢ tax to government, but only get back 5¢ of it from consumers. Therefore producers' share of the tax burden is $10,000 (10¢ × 100,000).

d See Fig. 6.5 Solution. In the dog biscuit market, the supply curve shifts up vertically by an amount equal to the tax (15¢). The original equilibrium price is 25¢ and quantity is

200,000. The new equilibrium price is 35¢ and quantity is 150,000. Total expenditure has increased, from $50,000 (25¢ × 200,000) to $52,500 (35¢ × 150,000).

FIGURE **6.5** SOLUTION

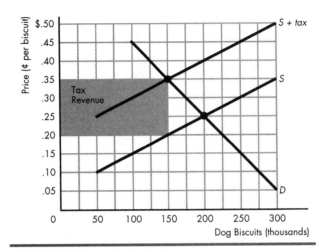

e Total tax revenue is 15¢ per dog biscuit × 150,000 units sold = $22,500 and is indicated by the shaded area on Fig. 6.5 Solution.

f As a result of the tax, the price to consumers has gone up by 10¢ (from 25¢ to 35¢). Consumers' share of the tax burden is $15,000 (10¢ × 150,000). Producers pay the 15¢ tax to government, and get back 10¢ of it from consumers. Therefore producers' share of the tax burden is $7,500 (5¢ × 150,000).

g You confidently recommend to Dr. More that the Ministry tax dog biscuits. An excise tax on dog biscuits meets both objectives: (1) it will raise more tax revenue than a tax on comic books ($22,500 versus $15,000), and (2) it will place more of the tax burden on consumers. In the dog biscuit market, consumers will pay $15,000, which is 67 percent of the tax burden. In the comic book market, consumers will pay only $5,000, which is 33 percent of the tax burden.

9 You are kicking yourself because you forgot that there is a relationship between elasticity of demand and both (1) a change in total revenue for a (tax-induced) increase in price, and (2) whether consumers or producers bear more of the burden of a tax.

a For the comic book market, the elasticity of demand calculation is

$$\eta = \left|\left(\frac{\Delta Q}{Q_{ave}}\right)\middle/\left(\frac{\Delta P}{P_{ave}}\right)\right|$$

$$= \left|\left(\frac{100-200}{150}\right)\middle/\left(\frac{.30-.25}{.275}\right)\right|$$

$$= \left|\left(\frac{-.667}{-.182}\right)\right| = 3.67$$

Demand is elastic.

b For the dog biscuit market, the elasticity of demand calculation is

$$\eta = \left|\left(\frac{\Delta Q}{Q_{ave}}\right)\middle/\left(\frac{\Delta P}{P_{ave}}\right)\right|$$

$$= \left|\left(\frac{150-200}{175}\right)\middle/\left(\frac{.35-.25}{.30}\right)\right|$$

$$= \left|\left(\frac{-.286}{.333}\right)\right| = 0.86$$

Demand is inelastic.

c You forgot that an increase in price increases total expenditure when demand is inelastic, and decreases total expenditure when demand is elastic. Thus you could have used elasticity data to predict that expenditure would increase in the dog biscuit market. An increase in expenditure is not the same as an increase in tax revenue, but if more money is being spent, there is more to be spent on taxes. You also forgot that the more inelastic demand is, the more of a tax consumers pay.

If you had thought of the elasticity approach without prompting, good for you! Dr. More will be calling on you again for advice. If you didn't think of it, time to return to Drs. Parkin and Bade for a refresher.

◑ 10 Refer to Fig. 6.6 Solution.

FIGURE **6.6** SOLUTION

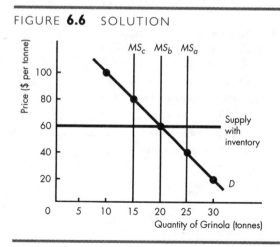

a When momentary supply is 25 tonnes, $P = \$40$. When momentary supply is 20 tonnes, $P = \$60$. When momentary supply is 15 tonnes, $P = \$80$.

b The expected future price is \$60. When momentary supply is 25 tonnes, the market price of \$40 would be below the expected future price so speculators buy grinola to store. They start buying at \$40, but their added demand pushes up the price until it quickly reaches \$60. The speculators buy 5 tonnes, paying somewhere between \$40 and \$60 per tonne. Consumers buy the remaining 20 tonnes, and the final market price is \$60.

c In this case, the expected future price and the market price are identical (\$60), so speculators take no action. The market price is \$60.

d The expected future price is \$60. When momentary supply is 15 tonnes, the market price of \$80 would be above the expected future price so speculators sell grinola from their inventories. They start selling at \$80, but their added supply pushes down the price until it quickly reaches \$60. The speculators sell 5 tonnes, receiving somewhere between \$80 and \$60 per tonne. Consumers buy 20 tonnes (15 from producers and 5 from speculators), and the final market price is \$60.

e Price fluctuations for consumers have been largely eliminated since, regardless of the momentary supply, the market price moves quickly to \$60.

f It is likely that the inventory speculators have made a profit. In part **b**, they bought 5 tonnes at a price somewhere between \$40 and \$60 per tonne. Therefore they spent between \$200 and \$300. They made no transactions in part **c**. In part **d**, they sold 5 tonnes at a price somewhere between \$80 and \$60 per tonne. Therefore they earned between \$400 and \$300. Their net profit is somewhere between a maximum of \$200 (\$400 – \$200) and a minimum of zero (\$300 – \$300).

PROBLEM

The finance minister has asked your boss at the finance department, Dr. Ina Lastic, to estimate the effects of levying a $24-per-carton tax on cigarettes. Dr. Lastic predicts that the tax will raise significant tax revenues (at least $30 million) because cigarette demand is inelastic.

Unfortunately, Dr. Lastic is unaware of a recent study you read in the *Globe and Mail* about past tax increases that found "that Ottawa has not received the entire tax windfall it expected from increased cigarette levies because of growing tobacco smuggling."

She has asked you to perform the following detailed analysis for her predictions. The demand and supply curves (without taxes) for cigarettes are given in Fig. P1.1. The before-tax price is $28 per carton, and the before-tax quantity is 2.25 million cartons per year.

a Draw the new $S + tax$ curve on Fig. P1.1.
b According to Dr. Lastic's predictions, what is the after-tax equilibrium price? equilibrium quantity?
c Calculate her predicted tax revenues.
d Check to see if Dr. Lastic's claim that the demand for cigarettes is inelastic is correct by calculating η between the before-tax equilibrium and the after-tax equilibrium. Was she right?

FIGURE **P1.1** CANADIAN CIGARETTE MARKET

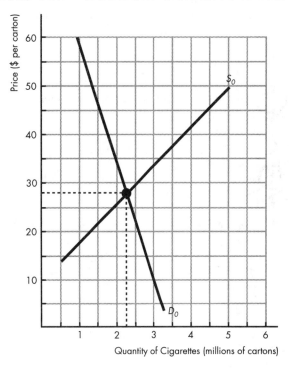

e Dr. Lastic gets high marks for economics so far. Nonetheless, you respectfully point out that her revenue prediction is wrong because she hasn't taken into account the effects of smuggling. Showing an uncharacteristic willingness to stretch herself, she replies, "I'm listening. What's *your* prediction of tax revenue?"

Here's your chance to impress the boss. You know that the supply curve of cigarettes in the United States is the same as the before-tax supply curve in Canada. You have estimated the cost of breaking the law (*CBL*) to suppliers at $16 per carton and risk to consumers of buying smuggled cigarettes is so small that their *CBL* is effectively zero. Use this information to answer the following questions.

i   Draw and label any appropriate new curve(s) on Fig. P1.1.

ii   What is *your* prediction of the after-tax price of a carton of cigarettes? the quantity of cigarettes sold legally? the quantity of smuggled cigarettes sold illegally? [*Hint*: the price of legal and illegal cigarettes will be equal because they are perfect substitutes.]

iii What is *your* prediction of tax revenue?

MIDTERM EXAMINATION

You should allocate 48 minutes for this examination (24 questions, 2 minutes per question). For each question, choose the one *best* answer.

1   The Canadian economy relies

a   exclusively on the market mechanism.
b   extensively on the market mechanism in a mixed economy.
c   exclusively on the command mechanism.
d   extensively on the command mechanism in a mixed economy.
e   equally on market and command mechanisms in a mixed economy.

2   Francesca makes $25 an hour as a welder. She must take 2 hours off work (without pay) to go to the dentist for a filling. The dentist charges $100. The opportunity cost of Francesca's trip to the dentist is

a $125.
b $100.
c $50.
d $150.
e   none of the above.

3   A conventional *PPF* shows that

a   there is a limit to the production of any one good.
b   to produce more of one good, we must produce less of another good.
c   there are limits to total production with given resources and technology.
d   all of the above are true.
e   none of the above is true.

4   If individuals *a* and *b* can both produce only goods *X* and *Y* and *a* does *not* have a comparative advantage in the production of either *X* or *Y*, then we know that

a   *b* has an absolute advantage in the production of *X* and *Y*.
b   *a* and *b* have the same opportunity cost for *X* and for *Y*.
c   *b* has a comparative advantage in the production of both *X* and *Y*.
d   there will be gains from trade.
e   **b** and **d**.

5   The magnitude of *both* the elasticity of demand and the elasticity of supply depends on

a   the factor substitution possibilities.
b   the proportion of income spent on a good.
c   the time elapsed since the price change.
d   the technological conditions of production.
e   none of the above factors.

6   If an increase in price causes a decrease in total revenue then price elasticity of demand is

a   negative.
b   zero.
c   greater than zero but less than one.
d   equal to one.
e   greater than one.

7   The data in Table P1.1 could *not* be represented by

a   two one-variable time-series graphs.
b   one two-variable time-series graph.
c   a three-variable time-series graph.
d   a scatter diagram.
e   any of the above.

TABLE **P1.1**

Year	x	y
1990	6.2	143
1991	5.7	156
1992	5.3	162

8 If the price of an umbrella is low and the number of rainy days is large, more umbrellas will be sold. If the price of an umbrella is high and there are few rainy days, fewer umbrellas will be sold. On the basis of this information, the number of

a umbrellas sold and the price of an umbrella are positively related, holding the number of rainy days constant.

b umbrellas sold and the price of an umbrella are negatively related, holding the number of rainy days constant.

c rainy days and the number of umbrellas sold are negatively related, holding the price of an umbrella constant.

d rainy days and the price of an umbrella are negatively related, holding the number of umbrellas sold constant.

e times you scratch your head over this question is 44.

9 Inventory holders

a sell goods from inventory when price is less than the expected future price.

b buy goods to put into inventory when price is greater than the expected future price.

c make the market supply curve perfectly elastic at the inventory holders' expected future price.

d do all of the above.

e do none of the above.

10 The tax burden on consumers will be greater the more

1 elastic is demand.
2 inelastic is demand.
3 elastic is supply.
4 inelastic is supply.

a 2 only
b 1 and 3
c 1 and 4
d 2 and 3
e 2 and 4

Suppose a society produces only two goods—guns and butter. Three alternative combinations on its *PPF* are given in Table P1.2. Use the information in Table P1.2 to answer Questions 11 and 12.

TABLE **P1.2** PRODUCTION POSSIBILITIES

Possibility	Units of Butter	Units of Guns
a	8	0
b	6	1
c	0	3

11 In moving from combination *b* to combination *c*, the opportunity cost of producing *one* additional unit of guns is

a 2 units of butter.
b 1/2 unit of butter.
c 6 units of butter.
d 1/6 unit of butter.
e 3 units of butter.

12 According to this *PPF*

a a combination of 6 butter and 1 gun would not employ all resources.

b a combination of 0 butter and 4 guns is attainable.

c resources are homogeneous.

d the opportunity cost of producing guns increases as more guns are produced.

e the opportunity cost of producing guns decreases as more guns are produced.

13 Which of the following is a normative statement?

a Pollution is an example of an external cost.
b Pollution makes people worse off.
c Firms that pollute should be forced to shut down.
d Pollution imposes opportunity costs on others.
e None of the above.

14 Economic decisions in markets are *coordinated* by

a firms.
b households.
c governments.
d price adjustments.
e all of the above.

15 If both demand and supply increase, then equilibrium price

a will rise and quantity will increase.
b will fall and quantity will increase.
c could rise or fall and quantity will increase.
d will rise and quantity could either increase or decrease.
e will fall and quantity could either increase or decrease.

16 If turnips are an inferior good, then, *ceteris paribus*, an increase in the price of turnips will cause

a a decrease in the demand for turnips.
b an increase in the demand for turnips.
c a decrease in the supply of turnips.
d an increase in the supply of turnips.
e none of the above.

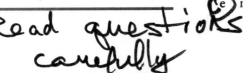
Read questions carefully

17 In Fig. P1.2, if the minimum wage is set at $6 per hour, what is the level of unemployment in millions of hours?

a 50
b 40
c 0
d 10
e 20

FIGURE **P1.2**

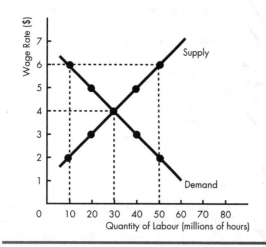

18 A price floor set below the equilibrium price results in

a excess supply.
b excess demand.
c the equilibrium price.
d an increase in supply.
e a decrease in demand.

19 If a 10 percent increase in income causes a 10 percent decrease in the consumption of widgets (at a constant price), then

a the price elasticity of demand for widgets equals 1.
b the income elasticity of demand for widgets is negative.
c the income elasticity of demand for widgets equals 1.
d widgets are a normal good.
e none of the above is true.

20 A decrease in the price of X from $6 to $4 causes an increase in the quantity of Y demanded (at the current price of Y) from 900 to 1,100 units. What is the cross elasticity of demand between X and Y?

a 0.5
b −0.5
c 2
d −2
e **a** or **b**, depending on whether X and Y are substitutes or complements

21 The graph of the relationship between two variables that are negatively related

a is horizontal.
b slopes upward to the right.
c is vertical.
d slopes downward to the right.
e is linear.

22 In Fig. P1.3, the slope of the line is

a 1.00.
b 1.25.
c 1.50.
d 0.75.
e 0.50.

FIGURE **P1.3**

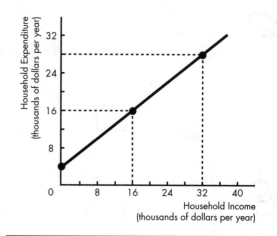

23 A decrease in quantity supplied is represented by a

a movement down the supply curve.
b movement up the supply curve.
c leftward shift of the supply curve.
d rightward shift of the supply curve.
e rightward shift of the demand curve.

24 Farmland can be used to produce either cattle or corn. If the demand for cattle increases then

a demand for corn will increase.
b supply of corn will increase.
c demand for corn will decrease.
d supply of corn will decrease.
e **b** and **c**.

A N S W E R S

Problem

a See Fig. P1.1 Solution. Ignore the curve $S + CBL$ for now.

FIGURE **P1.1** SOLUTION
CANADIAN CIGARETTE MARKET

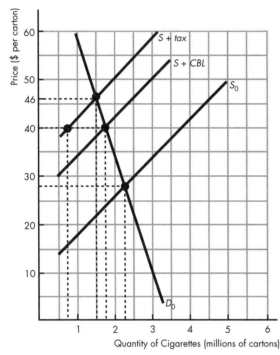

b The after-tax equilibrium price is $46 per carton. The after-tax equilibrium quantity is 1.5 million cartons per year.
c Tax revenue is 1.5 million cartons × $24 per carton = $36 million per year.

d $$\eta = \left| \frac{\frac{\Delta Q}{Q_{ave}}}{\frac{\Delta P}{P_{ave}}} \right|$$

$$\eta = \left| \frac{\frac{-0.75}{1.875}}{\frac{18}{37}} \right| = \frac{.4}{.486} = .82$$

The demand curve is inelastic ($\eta < 1$) between the two equilibrium points. Dr. Lastic's predictions about tax revenue (without smuggling) and elasticity were correct.

e **i** See Fig. P1.1 Solution. Since the *CBL* to consumers is zero, the demand curve does not shift. The smugglers' supply curve is $S + CBL$.
ii Since consumers can buy cigarettes from smugglers at a price of $40 per carton, no one is willing to buy at the higher legal price of $46. The legal price is bid down to $40. At that price, legal suppliers will supply 0.75 million cartons, and total market demand is 1.75 million cartons. Smugglers supply the difference, 1 million cartons.
iii Tax revenue is 0.75 million cartons × $24 per carton = only $18 million per year.

Dr. Lastic is impressed. She says, "When I studied economics, we were taught that illegal activities were the business of law enforcement officials, not economists. What you have shown is that almost any activity can be analysed from an economic perspective. Well done. Let's draft our reply to the minister."

Midterm Examination

1 **b** Definition. (19–20)
2 **d** $100 which could have been spent on other goods plus time cost ($25 × 2 hours). (8–9)
3 **d** **a** and **b** show scarcity, **c** shows opportunity cost. (44–46)
4 **b** No comparative advantage means equal opportunity cost. No information on absolute advantage. (53–56)
5 **c** **a**, **d** affect η_s only. **b** affects η only. (103–105, 110–111)
6 **e** Total revenue test. (105–106)
7 **c** There are two variables plus time, which could be represented by **a**, **b**, or **d**.(27–31)
8 **b** **c** would be true if change "negatively" to "positively." Can't judge **d** without additional information. (38–39)
9 **c** **a** and **b** would be true if reversed "less" and "greater." (134–135)
10 **d** Definition. (127–130)
11 **e** Give up 6 butter to get 2 guns: 6/2 = 3 butter per gun. (47–48)

12 d Opportunity cost gun between a and $b = 2$
       butter; between b and $c = 3$ butter. **a** on *PPF*,
       b outside *PPF*. (47–48)

13 c **a** and **b** are true statements; **d** is a positive
       statement that can be tested. (12–13)

14 d Price adjustments coordinate choices made by
       firms, households, and governments. (19–20)

15 c Rightward shifts demand and supply must
       $\rightarrow \uparrow$ equilibrium quantity, but effect on price
       indeterminate. (82–83)

16 e $\uparrow P \rightarrow$ movement along demand curve.
       (72–73)

17 b Quantity supplied (50) > quantity demanded
       (10). (125–126)

18 c Draw graph. Floor doesn't prevent $\uparrow P$ from
       excess demand. (124–126)

19 b $\eta_y = (\% \Delta Q_D)/(\% \Delta \text{ income}) = -10/10 =$
       -1; widgets inferior good. (107–108)

20 b $\eta_x = (\% \Delta Q_D^Y)/(\% \Delta P^X) =$
       $(200/1{,}000)/(-2/5) = -0.5.$ (107)

21 d As $x \uparrow$, $y \downarrow$. (33–34)

22 d For example, using points (0, 4) and (16, 16):
       $\Delta y = 12$ (16 − 4), $\Delta x = 16$ (16 − 0). (36–37)

23 a Illustration of law of supply. (74–77)

24 d Cattle and corn substitutes in production.
       $\uparrow$ demand for cattle $\rightarrow \uparrow$ price cattle $\rightarrow$
       $\downarrow$ supply corn. (75–76)

12/25

Household Consumption Choices

Household consumption choices are determined by

◆ Budget constraint

- Income and prices (*P*) of goods and services are given.
- Budget line marks boundary between affordable (points on line or inside) and unaffordable (outside line) choices.

◆ Preferences—likes and dislikes based on utility.

Utility is benefit or satisfaction from consumption.

◆ **Total utility** (*TU*) is total benefit or satisfaction from consumption of goods and services. ↑ consumption → ↑ total utility.

◆ **Marginal utility** (*MU*) is Δ total utility from one-unit increase in quantity good consumed. *MU* positive, but due to **diminishing marginal utility**, ↓ as consumption good ↑.

Maximizing Utility

Consumers strive for utility maximization.

◆ Given income and the prices of goods and services, **consumer equilibrium** occurs when consumer allocates income in way that maximizes total utility.

◆ Total utility is maximized when all income is spent and **marginal utility per dollar spent** is equal for all goods. For substitute goods movies (*m*) and pop (*p*), this occurs when

$$\frac{MU_m}{P_m} = \frac{MU_p}{P_p}$$

The power of marginal analysis for predicting economic choices stems from a simple rule—if the marginal gain from an action exceeds the marginal loss, take the action.

◆ The rule applied to the utility maximization example is—if the marginal utility per dollar spent on movies exceeds the marginal utility per dollar spent on pop, buy more movies and less pop.

◆ The marginal gain from more movies exceeds the marginal loss from less pop.

Predictions of Marginal Utility Theory

Ceteris paribus, ↓ P_m → ↑ Q_m consumed (movement down along demand curve for movies) and → leftward shift demand curve for pop.

Ceteris paribus, ↑ P_p → ↓ Q_p consumed (movement up along demand curve for pop) and → rightward shift demand curve for movies.

Movies and pop normal goods. *Ceteris paribus*, ↑ income → ↑ consumption movies and pop (rightward shifts both demand curves).

Marginal utility theory allows us to derive and predict the above results which, in Chapter 4, were just *assumptions* about consumer demand.

Individual and market demand:

◆ Individual demand—relationship between quantity demanded and price for single individual.

◆ **Market demand**—sum of individual demands; relationship between total quantity demanded and price.

◆ Market demand curve—horizontal sum of individual demand curves.

Criticisms of Marginal Utility Theory

Utility can't be observed. But utility does not need to be observed to be used. We do observe incomes and quantities and prices of goods and services. Utility theory allows us to understand consumption choices and predict effects of changes in prices and incomes on these choices.

Consumers aren't as smart as the theory implies. But the theory makes no predictions about real consumers' thought processes. It simply predicts real consumers' *actions*.

Implications of Marginal Utility Theory

Consumer surplus:

◆ **Value** of a good is maximum amount person would be willing to pay for it.

◆ **Consumer surplus** is the value of a good minus its price.

◆ Consumer surplus is the area under the demand curve, but above market price (see Text Fig. 7.7, page 161).

Distinction between total utility and marginal utility resolves diamond–water paradox.

◆ Diamonds, though less useful (low TU) than water, have higher price (high MU).

◆ Water more useful (high TU), but has lower price (low MU).

HELPFUL HINTS

I Utility is an extremely useful abstract concept that allows us to think more clearly about consumer choice. Do not be confused by the fact that arbitrary units are used to measure utility. The only important basis for marginal utility theory is that you are able to judge whether the additional satisfaction per dollar spent on good X is greater or less than the additional satisfaction per dollar spent on Y. If it is greater, then you decide to consume an additional unit of X. How much greater is irrelevant for the decision.

2 The marginal utility per dollar spent on good X can be written as MU_X/P_X where MU_X is the marginal utility of the last unit of X consumed and P_X is the price of a unit of good X. The consumer equilibrium (utility-maximizing)

condition for goods X and Y can thus be written

$$\frac{MU_X}{P_X} = \frac{MU_Y}{P_Y}$$

This implies that, in consumer equilibrium, the ratio of marginal utilities will equal the ratio of prices of the two goods:

$$\frac{MU_X}{MU_Y} = \frac{P_X}{P_Y}$$

This result is often useful.

3 If an individual is not in consumer equilibrium, then the preceding equation is not satisfied. For example, consider spending all of one's income on a consumption plan where

$$\frac{MU_X}{P_X} > \frac{MU_Y}{P_Y}$$

or, equivalently,

$$\frac{MU_X}{MU_Y} > \frac{P_X}{P_Y}$$

Since P_X and P_Y are given, this means that MU_X is "too large" and MU_Y is "too small." Utility can be increased by increasing consumption of X (and thereby decreasing MU_X due to the principle of diminishing marginal utility) and decreasing consumption of Y (and thereby increasing MU_Y due to diminishing marginal utility).

4 Text Table 7.7 on page 157 is a good review device.

SELF-TEST

True/False/Uncertain and Explain

I The market demand curve is the horizontal sum of all individual demand curves.

2 The principle of diminishing marginal utility means that as consumption of a good increases, total utility increases but at a decreasing rate.

3 When the price of good X rises, the marginal utility from the consumption of X decreases.

4 If the marginal utilities from consuming two goods are not equal, then the consumer cannot be in equilibrium.

5 If the marginal utility per dollar spent on good X exceeds the marginal utility per dollar spent on good Y, total utility will increase by increasing consumption of X and decreasing consumption of Y.

6 When income decreases, the marginal utility derived from a good will increase.

7 Because utility cannot be observed or measured, marginal utility theory is essentially useless.

8 The value of a good is equal to the price of the good.

9 Consumer surplus for relatively cheap goods like water will be relatively low.

10 If a shift in supply decreases the price of a good, consumer surplus increases.

Multiple-Choice

1 If Ms. Petersen is maximizing her utility in the consumption of goods A and B, which of the following statements must be *true*?

a $MU_A = MU_B$

b $\dfrac{MU_A}{P_A} = \dfrac{MU_B}{P_B}$

c $\dfrac{MU_A}{P_B} = \dfrac{MU_B}{P_A}$

d $TU_A = TU_B$

e $\dfrac{TU_A}{P_A} = \dfrac{TU_B}{P_B}$

2 Samir consumes apples and bananas and is in consumer equilibrium. The marginal utility of the last apple is 10 and the marginal utility of the last banana is 5. If the price of an apple is $0.50, then what is the price of a banana?

a $0.05
b $0.10
c $0.25
d $0.50
e $1.00

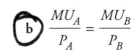

$$\frac{10}{0.5} \qquad \frac{5}{P_B}$$

$$P_B = 0.25$$

3 Market demand is the

a sum of the prices that each individual is willing to pay for each quantity demanded.
b sum of the quantities demanded by each individual at each price.
c sum of the consumer surplus of each individual.
d difference between the maximum amount each individual is willing to pay for a good and the market price.
e difference between the market price and the maximum amount each individual is willing to pay for a good.

4 If Soula is maximizing her utility and two goods have the same marginal utility then she will

a buy only one.
b buy equal quantities of both.
c be willing to pay the same price for each.
d get the same total utility from each.
e do none of the above.

5 Bikes and roller blades are substitutes. Marginal utility theory predicts that when the price of bikes increases, the quantity demanded of bikes

a decreases and the demand curve for roller blades shifts rightward.

b decreases and the demand curve for roller blades shifts leftward.

c decreases and the demand curve for roller blades will not shift.

d increases and the demand curve for roller blades shifts rightward.

e increases and the demand curve for roller blades shifts leftward.

maybe

6 Total utility is always

a greater than marginal utility.

b less than marginal utility.

c decreasing when marginal utility is decreasing.

d decreasing when marginal utility is increasing.

e increasing when marginal utility is positive.

7 Bill and Ted consume 15 chocolate bars each at the current price. If Bill's demand curve is more elastic than Ted's demand curve, then

a Bill's willingness to pay for the last chocolate bar is greater than Ted's.

b Ted's willingness to pay for the last chocolate bar is greater than Bill's.

c Bill's consumer surplus is greater than Ted's.

d Ted's consumer surplus is greater than Bill's.

e Bill's consumer surplus equals Ted's.

8 If a consumer is in equilibrium, then

a total utility is maximized given the consumer's income and the prices of goods.

b marginal utility is maximized given the consumer's income and the prices of goods.

c marginal utility per dollar spent is maximized given the consumer's income and the prices of goods.

d the marginal utility of each good will be equal.

e none of the above is true.

9 Squid costs $2 per kilogram and octopus costs $1 per kilogram. Jacques buys only octopus and gets 10 units of utility from the last kilogram he buys. Assuming that Jacques has maximized his utility, his marginal utility, in units, from the first kilogram of squid must be

a more than 10.

b less than 10.

c more than 20.

d less than 20.

e zero.

use ev in $\frac{10}{1}$ use your fucking head

10 Suppose that Arnie spends his entire income of $10 on law books and silk ties. Law books cost $2 and silk ties cost $4 (see Table 7.1). The marginal utility of each good is independent of the amount consumed of the other good.

TABLE **7.1**

Quantity	Marginal Utility	
	Law Books	Silk Ties
1	12	16
2	10	12
3	8	8
4	6	4

If Arnie is maximizing his utility, how many silk ties does he buy?

a 0

b 1

c 2

d 3

e 4

$$\frac{MU}{P_2} = \frac{MU}{P_4}$$

11 Total utility equals

a the sum of the marginal utilities of each unit consumed.

b the area below the demand curve but above the market price.

c the slope of the marginal utility curve.

d the marginal utility of the last unit divided by price.

e the marginal utility of the last unit consumed multiplied by the total number of units consumed.

12 A household's consumption choices are determined by

a prices of goods and services.

b income.

c preferences.

d all of the above.

e a and b only.

13 The high price of diamonds relative to the price of water reflects the fact that at typical levels of consumption

a the total utility of water is relatively low.

b the total utility of diamonds is relatively high.

c the marginal utility of water is relatively high.

d the marginal utility of diamonds is relatively low.

e none of the above is true.

14 The demand schedule for marbles is shown in Table 7.2.

TABLE **7.2** DEMAND SCHEDULE FOR MARBLES

Price ($ per marble)	Quantity Demanded
10	1
9	2
8	3
7	4
6	5

If the actual price is $7, what is total consumer surplus?

a $3
b $4
c $6
d $12
e $27

15 Sergio is maximizing his utility in his consumption of beer and bubblegum. If the price of beer is greater than the price of bubblegum, then we know with *certainty* that

a Sergio buys more beer than bubblegum.
b Sergio buys more bubblegum than beer.
c the marginal utility of the last purchased beer is greater than the marginal utility of the last purchased bubblegum.
d the marginal utility of the last purchased bubblegum is greater than the marginal utility of the last purchased beer.
e the marginal utilities of the last purchased beer and bubblegum are equal.

16 Chuck and Barry have identical preferences but Chuck has a much higher income. If each is maximizing his utility, then

a they will have equal total utilities.
b Chuck will have lower total utility than Barry.
c Chuck will have lower marginal utility than Barry for most goods.
d Chuck will have higher marginal utility than Barry for most goods.
e they will have equal marginal utilities for most goods.

17 Which of the following is *not* a prediction of marginal utility theory?

a other things remaining the same, the higher the price of a good, the lower is the quantity demanded
b other things remaining the same, the higher the price of a good, the higher is the consumption of substitutes for that good
c other things remaining the same, the lower the price of a good, the lower is the consumption of substitutes for that good
d the law of demand
e diminishing marginal utility

18 According to the principle of diminishing marginal utility, as consumption of a good increases, total utility

a decreases and then eventually increases.
b decreases at an increasing rate.
c decreases at a decreasing rate.
d increases at an increasing rate.
e increases at a decreasing rate.

19 Suppose that Madonna spends her entire income of $6 on purple nail polish and leather outfits. Nail polish costs $1 per unit and outfits cost $2 per unit (see Table 7.3). The marginal utility of each good is independent of the amount consumed of the other good.

TABLE **7.3**

| Quantity | Marginal Utility | |
	Nail Polish	Outfits
1	8	16
2	6	12
3	4	10
4	3	6

If Madonna is maximizing her utility, what is her *total* utility?

a 19
b 28
c 38
d 42
e none of the above

20 In consumer equilibrium, a consumer equates the

a total utility from each good.
b marginal utility from each good.
c total utility per dollar spent on each good.
d marginal utility per dollar spent on each good.
e total income spent on each good with total utility from each good.

21 The relative prices of beer to back bacon are 2:1. If Bob's current consumption is at a level where $MU_{beer}/MU_{back\ bacon}$ is 1:2, then to achieve maximum utility Bob must

a consume more beer and less back bacon.

b not change his current consumption of beer and back bacon.

c consume less beer and more back bacon.

d increase the price of beer.

e consume twice as much beer and one-half as much back bacon.

22 The value of a good is defined as the

a market price.

b average price paid by individuals in a market.

c cost of producing the good.

d highest price an individual is willing to pay.

e total utility to an individual of all units of the good.

23 If potato chips were free, individuals would consume

a an infinite quantity of chips.

b the quantity of chips at which total utility from chips falls to zero.

c the quantity of chips at which marginal utility from chips falls to zero.

d zero chips since this equates marginal utility and price.

e none of the above.

24 Broomhilda is initially maximizing her utility in her consumption of goods X and Y. The price of good X doubles, *ceteris paribus*. For Broomhilda to once again maximize her utility, her *quantity of X* consumed must

a rise until the marginal utility of X has doubled.

b fall to one-half its previous level.

c fall until the marginal utility of X has doubled.

d fall until the marginal utility of X falls to one-half its previous level.

e yield infinite bliss.

25 Beverly is currently in consumer equilibrium. An increase in her income will

a increase her total utility.

b decrease her total utility.

c increase her marginal utility of all goods.

d decrease her marginal utility of all goods.

e increase her consumption of all goods.

Short Answer Problems

1 A consumer is initially maximizing his utility in the consumption of goods A and B so that

$$\frac{MU_A}{P_A} = \frac{MU_B}{P_B}$$

The price of A then rises as a result of the shift in supply shown in Fig. 7.1.

FIGURE **7.1**

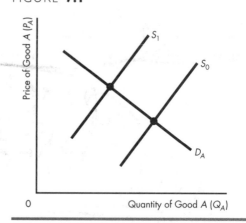

Use the above condition for utility maximization to explain how the consumer will move to a new utility-maximizing equilibrium. Show the connection between your explanation and the change on the diagram.

2 Consider the following information relevant to a consumer who is trying to allocate her income between goods X and Y so as to maximize utility. The price of X is $2 and the price of Y is $1 per unit. When all income is spent, the marginal utility of the last unit of X is 20 and the marginal utility of the last unit of Y is 16.

a Why is the consumer not in equilibrium?

b To increase utility, which good should this consumer consume more of and which less of?

3 Explain why the consumer equilibrium condition and the principle of diminishing marginal utility imply the law of demand.

4 An apparent paradox that bothers many people is that although childcare workers are usually paid low salaries, it is often said that "they have the most important job in the world." Use economic reasoning to resolve this paradox.

5 Table 7.4 gives the demand schedules for broccoli for three individuals: Tom, Jana, and Ted.

TABLE **7.4** INDIVIDUAL DEMAND FOR BROCCOLI

Price ($ per kilogram)	Quantity Demanded (kilograms per week)		
	Tom	Jana	Ted
0.50	10	4	10
0.75	9	2	7
1.00	8	0	4
1.25	7	0	1

a Calculate the market demand schedule.
b On a single diagram, draw the individual demand curves for Tom, Jana, and Ted, as well as the market demand curve.

6 Tables 7.5 and 7.6 give Amy's utility from the consumption of popcorn and candy bars during a week.

TABLE **7.5** AMY'S UTILITY FROM POPCORN

Bags of Popcorn	Total Utility	Marginal Utility
1	20	
2	36	
3	50	
4		12
5	72	
6	80	

TABLE **7.6** AMY'S UTILITY FROM CANDY BARS

Number of Candy Bars	Total Utility	Marginal Utility
1	14	
2	26	
3		10
4	44	
5	51	
6	57	

a Complete the tables.
b Suppose the price of a bag of popcorn is $1.00 and the price of a candy bar is $0.50. Given the information in Tables 7.5 and 7.6, complete Table 7.7 where *MU/P* means marginal utility divided by price, which is equivalent to marginal utility per dollar spent.

TABLE **7.7**

Bags of Popcorn	MU/P	Number of Candy Bars	MU/P
1		1	
2		2	
3		3	
4		4	
5		5	
6		6	

c Amy's weekly allowance is $4.00. Answer the following if she spends her entire allowance on popcorn and candy.
 i How much popcorn and how many candy bars will Amy consume each week if she maximizes her utility?
 ii Show that the utility maximum condition is satisfied.
 iii What is total utility?
 iv If, instead, Amy consumed 3 bags of popcorn and 2 candy bars, explain why she would not be maximizing her utility using figures for both total utility and for the terms *MU/P*.

7 Suppose that Amy's preferences remain as they were in Short Answer Problem **6**, but the price of a candy bar doubles to $1.00.
a Construct a new table (similar to Table 7.7) of *MU/P* for popcorn and candy bars.
b Amy's allowance continues to be $4.00. After the price change, how much popcorn and how many candy bars will she consume each week?
c Are popcorn and candy bars substitutes or complements for Amy? Why?
d Based on the information you have obtained, draw Amy's demand curve for candy bars.

e Suppose that both bags of popcorn and candy bars continue to sell for $1.00 each, but now Amy's allowance increases to $6.00 per week.
  i   How many candy bars and bags of popcorn will Amy choose to consume per week under the new situation?
  ii   Are popcorn and candy bars normal goods? Why or why not?

8 Suppose that Andre Agassi spends his entire income of $8 on hairbands and toy tennis rackets (see Table 7.8). The price of a hairband is $2 and the price of a tennis racket is $4. The marginal utility of each good is independent of the amount consumed of the other good.

TABLE **7.8**

| Quantity | Marginal Utility | |
	Hairbands	Rackets
1	20	36
2	18	32
3	16	20
4	8	16

a If Andre is maximizing his utility, how many units of each good should he purchase?
b If Andre's income rises to $24, how many units of each good should he purchase?
c Using the information above, calculate Andre's income elasticity of demand for hairbands.

9 Suppose that Igor maximizes his utility by spending his entire income on bats and lizards (see Table 7.9). The marginal utility of each good is independent of the amount consumed of the other good.

TABLE **7.9**

| Quantity | Marginal Utility | |
	Bats	Lizards
1	20	45
2	18	40
3	16	25
4	8	20

Igor's income is $16. The price of a bat is $2, and he buys 3 bats. If the marginal utility of the last lizard he buys is 40, calculate the price of a lizard using *two* separate methods.

10 Andy's weekly demand schedule for pizza is shown in Table 7.10.

TABLE **7.10**   DEMAND SCHEDULE FOR PIZZA

Price ($ per pizza)	Quantity Demanded
15	1
12	2
10	3
9	4
8	5

If the price of a pizza is $9, what is Andy's consumer surplus for the following number of pizzas that he buys at that price?
a first pizza
b second pizza
c total number of pizzas

ANSWERS

True/False/Uncertain and Explain

1 T   Definition. (158)
2 T   Because MU positive but diminishing. (150–151)
3 F $\uparrow P \rightarrow \downarrow Q \rightarrow \uparrow MU$. (154–156)
4 F   If prices unequal, then marginal utilities unequal in consumer equilibrium. (152–153)
5 T $\uparrow$ consumption $X \rightarrow \downarrow MU_X$. $\downarrow$ consumption $Y \rightarrow \uparrow MU_Y$. Moves ratios MU/P toward equality. (152–154)
6 U   True for normal good; may be false for inferior good. (157)
7 F   Theory makes predictions that can be tested against observed data. (159–160)
8 U   True if last unit consumed, false (value > price) otherwise. (160–161)
9 F   Since many units consumed, many earlier units have willingness to pay > price. (160–161)
10 T   Rightward shift supply ($\rightarrow \downarrow P$) $\rightarrow$ $\uparrow$ quantity consumed, so more units with willingness to pay > price. (160–161)

Multiple-Choice

1 b   Definition. (152–153)
2 c   Solve $10/.5 = 5/P_b$ for P_b. (152–153)
3 b   See text discussion. (158)

4 c *From maximum condition of equal *MU/P*. No necessary relation between *MU* and quantity or *TU*. (152–154)

5 a See text discussion. (155–156)

6 e *TU* ↑ when *MU* positive, whether *MU* ↓ or ↑. *TU* may be $\lesseqgtr$ *MU*. (150–151)

7 d Ted's steeper demand curve → ↑ willingness to pay for previous units. Willingness to pay for last unit equal. (160–161)

8 a Consumers maximize *TU*. **c** and **d** wrong because *MU/P* equal for *TU* maximization. (152–154)

9 d For octopus, $MU_o/P_o = 10$. For squid, $MU_s/2$ would need to be = 10, so MU_s must be < 20. (152–153)

10' b Buys 1 tie (*MU/P* = 16/4) and 3 books (*MU/P* = 8/2). (152–154)

11 a **b** is consumer surplus. For **c**, *MU* = slope *TU* curve. **d** and **e** nonsense. (150–151)

12 d Preferences and constraints. (149–150)

13 e For diamonds: *TU* relatively low, *MU* relatively high. For water: *TU* relatively high, *MU* relatively low. (160–161)

14 c For 4 marbles consumed, consumer surplus (in $) = (10 – 7) + (9 – 7) + (8 – 7) + (7 – 7). (160–161)

15 c From maximum condition of equal *MU/P*. No necessary relation between *MU* and quantity. (152–154)

16 c Chuck consumes greater quantities of each good, so *MU* lower. (157)

17 e ↓ *MU* is *assumption* of theory. (154–157)

18 e Because marginal utility is positive but diminishing with ↑ consumption. (150–151)

19 d Buys 2 polish and 2 outfits. *TU* = 8 + 6 + 16 + 12. (150–153)

20 d Definition. *MU/P* key to utility maximization. (152–153)

21 c To equalize *MU/P* must ↑ MU_{beer} and ↓ $MU_{back\ bacon}$. **d** wrong because no control over prices. (152–154)

22 d Definition. (160)

23 c Maximizes *TU*. With fewer chips, *MU* still positive, so *TU* could ↑. With more, *MU* turns negative so *TU* would ↓. (152–154)

24 c From maximum condition of equal *MU/P*. No necessary relation between *MU* and quantity consumed. (152–154)

25 a For inferior goods, consumption may ↓ and *MU* ↑. (157)

Short Answer Problems

1 When the price of *A* rises, *ceteris paribus*:

$$\frac{MU_A}{P_A} < \frac{MU_B}{P_B}$$

The consumer is no longer in equilibrium. In order to restore the equality in the equilibrium condition, the consumer must change his consumption to make MU_A rise and MU_B fall. (The consumer cannot change the prices of *A* and *B*.) Since marginal utility diminishes with increases in quantity consumed, the consumer must decrease consumption of *A* and increase consumption of *B*. Decreased consumption of *A* moves the consumer up to the left on the demand curve, from the initial intersection of *D* and S_0 to the new intersection of *D* and S_1. In the new consumer equilibrium, equality will be restored in the equilibrium condition.

2 a This consumer is not in equilibrium because the marginal utility per dollar spent is not the same for goods *X* and *Y*. The marginal utility per dollar spent on *X* is $MU_X/P_X = 20/2 = 10$, which is less than the marginal utility per dollar spent on *Y*: $MU_Y/P_Y = 16$.

b To equate the marginal utilities per dollar spent (and thus increase utility), this consumer should increase consumption of *Y* and decrease consumption of *X*. The principle of diminishing marginal utility implies that this will decrease the marginal utility of *Y* and increase the marginal utility of *X*.

3 Suppose we observe an individual in consumer equilibrium consuming X_0 units of good *X* and Y_0 units of good *Y* with the prices of *X* and *Y* given by P_X and P_Y respectively. This means that at consumption levels X_0 and Y_0, the marginal utility per dollar spent on *X* equals the marginal utility per dollar spent on *Y*. Now let the price of *X* increase to P^1_X. The marginal utility per dollar spent on *X* declines and thus is now less than the marginal utility per dollar spent on *Y*. To restore equilibrium, our consumer must increase the marginal utility of *X* and decrease the marginal utility of *Y*. From the principle of diminishing marginal utility we know that the only way to do this is to decrease the consumption of *X* and increase the consumption of *Y*. This demonstrates the law of demand since an increase in the price of *X* has been shown to require a decrease in the consumption of *X* to restore consumer equilibrium.

4   While most parents place a high value on childcare services, there are many childcare workers willing to provide those services. While the total utility provided by the services of childcare workers is high, the marginal utility of those (abundantly supplied) services is low.

5 a The market demand schedule is obtained by adding the quantities demanded by Tom, Jana, and Ted at each price (see Table 7.11).

TABLE **7.11**   MARKET DEMAND
SCHEDULE FOR BROCCOLI

Price ($ per kilogram)	Quantity Demanded (kilograms per week)
0.50	24
0.75	18
1.00	12
1.25	8

b   Figure 7.2 illustrates the individual demand curves for Tom, Jana, and Ted as well as the market demand curve.

FIGURE **7.2**

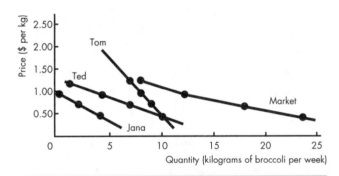

6 a The tables are completed in Table 7.5 Solution and Table 7.6 Solution.

TABLE **7.5**   SOLUTION
AMY'S UTILITY FROM POPCORN

Bags of Popcorn	Total Utility	Marginal Utility
1	20	20
2	36	16
3	50	14
4	62	12
5	72	10
6	80	8

TABLE **7.6**   SOLUTION
AMY'S UTILITY FROM CANDY BARS

Number of Candy Bars	Total Utility	Marginal Utility
1	14	14
2	26	12
3	36	10
4	44	8
5	51	7
6	57	6

b   The table is completed in Table 7.7 Solution.

TABLE **7.7**   SOLUTION

Bags of Popcorn	MU/P	Number of Candy Bars	MU/P
1	20	1	28
2	16	2	24
3	14	3	20
4	12	4	16
5	10	5	14
6	8	6	12

c i   2 bags of popcorn and 4 candy bars.
ii   The utility maximum condition is satisfied since Amy spends all of her income ($4.00), and the marginal utility per dollar spent is the same for popcorn and candy bars (16).
iii   Total utility is the utility from the consumption of 2 bags of popcorn (36) plus the utility from the consumption of 4 candy bars (44) = 80.
iv   If Amy consumed 3 bags of popcorn and 2 candy bars, total utility would be 76, which is less than 80, the total utility from the consumption of 2 bags of popcorn and 4 candy bars. For the combination of 3 bags of popcorn and 2 candy bars, *MU/P* for popcorn is 14 while *MU/P* for candy bars is 24. Since *MU/P* is not the same for both goods, this combination does not meet the condition for utility maximization.

7 a See Table 7.12.

TABLE **7.12**

Bags of Popcorn	MU/P	Number of Candy Bars	MU/P
1	20	1	14
2	16	2	12
3	14	3	10
4	12	4	8
5	10	5	7
6	8	6	6

b 3 bags of popcorn and 1 candy bar. Amy spends all of her income ($4.00) and the marginal utility per dollar spent is the same for popcorn and candy bars (14).

c Popcorn and candy bars are substitutes for Amy, since an increase in the price of a candy bar causes an increase in the demand for popcorn.

d Amy's demand curve for candy bars is given in Fig. 7.3. Two points on the demand curve have been identified: when the price of a candy bar is $1.00, 1 candy bar will be demanded, and when the price is $0.50, 4 candy bars will be demanded. The demand curve is a line through these two points.

FIGURE **7.3**

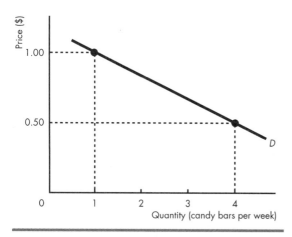

e i Now, Amy will choose to consume 4 bags of popcorn and 2 candy bars (instead of 3 bags of popcorn and 1 candy bar). Amy spends all of her income ($6.00) and the marginal utility per dollar spent is the same for popcorn and candy bars (12).

ii Popcorn and candy bars are both normal goods for Amy since the increase in income (allowance) leads to increases in the demand for both goods.

8 a The utility-maximizing combination of goods is shown in Table 7.13.

TABLE **7.13**

Quantity	MU/P	
	Hairbands	Rackets
1	10	9
2	9	8
3	8	5
4	4	4

Andre should purchase 2 hairbands and 1 racket. Andre spends all of his income ($8), and the marginal utility per dollar spent is the same for hairbands and rackets (9).

b Andre should purchase 4 hairbands and 4 rackets. He spends all of his income ($24), and the marginal utility per dollar spent is the same for hairbands and rackets (4).

c The income elasticity of demand for hairbands is

$$\eta_y = \frac{\dfrac{\Delta Q}{Q_{ave}}}{\dfrac{\Delta Y}{Y_{ave}}} = \frac{\dfrac{4-2}{\frac{1}{2}(4+2)}}{\dfrac{24-8}{\frac{1}{2}(24+8)}} = \frac{\dfrac{2}{3}}{\dfrac{16}{16}} = \frac{2}{3}$$

9 There are two methods for calculating the price of a lizard. One method is based on the fact that Igor spends all of his income on bats and lizards. This means that

$$Y = P_B Q_B + P_L Q_L$$

where Y = income, P_B = the price of a bat, Q_B = the quantity of bats purchased, P_L = the price of a lizard, and Q_L = the quantity of lizards purchased. We know $Y = 16$, $P_B = 2$, $Q_B = 3$, and if the marginal utility of the last lizard is 40, then $Q_L = 2$. Substituting in these values, we can solve for P_L.

$$16 = 2(3) + P_L(2)$$
$$10 = P_L(2)$$
$$5 = P_L$$

The second method uses the condition for utility maximization:

$$\frac{MU_B}{P_B} = \frac{MU_L}{P_L}$$

We know that $MU_L = 40$, $P_B = 2$, and if Igor buys 3 bats, $MU_B = 16$. Substituting in these values, we can solve for P_L.

$$\frac{16}{2} = \frac{40}{P_L}$$
$$80 = 16P_L$$
$$5 = P_L$$

10 a The most Andy would be willing to pay for the first pizza is $15, but the price is only $9. His consumer surplus is $6 ($15 − $9).

   b Andy's consumer surplus on the second pizza is the difference between the most he would be willing to pay ($12) and the price ($9). His consumer surplus is $3.

   c At a price of $9, Andy will buy 4 pizzas. He will receive consumer surplus on the first three pizzas in the amount of $6, $3, and $1, respectively. Thus, his total consumer surplus is $10.

$$\frac{MU}{P} = \frac{MU}{P}$$

Possibilities, Preferences, and Choices

KEY CONCEPTS

Consumption Possibilities

Budget line shows limits to household consumption, given income, and prices of goods and services. Consider example of movies (horizontal axis) and pop (vertical axis).

$$Q_p = \frac{y}{P_p} - \frac{P_m}{P_p} Q_m$$

◆ Budget equation is

$$Q_p = \frac{y}{P_p} - \frac{P_m}{P_p} Q_m$$

◆ Magnitude of slope of budget equation (P_m/P_p) equals **relative price** of movies in terms of pop.

◆ Intercepts measure household's **real income** in movies (x-intercept) and pop (y-intercept).

◆ $\uparrow P_m \rightarrow$ steeper budget line, fixed pop-intercept.

◆ $\uparrow P_p \rightarrow$ flatter budget line, fixed movie-intercept.

◆ $\uparrow y \rightarrow$ rightward parallel shift budget line.

Preferences and Indifference Curves

Indifference curve maps household preferences, joining combinations goods giving equal satisfaction.

◆ Indifference curves generally slope downward and bow towards the origin (convex).

◆ Indifference curves farther from the origin represent higher levels of satisfaction.

◆ Indifference curves never intersect.

◆ **Marginal rate of substitution** (MRS) is magnitude of slope of indifference curve—rate at which household gives up good y (pop) for additional unit good x (movies) and still remains indifferent.

◆ **Diminishing marginal rate of substitution** is tendency for MRS to $\downarrow$ as move down along an indifference curve. Accounts for bowed-towards-the-origin shape of indifference curves.

◆ $\uparrow$ substitutability between goods $\rightarrow$ straighter indifference curves.
$\downarrow$ substitutability between goods $\rightarrow$ more tightly curved indifference curves.

The Household's Consumption Choice

Given income and prices of goods, household allocates income to maximize satisfaction. Household chooses best affordable point, which is on budget line and on highest possible indifference curve. At the best affordable point

◆ household spends all its income and achieves maximum satisfaction.

◆ budget line and indifference curve are tangent and have same slope—MRS equals the relative price.

Predicting Consumer Behaviour

Price effect is Δ consumption resulting from Δ price of a good. Price effect = substitution effect + income effect.

◆ **Substitution effect**—Δ consumption resulting from Δ price accompanied by (hypothetical) Δ income leaving household indifferent between initial and new situations. For normal and inferior goods, substitution effect of $\downarrow$ price $\rightarrow$ $\uparrow$ consumption.

◆ **Income effect**—Δ consumption resulting from (hypothetically) restoring original income but keeping prices constant at new level. For normal goods, income effect of (hypothetical) ↑ income → ↑ consumption. For inferior goods, (hypothetical) ↑ income → ↓ consumption.

◆ The downward-sloping demand curve is a consequence of the consumer choosing his best affordable combination of goods. The demand curve can be derived from the price effect—by tracing the best affordable quantity of a good as its price changes.

For normal goods, substitution and income effects work in same direction, so ↓ price → ↑ consumption.

For inferior goods, substitution and income effects work in opposite directions, but net effect of ↓ price usually → (smaller) ↑ consumption.

HELPFUL HINTS

1 Although the analysis in this chapter may seem restrictive, it is helpful to maintain a broad perspective. From a general economic perspective, the consumer's problem is to do the best given the constraints faced. These constraints, which limit the range of possible choices, depend on income and the prices of goods and are represented graphically by the budget line. Doing the best means finding the most preferred outcome consistent with those constraints. In this chapter, preferences are represented graphically by indifference curves.

Graphically, the consumer problem is to find the highest indifference curve attainable given the budget line. To make graphical analysis feasible, we restrict ourselves to choices between only two goods, but the same principles apply in the real world to a broader array of choices.

2 The budget equation for pop and movies on text page 170 is

$$Q_p = \frac{y}{P_p} - \frac{P_m}{P_p} Q_m$$

This is the type of straight line equation ($y = a + bx$) that we discussed in Chapter 2. The differences are that Q_p is the dependent variable (instead of y) and Q_m is the independent variable (instead of x). We can use the budget equation to graph the budget line by finding the Q_p-intercept (where the line intersects the

vertical Q_p axis), finding the Q_m-intercept (where the line intersects the horizontal Q_m axis), and then connecting those two points with a straight line.

To find the Q_p-intercept, set $Q_m = 0$.

$$Q_p = \frac{y}{P_p} - \frac{P_m}{P_p}(0)$$

$$Q_p = \frac{y}{P_p}$$

To find the Q_m-intercept, set $Q_p = 0$.

$$0 = \frac{y}{P_p} - \frac{P_m}{P_p} Q_m$$

$$\frac{P_m}{P_p} Q_m = \frac{y}{P_p}$$

$$Q_m = \frac{y}{P_m}$$

The Q_p-intercept, $Q_p = y/P_p$, is the consumer's real income in terms of pop. It tells us how much pop could be purchased if all income was spent on pop. The Q_m-intercept, $Q_m = y/P_m$, is the consumer's real income in terms of movies. It tells us how many movies could be purchased if all income was spent on movies. These intercepts provide an easy method for drawing a budget line. Each of the two endpoints (the intercepts) is just income divided by the price of the good on that axis. Connecting those endpoints with a straight line yields the budget line.

The slope of the budget line provides additional information for the consumer's choice. The magnitude (absolute value) of the slope equals the relative price (or opportunity cost) of movies in terms of pop. In other words, the magnitude of the slope equals the number of units of pop it takes to buy one movie. More generally, the magnitude of the slope of the budget line (P_x/P_y) equals the relative price (or opportunity cost) of the good on the horizontal x-axis in terms of the good on the vertical y-axis; or the number of units of vertical-axis goods it takes to buy one unit of the horizontal-axis good.

3 The marginal rate of substitution (MRS) is the rate at which a consumer gives up good Y for an additional unit of good X and still remains indifferent. The MRS equals the magnitude of the slope of the indifference curve, $\Delta Q_Y / \Delta Q_X$.

Because indifference curves are bowed towards the origin (convex), the magnitude of the slope and hence the MRS diminish as we move down an indifference curve. The diminishing MRS means that the consumer is willing to give up less of good Y for each additional unit of good X. As the consumer moves down an indifference curve, she is coming to value good Y more and value good X less. This is easily explained by the principle of diminishing marginal utility, which underlies the following equation (which also appear in the website appendix to the chapter).

$$\text{Marginal rate of substitution} = \frac{MU_X}{MU_Y}$$

At the top of the indifference curve, the consumer is consuming little X and much Y, so the marginal utility of X (MU_X) is high and the marginal utility of Y (MU_Y) is low. Moving down the curve, as the quantity of X consumed increases, MU_X decreases; and as the quantity of Y consumed decreases, MU_Y increases. Thus the principle of diminishing marginal utility provides an intuitive understanding of why the MRS diminishes as we move down an indifference curve.

4 At the consumer's best affordable point, the budget line is just tangent to the highest affordable indifference curve, so the magnitude of the slope of the budget line equals the magnitude of the slope of the indifference curve. Combining the information from Helpful Hint **2** (the magnitude of the slope of the budget line equals P_X/P_Y) and Helpful Hint **3** (the magnitude of the slope of the indifference curve equals MU_X/MU_Y) yields

$$\frac{P_X}{P_Y} = \frac{MU_X}{MU_Y}$$

Rearranging terms yields

$$\frac{MU_X}{P_X} = \frac{MU_Y}{P_Y}$$

This is the equation for utility maximization from Chapter 7. You can now see why the budget equation/indifference curve analysis of consumer choice developed here complements the marginal utility analysis of Chapter 7.

5 Understanding the distinction between the income and substitution effects of a change in the price of a good is often challenging for students. Consider a decrease in the price of good A. This has two effects that will influence the consumption of A. First, the decrease in the price of A will reduce the relative price of A and, second, it will increase real income. The substitution effect is the answer to the question: How much would the consumption of A change as a result of the relative price decline if we also (hypothetically) reduce income by enough to leave the consumer indifferent between the new and original situations? The income effect is the answer to the question: How much more would the consumption of A change if we (hypothetically) restore the consumer's real income but leave relative prices at the new level?

SELF-TEST

True/False/Uncertain and Explain

1 The graph of a budget line will be bowed towards the origin.

2 *Ceteris paribus*, an increase in the price of goods means that real income falls.

3 We assume that more of any good is preferred to less of the good.

4 Higher indifference curves represent higher levels of income.

5 The principle of the diminishing marginal rate of substitution explains why indifference curves are bowed towards the origin.

6 Perfect substitutes will have L-shaped indifference curves.

7 At the best affordable consumption point of movies and pop, the marginal rate of substitution equals the ratio of the price of movies to the price of pop.

8 When the relative price of a good decreases, the income effect leads to increased consumption of the good.

9 The law of demand can be derived from an indifference curve model by tracing the impact on quantity demanded of an increase in price.

10 The theory of consumer choice claims that people actually compute marginal rates of substitution and set them equal to relative prices in order to make spending decisions.

Multiple-Choice

1 Which of the following statements best describes a consumer's budget line?

a the amount of each good a consumer can purchase

b the limits to a consumer's set of affordable consumption choices

c the desired level of consumption for the consumer

d the consumption choices made by a consumer

e the set of all affordable consumption choices

2 Real income is measured in

a monetary units.

b price units.

c units of satisfaction.

d units of indifference.

e units of goods.

3 For an increase in price, the substitution effect

a always increases consumption.

b increases consumption for normal goods only.

c decreases consumption for normal goods only.

d decreases consumption for inferior goods only.

e does none of the above.

watch out realize that, they are saying

4 If two goods are perfect substitutes, then their

a indifference curves are positively sloped straight lines.

b indifference curves are negatively sloped straight lines.

c indifference curves are L-shaped.

d marginal rate of substitution is zero.

e marginal rate of substitution is infinity.

5 Consider the budget line and indifference curve in Fig. 8.1. If the price of good X is $2, what is the price of good Y?

a $0.37

b $0.67

c $1.50

d $2.67

e impossible to calculate without additional information

$$Y = mx + b$$
$$0 = m6 + 8 \qquad -8/6 = -4/3$$
$$Y = -4/3(2) + 8$$
$$= -8/3 + 8$$
$$= \frac{24-8}{3}$$
$$= 16/3$$

FIGURE **8.1**

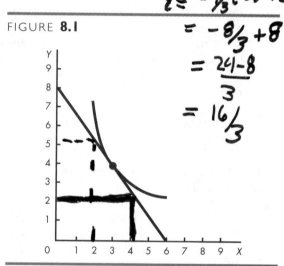

6 The initial budget equation for pop and movies is $Q_p = 20 - 4Q_m$, and the price of pop (P_p) is $5. If the price of pop falls to $4, which of the following is the new budget equation?

a $Q_p = 25 - 2Q_m$

b $Q_p = 25 - 4Q_m$

c $Q_p = 25 - 5Q_m$

d $Q_p = 20 - 5Q_m$

e none of the above

$$\frac{x}{5} = 20$$
$$\frac{y}{5} = 4 \qquad 10\%$$

7 Which of the following statements is *false*?

a indifference curves are negatively sloped

b a preference map consists of a series of nonintersecting indifference curves

c indifference curves are bowed out from the origin

d the marginal rate of substitution is the magnitude of the slope of an indifference curve

e the marginal rate of substitution increases with movement up an indifference curve

8 The initial budget line labelled *RS* in Fig. 8.2 would shift to *RT* as a result of a(n)

a increase in the price of good *X*.
b decrease in the price of good *X*.
c decrease in preferences for good *X*.
d increase in the price of good *Y*.
e increase in real income.

FIGURE **8.2**

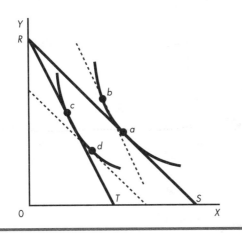

9 When the initial budget line labelled *RS* in Fig. 8.2 shifts to *RT*, the substitution effect is illustrated by the move from point

a *a* to *b*.
b *a* to *c*.
c *a* to *d*.
d *b* to *d*.
e *d* to *c*.

10 When the initial budget line labelled *RS* in Fig. 8.2 shifts to *RT*, the income effect is illustrated by the move from point

a *a* to *b*.
b *a* to *c*.
c *a* to *d*.
d *b* to *c*.
e *b* to *d*.

11 Zarina's income allows her to afford 3 tomatoes and no toothbrushes, or 2 toothbrushes and no tomatoes. The relative price of toothbrushes (price toothbrush/price tomato) is

a 2/3.
b 3/2.
c 6/1.
d 1/6.
e impossible to calculate without additional information.

12 In general, as a consumer moves down an indifference curve, increasing consumption of good *X* (measured on the horizontal axis),

a more of *Y* must be given up for each additional unit of *X*.
b a constant amount of *Y* must be given up for each additional unit of *X*.
c less of *Y* must be given up for each additional unit of *X*.
d the relative price of *Y* increases.
e the relative price of *Y* decreases.

13 If the price of the good measured on the vertical axis increases, the budget line will

a become steeper.
b become flatter.
c shift leftward but parallel to the original budget line.
d shift rightward but parallel to the original budget line.
e shift leftward and become steeper.

14 Which of the following statement(s) about Fig. 8.3 is/are *true*?

a Point *s* is preferred to point *q*, but *s* is not affordable.
b Points *q* and *r* yield the same utility, but *q* is more affordable.
c Point *t* is preferred to point *q*, but *t* is not affordable.
d Points *q* and *s* cost the same, but *q* is preferred to *s*.
e All of the above statements are true.

FIGURE **8.3**

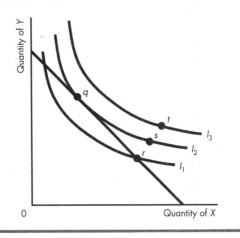

15 If income increases, the budget line will

a become steeper.

b become flatter.

c shift leftward but parallel to the original budget line.

d shift rightward but parallel to the original budget line.

e shift parallel but leftward or rightward depending on whether a good is normal or inferior.

16 If the price of good X (measured on the horizontal axis) falls, the substitution effect is represented by a movement to a

a higher indifference curve.

b lower indifference curve.

c steeper part of the same indifference curve.

d flatter part of the same indifference curve.

e flatter part of a higher indifference curve.

17 A change in the price of the good measured on the horizontal (x) axis changes which aspect(s) of the budget equation?

a slope and y-intercept

b slope and x-intercept

c x- and y-intercepts but not slope

d slope only

e none of the above

18 Bill consumes apples and bananas. Suppose Bill's income doubles and the prices of apples and bananas also double. Bill's budget line will

a shift left but not change slope.

b remain unchanged.

c shift right but not change slope.

d shift right and become steeper.

e shift right and become flatter.

19 When the price of an inferior good falls, the

1 income and substitution effects both move quantity demanded in the same direction.

2 income and substitution effects move quantity demanded in opposite directions.

3 income effect is usually larger than the substitution effect.

4 substitution effect is usually larger than the income effect.

a 1 and 2

b 1 and 4

c 2 and 3

d 2 and 4

e none of the above

20 Which of the following statements about the budget line is *false*? The budget line

a divides affordable from unaffordable consumption points.

b is based on fixed prices.

c is based on fixed income.

d is based on fixed quantities.

e constrains consumer choices.

21 When Clark Gable took off his shirt in *It Happened One Night*, he was not wearing an undershirt. As a result, men's undershirt sales plummeted. *Ceteris paribus*, we can conclude that men's undershirt

a preferences changed when prices changed.

b preferences changed when income changed.

c choices changed when preferences changed.

d choices changed when prices changed.

e choices changed when income changed.

22 In moving down along an indifference curve, the marginal rate of substitution (MRS) for complements will

a increase faster than the MRS for substitutes.

b increase more slowly than the MRS for substitutes.

c be relatively constant.

d decrease faster than the MRS for substitutes.

e decrease more slowly than the MRS for substitutes.

23 The income effect

a usually dominates the substitution effect.

b usually dominates the price effect.

c plus the price effect equals the substitution effect.

d minus the price effect equals the substitution effect.

e plus the substitution effect equals the price effect.

24 The budget line depends on

a income.

b prices.

c income and prices.

d preferences.

e preferences and prices.

25 The shape of an indifference curve depends on

a the prices of goods.

b household income.

c the substitutability between goods for the household.

d the level of satisfaction for the household.

e all of the above.

Short Answer Problems

1 Why is an indifference curve negatively sloped?

2 Explain why it is logically impossible for indifference curves to intersect each other, by comparing points *a*, *b*, and *c* in Fig. 8.4.

FIGURE **8.4**

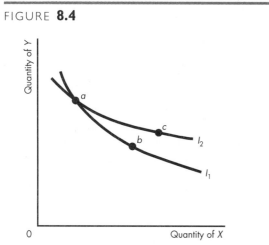

@ 3 In Helpful Hint **3** (as well as in the website Appendix to Chapter 8), it is established that the

$$\text{Marginal rate} \atop \text{of substitution} = \frac{\text{marginal utility of movies}}{\text{marginal utility of pop}}$$

As we move down an indifference curve, use the principle of diminishing marginal utility to explain why the marginal rate of substitution diminishes.

4 For normal goods,

* an increase in income causes an *increase in demand* (demand curve shifts to the right).
* the income effect (due to a decrease in price) causes *an increase in quantity demanded*.

Explain why these two statements are or are not contradictory. Be sure to define clearly any important concepts.

5 Jan and Dan both like bread and peanut butter and have the same income. Since they face the same prices, they have identical budget lines. Currently, Jan and Dan consume exactly the same quantities of bread and peanut butter; they have the same best affordable consumption point. Jan, however, views bread and peanut butter as close (though not perfect) substitutes, while Dan considers bread and peanut butter to be quite (but not perfectly) complementary.

a On the same diagram, draw a budget line and representative indifference curves for Jan and Dan. (Measure the quantity of bread on the horizontal axis.)

b Now, suppose the price of bread declines. Graphically represent the substitution effects for Jan and Dan. For whom is the substitution effect greater?

@ 6 Figure 8.5 illustrates a consumer's indifference map for food and clothing.

FIGURE **8.5**

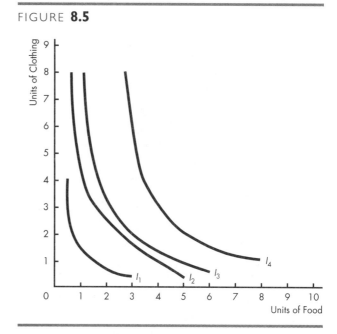

a i Initially, the price of a unit of clothing is $P_c = \$1.00$ and the price of a unit of food is $P_f = \$1.50$. If income is $y = \$9.00$, draw the consumer's budget line on Fig. 8.5 and label the best affordable point as point *a*. What is the quantity of food consumed?
ii What is the equation of the budget line in terms of P_c, P_f, and y? What is the equation of the budget line in numerical terms? Express the magnitude (absolute value) of the slope of the budget line as a ratio of P_c and P_f.
iii At point *a*, what is the value of the marginal rate of substitution (or equivalently, MU_f/MU_c)?
iv Use your answers in parts **ii** and **iii** to derive the formula for utility maximization. Explain.

b If P_f increases to $3.00 per unit while income and P_c remain unchanged, draw the new budget line and label the new best affordable point as point *b*. What is the new quantity of food consumed?

c If P_f increases again to $4.50 per unit while income and P_c remain unchanged, draw the corresponding budget line and label the best affordable point as point *c*. What is the quantity of food consumed?

d On a separate graph, plot and draw the demand curve for food that corresponds to points *a, b,* and *c*. Be sure to clearly label the axes.

e Suppose prices remain at their initial values ($P_c = \$1.00$, $P_f = \$1.50$) but income falls to $3.00. Draw the new budget line and label the best affordable point as point *z*. What is the quantity of food consumed? Is food a normal or inferior good? Explain. On your demand curve graph from part **d**, plot point *z* and roughly sketch a demand curve corresponding to the new income level.

7 Sharon, a fitness fanatic, plays squash and takes aerobics classes at her health club. Squash courts rent for $2 per hour and aerobics classes are $1 per hour. Sharon has decided to spend $12 per week for fitness activities. Figure 8.6 illustrates several indifference curves for squash and aerobics on Sharon's preference map.

FIGURE **8.6**

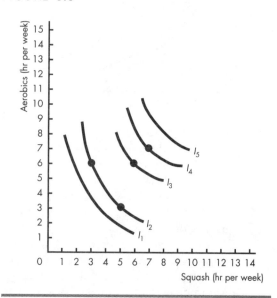

a How many hours of squash and aerobics will Sharon consume at her best affordable point?

b Suppose that squash rentals fall to $1 per hour.
   i How many hours of squash and aerobics will Sharon now consume? What is the increase in her hours of squash?
   ii Of the total increase in hours of squash, how many hours are due to the substitution effect of the price fall?
   iii Of the total increase in hours of squash, how many hours are due to the income effect of the price fall?

c On a separate graph, plot two points on Sharon's demand curve for squash and draw her straight line demand curve.

d The price of squash continues to be $1 but Sharon's fitness budget increases to $14. How many hours of squash and aerobics will Sharon now consume?

8 Ms. Muffet consumes both curds and whey. The initial price of curds is $1.00 per unit, and the price of whey is $1.50 per unit. Ms. Muffet's initial income is $12.00.

a What is the relative price of curds?

b Derive Ms. Muffet's budget equation and draw her budget line on a graph. (Measure curds on the horizontal axis.)

c On your graph, draw an indifference curve so that the best affordable point corresponds to 6 units of curds and 4 units of whey.

d What is the marginal rate of substitution of curds for whey at this point?

e Show that any other point on the budget line is inferior.

9 Given the initial situation described in Short Answer Problem 8, suppose Ms. Muffet's income now increases.

a Illustrate graphically how the consumption of curds and whey are affected if both goods are normal. (Numerical answers are not necessary. Just show whether consumption increases or decreases.)

b Draw a new graph showing the effect of an increase in Ms. Muffet's income if whey is an inferior good.

10 Return to the initial circumstances described in Short Answer Problem 8. Now, suppose the price of curds doubles to $2.00 a unit, while the price of whey remains at $1.50 per unit and income remains at $12.00.

a Draw the new budget line.

b Why is the initial best affordable point (label it point *r*) no longer the best affordable point?

c Using your graph, show the new best affordable point and label it *t*. What has happened to the consumption of curds?

d Decompose the effect on the consumption of *X* into the substitution effect and the income effect. On your graph, indicate the substitution effect as movement from point *r* to point *s* (which you must locate) and indicate the income effect as movement from point *s* to point *t*.

12/25

ANSWERS

True/False/Uncertain and Explain

1 F Budget lines straight. Indifference curves bowed towards origin. (169–170)
2 T Real income = income/price goods. (170–171)
3 T See text discussion. (172–173)
4 F Represent higher levels satisfaction. (172–173)
5 T See text discussion. (173–174)
6 F True for perfect complements. (175–176)
7 T Budget line tangent to indifference curve. (176–177)
8 U True for normal, false for inferior goods. (177–181)
9 T See text discussion. (177–178)
10 F Claims only choices made by real people resemble choices predicted by model. (159–160)

Multiple-Choice

1 b **a** should be combinations of goods; **c** about indifference curves; **d** about best affordable point; **e** includes area inside budget line. (169–170)
2 e See text discussion. (170)
3 e For ↑ price, substitution effect always → ↓ consumption for both normal and inferior goods. (179–181)
4 b With constant slope = 1. (175–176)
5 c Income = $12 ($2 × 6 units X), so price Y = $12/8 units Y. (169–171)
6 c From $Q_p = (y/P_p) - (P_m/P_p)Q_m$. If P_p = $5, then y = $100 and P_m = $20. Then recalculate Q_p equation for P_p = $4. (170–171)
7 c Indifference curves bow in towards the origin. (172–174)
8 a With same income, ↓ X can be purchased. **c** relates to indifference curves. ↑ real income is move from point b to c. (170–171)
9 a Budget line with new prices tangent to original indifference curve. (179–181)
10 d Hypothetically restore original income (reverse ↑ real income) but keep prices constant at new level. (179–181)
11 b (3 × price tomato) = (2 × price toothbrush). Divide both sides equation by price tomato and by 2. (169–171)
12 c Due to diminishing MRS. **d** and **e** wrong since relative price relates to budget line, not indifference curve. (172–174)
13 b y-intercept shifts down, x-intercept unchanged. (170–171)
14 c t on higher indifference curve, but outside budget line. s and q yield same utility so **a, d** wrong. q preferred to r so **b** wrong. (176–177)
15 d ↑ income does not change slope but ↑ x- and y-intercepts. (170–171)
16 d New budget line flatter and drawn tangent to same indifference curve. (179–181)
17 b See Helpful Hint 2 and analyse ΔP_m (movies on horizontal axis). (170–171)
18 b Numerators and denominators of both intercepts double, so intercepts do not change. (170–171)
19 d See text discussion. (181)
20 d Quantities vary along budget line. (169–170)
21 c Gable's influence → ↓ preference undershirts. Combined with unchanged prices and incomes → ↓ consumption. (172–173)
22 d MRS always ↓ moving down indifference curve. Complements have more tightly curved indifference curves. (175–176)
23 e See text discussion. Reverse of **a, b** true. (179–181)
24 c See text discussion. (169–170)
25 c Budget line depends on **a** and **b**. At any level satisfaction, indifference curve could be any shape. (175–176)

Short Answer Problems

1 An indifference curve tells us how much the consumption of one good must increase as the consumption of another good decreases in order to leave the consumer indifferent (no better or worse off). It is negatively sloped because the goods are both desirable. As we *decrease* the consumption of one good, in order to not be made worse off, consumption of the other good must *increase*. This implies a negative slope.

2 The explanation takes the form of a proof by contradiction. Since points a and b are on the same indifference curve (I_1), the consumer is indifferent between them. Since points a and c are on the same indifference curve (I_2), the consumer is also indifferent between them. If the consumer is indifferent between a and b and between a and c, this implies an indifference between b and c. But indifference between points b and c is logically impossible, because we assume that more of any good is preferred to less of that good. Since point c has more of both good X and good Y than point b, the consumer cannot be indifferent between b and c. Indifference between b and c contradicts the assumption that more is preferred to less. Hence indifference curves cannot intersect.

e 3   As we move down an indifference curve for pop and movies, such as in Text Fig. 8.5 on page 174, we increase the quantity of movies consumed and decrease the quantity of pop consumed. As movie consumption increases, each additional movie yields lower marginal utility because of the principle of diminishing marginal utility. Thus the value of the numerator on the right-hand side of the equation below decreases.

$$\begin{array}{c} \text{Marginal rate} \\ \text{of substitution} \end{array} = \frac{\text{marginal utility of movies}}{\text{marginal utility of pop}}$$

As pop consumption decreases, each previous pop consumed yields higher marginal utility. Thus, the value of the denominator on the right-hand side of the equation increases. The combined effect of a decrease in the numerator and an increase in the denominator is that the ratio MU_{movies}/MU_{pop} falls as we move down an indifference curve, corresponding to a diminishing marginal rate of substitution on the left-hand side of the equation.

4   These statements appear to be contradictory because an increase in income leads, in the first statement, to a shift of the demand curve but, in the second statement, to a movement along the demand curve. The reason the statements are *not* contradictory has to do with a crucial distinction between *nominal* income and *real* income.

The first statement (an increase in income causes an increase in *demand* [demand curve shifts rightward]) describes how an increase in *nominal* income shifts the demand curve. *Nominal* income is measured in dollars.

The second statement (the income effect [due to a decrease in price] causes an increase in *quantity demanded*) describes how an increase in *real* income causes a movement along the stationary demand curve.

Real income is measured in purchasing power, or the quantities of goods that nominal income can buy. When the price of a good decreases, your *real* income goes up because you can now purchase more of that good with the same, unchanged, *nominal* income. Because *nominal* income is unchanged in the second statement, the demand curve does not shift. But because *real* income has increased, the decrease in price leads to an increase in *quantity demanded*.

5 a   Initially, Jan and Dan are at point *c* on the budget line labelled *AB* in Fig. 8.7. Jan's indifference curve is illustrated by I_J. Note that her indifference curve is close to a straight line reflecting the fact that bread and peanut butter are close substitutes. On the other hand, since Dan considers bread and peanut butter to be complementary, his indifference curve, I_D, is more tightly curved.

FIGURE **8.7**

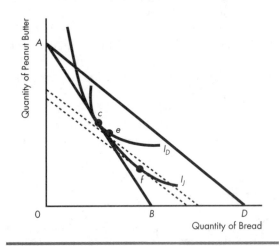

b   If the price of bread declines, the budget line will become flatter, such as the line labelled *AD* in Fig. 8.7. In order to measure the substitution effect, find the point on the original indifference curve that has the same slope as the new budget line. Since Dan's indifference curve is more sharply curved, it becomes flatter quite rapidly as we move away from point *c*. Thus the substitution effect is quite small, from *c* to point *e*. Since Jan's indifference curve is almost a straight line, the substitution effect must be much larger, from *c* to point *f*.

d 6   The consumer's budget line is shown in Fig. 8.5 Solution.

FIGURE **8.5**   SOLUTION

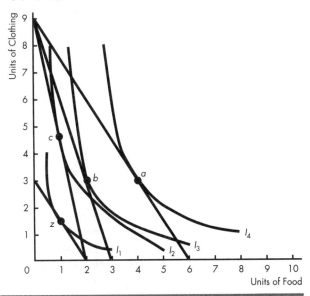

a **i** 4 units of food

  ii The consumer's budget is given by

$$P_c Q_c + P_f Q_f = y$$

To obtain the budget equation, follow the calculation procedure on text page 170. Divide by P_c to obtain

$$Q_c + \frac{P_f}{P_c} Q_f = \frac{y}{P_c}$$

Subtract $(P_f/P_c) Q_f$ from both sides to obtain

$$Q_c = \frac{y}{P_c} - \frac{P_f}{P_c} Q_f$$

To obtain the budget equation in numerical terms, substitute in the values $P_c = \$1.00$, $P_f = \$1.50$, and $y = \$9.00$.

$$Q_c = \frac{9}{1} - \frac{1.50}{1} Q_f$$

$$Q_c = 9 - 3/2 Q_f$$

The magnitude (absolute value) of the slope of the budget line is 3/2, which is the ratio of P_f/P_c. Note that this price ratio cannot be read directly off the graph since the axes measure quantities, not prices.

  iii The marginal rate of substitution at point a is defined as the magnitude of the slope of the indifference curve at point a. Since the slope of the indifference curve at point a is equal to the slope of the tangent at a, and since the budget line is tangent at a, the magnitude of the slope of the indifference curve is 3/2. This magnitude is equivalent to MU_f/MU_c.

  iv The magnitude of the slope of the budget line is P_f/P_c and the magnitude of the slope of

the indifference curve at a is MU_f/MU_c. Since the two magnitudes are equal, $P_f/P_c = MU_f/MU_c$ or $MU_f/P_f = MU_c/P_c$.

b See Fig. 8.5 Solution: 2 units of food.

c See Fig. 8.5 Solution: 1 unit of food.

d The demand curve for food is shown in Fig. 8.8.

FIGURE **8.8**

e See Fig. 8.5 Solution. 1 unit of food. Food is a *normal* good because a *decrease* in income (with prices constant) causes a decrease in food consumption (from 4 units to 1 unit). See Fig. 8.8 for the new demand curve (income = $3).

7 a In order to find Sharon's best affordable point, draw the budget line in Fig. 8.6 Solution. The initial budget line is labelled AB and Sharon's best affordable point is point c on indifference curve I_2. Thus Sharon consumes 3 hours of squash and 6 hours of aerobics per week.

FIGURE **8.6**   SOLUTION

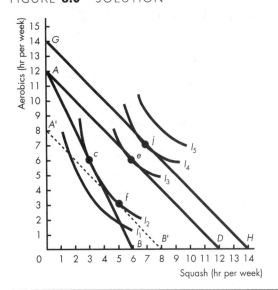

b If the price of squash falls to $1, the budget line becomes *AD*.

i Now Sharon's best affordable point is point *e* on indifference curve I_3. This corresponds to consumption of 6 hours of squash and 6 hours of aerobics per week. Her squash consumption has increased by 3 hours.

ii To measure the substitution effect, shift the new budget line leftward in parallel fashion until it is tangent to the indifference curve I_2, where Sharon was before the fall in the price of squash. In effect, budget line *A'B'* removes the increase in real income due to the price fall in order to isolate the substitution effect of the price fall on Sharon's consumption of squash. Point *f* is what Sharon would have consumed at the new prices if her income fell just enough to return her to her original indifference curve. The substitution effect of the fall in the price of squash is the movement from initial point *c* to point *f*, which is an increase in squash hours consumed of 2 (from 3 to 5 hours).

iii To measure the income effect, shift the budget line *A'B'* rightward in parallel fashion until it is tangent to the indifference curve I_3, where Sharon was before we hypothetically reduced her real income. In effect, this shift isolates the income effect by restoring the increase in real income due to the price fall while keeping prices constant at their new values. The income effect of the fall in the price of squash is the movement from point *f* to point *e*, which is an increase in squash hours consumed of 1 (from 5 to 6 hours).

The results are summarized in Table 8.1.

TABLE **8.1** PRICE EFFECT FROM FIGURE 8.6 SOLUTION

Effect	Move from Point	↑ Hours Squash
Substitution effect	c to f	2
+ Income effect	f to e	1
= Price effect	c to e	3

c In parts **a** and **b**, income spent on fitness was constant at $12 and the price of aerobics was constant at $1 per hour. When the price of squash was $2 per hour, Sharon wanted to consume 3 hours of squash and when the price of squash was $1, Sharon wanted to consume 6 hours of squash. This gives us two points on Sharon's demand curve for squash, which are labelled *a* and *b* in Fig. 8.9. Drawing a line passing through these points allows us to obtain her straight line demand curve, labelled *D*.

FIGURE **8.9**

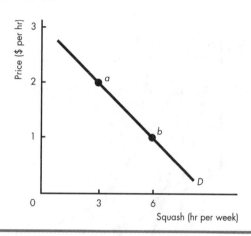

d When Sharon's fitness budget increases to $14, the budget line shifts right to the line labelled *GH* in Fig. 8.6 Solution. Sharon's best affordable point is now at *j*, which corresponds to 7 hours of squash and 7 hours of aerobics consumed per week.

8 a The relative price of curds is the price of curds divided by the price of whey:

$$\frac{\$1.00}{\$1.50} = \frac{2}{3}$$

b Let P_c = the price of curds, P_w = the price of whey, Q_c = quantity of curds, Q_w = quantity of whey, and y = income. The budget equation, in general form, is

$$Q_w = \frac{y}{P_w} - \frac{P_c}{P_w} Q_c$$

Since $P_c = \$1.00$, $P_w = \$1.50$, and $y = \$12.00$, Ms. Muffet's budget equation is specifically given by

$$Q_w = 8 - 2/3 \ Q_c$$

The graph of this budget equation, the budget line, is given by the line labelled *AB* in Fig. 8.10.

FIGURE **8.10**

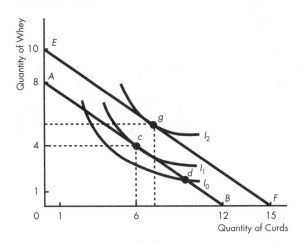

FIGURE **8.11**

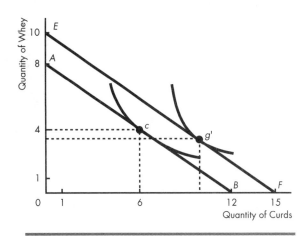

c If the best affordable point corresponds to 6 units of curds and 4 units of whey, then the relevant indifference curve must be tangent to (just touch) the budget line *AB* at *c*, which is indifference curve I_1.

d The marginal rate of substitution is given by the magnitude of the slope of the indifference curve at point *c*. We do not know the slope of the indifference curve directly, but we can easily compute the slope of the budget line. Since, at point *c*, the indifference curve and the budget line have the same slope, we can obtain the marginal rate of substitution of curds for whey. Since the slope of the budget line is –2/3, the marginal rate of substitution is 2/3. For example, Ms. Muffet is willing to give up 2 units of whey in order to receive 3 additional units of curds and still remain indifferent.

e Since indifference curves cannot intersect each other and since indifference curve I_1 lies everywhere above the budget line (except at point *c*), we know that every other point on the budget line is on a lower indifference curve. For example, point *d* lies on indifference curve I_0. Thus every other point on the budget line is inferior to point *c*.

9 a An increase in income will cause a parallel rightward shift of the budget line, for example, to *EF* in Fig. 8.10. If both curds and whey are normal goods, Ms. Muffet will move to a point like *g* at which the consumption of both goods has increased.

b If whey is an inferior good, then its consumption will fall as income rises. This is illustrated in Fig. 8.11. Once again the budget line shifts from *AB* to *EF*, but Ms. Muffet's preferences are such that her new consumption point is given by a point like *g'* where the consumption of whey has actually declined.

10 a Ms. Muffet's initial budget line is *AB* and the initial best affordable point is *r* in Fig. 8.12. Note that point *r* in Fig. 8.12 is the same as point *c* in Fig. 8.10. The new budget line following an increase in the price of curds to $2.00 (income remains at $12.00) is *AH*.

FIGURE **8.12**

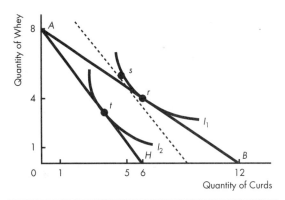

b After the price increase, point *r* is no longer the best affordable point since it is no longer even affordable.

c The new best affordable point (labelled *t* in Fig. 8.12) indicates a decrease in the consumption of curds.

d The substitution effect of the increase in the price of curds is indicated by the movement from *r* to *s* in Fig. 8.12. This gives the effect of the change in relative prices while keeping Ms. Muffet on the same indifference curve. The income effect is indicated by movement from *s* to *t*.

Chapter 9

Organizing Production

The Firm and Its Economic Problem

A **firm** is an institution that hires and organizes factors of production to produce and sell goods and services. Firms strive for maximum profit and efficient, lowest-cost production. Firms organize production by using

◆ Command systems based on a managerial hierarchy.

◆ Incentive systems to overcome problems of uncertainty and incomplete information.

With incomplete information, the **principal–agent problem** arises when agents (those employed by others) do not act in the best interests of the principals (employers of the agents).

◆ Strategies for coping with the principal–agent problem and inducing agents to act in the best interests of the principals include ownership, incentive pay, and long-term contracts.

◆ To cope with uncertainty and incomplete information, firms have devised different forms of business organization:

 • *Sole proprietorship*—single owner with unlimited liability.
 • *Partnership*—two or more owners with unlimited liability.
 • *Corporation*—owned by limited liability stockholders.

Business Finance

Firms finance expenses by

◆ Selling stock. Corporations raise **equity** by selling shares of stock. The shareholders are owners of a corporation, and an owner's stake in a business is called equity.

◆ Selling bonds. A **bond** is a legally enforceable obligation to pay specified money at future dates.

 • **Capital gain** is income received by selling a stock or bond for a higher price than the original price paid for it.

Present value of future amount of money is amount which, if invested today, will grow as large as the future amount, taking account of earned interest. **Discounting** is the conversion of a future amount of money to its present value.

◆ $\text{Present value} = \dfrac{\text{amount money available } n \text{ years}}{(1 + r)^n}$

◆ Firms decide whether or not to borrow by evaluating net benefit of borrowing = (marginal benefit – marginal cost). Present value of net benefit is net present value. If net present value is positive, firm ↑ profit by borrowing.

Opportunity Cost and Economic Profit

A firm's opportunity costs of production consist of explicit costs (paid directly in money) and *implicit costs* (opportunities forgone but not paid for directly in money). Major implicit costs include

◆ Cost of capital—the **economic depreciation** of capital is the change in market price of a capital asset. (Accountants apply conventional depreciation rates to the purchase price to calculate depreciation.) Other cost of capital is forgone interest.

 • **Implicit rental rate** (= economic depreciation + forgone interest).
 • **Sunk cost** (= past economic depreciation) is *not* an opportunity cost of capital.

◆ Cost of inventories—must be replaced when used.

- Cost of owner's resources—owners supply entrepreneurial ability. **Normal profit** is the expected return to entrepreneurial ability and is part of a firm's opportunity costs of production.

Economists' costs and profits:

- *Opportunity costs* = explicit costs + implicit costs
- **Economic profits** = revenues – (explicit costs + implicit costs)
- Because normal profits are part of implicit costs, economic profits (when positive) are over and above normal profits.

Accountants' costs and profits:

- Accounting costs = explicit costs + conventional depreciation
- Accounting profits = revenues – (explicit costs + conventional depreciation)
- Accounting profits do *not* subtract normal profits or other implicit costs.

Economic Efficiency

Technological efficiency—not possible to ↑ output without ↑ inputs.

Economic efficiency—lowest possible cost of producing given output.

Firms and Markets

Firms coordinate economic activity when perform!tasks more efficiently than markets. Firms often have advantages of

- lower **transactions costs**—costs arising from finding someone with whom to do business.
- **economies of scale**—↓ unit cost of producing good as output rate ↑.
- economies of team production—individuals in production process specializing in mutually supportive tasks.

HELPFUL HINTS

1 The concept of *present value* is fundamental in thinking about the value today of an investment or of future amounts of money. It gives us a method of comparing investments that have payments that occur at different points in time. The intuition behind present value is that a dollar today is worth more than a dollar in the future because today's dollar can be invested to earn interest. To calculate the value *today* of an amount of money that will be paid in the future, we must discount that future amount to compensate for the forgone interest. The *present value* of a future amount of money is the amount that, if invested today, will grow as large as that future amount, taking into account the interest that it will earn.

2 In this chapter, we again meet our old friend opportunity cost. Here we look at the costs firms face with a special emphasis on the differences between *opportunity cost* measures used by economists and *accounting cost* measures. Opportunity cost, which is the concept of cost relevant for economic decisions, includes *explicit* and *implicit costs*. Important examples of implicit costs include the owner's/investor's forgone interest, implicit rent, economic depreciation, and normal profits. Accounting cost includes only explicit, out-of-pocket costs and conventional depreciation. These differences in cost measures between accountants and economists lead to differences in profit measures as well, as outlined here.

Economists
Opportunity costs = explicit costs + implicit costs
Economic profits = revenues – (explicit costs + implicit costs)

Accountants
Accounting costs = explicit costs + conventional depreciation
Accounting profits = revenues – (explicit costs + conventional depreciation)

Implicit costs, which economists include but accountants exclude, are the key to difference between economists' and accountants' measures of cost and profit. Accounting profits do *not* subtract normal profits or other implicit costs, so accounting profits are generally greater than economic profits.

Because normal profits are part of implicit costs, economic profits are profits over and above normal profits. If we think of normal profits as average profits, economic profits are *above-average* profits. Economic profits are a signal to firms that they are earning a greater return on investment than could be earned on average elsewhere in the economy.

Economic profits can also be negative if revenues are less than opportunity costs. As we will see in Chapter 11, such *economic losses* are a signal to firms that they are earning a *lower* return on investment than could be earned on average elsewhere.

3 It is important to distinguish between *technological efficiency* and *economic efficiency*. The difference is critical since economic decisions will be made only on the basis of economic efficiency. Technological efficiency is an engineering concept and occurs when it is not possible to increase output without increasing inputs. There is no consideration of input costs. Economic efficiency occurs when the *cost* of producing a given output is at a minimum. All technologically efficient production methods are not economically efficient. But all economically efficient methods are also technologically efficient. Competition favours firms that choose economically efficient production methods, and penalizes firms that do not.

SELF-TEST

True/False/Uncertain and Explain

1 Giving corporate managers stock in their companies is a strategy for coping with a principal–agent problem.

2 Normal profit is the expected return for supplying entrepreneurial ability.

3 If the interest rate is 10 percent a year, then the present value of $100 received in one year is $110.

4 In a principal–agent relationship between the stockholders and managers of Scotiabank, the stockholders are agents and the managers are principals.

5 Opportunity cost is greater than accounting cost.

6 When a firm produces using its own machine, its opportunity cost is lower than if it had rented the machine.

7 The opportunity cost of using inventories is the current market price.

8 An economically efficient production process becomes economically inefficient if the relative prices of inputs change.

9 For a capital asset, economic depreciation is less than conventional depreciation.

10 Markets will coordinate economic activity in situations where there are economies of scale.

Multiple-Choice

1 Which of the following statements is *not* true of firms?
a Firms and markets are institutions for coordinating economic activity.
b Firms organize factors of production in order to produce goods and services.
c Firms sell goods and services.
d Technologically efficient firms can eliminate scarcity.
e Firms use command systems to organize production.

2 A firm that has two or more owners with joint unlimited liability is
a a proprietorship.
b a partnership.
c a conglomerate.
d a corporation.
e none of the above.

3 Which of the following may vary over the term of a bond?

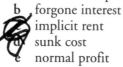

a present value
b redemption value
c redemption date
d annual coupon value
e none of the above

4 Bart buys a bow tie business for $100,000. To pay for the business, he borrows $60,000 from the bank at 12 percent interest and sells $40,000 worth of bonds. The bonds pay 10 percent interest per year. The opportunity cost of running the business in its first year includes

a only the $7,200 interest paid to the bank.
b only the $4,000 interest paid to bondholders.
c both the $7,200 bank interest and the $4,000 bondholders' interest.
d neither the $7,200 bank interest nor the $4,000 bondholders' interest.
e none of the above.

5 In general,
1 opportunity cost is greater than accounting cost.
2 opportunity cost is less than accounting cost.
3 economic profit is greater than accounting profit.
4 economic profit is less than accounting profit.

a 1 only
b 1 and 3
c 1 and 4
d 2 and 3
e 2 and 4

6 The rate of interest is 10 percent per year. You invest $50,000 of your own money in a business and earn *accounting* profits of $20,000 after one year. *Ceteris paribus*, what are your *economic* profits?

a $20,000
b $15,000
c $5,000
d $2,000
e – $15,000

7 The owner's stake in a business is called

a present value.
b redemption value.
c sunk cost.
d equity.
e inventories.

8 Which of the following is *not* an implicit cost?

a economic depreciation
b forgone interest
c implicit rent
d sunk cost
e normal profit

9 In Table 9.1, which method(s) of making a photon torpedo is/are technologically efficient?

a 1
b 2
c 3
d all of the above
e 1 and 3 only

TABLE **9.1** THREE METHODS OF MAKING ONE PHOTON TORPEDO

| | Quantities of Inputs | |
Method	Labour	Capital
1	5	10
2	10	7
3	15	5

10 Refer to Table 9.1. If the price of labour is $10 per unit and the price of capital is $20 per unit, which method(s) is/are economically efficient?

a 1
b 2
c 3
d all of the above
e 1 and 3 only

11 What is a *disadvantage* of a corporation relative to a proprietorship or partnership?

a owners have unlimited liability
b profits are taxed as corporate profits and as dividend income to stockholders
c there is difficulty in raising money
d perpetual life
e none of the above

12 Which of the following statements is *true*?

a All technologically efficient methods are also economically efficient.
b All economically efficient methods are also technologically efficient.
c Technological efficiency changes with changes in relative input prices.
d Technologically efficient firms will be more likely to survive than economically efficient firms.
e None of the above.

13 Firms will be more efficient than the market as a coordinator of economic activity when firms have

a lower transactions costs.
b lower monitoring costs.
c economies of scale.
d economies of team production.
e all of the above.

14 If the annual rate of interest is 10 percent, what is the present value of $100 received one year from now?

a $90.00
b $90.91
c $95.45
d $100.00
e $110.00

15 The possibility that an employee may not work hard is an example of the

a limited liability problem.
b principal–agent problem.
c transactions cost problem.
d technological efficiency problem.
e partnership problem.

16 Which of the following types of firms issue(s) shares of stock?

a proprietorship
b partnership
c corporation
d all of the above
e b and c only

17 Which of the following groups is the residual claimant of a corporation?

a stockholders
b bondholders
c banks and other creditors
d government taxing agencies
e managers

18 The construction cost of a building is $100,000. The conventional depreciation allowance is 5 percent per year. At the end of the first year the market value of the building is $80,000. For the first year, the depreciation cost is

a $20,000 to an accountant or an economist.
b $5,000 to an accountant or an economist.
c $5,000 to an accountant but $20,000 to an economist.
d $20,000 to an accountant but $5,000 to an economist.
e none of the above.

19 Abdul operates his own business and pays himself a salary of $20,000 per year. He refused a job that pays $30,000 per year. What is the opportunity cost of Abdul's time in the business?

a $10,000
b $20,000
c $30,000
d $50,000
e zero

20 Economic profit is revenues minus

a explicit costs.
b implicit costs.
c opportunity costs.
d accounting costs.
e (explicit costs + conventional depreciation).

21 Economies of scale exist when

a transactions costs are high.
b transactions costs are low.
c hiring additional inputs does not increase the price of inputs.
d the cost of producing a unit of output falls as the output rate increases.
e the firm is too large and too diversified.

22 Suppose that the trademark "Vice–President's Choice" currently has a market value of $10,000. After one year, the market value increases to $15,000. The opportunity cost of using the trademark during the year is

a zero
b –$5,000
c $5,000
d $10,000
e $15,000

23 The present value of a future payment of money will be higher the

a higher the interest rate or the further in the future the payment.
b lower the interest rate or the further in the future the payment.
c higher the interest rate or the nearer the date of the future payment.
d lower the interest rate or the nearer the date of the future payment.
e lower the interest rate and independent of the date of the future payment.

24 If the present value of $500 received one year from now is $463, what is the annual interest rate?

a 5 percent
b 8 percent
c 10 percent
d 20.8 percent
e 37 percent

25 If the annual interest rate is 10 percent, what is the present value of $100 *two* years from now?

a $80.00
b $82.64
c $90.91
d $120.00
e $121.00

Short Answer Problems

1 Give the meaning of present value by explaining (in words) why $110 received one year from now has a present value of $100 if the interest rate is 10 percent per year.

2 The standard tip in a restaurant is 15 percent. Restaurants could raise their prices 15 percent, set a no-tipping policy, and pay servers the extra 15 percent. Use principal–agent analysis to explain why most restaurants prefer tipping.

3 Compare the accounting cost and opportunity cost approaches in each of the following cases:
a depreciation cost.
b the firm borrows money to finance its operation.
c the firm uses its own funds rather than borrowing.
d the value of the firm's owner's resources.

4 Distinguish between technological efficiency and economic efficiency.

5 Markets and firms are alternative ways of coordinating economic activity that arise because of scarcity. Why do both firms and markets exist?

6 Complete Table 9.2 by computing the present value of each of three future payment sequences, first assuming the annual interest rate is 10 percent ($r = 0.1$), then assuming it is 5 percent ($r = 0.05$). The three future payment sequences are
A: $100 paid after one year.
B: $100 paid after two years.

C: A 2-year, $1,000 bond with a coupon payment of $100 per year. For example, the bondholder will receive a $100 coupon payment at the end of one year and again at the end of two years. At the end of two years, the bondholder will also receive $1,000 (the face value of the bond).

TABLE **9.2**

Future Payment	Present Value ($)	
Sequence	$r = 0.1$	$r = 0.05$
A		
B		
C		

7 Bonds *A* and *B* are described as follows.
  A: Pays $220 after two years.
  B: Pays $110 after one year and $110 after two years.
  For which of these bonds would you be willing to pay more? Why? [*Hint:* You do not need to know the interest rate to answer this question.]

8 A year ago, Frank, the bricklayer, decided to start a business manufacturing doll furniture. Frank has two sisters; Angela is an accountant and Edith is an economist. (Both sisters are good with numbers, but Edith doesn't have enough personality to be an accountant.) Each of the sisters computes Frank's cost and profit for the first year using the following information.

1. Frank took no income from the firm. He has a standing offer to return to work as a bricklayer for $30,000 per year.
2. Frank rents his machinery for $9,000 a year.
3. Frank owns the garage in which he produces, but could rent it out at $3,000 per year.
4. To start the business, Frank used $10,000 of his own money and borrowed $30,000 at the market rate of interest of 10 percent per year.
5. Frank hires one employee at an annual salary of $20,000.
6. The cost of materials during the first year is $40,000.
7. End of year inventory is zero.
8. Frank's entrepreneurial abilities are worth $14,000.
9. Frank's revenue for his first year is $100,000.

a Set up a table indicating how Angela and Edith would compute Frank's cost. Ignore any depreciation. What is Frank's cost as computed by Angela? by Edith?

b What is Frank's profit (or loss) as computed by Angela? by Edith?

9 According to your roommate, it is always more economically efficient to produce wheat using some machinery than using only labour. Suppose that there are two technologically efficient methods of producing one tonne of wheat.

Method 1 requires 20 machine hours plus 20 hours of labour.

Method 2 requires 100 hours of labour.

Country *A* has a highly developed industrial economy, while country *B* is less developed. In country *A* the price of an hour of labour (the wage rate) is $8, while the wage rate in country *B* is $4. The price of a machine hour is $20 in both countries. Which method is economically efficient in country *A*? in country *B*? Explain.

10 Consider countries *A* and *B* described in Short Answer Problem 9.

a What wage rate in country *B* would make the two methods equally efficient in country *B*?

b What price of a machine hour would make the two methods equally efficient in country *A*?

A N S W E R S

True/False/Uncertain and Explain

1 T Makes managers' (agents) incentives same as shareholders' (principal). (189–190)

2 T Definition. (198)

3 F *PV* of $110 received in one year is $100. (194–196)

4 F Stockholders' (principals) profits depend on job done by managers (agents). (190–192)

5 U Usually true, but depends on existence of implicit costs and differences between economic and conventional depreciation. (196–199)

6 F Opportunity cost equal for ownership or rental. (196–197)

7 T See text discussion. (198)

8 U Depends on magnitude price change. (200–201)

9 U Depends on whether ↓ market value is ⋛ conventional depreciation calculation. (196–197)

10 F Firms more efficient if economies of scale. (202–203)

Multiple-Choice

1 d Scarcity can never be eliminated. (189–190)

2 b Definition. (191–192)

3 a *PV* changes with changes in *r*. All other parameters fixed. (194–195)

4 c Both explicit costs, part of opportunity cost. (196–197)

5 c See formulae in Helpful Hint 2. (196–199)

6 b Economic profits = accounting profits − implicit costs = $20,000 − (0.10 × $50,000). (196–199)

7 d Definition. (193)

8 d Sunk cost is past economic depreciation; past forgone opportunity cannot be retrieved. (196–198)

9 d No method has more of one input and same amount of other input, compared with alternative method. (200–201)

10 b 2 costs $240 while 1 and 3 cost $250. (200–201)

11 b d advantage. a, c disadvantages proprietorship and partnership. (191–192)

12 b c true for economic efficiency. Reverse of d true. (200–201)

13 e See text discussion. (202–203)

14 b $PV = \$100/(1 + 0.1)$. (194–195)

15 b See text discussion. (190–191)

16 c See text discussion. (191–192)

17 a Others have fixed claims. (191–192)

18 c Accountant's depreciation = (5 %) × $100,000. Economist's depreciation = Δ market value. (197–198)

19 c Forgone income. (198)

20 c Definition. (198)

21 d See text discussion. (203)

22 b ↑ value = negative opportunity cost. (196–198)

23 d Since $(1 + r)^n$ in denominator of *PV* formula, lower *r* and *n* make *PV* higher. (194–196)

24 b $463 = $500/(1 + *r*)$. Solve for *r*. (194–196)

25 b $PV = \$100/(1 + 0.1)^2$. (194–196)

Short Answer Problems

1 The present value of $110 received one year from now is the amount that, if invested today at the market rate of interest, would grow to be $110 in one year. Since the interest rate is 10 percent, $100 invested today at 10 percent would grow to be $110 in one year. Thus $100 is the present value of $110 in one year.

2 Restaurants face a classic principal–agent problem because servers may provide poor service to customers and drive away future business. Instead of having managers try to closely monitor each server, it is more efficient to delegate monitoring to customers. Customers tip based on quality of service, creating an incentive for the server—the agent—to provide good service. This is exactly what the restaurant owner—the principal—wants.

3 a From the accounting cost approach, depreciation cost is computed as a prespecified percentage of the original purchase price of the capital good, with no reference to current market value. The opportunity cost approach measures economic depreciation cost as the change in the market value of the capital good over the period in question.
  b If a firm borrows money, the accounting and opportunity cost approaches will be the same; both will include the explicit interest payments.
  c If a firm uses its own funds rather than borrowing, the accounting and opportunity cost approaches will differ. The accounting cost will be zero since there are no explicit interest payments. The opportunity cost approach recognizes that those funds could have been loaned and thus the (implicit) interest income forgone is the opportunity cost.
  d If the owner could have worked elsewhere, the forgone wages are an opportunity cost but not an accounting cost. If the owner pays herself a salary, that will be counted as both an opportunity and accounting cost. In addition to supplying labour, the owner supplies entrepreneurial ability that also could be applied elsewhere. The cost of entrepreneurial ability is normal profit, which is an opportunity cost but not an accounting cost.

4 A method is technologically efficient if it is not possible to increase output without increasing inputs. A method is economically efficient if the cost of producing a given level of output is as low as possible. Technological efficiency is independent of prices while economic efficiency depends on the prices of inputs. An economically efficient method of production is always technologically efficient, but a technologically efficient method is not necessarily economically efficient.

5 As we saw in the example on text page 203, car repair can be coordinated by the market or by a firm. The institution (market or firm) that actually coordinates in any given case will be the one that is more efficient. In cases where there are significant transactions costs, economies of scale, or economies of team production, firms are likely to be more efficient, and firms will dominate the coordination of economic activity. But the efficiency of firms is limited, and there are many circumstances where market coordination of economic activity dominates because it is more efficient.

6 The completed table is shown here as Table 9.2 Solution. While each answer is a straightforward application of the present value formula, here are details for computing the present value of future payment sequence C when $r = 0.05$. Payment sequence C is best thought of as a two-part promise: (1) $100 after one year and (2) $1,100 after two years (the sum of value of the bond and the second coupon payment). The present value is then the sum of the present values of the two parts. The present value of (1) is $100/1.05 = $95.24, and the present value of (2) is $1,100/(1.05)^2 = $997.73. Therefore, the present value of the two-year bond is the sum $95.24 + $997.73 = $1,092.97.

TABLE **9.2** SOLUTION

Future Payment Sequence	Present Value ($)	
	$r = 0.1$	$r = 0.05$
A	90.91	95.24
B	82.64	90.70
C	1,000.00	1,092.97

7 A bondholder would be willing to pay more for bond B than bond A because bond B has a higher present value. While both bonds pay the same total dollar amount over two years, bond B pays half of that amount after only one year. A holder of bond A, however, must wait two years for the full amount.

  If we think of the $220 payment of bond A as two $110 payments, each paid after two years, each payment is discounted by (divided by) $(1 + r)^2$. The second $110 payment of bond B is also paid after two years and is also discounted by $(1 + r)^2$. So one $110 payment from bond A and one $110 payment from bond B have equal present values. But the first $110 payment of bond B is paid after one year and is therefore only discounted by $(1 + r)$, which is a smaller number than the discount of $(1 + r)^2$ which applies to the other \$110 payment of bond A. Since this discount factor is in the denominator of the present value formula, the smaller denominator for the bond B calculation means a higher present value than for the bond A calculation. This result is shown in the following expression comparing the present values of bond A (PV_A) and bond B (PV_B).

$$PV_B = \frac{110}{1 + r} + \frac{110}{(1 + r)^2} \qquad \text{is greater than}$$

$$PV_A = \frac{110}{(1 + r)^2} + \frac{110}{(1 + r)^2} = \frac{220}{(1 + r)^2}$$

8 a Table 9.3 gives the cost as computed by Angela and Edith. The item numbers correspond to the item numbers in the problem.

TABLE **9.3**

Item Number	Angela's Accounting Computation (accounting cost)	Edith's Economic Computation (opportunity cost)
1.	\$0	\$30,000
2.	9,000	9,000
3.	0	3,000
4.	3,000	4,000
5.	20,000	20,000
6.	40,000	40,000
7.	0	0
8.	0	\$14,000
Total Cost	\$72,000	\$120,000

b Revenue is \$100,000. Angela's accounting computation of profit uses this formula:

Accounting profits = revenues − explicit costs
= \$100,000 − \$72,000
= \$28,000

Edith's economic computation of profit uses this formula:

Economic profits = revenues − opportunity costs
= \$100,000 − \$120,000
= − \$20,000 (an economic loss)

9 Both production methods are technologically efficient. The economically efficient production method has the lower cost of producing a tonne of wheat. In country A, the price of an hour of labour is \$8 and the price of a machine hour is \$20. The cost of producing a tonne of wheat is \$560 using method 1 and \$800 using method 2.

Therefore method 1 is economically efficient for country A.

The price of an hour of labour is \$4 in country B, and thus it will face different costs of producing a tonne of wheat. Under method 1, the cost will be \$480 but under method 2, which uses only labour, the cost will be \$400. So method 2 is economically efficient for country B.

The reason for this difference is that economic efficiency means producing at lowest cost. If the relative prices of inputs are different in two countries, there will be differences in the relative costs of production using alternative methods. Therefore your roommate is wrong.

10 a If the wage rate in country B were to increase to \$5 an hour, then production of a tonne of wheat would be \$500 under either method. How did we obtain this answer? Express the cost under method 1 (C_1) and the cost under method 2 (C_2) as follows:

$$C_1 = 20P_m + 20P_h$$
$$C_2 = 100P_h$$

where P_m is the price of a machine hour and P_h is the price of an hour of labour (the wage rate). We are given that $P_m = \$20$ and asked to find the value of P_h that makes the two methods equally efficient; the value of P_h that makes $C_1 = C_2$. Thus we solve the following equation for P_h:

$$20P_m + 20P_h = 100P_h$$
$$20(\$20) + 20P_h = 100P_h$$
$$\$400 = 80P_h$$
$$\$5 = P_h$$

b If the price of a machine hour is \$32, production of a tonne of wheat would be \$800 under either method in country A. This question asks: Given the wage rate of \$8 (P_h) in country A, what value of P_m makes $C_1 = C_2$? Thus we solve the following equation for P_m:

$$20P_m + 20P_h = 100P_h$$
$$20P_m + 20(\$8) = 100(\$8)$$
$$20P_m = \$640$$
$$P_m = \$32$$

Chapter 10

Output and Costs

The Firm's Objective and Constraints

Firm's objective is profit maximization. Limits to profit maximization are

◆ Market constraints

- Limited demand for firm's output and limited supply factor inputs.
- For small firms, market constraints take form of given prices for outputs and inputs.

◆ Technology constraints

Firm has two planning horizons.

◆ **Short run**—at least one fixed input. Other inputs are variable inputs.

◆ **Long run**—all inputs are variable.

Short-Run Technology Constraint

Short-run production described by

◆ **Total product** curve (TP)—maximum attainable output with fixed quantity capital as quantity labour varies.

◆ **Marginal product** curve (MP)—ΔTP resulting from one-unit ↑ variable input.

◆ **Average product** curve (AP)—TP per unit variable input.

◆ As ↑ variable input, MP ↑ (**increasing marginal return**), reaches maximum, and then ↓ (**decreasing marginal return**). When $MP > AP$, AP ↑. When $MP < AP$, AP ↓. When $MP = AP$, maximum AP.

◆ **Law of diminishing returns**—with quantity fixed inputs constant, as firm uses more variable input, its MP eventually diminishes.

Short-Run Cost

Short-run cost curves determined by technology and product curves.

◆ **Total cost** (TC) = $TFC + TVC$.

- **Total fixed cost** (TFC)—cost of fixed inputs.
- **Total variable cost** (TVC)—cost of variable inputs.
- **Marginal cost** (MC)—ΔTC resulting from one-unit ↑ output.

◆ **Average total cost** (ATC) = $AFC + AVC$.

- **Average fixed cost** (AFC)—total fixed cost per unit output.
- **Average variable cost** (AVC)—total variable cost per unit output.
- AFC curve ↓ constantly as output ↑.
- AVC, ATC, and MC curves are U-shaped.
- As ↑ output, MC ↓, reaches minimum, and then ↑.
- When $MC < ATC$, ATC ↓. When $MC > ATC$, ATC ↑. When $MC = ATC$, minimum ATC. Same relation MC and AVC.

Plant Size and Cost

Long-run cost—cost of production when all inputs, including plant size, adjusted to economically efficient levels.

Production function—relationship between maximum attainable output and quantities of inputs when *all* inputs variable.

◆ **Returns to scale**—↑ output resulting from ↑ all inputs by same percentage. Three possibilities:

- **Constant returns to scale**—percentage ↑ firm's output = percentage ↑ inputs.
- **Increasing returns to scale (economies of scale)**—percentage ↑ firm's output > percentage ↑ inputs.
- **Decreasing returns to scale (diseconomies of scale)**—percentage ↑ firm's output < percentage ↑ inputs.

◆ **Long-run average cost curve (*LRAC*)**—traces U-shaped relation between lowest attainable *ATC* and output when all inputs variable. When *LRAC* ↓, increasing returns to scale. When *LRAC* horizontal, constant returns to scale. When *LRAC* ↑, decreasing returns to scale.

H E L P F U L   H I N T S

I This chapter introduces many new concepts and graphs and may at first appear overwhelming. Don't get lost among the trees and lose sight of the forest. There is a simple and fundamental relationship between production functions and cost functions.

The chapter begins with the short-run production function and concepts of total product, marginal product, and average product. This is followed by the short-run cost function and concepts of total cost, marginal cost, average variable cost, and average total cost.

But all of these seemingly disparate concepts are related to the law of diminishing returns. The law states that as a firm uses additional units of a variable input, while holding constant the quantity of fixed inputs, the marginal product of the variable input will eventually diminish. This law explains why the marginal product and average product curves eventually fall, and why the total product curve becomes flatter. When productivity falls, costs increase, and the law explains the eventual upward slope of the marginal cost curve. When marginal product falls, marginal cost increases.

The marginal cost curve, in turn, explains the U-shape of the average variable cost and average total cost curves. When the marginal cost curve is below the average variable (or total) cost curve, the average variable (or total) cost curve is falling. When marginal cost is above the average variable (or total) cost curve, the average variable (or total) cost curve is rising. The marginal cost curve intersects the average variable (or total) cost curve at the minimum point on the average variable (or total) cost curve.

Use the law of diminishing returns as the key to understanding the relationships between the many short-run concepts and graphs in the chapter. But all concepts and graphs are not equally important. Pay most attention to the unit cost concepts and graphs—especially marginal cost, average variable cost, and average total cost—because these will be used the most in later chapters to analyse the behaviour of firms.

2 Be sure to thoroughly understand Fig. 10.1 (Text Fig. 10.5b on page 218). It is the most important graph in the chapter and one of the most important graphs in all of microeconomics.

FIGURE **10.1**

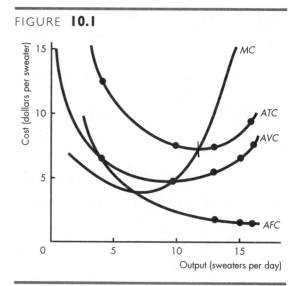

The curves for average total cost (*ATC*), average fixed cost (*AFC*), and average variable cost (*AVC*) are derived by taking the values for *TC*, *TFC*, and *TVC* and dividing by quantity of output. Since these are average values for a fixed quantity of output, they are plotted directly above the corresponding units of output. On the other hand, marginal cost (*MC*) is the *change* in total cost (or equivalently, in total variable cost) resulting from a one-unit increase in output. It is plotted *midway* between the corresponding units of output. The *ATC*, *AVC*, and *MC* curves are crucially important. The *ATC* and *AVC* curves are both U-shaped. The *MC* curve is also U-shaped and intersects the *ATC* and *AVC* curves at their minimum points. The *MC* curve is below the *ATC* and *AVC* curves when *ATC* and *AVC* are falling, and above the *ATC* and *AVC* curves when they are rising. The less important *AFC* curve falls continuously as output increases.

3 You will probably draw a graph like the one in Fig. 10.1 at least one hundred times in this course. Here are some hints on drawing the graph quickly and easily.

Be sure to label the axes; quantity of output (*Q*) on the horizontal axis and average cost on the vertical axis.

Draw an upward-sloping marginal cost curve, as shown here in Fig. 10.2. The marginal cost curve can have a small downward-sloping section at first, but this is not important for subsequent analysis. Next, draw a shallow U-shaped curve that falls until it intersects the marginal cost curve, and then rises. Then pick a point further up the marginal cost curve. Draw another shallow U-shaped curve whose minimum point passes through your second point. Finally, label the curves.

Any time a test question (including those in the Self-Test) asks about these curves, *draw a graph* before you answer.

FIGURE **10.2**

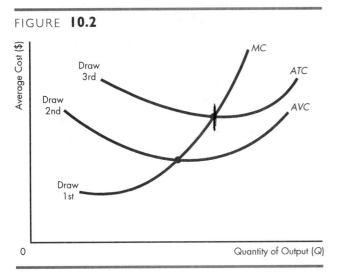

4 Be sure to understand how economists use the terms *short run* and *long run*. These terms do *not* refer to any notion of calendar time. They are better thought of as planning horizons. The short run is a planning horizon short enough that while some inputs are variable, at least one input cannot be varied but is fixed. The long run refers to a planning horizon that is long enough that all inputs can be varied.

5 The later sections of the chapter explain the long-run production function and cost function when plant size is variable. While diminishing returns was the key for understanding short-run costs, the concept of returns to scale is the key for understanding long-run costs. Returns to scale are the increase in output relative to the increase in inputs when *all inputs* are increased by the same percentage. Returns to scale can be increasing, constant, or decreasing, and correspond to the downward-sloping, horizontal, and upward-sloping sections of the long-run average cost curve.

SELF-TEST

True/False/Uncertain and Explain

1 Limitations on the feasible ways in which inputs can be converted into outputs is an example of a market constraint on firm profitability.

2 Given a fixed quantity of capital, if 2 additional labourers produce 15 additional units of output, the marginal product of labour is 15 units of output.

3 The average product curve cuts the marginal product curve from above at the maximum point on the marginal product curve.

4 The law of diminishing returns implies that eventually the marginal product curve will be negatively sloped as the variable input increases.

5 The law of diminishing returns implies that we will not observe a range of increasing marginal returns.

6 Average variable cost reaches its minimum at the same level of output at which average product is a maximum.

7 If average variable cost is decreasing then marginal cost is decreasing.

8 No part of any short-run average total cost curve can lie below the long-run average cost curve.

9 Increasing returns to scale means that the long-run average cost curve is negatively sloped.

10 In the long run, the total cost and total variable cost curves are the same.

Multiple-Choice

1 In economics, the short run is a time period in which
a one year or less elapses.
b all inputs are variable.
c all inputs are fixed.
d there is at least one fixed input and at least one variable input.
e all inputs are variable but the technology is fixed.

2 The marginal cost (*MC*) curve intersects the
a *ATC, AVC,* and *AFC* curves at their minimum points.
b *ATC* and *AFC* curves at their minimum points.
c *AVC* and *AFC* curves at their minimum points.
d *ATC* and *AVC* curves at their minimum points.
e *TC* and *TVC* curves at their minimum points.

3 Marginal cost is the amount that
a total cost increases when one more labourer is hired.
b fixed cost increases when one more labourer is hired.
c variable cost increases when one more labourer is hired.
d total cost increases when one more unit of output is produced.
e fixed cost increases when one more unit of output is produced.

4 A rise in the price of a fixed input will cause a firm's
a average variable cost curve to shift up.
b average total cost curve to shift up.
c average total cost curve to shift down.
d marginal cost curve to shift up.
e marginal cost curve to shift down.

5 A field of ripe corn is waiting to be harvested. Labour is the only variable input, and the total product (in bushels) of various numbers of labourers is given in Table 10.1.

TABLE **10.1**

Number of Labourers	Total Product
0	0
1	3
2	7
3	10
4	12

Diminishing returns *begin* when you add which labourer?
a 1st labourer
b 2nd labourer
c 3rd labourer
d 4th labourer
e there are no diminishing returns since total product always rises

6 When the marginal product of labour is less than the average product of labour,
a the average product of labour is increasing.
b the marginal product of labour is increasing.
c the total product curve is negatively sloped.
d the firm is experiencing diminishing returns.
e none of the above is true.

7 If all inputs are increased by 10 percent and output increases by less than 10 percent, it must be the case that
a average total cost is decreasing.
b average total cost is increasing.
c the *LRAC* curve is negatively sloped.
d there are increasing returns to scale.
e there are decreasing returns to scale.

8 A technological advance will shift
1 *TP, AP,* and *MP* curves up.
2 *TP, AP,* and *MP* curves down.
3 *TC, ATC,* and *MC* curves up.
4 *TC, ATC,* and *MC* curves down.

a 1 and 3
b 1 and 4
c 2 and 3
d 2 and 4
e none of the above

9 The vertical distance between the *TC* and *TVC* curves is

a decreasing as output increases.
b increasing as output increases.
c equal to *AFC.*
d equal to *TFC.*
e equal to *MC.*

10 Total cost is $20 at 4 units of output and $36 at 6 units of output. Between 4 and 6 units of output, marginal cost

a is less than average total cost.
b is equal to average total cost.
c is equal to average variable cost.
d is greater than average total cost.
e cannot be compared with any average cost without additional information.

11 The long-run average cost curve

a shifts up when fixed costs increase.
b shifts down when fixed costs increase.
c is the short-run average total cost curve with the lowest cost.
d traces the minimum points on all the short-run average total cost curves for each scale of plant.
e traces the minimum short-run average total cost for each output.

12 The average variable cost curve will shift up if

a there is an increase in fixed costs.
b there is a technological advance.
c the price of variable input decreases.
d the price of output increases.
e none of the above occurs.

13 A firm's fixed costs are $100. If total costs are $200 for one unit of output and $310 for two units, what is the marginal cost of the second unit?

a $100
b $110
c $200
d $210
e $310

14 A firm will want to increase its scale of plant if

a it persistently produces on the upward-sloping part of its short-run average total cost curve.
b it persistently produces on the downward-sloping part of its short-run average total cost curve.
c it is producing below capacity.
d marginal cost is below average total cost.
e marginal cost is below average variable cost.

15 If *ATC* is falling then *MC* must be

a rising.
b falling.
c equal to *ATC.*
d above *ATC.*
e below *ATC.*

16 In the long run,

a only the scale of plant is fixed.
b all inputs are variable.
c all inputs are fixed.
d a firm must experience decreasing returns to scale.
e none of the above is true.

17 Constant returns to scale means that as all inputs are increased,

a total output remains constant.
b average total cost remains constant.
c average total cost increases at the same rate as inputs.
d long-run average cost remains constant.
e long-run average cost rises at the same rate as inputs.

18 According to the law of diminishing returns,

1 marginal productivity eventually rises.
2 marginal productivity eventually falls.
3 marginal cost eventually rises.
4 marginal cost eventually falls.

a 1 and 3
b 1 and 4
c 2 and 3
d 2 and 4
e 4 only

19 The average product of labour is

a the slope of the total product curve.
b the slope of the marginal product curve.
c the increase in total product divided by the increase in labour employed.
d the total product divided by the quantity of labour employed.
e none of the above.

20 In the short run, a profit-maximizing firm is constrained by

a limited demand for its product.
b limited input supplies.
c limited number of technologically efficient production methods.
d limited planning horizon.
e all of the above.

21 Which of the following does *not* cause decreasing *ATC*?

a decreasing marginal cost
b decreasing average variable cost
c decreasing average fixed cost
d increasing marginal product
e increasing returns to scale

22 Refer to Fig. 10.3 illustrating Swanky's short-run total product curve. Which of the following statements is *true*?

a Points above the curve are attainable and are inefficient.
b Points below the curve are attainable and are inefficient.
c Points below the curve are unattainable and are inefficient.
d Points on the curve are unattainable and are efficient.
e Points on the curve all have equal marginal products.

FIGURE **10.3**

23 Refer to Fig. 10.3 illustrating Swanky's short-run total product curve. Marginal product reaches a maximum when you add which labourer?

a 1st labourer
b 2nd labourer
c 3rd labourer
d 4th labourer
e 5th labourer

24 Average variable cost is at a minimum at the same output where

a average product is at a maximum.
b average product is at a minimum.
c marginal product is at a maximum.
d marginal product is at a minimum.
e marginal cost is at a minimum.

25 Which of the following statements by a restaurant owner refers to the law of diminishing returns?

a "The higher the quality of the ingredients we use, the higher the cost of producing each meal."
b "If we double the size of our premises and double everything else—kitchen staff, serving staff, equipment—we can increase the number of meals we serve, but not to double current levels."
c "We can increase the number of meals we serve by just adding more kitchen staff, but each additional worker adds fewer meals than the previous worker because traffic in the kitchen will get worse."
d "We can serve the same number of meals with fewer kitchen staff, but we would have to buy more labour-saving kitchen equipment."
e "We can serve the same number of meals with less kitchen equipment, but we would have to hire more kitchen staff."

Short Answer Problems

1 Why must the marginal product curve intersect the average product curve at the maximum point of the average product curve?

2 Why must the marginal cost curve intersect the average total cost curve at the minimum point of the average total cost curve?

3 Explain the connection, if any, between the U-shape of the average total cost curve and (a) fixed costs, and (b) the law of eventually diminishing returns.

4 Use the concepts of marginal and average to answer the following question. Suppose the worst student at Hubertville High School transfers to Histrionic High School. Is it possible that the average grade-point of the students at each school rises? Explain.

5 What is the difference, if any, between diminishing returns and decreasing returns to scale?

6 How is the long-run average cost curve obtained and how does it differ from Jacob Viner's mistaken conception of it?

7 For a given scale of plant, Table 10.2 gives the total monthly output of golf carts attainable using varying quantities of labour.

TABLE **10.2** MONTHLY GOLF CART PRODUCTION

Labourers (per month)	Output (units per month)	Marginal Product	Average Product
0	0		
1	1		
2	3		
3	6		
4	12		
5	17		
6	20		
7	22		
8	23		

a Complete the table for the marginal product and average product of labour. (Note that marginal product should be entered *midway* between rows to emphasize that it is the result of *changing* inputs—moving from one row to the next. Average product corresponds to a *fixed* quantity of labour and should be entered on the appropriate row.)

b Label the axes and draw a graph of the total product curve (*TP*).

c On a separate piece of paper, label the axes and draw a graph of both marginal product (*MP*) and average product (*AP*). (Marginal product should be plotted *midway* between the corresponding units of labour, as in Text Fig. 10.2(b) on page 213, while average product should be plotted directly above the corresponding units of labour, as in Text Fig. 10.3 on page 214.)

8 Now let's examine the short-run costs of golf cart production. The first two columns of Table 10.2 are reproduced in the first two columns of Table 10.3. The cost of 1 labourer (the only variable input) is $2,000 per month. Total fixed cost is $2,000 per month.

TABLE **10.3** SHORT-RUN COSTS (MONTHLY)

L	Q	TFC ($)	TVC ($)	TC ($)	MC ($)	AFC ($)	AVC ($)	ATC ($)
0	0	2,000						
1	1							
2	3							
3	6							
4	12							
5	17							
6	20							
7	22							
8	23							

a Given this information, complete Table 10.3 by computing total fixed cost (*TFC*), total variable cost (*TVC*), total cost (*TC*), marginal cost (*MC*), average fixed cost (*AFC*), average variable cost (*AVC*), and average total cost (*ATC*). Your completed table should look like Text Table 10.2 on page 217, with marginal cost entered *midway* between the rows.

b Label the axes and draw the *TC*, *TVC*, and *TFC* curves on a single graph.

c Label the axes and draw the *MC*, *ATC*, *AVC*, and *AFC* curves on a single graph. Be sure to plot *MC midway* between the corresponding units of output.

d Now suppose that the price of a labourer increases to $2,500 per month. Construct a table for the new *MC* and *ATC* curves (output, *MC*, *ATC*). Label the axes and draw a graph of the new *MC* and *ATC* curves. What is the effect of the increase in the price of the variable input on these curves?

9 Return to the original price of labour of $2,000 per month. Now suppose that we double the quantity of fixed inputs so that total fixed costs also double to $4,000 per month. This increases the monthly output of golf carts for each quantity of labour as indicated in Table 10.4.

TABLE **10.4** NEW MONTHLY PRODUCTION
OF GOLF CARTS

Labourers (per month)	Output (units per month)
0	0
1	1
2	4
3	10
4	19
5	26
6	31
7	34
8	36

a Construct a table for the new *MC* and *ATC* curves (output, *MC*, *ATC*). Label the axes and draw a graph of the new *MC* and *ATC* curves.

b What is the effect on these curves (compared with the original *MC* and *ATC* curves in Short Answer Problem 8c) of an increase in "plant size"? Are there economies of scale?

c Draw the long-run average cost (*LRAC*) curve if these are the only two plant sizes available.

10 Figure 10.4 gives a sequence of short-run *ATC* curves numbered 1 through 7 corresponding to seven different plant sizes.

FIGURE **10.4**

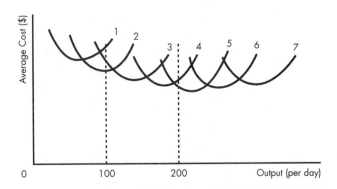

a Draw the long-run average cost curve on Fig. 10.4.

b If the desired level of output is 100 units per day, what is the best plant size? (Give the number of the associated short-run *ATC* curve.) What if the desired level of output is 200 units per day?

ANSWERS

True/False/Uncertain and Explain

1 F Example of technology constraint. (211)
2 F $\Delta TP/\Delta L = 15/2 = 7.5$. (212–214)
◓3 F True if switch terms "average product" and "marginal product." (214)
4 T *MP* must eventually ↓ with ↑ *L*. (215)
5 F *Eventually* diminishing returns. *MP* can initially ↑. (215)
◓6 T $AVC = TVC/Q = WL/Q = W/(Q/L) = W/AP$. (219)
◓7 U *MC* must be below *AVC*, but *MC* may be ↑ or ↓. (218–219)
8 T Definition *LRAC*. (224)
9 T See text discussion. (222–225)
10 T All costs variable in long run. (211)

Multiple-Choice

1 d Definition. (211)
2 d *AFC* always ↓, *TC* and *TVC* always ↑. (217–219)
3 d Definition. (216–217)
4 b Won't affect *AVC* or *MC*. (220)
5 c *MP* 1st = 3, *MP* 2nd = 4, *MP* 3rd = 3. (215)
6 d When *MP* < *AP*, *MP* ↓ (diminishing returns), *AP* ↓, and *TP* positively sloped. (213–214)
7 e Definition. Since all inputs variable, **a** and **b** irrelevant. (222–225)
8 b Productivity ↑, costs ↓. (219–220)
9 d *TC* = *TFC* + *TVC*. Distance constant. (217–218)
◓10 d $MC = 16/2 = 8$. *ATC* is $5 at 4 units and $6 at 6 units. (216–218)
11 e Definition. **d** is Jacob Viner's mistake. **a** and **b** short run since fixed costs. (224)
12 e **a** and **d** don't affect *AVC*. **b** and **c** shift *AVC* down. (220)
13 b Fixed costs irrelevant. $\Delta TC/\Delta Q = (\$310 - \$200)/(2 - 1)$. (216–217)
14 a **b** and **c** plant too big. **d** and **e** relate to short run. (224–225)
◓15 e *MC* could be ↑ or ↓ below *ATC* when *ATC* ↓. (218–219)
16 b Definition. All returns to scale possible in long run. (211, 222)
17 d *LRAC* horizontal. (225)
18 c ↓ *MP* → ↑ *MC*. (218–219)
19 d Definition. (212–214)
20 e Market constraints and technology constraints. (211)

21 e ↑ returns to scale is long-run concept; *ATC* is short-run concept. (218–219)

22 b Attainable but not maximum *TP*. (212–213)

23 b *MP* = slope *TP* curve = 6 for 2nd labourer. (212–214)

24 a *AVC* ↓ as long as *AP* ↑. See Text Fig. 10.6. (219)

25 c *MP* ↓ as restaurant uses more variable input (labour). (215)

Short Answer Problems

1 Since the average product curve first rises and then falls, when average product is rising, marginal product must be greater than average product, and when average product is falling, marginal product must be lower than average product. Therefore the marginal product curve must intersect the average product curve at its maximum point. In order for average product to increase, it must have been *pulled up* by a larger increase in product from the last unit of input. Therefore marginal product is higher than average product. Similarly, when average product is falling, it must be that it has been *pulled down* by a lower marginal product. When average product is at its maximum, it is neither rising nor falling, so marginal product cannot be higher or lower than average product. Therefore marginal product must be equal to average product.

2 The answer to this problem is just the mirror image of the answer to Short Answer Problem 1. The average total cost curve is U-shaped, first falling and then rising as output increases. When average total cost is falling, marginal cost must be less than average total cost, and when average total cost is rising, marginal cost must be greater than average total cost. Therefore the marginal cost curve must intersect the average total cost curve at its minimum point. In order for average total cost to fall, it must have been *pulled down* by a smaller increase in cost from the last unit of output. Therefore marginal cost is lower than average total cost. Similarly, when average total cost is rising, it must be that it has been *pulled up* by a higher marginal cost. When average total cost is at its minimum, it is neither falling nor rising, so marginal cost cannot be lower or higher than average total cost. Therefore, marginal cost must be equal to average total cost.

3 The U-shape of the average total cost (*ATC*) curve arises from the opposing forces of (a) spreading fixed costs over a larger output and (b) the law of eventually diminishing returns.

As output increases, fixed costs are spread over a larger output so average fixed cost (*AFC*) falls. Initially, as output increases, the marginal productivity of the variable factor rises, causing average variable cost (*AVC*) to fall. Falling *AVC*, together with falling *AFC*, cause average total cost (*ATC*) to fall, contributing to the downward-sloping portion of *ATC*. Eventually, as output increases, diminishing returns set in, marginal productivity falls, and *AVC* rises. Eventually, *AVC* rises more quickly than *AFC* falls, contributing to the upward sloping portion of *ATC*.

4 Yes, it is possible that the average grade-point of the students at each school rises. Think of the transferring student as the *marginal* student. If his grade-point average, although the lowest at Hubertville High, is higher than the *average* grade-point at Histrionic High, then the results are: the *average* grade-point at Hubertville High rises with the elimination of the lowest grade-point; and the *average* grade-point at Histrionic High rises because the transferring (*marginal*) student's grade-point pulls up the *average* grade-point.

5 The law of diminishing returns states that as a firm uses additional units of a variable input, *while holding constant the quantity of fixed inputs,* the marginal product of the variable input will eventually diminish. Decreasing returns to scale occur when a firm increases *all of its inputs by an equal percentage,* and this results in a lower percentage increase in output. Diminishing (marginal) returns is a short-run concept since there must be a fixed input. Decreasing returns to scale is a long-run concept since all inputs must be variable.

6 Any given level of output can be produced using alternative scales of plant, but for each level of output, one scale of plant results in the lowest short-run average total cost. The scale of plant can be varied in the long run, and the long-run average cost curve traces out the lowest short-run average total cost at each level of output. Jacob Viner's mistaken conception of the long-run average cost curve was that (a) it must pass through the minimum point of each short-run average cost curve (which is incorrect) and, (b) it must not be above any short-run cost curve at any point (which is correct). The mistake is that these two properties cannot be satisfied simultaneously. Indeed, the long-run average cost curve does *not* pass through the minimum point of each of the short-run average cost curves.

7 a The completed Table 10.2 is shown here as Table 10.2 Solution.

TABLE **10.2** SOLUTION
MONTHLY GOLF CART PRODUCTION

Labourers (per month)	Output (units per month)	Marginal Product	Average Product
0	0		0
		 1	
1	1		1.00
		 2	
2	3		1.50
		 3	
3	6		2.00
		 6	
4	12		3.00
		 5	
5	17		3.40
		 3	
6	20		3.33
		 2	
7	22		3.14
		 1	
8	23		2.88

b Figure 10.5 gives the graph of the total product curve.

FIGURE **10.5**

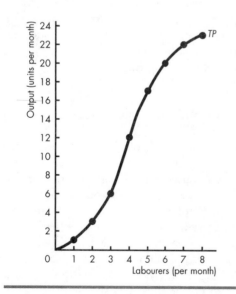

c Figure 10.6 gives the graphs of marginal product and average product.

FIGURE **10.6**

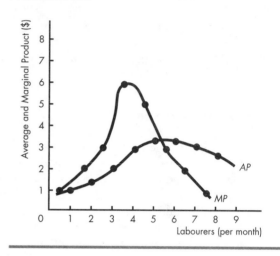

8 a Completed Table 10.3 is given here as Table 10.3 Solution.

TABLE **10.3** SOLUTION
SHORT-RUN COSTS (MONTHLY)

L	Q	TFC ($)	TVC ($)	TC ($)	MC ($)	AFC ($)	AVC ($)	ATC ($)
0	0	2,000	0	2,000		—	—	—
					2,000			
1	1	2,000	2,000	4,000		2,000	2,000	4,000
					1,000			
2	3	2,000	4,000	6,000		667	1,333	2,000
					667			
3	6	2,000	6,000	8,000		333	1,000	1,333
					333			
4	12	2,000	8,000	10,000		167	667	833
					400			
5	17	2,000	10,000	12,000		118	588	706
					667			
6	20	2,000	12,000	14,000		100	600	700
					1,000			
7	22	2,000	14,000	16,000		91	636	727
					2,000			
8	23	2,000	16,000	18,000		87	696	783

b The *TC*, *TVC*, and *TFC* curves are graphed in Fig. 10.7.

FIGURE **10.7**

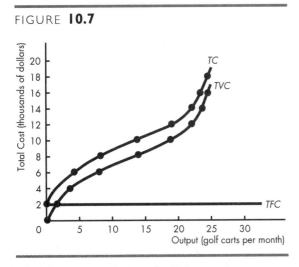

c The *MC, ATC, AVC,* and *AFC* curves are graphed in Fig. 10.8.

FIGURE **10.8**

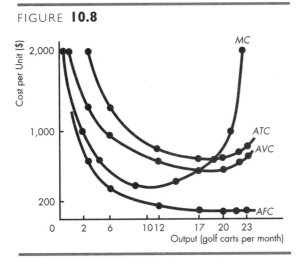

d The new *MC* and *ATC* curves (and the associated table) are given in Fig. 10.9. The original curves, MC_1 and ATC_1, are indicated for reference. The new curves are labelled MC_2 and ATC_2. Both curves have shifted up as a result of an increase in the price of labour.

FIGURE **10.9**

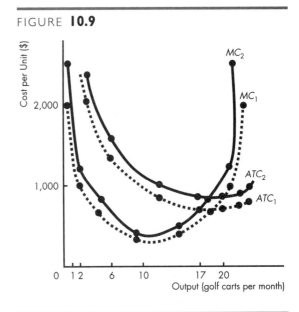

Output	MC ($)	ATC ($)
0		0
	2,500	
1		4,500
	1,250	
3		2,333
	833	
6		1,583
	417	
12		1,000
	500	
17		853
	833	
20		850
	1,250	
22		886
	2,500	
23		957

9 a The new *MC* and *ATC* curves (and the associated table) are given in Fig. 10.10. The new curves are labelled MC_3 and ATC_3. The original curves, MC_1 and ATC_1, are indicated for reference.

FIGURE **10.10**

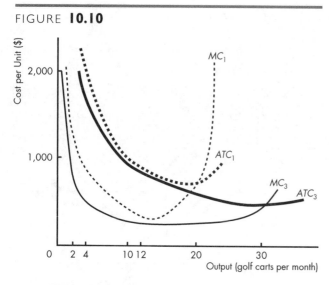

Output	MC ($)	ATC ($)
0		0
	2,000	
1		6,000
	667	
4		2,000
	333	
10		1,000
	222	
19		632
	286	
26		538
	400	
31		516
	667	
34		529

10 a The long-run average cost curve is indicated in Fig. 10.4 Solution by the heavy scalloped-shaped curve tracing out the lowest short-run average cost of producing each level of output.

b For output of 100 units, the best plant size is associated with short-run average total cost curve 2. For output of 200 units, the best plant size is associated with short-run average total cost curve 5.

FIGURE **10.4** SOLUTION

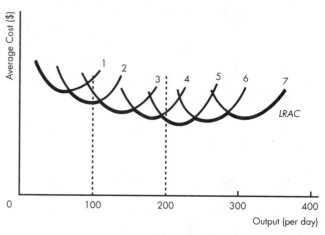

b The curves have shifted (generally) down and to the right as a result of increasing the plant size. There are economies of scale (increasing returns to scale) up to the level of output at which MC_3 intersects ATC_3 (approximately 32 units).

c The long-run average cost curve is indicated in Fig. 10.10 by the heavy line tracing out the lowest short-run average total cost of producing each level of output. In this example, that happens to correspond entirely to ATC_3.

Chapter 11

Competition

Perfect Competition

Perfect competition is a model that assumes many firms; identical products; many buyers; free entry; complete information.

◆ Each firm is a **price taker**.

◆ Each firm faces a perfectly elastic demand curve at the market price.

Firm maximizes profit (**normal profit + economic profit**).

◆ Normal profit = expected return to entrepreneurial ability.

◆ Economic profit = total revenue – total cost (total cost includes normal profit).

◆ **Total revenue** (*TR*)—price (*P*) × quantity (*Q*).

  • **Average revenue** (*AR*)—*TR/Q*.
  • **Marginal revenue** (*MR*)—$\Delta TR/\Delta Q$.
  • In perfect competition, *AR* = *MR* = *P*.

In short run, firm decides what quantity to produce or to shut down.

◆ Profit maximized at quantity where *MR* = *MC*:

  • If *MR* > *MC*, firm ↑ *Q* to ↑ profit.
  • If *MR* < *MC*, firm ↓ *Q* to ↑ profit.

◆ Three possible short-run profit-maximizing outcomes:

  • *P* (= *AR* = *MR*) > *ATC* → economic profits.
  • *P* (= *AR* = *MR*) = *ATC* → zero economic profits (*break-even point* at minimum *ATC*; firm just earning normal profits).
  • *P* (= *AR* = *MR*) < *ATC* → economic losses (firm earning less than normal profits).

◆ For firm suffering economic losses:

  • If *P* > *AVC*, firm will continue to produce.
  • If *P* < *AVC*, firm will temporarily shut down.
  • **Shutdown point** at minimum *AVC*.

Perfectly competitive firm's supply curve is its *MC* curve above minimum *AVC*.

Output, Price, and Profit in the Short Run

Short-run industry supply curve is horizontal sum of individual firm supply curves.

Equilibrium market price and quantity determined by industry demand and supply curves.

◆ In the short run, perfectly competitive firms can make an economic profit, normal profit (zero economic profit), or suffer an economic loss.

◆ In the short run, the number of firms and their plant size are fixed.

Output, Price, and Profit in the Long Run

In the long run, the number of firms in the industry and the plant size of each firm can adjust. Economic profits/losses are signals for firms to enter/exit the industry and cause reallocation of resources.

◆ Economic profits → new entry → rightward shift industry *S* → ↓ *P* → elimination profits.

◆ Economic losses → existing firms exit → leftward shift industry *S* → ↑ *P* → elimination losses.

In long-run competitive equilibrium

◆ *MR* = *P* = *MC*. Firms maximize short-run profits.

◆ *P* = minimum *ATC*. Economic profits are zero. No incentive for firms to enter or exit industry.

◆ $P =$ minimum $LRAC$. Optimum plant size. No incentive for firm to change plant size.

Changing Tastes and Advancing Technology

For a permanent shift in demand

◆ ↓ Demand → ↓ P, economic loss and exit → ↓ industry supply → ↑ P. In long run, enough firms exit so remaining firms earn normal profit.

◆ ↑ Demand → ↑ P, economic profit and entry → ↑ industry supply → ↓ P. In long run, enough firms enter so economic profit eliminated and firms earn normal profit.

The change in long-run equilibrium price from a permanent shift in demand depends on

◆ **external economies**—factors beyond control of firm that lower costs as *industry* output ↑ .

◆ **external diseconomies**—factors beyond control of firm that raise costs as *industry* output ↑ .

The shape of the **long-run industry supply curve** depends on existence of external economies or diseconomies. The long-run industry supply curve shows how industry quantity supplied varies as market price varies after all possible adjustments, including changes in plant size and number of firms. Shape may be

◆ horizontal for constant cost industry.

◆ upward sloping for increasing cost industry with external diseconomies.

◆ downward sloping for decreasing cost industry with external economies.

New technology → ↓ costs, ↑ industry supply → ↓ P. New technology firms make economic profit and enter. Old technology firms suffer economic loss and exit or switch to new technology. In long run, all firms use new technology and earn normal profit

Competition and Efficiency

Allocative efficiency—no one can be made better off without making someone else worse off; no wasted resources. Requires

◆ **Consumer efficiency**—maximum utility. All points on market demand curve achieve consumer efficiency if there are no **external benefits**— benefits accruing to people other than buyer of good.

◆ **Producer efficiency**—technological efficiency and economic efficiency. All points on market supply curve achieve producer efficiency if there are no **external costs**—cost borne by people other than producer of good.

◆ **Exchange efficiency**—all gains from trade realized. Total gains from trade are sum of

• **Consumer surplus**—value of goods to consumers – price paid = area below demand curve and above market price.

• **Producer surplus**—total revenue – opportunity cost = area below market price and above supply curve.

Perfect competition achieves allocative efficiency at the market equilibrium price and quantity if there are no external benefits and costs.

HELPFUL HINTS

1 Although perfectly competitive markets are rare in the real world, there are three important reasons to develop a thorough understanding of their behaviour.

First, many markets closely approximate perfectly competitive markets. The analysis in this chapter gives direct and useful insights into the behaviour of these markets.

Second, the theory of perfect competition allows us to isolate the effects of competitive forces that are at work in *all* markets, even in those that do not match the assumptions of perfect competition.

Third, the perfectly competitive model serves as a useful benchmark for evaluating relative allocative efficiency.

2 In the short run, a perfectly competitive firm cannot change the size of its plant—it has fixed inputs. The firm also is a price taker; it always sells at the market price, which it cannot influence. The only variable that the firm controls is its level of output. The short-run condition for profit maximization is to choose the level of output at which marginal revenue equals marginal cost. This is a general condition which, as we will see in subsequent chapters, applies to other market structures such as monopoly and monopolistic competition. Since for the perfectly competitive firm, marginal revenue is equal to price, this profit-maximizing condition takes a particular form; choose the level of output at which price is equal to marginal cost ($P = MC$).

3 Many students have trouble understanding why a firm continues to operate at the break-even point, where economic profits are zero. The key to understanding lies in the definition of which costs are included in the average total cost curve. Recall from Chapter 9 that the economist defines a firm's total costs as *opportunity costs*, which include both explicit costs and *implicit costs*.

Implicit costs include forgone interest, forgone rent, and forgone cost of the owner's resources. Owners supply their time, which could have been used to earn income elsewhere. Owners also supply entrepreneurial ability. Normal profit is the expected return to entrepreneurial ability and is part of a firm's implicit costs.

At the break-even point where total revenue equals total cost (or, equivalently, average revenue equals average total cost), the owners of the firm are still earning a return on their investment, time, and entrepreneurial ability, which is equal to the best return that they could earn elsewhere. That is the definition of opportunity cost—the best alternative forgone. As the phrase "normal profits" implies, these are profits that could normally be earned as a return to entrepreneurial ability, on average, in any other industry. At the break-even point, the firm is earning normal profits even though its economic profits (sometimes called "extra-normal," or "above-average," profits) are zero. In earning normal profits, the firm is earning just as much profit as it could anywhere else, and is therefore totally content to continue producing in this industry.

4 When the price of output falls below the break-even point, but is above the shutdown point, the firm will continue to produce even though it is suffering economic losses. In this price range, the firm is no longer earning normal profit and theoretically could earn more by switching to another industry. Nonetheless, the firm will continue to operate in the short run because switching has costs. In order to switch industries, the firm must shut down, which entails still paying its total fixed costs.

As long as price is above the shutdown point (minimum average variable cost), a firm will decide to produce since it will be covering total variable cost and part of total fixed cost. Its loss will be less if it continues to produce at the output where $P = MC$ than if it shuts down.

If price falls below the shutdown point, a firm that produces output will not only lose its total fixed costs, it will lose additional money on every unit of output produced, since average revenue is less than average variable cost. Thus when price is less than average variable cost, the firm will choose to minimize its loss by shutting down.

5 In the long run, fixed costs disappear, and the firm can switch between industries and change plant size without cost. Economic profits serve as the signal for the movement or reallocation of firm resources until long-run equilibrium is achieved. Firms will move out of industries with negative economic profits and into industries with positive economic profits. Only when economic profits are zero will there be no tendency for firms to exit or enter industries.

The fact that there are no restrictions on entry into the industry is what assures that economic profits will be zero and that firms will be producing at the minimum of their long-run average cost curves in long-run equilibrium.

6 In long-run equilibrium, three conditions are satisfied for each firm in an industry:
 i $MR = P = MC$. This implies that profits are maximized for each firm.
 ii $P = ATC$. This implies that economic profits are zero and each firm is just earning normal profit.
 iii $P = $ minimum $LRAC$. This implies that production takes place at the point of minimum long-run average cost.

S E L F - T E S T

True/False/Uncertain and Explain

1 The industry demand curve in a perfectly competitive industry is horizontal.

2 The objective of firms in a competitive industry is to maximize revenue.

3 Firms can make losses in the long run but not the short run.

4 A perfectly competitive industry will achieve allocative efficiency if there are no external costs or external benefits.

5 At prices below minimum average total cost, a firm will shut down.

6 The supply curve of a perfectly competitive firm gives the quantities of output supplied at alternative prices as long as the firm earns economic profits.

7 In long-run equilibrium, each firm in a perfectly competitive industry will choose the plant size associated with minimum long-run average cost.

8 If, in a competitive industry, there are external economies, the long-run industry supply curve is positively sloped.

9 Suppose a competitive industry is in long-run equilibrium when there is a substantial increase in total fixed costs. All firms will now be making economic losses and some firms will go out of business.

10 When the quantity of a good bought by a consumer at a given price is a point on the demand curve, consumer efficiency has occurred.

Multiple-Choice

1 Which of the following is *not* a characteristic of a perfectly competitive industry?
a downward-sloping industry demand curve
b perfectly elastic demand curve for each individual firm
c each firm decides its quantity of output
d slightly differentiated products
e many firms each supplying a small fraction of industry supply

2 If a firm faces a perfectly elastic demand for its product, then
a it is not a price taker.
b it will want to lower its price to increase sales.
c it will want to raise its price to increase total revenue.
d its marginal revenue curve is equal to the price of the product.
e it will always earn zero economic profits.

3 In a perfectly competitive industry, the market price is $10. An individual firm is producing the output at which $MC = ATC = \$15$. AVC at that output is $10. What should the firm do to maximize its short-run profits?
a shut down
b expand output
c contract output
d leave output unchanged
e insufficient information to answer

4 Refer to Fact 11.1. If the price of fiddleheads last month was $15 per bag, Franklin
a should have shut down because total revenue did not cover total variable cost.
b made an economic loss of $135.
c made zero economic profits.
d made an economic profit of $50.
e made an economic profit of $100.

FACT **11.1**

Franklin is a fiddlehead farmer. He sold 10 bags of fiddleheads last month, with total fixed cost of $100 and total variable cost of $50.

---

5 Refer to Fact 11.1. If fiddlehead prices fell to $10 per bag while production and cost figures remained the same, Franklin would
a shut down immediately.
b break even because total revenues just cover total fixed costs.
c be indifferent between producing and shutting down because his loss of $50 just covers total variable costs.
d continue producing despite his loss of $50.
e continue producing despite his loss of $100.

6 Refer to Fact 11.1. Suppose the price of fiddleheads is expected to stay at $10 per bag, and Franklin's production and cost figures are expected to stay the same. His total fixed cost consists entirely of rent on land, and his five-year lease on the land runs out at the end of the month. Should Franklin renew the lease?

a Yes, because total revenue will still cover total fixed cost.

b Yes, because total revenue will still cover total variable cost and a portion of total fixed cost.

c No, because total revenue must cover all costs for resources to remain in fiddlehead farming in the long run.

d No, because in the long run, zero economic profits are a signal to move resources out of fiddlehead farming.

e Insufficient information to answer.

7 In which of the following situations will a perfectly competitive firm earn economic profits?

a *MR > AVC*

b *MR > ATC*

c *ATC > MC*

d *ATC > AR*

e *AR > AVC*

8 In the price range below minimum average variable cost, a perfectly competitive firm's supply curve is

a horizontal at the market price.

b vertical at zero output.

c the same as its marginal cost curve.

d the same as its average variable cost curve.

e none of the above.

9 The short-run industry supply curve is

a the horizontal sum of the individual firms' supply curves.

b the vertical sum of the individual firms' supply curves.

c vertical at the total level of output being produced by all firms.

d horizontal at the current market price.

e none of the above.

10 Mugs can be produced from labour alone. Table 11.1 shows two output/input combinations.

TABLE **11.1**

Mugs	Labour-Hours
25	4
27	5

If the price of a mug is $100 and labour costs $50 per hour, what is the marginal cost of production in this range of output?

a $25

b $40

c $50

d $100

e none of the above

11 A firm in a perfectly competitive industry is maximizing its short-run profits by producing 500 units of output. At 500 units of output, which of the following *must be false*?

a *MC < AVC*

b *MC < ATC*

c *MC > ATC*

d *AR < ATC*

e *AR > AVC*

12 If a profit-maximizing firm in perfect competition is earning economic profits, then it must be producing a level of output where

a price is greater than marginal cost.

b price is greater than marginal revenue.

c marginal cost is greater than marginal revenue.

d marginal cost is greater than average total cost.

e average total cost is greater than marginal cost.

13 If an industry experiences external economies as the industry expands in the long run, the long-run industry supply curve will

a be perfectly inelastic.

b be perfectly elastic.

c have a positive slope.

d have a negative slope.

e have allocative inefficiency.

14 Under which of the following circumstances would a long-run equilibrium in a perfectly competitive industry *not* be allocatively efficient?

a firms are price takers

b new technologies are developed

c external economies or external diseconomies are present

d external costs or external benefits are present

e free entry to the industry

15 Figure 11.1 illustrates the cost curves for a perfectly competitive firm. The current market price is $11 and the firm has the plant size shown by $SRAC_1$. The firm's short-run equilibrium output is

a 7 units.
b 9 units.
c 10 units.
d 17 units.
e 18 units.

FIGURE **11.1**

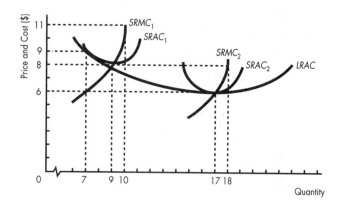

16 Refer to Fig. 11.1. The current market price is $11 and the firm has the plant size shown by $SRAC_1$. In the long run, the firm will
a exit from the industry.
b keep its current plant size, and other firms will enter the industry.
c keep its current plant size, and other firms will exit from the industry.
d increase its plant size, and other firms will enter the industry.
e increase its plant size, and other firms will exit from the industry.

17 Refer to Fig. 11.1. The long-run equilibrium price and quantity combination is
a $6 and 7 units.
b $6 and 17 units.
c $8 and 9 units.
d $8 and 18 units.
e $9 and 7 units.

18 A perfectly competitive industry is in short-run equilibrium with price below average total cost. Which of the following is *not* a prediction of the long-run consequences of such a situation?
a price will increase
b the output of the industry will increase
c firms will leave the industry
d the output of each remaining firm will increase
e economic profits will be zero

19 The supply curve for an individual firm in a perfectly competitive industry is $P = 1 + 2Q_S$. If the industry consists of 100 identical firms, then what is industry supply when $P = 7$?
a 300
b 400
c 600
d 800
e none of the above

20 If a perfectly competitive firm in the short run is able to pay its variable costs and part, but not all, of its fixed costs, then it is operating in the range on its marginal cost curve that is
a above the break-even point.
b below the break-even point.
c above the shutdown point.
d below the shutdown point.
e between the shutdown and break-even points.

21 A perfectly competitive firm is maximizing profit if
a marginal cost equals price and price is above minimum average variable cost.
b marginal cost equals price and price is above minimum average fixed cost.
c total revenue is at a maximum.
d average variable cost is at a minimum.
e average total cost is at a minimum.

22 The maximum loss a firm will experience in long-run equilibrium is
a zero.
b its total cost.
c its total variable cost.
d its average total cost.
e none of the above.

23 For a perfectly competitive firm in long-run equilibrium, which of the following is *not* equal to price?

a short-run average total cost
b short-run average variable cost
c short-run marginal cost
d long-run average cost
e average revenue

24 When economic profits are zero

a the product will not be produced in the short run.
b the product will not be produced in the long run.
c firms will leave the industry.
d revenues are not covering implicit costs.
e none of the above will occur.

25 Which of the following is *not* true of a new long-run equilibrium resulting from a new technology in a perfectly competitive industry?

a price will be lower
b industry output will be greater
c firm profits will be greater
d all firms in the industry will be using the new technology
e average total cost will be lower

Short Answer Problems

1 Why will a firm in a perfectly competitive industry choose *not* to charge a price either above or below the market price?

2 Why will economic profits tend to zero in long-run equilibrium in a perfectly competitive industry?

3 Suppose we observe a perfectly competitive industry in a long-run equilibrium when there is a permanent decrease in demand for the industry's product. There are no external economies or diseconomies. How does the industry adjust to a new long-run equilibrium? What happens to price, quantity, firm profits, and the number of firms during the adjustment process?

4 In a perfectly competitive industry with no external benefits or costs, suppose output is restricted to a quantity less than the equilibrium quantity. Explain why this level of output is allocatively inefficient.

5 Table 11.2 gives the total cost structure for one of many identical firms in a perfectly competitive industry.

a Complete the table by computing total variable cost, average total cost, average variable cost, and marginal cost at each level of output. [*Remember*: As in the problems in Chapter 10, marginal cost should be entered *midway* between rows.]

TABLE **11.2**

Quantity (units per day)	Total Cost ($)	Total Variable Cost ($)	Average Total Cost ($)	Average Variable Cost ($)	Marginal Cost ($)
0	12				
					...
1	24				
					...
2	32				
					...
3	42				
					...
4	54				
					...
5	68				
					...
6	84				

b Complete Table 11.3 by computing the profit (per day) for the firm at each level of output if the price of output is $9; $11; $15.

TABLE **11.3**

Quantity (units per day)	Profit P = $9	Profit P = $11	Profit P = $15
0			
1			
2			
3			
4			
5			
6			

c Consider the profit-maximizing output decision of the firm at alternative prices. How much will the firm produce if the price of output is $9? $11? $15? Explain each of your answers.

6 A firm will maximize profit if it produces every unit of output for which marginal revenue exceeds marginal cost. This is called the marginal approach to profit maximization. Using the marginal approach, determine the profit-maximizing level of output for the firm in Short Answer Problem 5 when the price of output is $15. How does your answer here compare with your answer in 5c?

7 This problem concerns a hypothetical pottery manufacturing firm that produces ceramic mugs for sale in a purely competitive market. With a plant of given size, the firm can turn out the quantities of ceramic mugs shown in Table 11.4, by varying the amount it uses of a single variable input, labour.

TABLE **11.4**

Number of Mugs	Labour-Hours (per day)
20	6.50
40	11.00
60	14.50
80	17.50
100	20.50
120	23.75
140	27.50
160	32.00
180	37.50
200	44.50
220	53.50
240	65.00
260	79.50
280	97.50

Suppose the firm can hire all the labour it would ever want at the going wage of $8 per labour-hour. The firm's total fixed costs are $64 per day.

a Draw a table showing output, total variable cost (*TVC*), total cost (*TC*), average variable cost (*AVC*), average total cost (*ATC*), and marginal cost (*MC*). [*Remember*: Marginal cost should be entered *midway* between rows of output.]

b On a graph with *Mugs (per day)* on the horizontal axis, draw the three "per-unit" cost curves, *AVC, ATC,* and *MC.* [Note that the marginal cost values from your table should be plotted on the graph *midway* between the corresponding units of output.]

c Consider (separately) the following alternative market prices that the firm might face: *P* = $3.20, *P* = $2, *P* = $1.65, *P* = $1.40. Assuming that the firm wants to maximize its profit, for *each* of the above prices, answer the following questions: Approximately how many mugs per day would the firm produce? How do you know? Is the firm making a profit at that price? And if so, approximately how much?

8 Suppose that the ceramic pottery mug industry consists of 60 firms, each identical to the single firm discussed in Short Answer Problem 7. Table 11.5 represents some points on the industry demand schedule for ceramic pottery mugs.

TABLE **11.5**

Price ($)	Quantity Demanded
1.00	15,900
1.60	14,400
2.20	12,900
2.80	11,400
3.40	9,900
4.00	8,400
4.60	6,900
5.20	5,400
5.80	3,900
6.40	2,400
7.00	900

a On a new graph, draw the industry short-run supply curve. Draw the industry demand curve on the same graph.

b What is the short-run equilibrium price of ceramic pottery mugs?

c Is the ceramic pottery mug industry in long-run equilibrium? Explain your answer.

9 A perfectly competitive industry has 100 identical firms in the short run, each of which has the short-run cost curves listed in Table 11.6.

TABLE **11.6**

Output (units)	Average Total Cost ($)	Average Variable Cost ($)	Marginal Cost ($)
11	20.5	13.1	
			12
12	19.8	13.0	
			14
13	19.3	13.1	
			16
14	19.1	13.3	
			18
15	19.0	13.6	
			20
16	19.1	14.0	
			22
17	19.2	14.5	
			24
18	19.5	15.0	
			26
19	19.8	15.6	
			28
20	20.3	16.2	
			30
21	20.7	16.9	

This short-run average total cost curve touches the long-run average cost curve at the minimum point on the long-run average cost curve as point *m* in Text Fig. 11.9 on page 245. The industry demand schedule is the same in the long and the short run. Table 11.7 represents some points on the demand schedule.

TABLE **11.7**

Price ($)	Quantity Demanded
11	3,200
13	3,000
15	2,800
17	2,600
19	2,400
21	2,200
23	2,000
25	1,800
27	1,600
29	1,400
31	1,200

a What is the quantity of output corresponding to the firm's break-even point? the shutdown point? Explain your answers.

b What is the short-run equilibrium price in this market? Show how you found your answer.

c What amount of profit or loss is being made by each firm at the short-run equilibrium price? Is this industry in long-run equilibrium at its present size? Why or why not?

d Exactly how many firms will exist in this industry in the long run? Explain your answer. How much economic profit will each firm earn in the long run?

10 Consider a perfectly competitive industry in long-run equilibrium. All the firms in the industry are identical.

a Draw a two-part graph illustrating the long-run equilibrium for the industry—part (a) on the left—and for the typical firm—part (b) on the right. The graph of the firm should include the *MC*, *ATC*, *MR*, and *LRAC* curves. Assume that the *LRAC* curve is U-shaped as it is in Text Fig. 11.9 on page 245. Label the equilibrium price P_0, the equilibrium industry quantity Q_0, and the output of the firm q_0.

b Now, suppose there is a decline in industry demand. Using your graphs from part **a**, show what happens to market price, firm output, firm profits, and industry equilibrium quantity in the short run (assume that the shutdown point is not reached).

Then show what happens to market price, firm output, firm profits, and industry equilibrium quantity in the long run (assume that there are no external economies or diseconomies). What has happened to the number of firms?

A N S W E R S

True/False/Uncertain and Explain

1 **F** Individual firm demand curve horizontal. Industry demand curve downward sloping. (234–235)

2 **F** Maximize total profit. (236–237)

3 **F** Losses in short run but not long run. (243–244)

4 **T** "Invisible hand" → economic efficiency and consumer efficiency. (249–251)

⊘5 **U** True if *P* < minimum *AVC*. False if *P* > minimum *AVC* but < minimum *ATC*. (240–241)

6 F As long as P > minimum AVC. (240–241)
7 T Otherwise firm driven out of business by lower-cost firms. (245)
8 F Negatively sloped. (247–248)
⊘9 T ATC shifts $\uparrow$ with no ΔMC. Economic losses $\rightarrow$ exit. (243–244)
10 T Definition. (249–250)

Multiple-Choice

1 d Identical products. (234–235)
2 d Firm can $\uparrow Q$ without ΔP, so MR from additional $Q = P$. (234–235)
⊘3 c Draw graph. Firm should choose lower Q where $P = MC$. If AVC at current $Q = \$10$, minimum AVC must be < $\$10$, so new Q > minimum AVC. (238–240)
4 c Profits = TR ($\$15 \times 100$) – TC ($\$100 + \$50$) = 0. (238–240)
⊘5 d TR ($\$10 \times 10$) – TC ($\$100 + \$50$) = –$\$50$. Shutting down would bring bigger loss of $\$100$ (fixed costs). (238–240)
⊘6 c He is making long-run decision. **a, b** refer to short run. **d** false because *losses* signal to move resources. (243–244)
7 b Since $MR = AR$, $AR > ATC$. Multiply by Q $\rightarrow TR > TC$, so economic profits. (238–240)
8 b Firm stays shut down ($Q = 0$) until P reaches minimum AVC. (240–241)
9 a Definition. **c** is momentary supply curve. **d** is demand curve facing individual firm. (240–241)
10 a $MC = \Delta TC/\Delta Q = \$50/2$. Mug price irrelevant. (216–217)
⊘11 a **a** implies shutdown. Other answers possible with losses (**b, d**) or profits (**c, e**). (238–240)
12 d ($MC = P =$) $AR > ATC$. **a, b, c** not consistent with profit maximization. **e** implies losses. (238–240)
13 d Because $\downarrow$ costs as industry $Q \uparrow$. (247–248)
14 d **a, e** conditions perfect competition. **b, c** affect shape long-run supply curve but not allocative efficiency. (249–250)
15 c Choose Q where $P = MC$. (238–240)
16 d Profits $\rightarrow$ new entry $\rightarrow \downarrow P$ and incentive to build larger, lower cost plant. (243–245)
17 b Long-run equilibrium at intersection $SRAC$, $SRMC$, and $LRAC$ curves. (243–245)
18 b As firms exit, supply shifts left $\rightarrow \downarrow$ industry Q and $\uparrow P \rightarrow \uparrow Q$ remaining firms. (243–244)
⊘19 a For one firm: $7 = 1 + 2Q_S$; $2Q_S = 6$; $Q_S = 3$. For 100 firms, $3 \times 100 = 300$. (241)
20 e If couldn't pay variable costs $\rightarrow$ below shutdown. If paying all variable and fixed costs $\rightarrow$ break even. (238–240)

21 a AFC irrelevant. Maximizing profit $\neq$ maximizing revenue. **d, e** might be true depending on P. (238–240)
22 a Definition long-run equilibrium $\rightarrow$ zero economic profits. (243–244)
23 b Long-run equilibrium at intersection ATC, MC, and $LRAC$ curves. (244–245)
⊘24 e Product produced in short and long run, revenues exactly cover all costs (including implicit). (243–245)
25 c In long-run equilibrium, economic profits always zero. (248–249)

Short Answer Problems

1 If a firm in a perfectly competitive industry charged a price even slightly higher than the market price, it would lose all of its sales. Thus it will not charge a price above the market price. Since it can sell all it wants at the market price, it would not be able to increase sales by lowering its price. Thus it would not charge a price below the market price since this would decrease total revenue and profits.

2 In a perfectly competitive industry, the existence of positive economic profits will attract the entry of new firms, which will shift the industry supply curve rightward, causing the market price to fall and firm profits to decline. This tendency will exist as long as there are positive economic profits. Similarly, the existence of economic losses will cause firms to exit from the industry, which will shift the industry supply curve leftward, causing the market price to rise and firm profits to rise (losses to decline). This tendency will exist as long as losses are being made. Thus, the only point of rest in the long run (the only equilibrium) occurs when economic profits are zero.

3 The decrease in market demand causes the market price to fall. Since, in the initial long-run equilibrium, each firm was earning zero economic profit, the fall in price means that profits will fall and firms will now be making losses. Since the decrease in demand is permanent, these losses will induce some firms to leave the industry. This will shift the industry supply curve leftward, causing an increase in market price. The increasing price causes profits to increase for the remaining firms, so their losses will decline. The exit of firms continues until losses are eliminated. Costs have not been affected by the decrease in demand, so if there are no external economies or diseconomies, the price must continue rising until it reaches its original level in the new long-run equilibrium. The output of each firm will also equal its original level, but the equilibrium quantity at the industry level will be less because the number of firms has declined.

4   Refer to Text Fig. 11.12 on page 250. If output is restricted to quantity Q_0, the value to consumers of an additional unit of the good is V_0, while producers would be willing to supply additional goods for any price at or above C_0. If more goods are produced and sold at any price in between V_0 and C_0, consumers will be better off because they value the goods more than the price paid, and producers will be better off because they receive a higher price than the minimum necessary to induce production. Consumers and producers could be made better off without making someone else worse off. Therefore at quantity Q_0, there are unrealized gains from trade (more consumer and producer surplus is possible), and this level of output is allocatively inefficient.

5 a   Completed Table 11.2 is shown here as Table 11.2 Solution.

TABLE **11.2**   SOLUTION

Quantity (units per day)	Total Cost ($)	Total Variable Cost ($)	Average Total Cost ($)	Average Variable Cost ($)	Marginal Cost ($)
0	12	0	—	—	
					... 12
1	24	12	24.00	12.00	
					... 8
2	32	20	16.00	10.00	
					... 10
3	42	30	14.00	10.00	
					... 12
4	54	42	13.50	10.50	
					... 14
5	68	56	13.60	11.20	
					... 16
6	84	72	14.00	12.00	

b   Completed Table 11.3 is given here as Table 11.3 Solution. The values for profit are computed as total revenue minus total cost, where total revenue is price times quantity and total cost is given in Table 11.2.

TABLE **11.3**   SOLUTION

Quantity (units per day)	Profit P = $9	Profit P = $11	Profit P = $15
0	**–12**	–12	–12
1	–15	–13	–9
2	–14	–10	–2
3	–15	**–9**	3
4	–18	–10	6
5	–23	–13	**7**
6	–30	–18	6

c   If the price is $9, profit is maximized (actually loss is minimized) when the firm shuts down and produces zero units. If the firm chooses to produce, its loss will be at least $14, which is greater than the fixed cost loss of $12. If the price is $11, the firm is still unable to make a positive economic profit. The loss is minimized (at $9) if the firm produces 3 units. At this price, all of variable cost and part of fixed cost can be recovered. At a price of $15, the firm will maximize profit (at $7) at an output of 5 units per day.

6   The marginal approach to profit maximization states that the firm should produce all units of output for which marginal revenue exceeds marginal cost. For a perfectly competitive firm, marginal revenue equals price, so (equivalently) the firm should produce every unit for which price exceeds marginal cost. If the price of output is $15, we can see from Table 11.2 Solution that the firm should produce 5 units. Since the marginal cost of moving from the 4th to the 5th unit ($14) is less than price ($15), the 5th unit should be produced. The marginal cost of moving to the 6th unit ($16), however, is greater than price. It should not be produced. The answer here is the same as the answer in 5c.

7 a With only one variable input (labour), *TVC* (for any level of output) = (labour hours × wage rate). The requested table is Table 11.8.

TABLE **11.8**

Output (per day)	TVC ($)	TC ($)	AVC ($)	ATC ($)	MC ($)
0	0	64	—	—	
					... 2.60
20	52	116	2.60	5.80	
					... 1.80
40	88	152	2.20	3.80	
					... 1.40
60	116	180	1.93	3.00	
					... 1.20
80	140	204	1.75	2.55	
					... 1.20
100	164	228	1.64	2.28	
					... 1.30
120	190	254	1.58	2.12	
					... 1.50
140	220	284	1.57	2.03	
					... 1.80
160	256	320	1.60	2.00	
					... 2.20
180	300	364	1.67	2.02	
					... 2.80
200	356	420	1.78	2.10	
					... 3.60
220	428	492	1.95	2.24	
					... 4.60
240	520	584	2.17	2.43	
					... 5.80
260	636	700	2.45	2.69	
					... 7.20
280	780	844	2.79	3.01	

b The graph appears in Fig. 11.2. It also illustrates the answers to part **c**.

FIGURE **11.2**

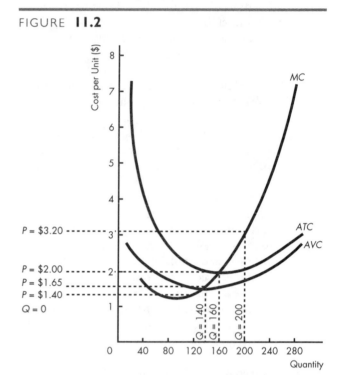

c In every case, at the profit-maximizing output, marginal revenue (which, for a price-taking firm in a perfectly competitive market, is the same as market price) is equal to marginal cost, provided that price is greater than average variable cost.

Profit "per unit of output" is the difference between average revenue (price) and average total cost at the level of output. Total profit is "per unit profit" × number of units of output. Economic profit might be zero or negative (a loss) and still be the best the firm can attain in the short run. The calculations of total profit at each price appear in Table 11.9.

TABLE **11.9**

Price ($)	Output Chosen	Per Unit Profit ($)	Total Profit ($)
3.20	200	1.10	220.00
2.00	160	0	0
1.65	140	−0.38	−53.20
1.40	0	0	−64.00

Note the following:

1. Marginal cost is $3.20 at approximately 200 units.

2. The per unit profit is $P - ATC$.

3. 160 units is the "break-even" level of output, where MC = minimum ATC and the firm is just covering all its opportunity costs.

4. At an output of 140 units, the firm continues to produce in the short run because it can more than cover its variable costs. If it produced zero units, its loss would be greater, $64, which is the amount of its fixed costs.

5. Any positive output increases losses when the price is below the shutdown price, which here is approximately $1.57. When price is less than minimum AVC, the firm would not only lose its fixed costs, it would also lose additional money on every unit it produced.

8 There are 60 identical price-taking firms. For every possible price (above minimum AVC of approximately $1.57), each firm will supply the quantity at which $P = MC$. We can derive (in Table 11.10) the industry supply schedule from the MC curve of an individual firm.

TABLE **11.10**

Price ($)	Quantity Supplied by 1 Firm	Quantity Supplied by 60 Firms
1.57	134	8,040
1.80	150	9,000
2.20	170	10,200
2.80	190	11,400
3.60	210	12,600
4.60	230	13,800
5.80	250	15,000
7.20	270	16,200

a The graph of the industry supply curve appears in Fig. 11.3, together with the industry demand curve.

FIGURE **11.3**

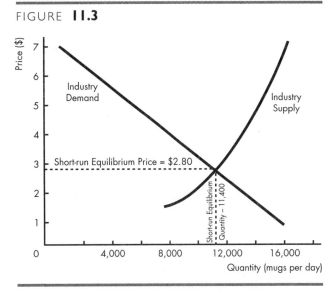

b The short-run equilibrium price is $2.80 (where a total of 11,400 mugs per day are supplied and sold; or 190 mugs per day supplied by each firm at MC of $2.80).

c At a price of $2.80 and output of 190, for each firm, $P > ATC$ where $ATC = \$2.06$. So all existing firms are making economic profits after covering *all* opportunity costs including a normal profit. (See Helpful Hint **3**.) The industry will attract new entrants because it offers more than normal profits. Even though the industry is in short-run equilibrium, it is *not* in long-run equilibrium because the number of firms has not "stabilized." New firms will enter the industry, the industry supply curve will shift rightward, and price will fall until no firm is making economic profits.

9 a The break-even point occurs at 15 units of output. At this level of output, ATC is at its minimum ($19) and is equal to MC. Since the MC of moving from the 14th to the 15th unit is $18, and the MC of moving from the 15th to the 16th units is $20, we can interpolate the MC exactly at 15 units as midway between $18 and $20, or as $19. The shutdown point occurs at 12 units of output. At this level of output, AVC is at its minimum ($13) and is equal to MC. The interpolated value of MC at exactly 12 units of output is midway between $12 and $14, or is $13.

b The short-run equilibrium price is $25. This is the price at which industry quantity supplied equals quantity demanded as shown in Table 11.11.

c At a price of $25, each firm produces 18 units of output. At 18 units, ATC is $19.50, so economic profits are being earned. The amount of profit is ($25 − $19.50 per unit =) $5.50 per unit. Total economic profit per *firm* is $5.50/unit × 18 units = $99. This means that new entrants will be attracted to the industry. We conclude that the industry is *not* in long-run equilibrium.

d Entry continues until economic profits are competed away, and all firms are operating at the minimum point of the $LRAC$ curve (which, in this problem, is also the minimum point of the given short-run average total cost curve).

　　Minimum ATC for each firm occurs at 15 units of output, when $ATC = MC = $19, so price in the long run *must* be $19. At a price of $19, consumers demand 2,400 units (from Table 11.11). It follows that when the industry is in long-run equilibrium, there must be 2,400 units/15 units per firm = 160 firms in the industry, each producing 15 units of output, at *zero economic profit*.

TABLE **11.11**

$P = MC$ ($)	Quantity Supplied by 1 Firm	Quantity Supplied by 100 Firms	Quantity Demanded
13	12	1,200	3,000
15	13	1,300	2,800
17	14	1,400	2,600
19	15	1,500	2,400
21	16	1,600	2,200
23	17	1,700	2,000
25	**18**	**1,800**	**1,800**
27	19	1,900	1,600
29	20	2,000	1,400

10 a A long-run equilibrium in a perfectly competitive industry is illustrated in Fig. 11.4.

　　Part (a) illustrates industry equilibrium at the intersection of industry demand (D_0) and industry supply (S_0): point *a*. The equilibrium industry quantity is labelled Q_0 and the equilibrium market price is labelled P_0.

　　Part (b) illustrates the situation for a single firm in long-run equilibrium. The firm is at point *a'*, the minimum point of both the short-run average total cost curve (ATC) and the long-run average cost curve ($LRAC$). The firm is producing the output labelled q_0 and earning zero economic profit.

FIGURE **11.4**

(a) Industry

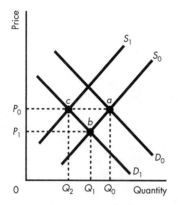

(b) Firm

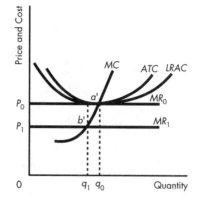

b The new short-run equilibrium is also illustrated in Fig. 11.4. The decrease in demand shifts the market demand curve leftward, from D_0 to D_1. The new market equilibrium is at point b. The price has fallen from P_0 to P_1 and the industry equilibrium quantity has fallen from Q_0 to Q_1. The fall in price induces firms to reduce output as shown by the move from point a' to point b' on the MC curve in part (b). Since P_1 is less than minimum ATC, firms are making losses in the new short-run equilibrium.

The new long-run equilibrium is also illustrated in Fig. 11.4. With short-run losses, firms will exit from the industry in the long run. This causes the industry supply curve to shift leftward, causing the price to rise and thus reducing losses. Firms continue to leave until the industry supply curve has shifted enough to eliminate losses, from S_0 to S_1. This gives a new long-run industry equilibrium at point c and the price has returned to its initial level, P_0, but industry quantity has fallen to Q_2.

As firms exit and the market price rises, remaining firms will increase their output (moving up the MC curve from point b' to point a') and their losses will be reduced. When sufficient firms have left the industry, the price will have risen (returned) to P_0 and firms will have returned to point a' in part (b). At this point, each firm is again earning zero economic profit and firm output has returned to q_0. But, since there are now fewer firms, industry equilibrium quantity is less.

KEY CONCEPTS

How Monopoly Arises

Monopoly—industry with one supplier of product with no close substitutes. Arises from

- **Barriers to entry**—impediments protecting firm from competition from potential new entrants.

  - Legal barriers to entry—for a **legal monopoly**, competition and entry restricted by public franchise, *government licence, patent,* or *copyright.*
  - Natural barriers to entry—a **natural monopoly** occurs when, due to economies of scale, one firm can supply the market at lower *ATC* than multiple firms can.

Single-Price Monopoly

Single-price monopoly charges same price for every unit output.

- Monopoly's demand curve is industry demand curve.

- Marginal revenue (*MR*) < price (*P*). To sell additional output, must lower *P* on *all* output.

- In moving down the monopoly's demand curve

  - when total revenue (*TR*) ↑, *MR* positive, η > 1.
  - when *TR* maximum, *MR* zero, η = 1.
  - when *TR* ↓, *MR* negative, η < 1.

- Monopoly's technology and costs like firm in perfect competition.

- Profit-maximizing monopoly chooses output at which *MR = MC*, charges maximum price consumers willing to pay (on demand curve).

- Monopoly never operates in inelastic range demand curve. Monopoly has no supply curve.

- Monopoly can make economic profits even in long run because barriers prevent entry of new firms.

Price Discrimination

Price discrimination—charging some customers lower price than others for *identical* good; or charging an individual customer a lower price on a large purchase than a small, even though selling costs are identical.

Price discrimination can increase profits by enabling firm to capture more of the consumer surplus.

- *Perfect price discrimination*—different price for each unit sold; obtains maximum price each consumer willing to pay.

  - *MR* curve same as demand curve. Same output as perfectly competitive industry.
  - But all consumer surplus captured as profit.

- Price discrimination requires

  - Good cannot be resold.
  - Charge lower *P* to higher elasticity group. Charge higher *P* to lower elasticity group.

- Price discriminating monopoly produces greater output than single-price monopoly.

Comparing Monopoly and Competition

Price and output

- Single-price monopoly *P* > competitive *P*.

- Single-price monopoly *Q* < competitive *Q*.

  - The more perfectly the monopoly can price discriminate, the closer its *Q* gets to competitive *Q*.

Allocative efficiency

♦ Allocative efficiency single-price monopoly
< competition. Monopoly prevents gains from
trade: restricts output, captures some consumer
surplus, but creates **deadweight loss**—total loss of
consumer surplus and **producer surplus** (revenue
– opportunity cost production) below efficient
levels.

♦ Perfect price discriminating monopoly captures
entire consumer surplus as profit, but achieves
competitive allocative efficiency—zero deadweight
loss.

Costs of monopoly

♦ Deadweight loss.

♦ Cost of resources used **rent seeking**—searching out
profitable monopoly opportunities.

♦ If no barriers to entry, cost of resources used rent
seeking = value monopoly profit (if there is rent
seeking).

♦ Social cost of monopoly = deadweight loss +
monopoly's economic profit (if there is rent
seeking).

Gains from monopoly

♦ *Economies of scale* (↓ *LRAC* through ↑ *Q*).

♦ **Economies of scope** (↓ *ATC* through ↑ range of
goods produced).

♦ ↑ innovation and technological change (in some
cases).

HELPFUL HINTS

1 The opposite extreme of perfect competition is
monopoly. While in perfect competition there
are many firms that can decide only on quantity
produced but not on price, a monopoly is a
single firm with the ability to set both quantity
and price. These differences create differences in
the revenue situation facing the monopoly. The
cost curves for the two market structures are
assumed to be the same.

Because there is only one firm, the industry
demand curve is also the firm demand curve.
Facing a negatively sloped demand curve, if a
single-price monopoly wants to sell one more
unit of output, it must lower its price. This has
two effects on revenue. First, the sale of an
additional unit will increase revenue by the
amount of the price. However, since the firm
must also *drop the price on previous units*, revenue

on these will decrease. The net change in
revenue, the marginal revenue, will be less than
price and the marginal revenue curve will lie
below the demand curve.

Combining this new revenue situation with
our familiar cost curves from Chapter 10 yields
the important Text Fig. 12.4(b), which is
reproduced below as Fig. 12.1. Notice the
following points about this graph.

FIGURE **12.1**

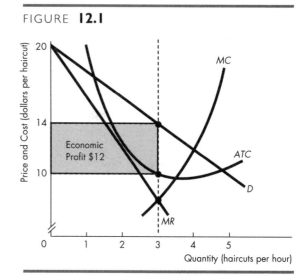

The profit maximization rule for a single-
price monopoly is to find the quantity of output
where *MR* = *MC*. This is the same rule that
applies to a perfectly competitive firm.

For a perfectly competitive firm *MR* is also
equal to price, so the intersection of *MR* and
MC yields the profit-maximizing output and
price. That is not true for the monopolist. *MR* is
not equal to price, and once the profit-
maximizing output is identified, the monopolist
still has to set the price.

To find the profit-maximizing price, draw
an imaginary vertical line up to the demand
curve from the intersection of *MR* and *MC*.
Then draw an imaginary horizontal line to the
price axis to read the price.

Understanding what the vertical and
horizontal distances of the economic profit area
represent will make you less likely to make
mistakes in drawing that area. The vertical
distance is between the demand (or average
revenue) curve and the average total cost curve.
That distance measures average revenue minus
average total cost, which equals average
economic profit, or economic profit per unit.
The horizontal distance is just the number of
units produced. So the area of the rectangle
(vertical distance × horizontal distance)
= economic profit per unit × number of units

= total economic profit. Do *not* make the mistake of drawing the vertical distance down to the intersection of *MC* and *MR*. That intersection has no economic meaning for the calculation of total economic profit.

2 There is an easy trick for drawing the marginal revenue curve corresponding to any linear demand curve. The price intercept (where *Q* = 0) is the same as for the demand curve, and the quantity intercept (where *P* = 0) is exactly *half* of the output of the demand curve. The marginal revenue curve is, therefore, a downward-sloping straight line whose slope is twice as steep as the slope of the demand curve.

3 Price discrimination can be profitable for a monopoly only if different consumer groups have different elasticities of demand for the good. If such differences exist, the price-discriminating monopolist treats the groups as different markets. The profit maximization rule for a price-discriminating monopoly is to find the quantity of output where *MR in each market* = *MC*. Then, in each market, charge the maximum price the consumer group is willing to pay for that output (on demand curve). With different elasticities of demand between groups, this rule will yield different prices in the two markets.

   If, however, the elasticities of demand in the two markets are equal, then marginal revenues are equal and the prices corresponding to the marginal revenues are also equal. There is no point in charging different prices, and the profit-maximizing rule for price discrimination collapses back into the rule for single-price monopoly.

4 The absence of entry barriers into a perfectly competitive industry is the basis for the prediction that any short-run economic profits in perfect competition will be competed away in the long run. Conversely, the presence of entry barriers in monopoly is the basis for the prediction that monopoly profits can persist in the long run. However, when rent-seeking activity is taken into account, there may be no long-run economic profits, even in monopoly. Rent seeking is any activity aimed at obtaining existing monopoly rights or creating new monopoly rights. Competition among rent seekers bids up the cost of rent seeking until it just equals the value of the potential monopoly profits, leaving the rent-seeker-turned-monopolist with little or no economic profit.

SELF-TEST

True/False/Uncertain and Explain

1 Over the output range where total revenue is decreasing, marginal revenue is positive.

2 The supply curve of a monopoly firm is its marginal cost curve.

3 A monopoly will make economic profits.

4 For a perfect price-discriminating monopolist, the demand curve is also the marginal revenue curve.

5 Price discrimination only works for goods that can be readily resold.

6 In moving from perfect competition to single-price monopoly, part of the deadweight loss is due to a reduction in producer surplus.

7 No deadweight loss results from monopoly because the monopoly gains everything the consumer loses.

8 Because of the existence of rent seeking, the social cost of monopoly is smaller than the deadweight loss.

9 When rent seeking is taken into account, economic profits from monopoly are guaranteed in the long run.

10 A monopoly industry with large economies of scale and scope may produce more output and charge a lower price than does a perfectly competitive industry.

Multiple-Choice

1 Which of the following is a *natural* barrier to the entry of new firms in an industry?

a   licensing of professions
b   economies of scale
c   issuing a patent
d   a public franchise
e   all of the above

2 In order to increase sales from 7 units to 8 units, a single-price monopolist must drop the price from $7 per unit to $6 per unit. What is marginal revenue in this range?

a $48
b $6
c $1
d   −$1
e   none of the above

3 If marginal revenue is negative at a particular output, then

a   price must be negative.
b   the monopolist should increase output.
c   the elasticity of demand is less than 1 at that output.
d   demand must be elastic at that output.
e   the monopolist should shut down.

4 *Disadvantages* of monopoly include

a   economies of scope.
b   economies of scale.
c   diffusion of technological advances.
d   rent-seeking behaviour.
e   all of the above.

5 Taking rent-seeking activity into account, the social cost of monopoly is equal to the

a   deadweight loss from monopoly.
b   monopoly profit.
c   deadweight loss plus monopoly profit.
d   deadweight loss minus monopoly profit.
e   consumer surplus lost plus producer surplus lost.

6 If a single-price monopoly has shut down, then at the level of output where marginal cost and marginal revenue intersect, it *must be true* that

a   marginal revenue is less than average variable cost.
b   marginal cost is less than average variable cost.
c   price is less than average variable cost.
d   total revenue is less than total cost.
e   all of the above are correct.

7 For the single-price monopoly depicted in Fig. 12.2, when profit is maximized, quantity is

a   3 and price is $3.
b   3 and price is $6.
c   4 and price is $4.
d   4 and price is $5.
e   5 and price is $4.

FIGURE **12.2**

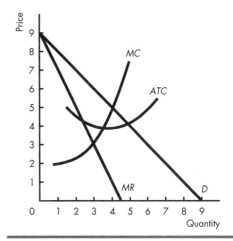

8 If the single-price monopoly depicted in Fig. 12.2 is maximizing profit, what is total economic profit?

a $3
b $4
c $6
d $9
e   none of the above

9 The output of a (not perfect) price-discriminating monopoly will be

a   less than a single-price monopoly.
b   more than a single-price monopoly, but less than a perfectly competitive industry.
c   the same amount as a perfectly competitive industry.
d   more than a perfectly competitive industry.
e   none of the above.

10 Consider the industry demand curve in Fig. 12.3. If the industry operates under perfect competition, which area in the diagram indicates consumer surplus?

a *aek*
b *dhk*
c *dik*
d *dih*
e none of the above

FIGURE **12.3**

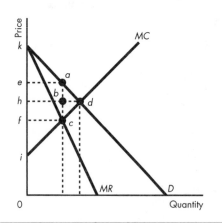

11 Consider the industry demand curve in Fig. 12.3. If the industry operates under perfect competition, which area in the diagram indicates producer surplus?

a *aek*
b *dhk*
c *dik*
d *dih*
e none of the above

12 Consider the industry demand curve in Fig. 12.3. Which area in the diagram indicates the deadweight loss from a single-price monopoly?

a *eacf*
b *acd*
c *abd*
d *bcd*
e none of the above

13 Which area in Fig. 12.3 indicates the deadweight loss from a perfect price-discriminating monopoly?

a *eacf*
b *acd*
c *abd*
d *bcd*
e none of the above

14 Four monopolists were overheard talking at an expensive restaurant. Which of their statements below contains a correct strategy for maximizing profits?

a "In my company, we don't increase output unless we know that the larger output will raise total revenue."
b "I think cost minimization is the key to maximizing profits."
c "We try to make the most of our equipment by producing at maximum capacity."
d "I don't really keep close tabs on total profits, but I don't approve any business deal unless it increases my revenue more than it increases my costs."
e None of the above.

15 A monopoly has economies of scope if

a average total cost declines as the firm's scale increases.
b average total cost declines as output increases.
c total profit declines as output increases.
d average total cost declines as the number of different goods produced increases.
e total profit declines as the number of different goods produced increases.

16 If a profit-maximizing monopoly is producing at an output at which marginal cost exceeds marginal revenue, it

a should raise price and lower output.
b should lower price and raise output.
c should lower price and lower output.
d is making losses.
e is maximizing profit.

17 A profit-maximizing monopoly will never produce at an output level

a at which it would make economic losses.
b where marginal revenue is less than price.
c at which average cost is greater than marginal cost.
d in the inelastic range of its demand curve.
e in the inelastic range of its marginal revenue curve.

18 A perfect price-discriminating monopoly

a has a demand curve which is also its average revenue curve.
b will maximize revenue.
c is assured of making a profit.
d will produce the quantity at which the marginal cost curve intersects the demand curve.
e will be allocatively inefficient.

19 A monopoly will go out of business in the short run if

a it is making an economic loss.

b *MR* is less than *AVC.*

c the price is less than *AVC.*

d the profit-maximizing level of output is in the elastic range of the demand curve.

e *MR* is less than *AR.*

20 Table 12.1 lists marginal costs for the XYZ firm. If XYZ sells 3 units at a price of $6 each, what is its producer surplus?

a $2

b $6

c $7

d $9

e $12

TABLE **12.1**

Quantity	Marginal Cost
1	2
2	3
3	4
4	5

21 A single-price monopolist will maximize profits if it produces the output where

a price equals marginal cost.

b price equals marginal revenue.

c marginal revenue equals marginal cost.

d average revenue equals marginal cost.

e average revenue equals marginal revenue.

22 Many video stores charge a lower rental for Wednesday nights compared with weekends. This price discrimination is profitable only if the elasticity of demand for videos on Wednesdays is

a greater than the elasticity of demand for videos on weekends.

b less than the elasticity of demand for videos on weekends.

c positive and the elasticity of demand for videos on weekends is negative.

d negative and the elasticity of demand for videos on weekends is positive.

e equal to one.

23 Activity for the purpose of creating monopoly is

a called rent seeking.

b illegal in Canada.

c called price discrimination.

d called legal monopoly.

e costless.

24 Which of the following is true for a producing single-price monopolist but not for a producing perfect competitor?

a The firm maximizes profit by setting marginal cost equal to marginal revenue.

b The firm is a price-taker.

c The firm can sell any level of output at any price it sets.

d The firm's marginal cost is less than average revenue.

e None of the above statements is true.

25 When perfect price discrimination occurs, which of the following statements is *false*?

a Buyers cannot resell the product.

b The firm can distinguish between buyers.

c The firm sets prices.

d The firm captures consumer surplus.

e Allocative efficiency is worse than with single-price monopoly.

Short Answer Problems

1 Why is marginal revenue less than price for a single-price monopoly?

2 Explain why the output of a competitive industry will always be greater than the output of the *same* industry under single-price monopoly.

3 The price of the last unit sold and the quantity sold are exactly the same in an industry under perfect competition and under a perfect price-discriminating monopoly. Are consumers therefore indifferent between the two? Explain.

4 Under what circumstances would a monopoly be more efficient than a large number of competitive firms? Illustrate graphically such a situation where a monopoly produces more and charges a lower price than would be the case if the industry consisted of a large number of perfectly competitive firms.

5 A single-price monopoly is the only seller of skyhooks in the Canadian market. The firm's total fixed cost is $112 per day. Its total variable costs and total costs (both in dollars per day) are shown in Table 12.2.

a Complete the table by computing marginal cost, average variable cost, and average total cost. [*Remember*: Marginal cost should be entered *midway* between rows of output.]

TABLE **12.2**

Quantity	Total Variable Cost (TVC)	Total Cost (TC)	Marginal Cost (MC)	Average Variable Cost (AVC)	Average Total Cost (ATC)
9	135	247			
10	144	256			
11	155	267			
12	168	280			
13	183	295			
14	200 ·	312			
15	219	331			
16	240	352			
17	263	375			
18	288	400			
19	315	427			
20	344	456			

TABLE **12.3**

Price (P)	Quantity Demanded (Q_D)	Total Revenue (TR)	Marginal Revenue (MR)	Total Cost (TC)	Marginal Cost (MC)	Economic Profit (TR–TC)
57	9			247		
56	10			256		
55	11			267		
54	12			280		
53	13			295		
52	14			312		
51	15			331		
50	16			352		
49	17			375		
48	18			400		
47	19			427		
46	20			456		

b Table 12.3 lists some points on the demand curve facing the firm, as well as the total cost information from part **a**. Complete the table by copying your values for marginal cost from Table 12.2 and by computing total revenue, marginal revenue, and economic profit. [*Remember:* Marginal revenue, like marginal cost, should be entered *midway* between rows of output.]

What is the firm's profit-maximizing quantity of output? At what price will it sell skyhooks? What will be its total economic profit? Explain your answers.

c On the graph in Fig. 12.4, plot the demand curve and the *MR, AVC, ATC,* and *MC* curves corresponding to the data in parts **a** and **b**. Show the equilibrium output and the area of economic profit on your diagram.

FIGURE **12.4**

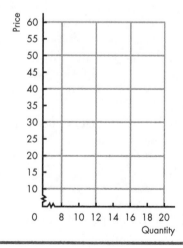

d The firm's cost curves are unchanged, but now consumer demand shifts. Table 12.4 lists some points on the new demand curve, as well as the total cost information from part **a**. Complete the table by copying your values for marginal cost from Table 12.2, and by computing the new values for total revenue, marginal revenue, and economic profit.

TABLE **12.4**

Price (P)	Quantity Demanded (Q_D)	Total Revenue (TR)	Marginal Revenue (MR)	Total Cost (TC)	Marginal Cost (MC)	Economic Profit (TR–TC)
24.50	9			247		
24.00	10			256		
23.50	11			267		
23.00	12			280		
22.50	13			295		
22.00	14			312		
21.50	15			331		
21.00	16			352		
20.50	17			375		
20.00	18			400		
19.50	19			427		
19.00	20			456		
18.50	21			487		

What is the firm's new profit-maximizing quantity of output? At what price will it now sell skyhooks? What will be its total economic profit? Explain your answers.

e On the graph in Fig. 12.5, plot the new demand curve and *MR* curve. Copy the *AVC*, *ATC*, and *MC* curves from Fig. 12.4. Show the new equilibrium output and the area of economic profit on your diagram.

FIGURE **12.5**

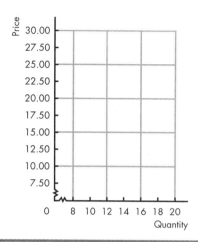

f Suppose demand falls even further so that the new demand curve equation is $P = 19 - 1/2Q_D$. On the graph in Fig. 12.6, plot this demand curve and copy the *AVC* curve from Fig. 12.4. Explain why the monopolist will shut down in the short run.

FIGURE **12.6**

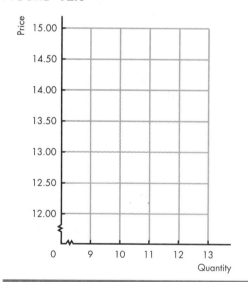

6 You are given the following information about an industry consisting of 100 identical firms. The demand curve facing the industry is

$$P = 36 - 0.01Q$$

The marginal revenue curve facing the industry is

$$MR = 36 - 0.02Q$$

The marginal cost curve of an individual firm is

$$MC = -12 + 2Q$$

The horizontal sum of the marginal cost curves of all of the firms in the industry is

$$MC = -12 + 0.02Q$$

Use this information to answer the following questions.

a Suppose all 100 firms are controlled by a single-price monopolist. Calculate the profit-maximizing quantity of output for the monopolist. Calculate the price per unit of output that the monopolist will charge.

b Suppose instead that the 100 firms operate independently as a perfectly competitive industry. Calculate the short-run equilibrium quantity of output for the industry as a whole. Calculate the short-run equilibrium price for the industry.

c *Without* using your answer about industry output to part **b**, calculate the short-run equilibrium output per firm.

d Compare the monopoly price and quantity outcomes with the perfect competition price and quantity outcomes.

7 Barney's Bistro has two kinds of customers for lunch: stockbrokers and retired senior citizens. The demand schedules for lunches for the two groups are given in Table 12.5.

Barney has decided to price discriminate between the two groups by treating each demand separately and charging the price that maximizes profit in each of the two submarkets. Marginal cost and average total cost are equal and constant at $2 per lunch.

a Complete Table 12.5 by computing the total and marginal revenue associated with stockbroker demand (TR_{SB} and MR_{SB}) as well as the total and marginal revenue associated with senior citizen demand (TR_{SC} and MR_{SC}). [*Remember*: Marginal revenue should be entered *midway* between rows.]

b What are the profit-maximizing output and price for stockbrokers?

c What are the profit-maximizing output and price for senior citizens?

d What is total economic profit?

e Show that the total economic profit in part **d** is the maximum by comparing it with total economic profit if instead Barney served: 1 additional lunch *each* to stockbrokers and senior citizens; 1 less lunch *each* to stockbrokers and senior citizens.

f What is the consumer surplus for stockbrokers? for senior citizens? for all customers?

8 The stockbrokers complain bitterly about Barney's discriminatory pricing policy, and threaten to bring bag lunches unless Barney charges a uniform price to all customers. Barney buckles under the pressure, and sits down with

TABLE **12.5**

	Stockbrokers			Senior Citizens		
Price (P)	Quantity Demanded (Q_D)	Total Revenue (TR_{SB})	Marginal Revenue (MR_{SB})	Quantity Demanded (Q_D)	Total Revenue (TR_{SC})	Marginal Revenue (MR_{SC})
8	0			0		
7	1			0		
6	2			0		
5	3			1		
4	4			2		
3	5			3		
2	6			4		
1	7			5		
0	8			6		

his calculator to figure out his profit-maximizing output and price as a single-price monopolist. Using the previous information in Short Answer Problem 7, can you figure it out for him *without* looking at the hints below? If not, answer these questions.

a Calculate Barney's demand schedule by adding up the quantity demanded by stockbrokers and senior citizens at each price. Construct a table similar to Table 12.3, with columns for price, quantity demanded, total revenue, and marginal revenue. [*Remember*: Marginal revenue should be entered *midway* between rows.]

b Marginal cost and average total cost remain unchanged at $2 per lunch. What are Barney's profit-maximizing output and price?

c What is Barney's total economic profit as a single-price monopolist? How does this compare with his total economic profit as a price-discriminating monopolist?

d What is the consumer surplus for all customers? How does this compare with the consumer surplus for all customers when Barney price discriminated?

9 Figure 12.7 gives the demand, marginal revenue, and marginal cost curves for a certain industry. Your task is to illustrate how consumer and producer surplus are distributed under each of four ways of organizing the industry. In each case redraw any relevant part of Fig. 12.7 and then (1) indicate the region of the graph corresponding to consumer surplus by drawing horizontal lines through it; (2) indicate the region corresponding to producer surplus by drawing vertical lines through it; and (3) indicate the region (if any) corresponding to deadweight loss by putting dots in the area.

a The industry consists of many perfectly competitive firms.

b The industry is a single-price monopoly.

c The industry is a price-discriminating monopoly charging two prices: P_1 and P_3.

d The industry is a perfect price-discriminating monopoly.

FIGURE **12.7**

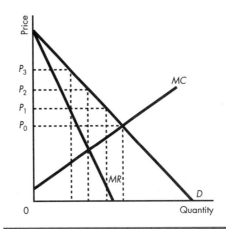

10 Before every Olympic Games, the International Olympic Committee (IOC) auctions off the rights to televise the Games to the highest bidder. NBC won the bid for the Summer 1996 Olympics, paying US$456 million. The television rights gave NBC a monopoly. Yet analysts (correctly) predicted that NBC would not make a profit. Their prediction was reasonable, since NBC failed to make a profit on similar telecasts of the 1988 and 1992 Olympics. The questions below will help to understand this apparent paradox.

a What kind of monopoly does NBC have?

b NBC earns revenue by selling airtime to commercial sponsors. Assume that NBC faces a normal, downward-sloping demand curve in selling 30-second commercial spots. Let's ignore for the moment the payment to the IOC and assume that marginal cost and average total cost of delivering the airtime are equal and constant. Draw a diagram representing NBC's profit-maximizing decision. Although you do not have enough information to calculate precise numbers, indicate generally the quantity of commercial spots sold and the price per commercial spot.

c On your diagram, indicate the area representing economic profit. If the analysts' predictions were correct, what is the value of this area?

d Why did NBC fail to realize this economic profit?

ANSWERS

True/False/Uncertain and Explain

1 F *MR* is negative. (263–264)
2 F Monopolist has no supply curve. (265–266)
3 U Monopoly no guarantee of profits if rent seeking is costly enough. (275–276)
4 T Demand curve gives revenue for each successive unit. (269–271)
5 F Can*not* be readily resold. (271)
6 T Area below competitive price and above *MC.* (273–274)
7 U True for perfect price-discriminating monopoly, false for all other monopoly. (273–275)
8 F Greater. Resources used in rent-seeking cost to society. (275–276)
9 F In equilibrium, economic profits may be totally eliminated by rent-seeking costs. (275–276)
10 T Advantages of monopoly. (276–277)

Multiple-Choice

1 b Others are legal barriers. (260–261)
2 d *TR* (*P* = $7) = $7 × 7 = $49. *TR* (*P* = $6) = $6 × 8 = $48. *MR* = Δ*TR* = $48 – $49. (261–263)
3 c See text discussion. Should ↓ output. Shutdown decision premature since monopolist can change price. (261–264)
4 d Others are advantages. Rent seeking diverts resources that could be used productively. (275–277)
5 c Monopoly profit = resources used rent seeking. (275–276)
6 c a, b irrelevant comparisons marginal and average quantities. d true *if TR* < *TVC.* (265–266)
7 b *Q* where *MR* = *MC.* Highest *P* consumers will pay for 3 units. (265–266)
8 c (*AR* – *ATC*) × *Q* = ($6 – $4) × 3. (265–266)
9 b c true for perfect price discrimination. (272–273)
10 b Area above price but below demand (willingness to pay). (273–274)
11 d Area below price but above *MC.* (273–274)
12 b Sum of lost producer (*bcd*) and consumer (*abd*) surplus compared to competitive outcome. (273–274)
13 e Deadweight loss is zero. (273–274)
14 d *MR* – *MC* comparisons are key. Revenue **a** and cost **b** are important, but must be *compared* for profitability. (265–266)
15 d Definition. (276–277)
16 a Draw graph. $Q_{current}$ > *Q* corresponding to *MR* = *MC.* (265–266)
17 d *TR* would be ↓ needlessly. Monopolist could ↓ *Q* and ↑ *P* to ↑ *TR.* (263–264)
18 d Same outcome as perfectly competitive industry, so **e** wrong. *D* = *MR* so **a** wrong. Profit maximizing so **b** wrong. (269–271)
19 c Shutdown rule same as perfect competition. (265–266)
20 d Sum of (*P* – *MC*) for each unit output. (273–274)
21 c Rule for choosing output. (265–266)
22 a Charge lower price with higher η and higher price with lower η. (268–271)
23 a Definition. Activity has costs. (275–276)
24 d **a** true for both. **b** true competitor only. **c** false for both. (265–266)
25 e Allocative efficiency same as perfect competition. (273–274)

Short Answer Problems

1 In order to sell an additional unit of output, a monopoly must drop the price. This has two effects on revenue: one positive and equal to price, and the other negative. Marginal revenue is the net effect, which must be less than price. First, the additional unit sold at the new lower price adds an amount to revenue equal to the price. But, a single-price monopoly must also lower the price to previous customers who would have paid more. The net effect on marginal revenue is equal to the price minus the loss of revenue from lowering the price to previous customers. This difference must necessarily be less than price.

2 A competitive industry will produce the level of output at which the industry marginal cost curve intersects the demand curve facing the industry. A single-price monopoly will produce at the level of output at which the industry marginal cost curve intersects the monopoly marginal revenue curve. Since the marginal revenue curve lies below the demand curve, this implies a lower level of output in the monopoly industry.

3 While the quantity sold and the price charged to the last customer are the same in the cases of perfect competition and a perfect price discriminator, the distribution of consumer surplus is not the same. Since a perfect price

discriminator charges each customer the most she is willing to pay, there is no consumer surplus. Any consumer surplus that would have occurred under perfect competition now accrues to the monopoly. Consumers would like to obtain more consumer surplus, and therefore pay less for the same amount. Consequently, consumers prefer perfect competition.

4 A monopoly would be more efficient than perfect competition if the monopoly has sufficient economies of scale and/or scope. Those economies must be large enough that the monopoly produces more than the competitive industry and sells it at a lower price. Figure 12.8 illustrates such a situation. The important feature is that the marginal cost curve for the monopoly must not only be lower than the supply curve of the competitive industry, but it must also be sufficiently lower so that it intersects the MR curve at an output greater than C (the competitive output). Such a situation could arise if there are extensive economies of scale and/or scope.

FIGURE **12.8**

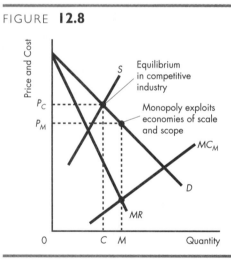

5 a Completed Table 12.2 is given here as Table 12.2 Solution.

TABLE **12.2** SOLUTION

Quantity	Total Variable Cost (TVC)	Total Cost (TC)	Marginal Cost (MC)	Average Variable Cost (AVC)	Average Total Cost (ATC)
9	135	247		15.00	27.44
			... 9		
10	144	256		14.40	25.60
			... 11		
11	155	267		14.09	24.27
			... 13		
12	168	280		14.00	23.33
			... 15		
13	183	295		14.08	22.69
			... 17		
14	200	312		14.29	22.29
			... 19		
15	219	331		14.60	22.07
			... 21		
16	240	352		15.00	22.00
			... 23		
17	263	375		15.47	22.06
			... 25		
18	288	400		16.00	22.22
			... 27		
19	315	427		16.58	22.47
			... 29		
20	344	456		17.20	22.80

b Completed Table 12.3 is shown here as Table 12.3 Solution.

TABLE **12.3**   SOLUTION

Price (P)	Quantity Demanded (Q_D)	Total Revenue (TR)	Marginal Revenue (MR)	Total Cost (TC)	Marginal Cost (MC)	Economic Profit (TR–TC)
57	9	513		247		266
			... 47		... 9	
56	10	560		256		304
			... 45		... 11	
55	11	605		267		338
			... 43		... 13	
54	12	648		280		368
			... 41		... 15	
53	13	689		295		394
			... 39		... 17	
52	14	728		312		416
			... 37		... 19	
51	15	765		331		434
			... 35		... 21	
50	16	800		352		448
			... 33		... 23	
49	17	833		375		458
			... 31		... 25	
48	18	864		400		464
			... 29		... 27	
47	19	893		427		466
			... 27		... 29	
46	20	920		456		464

Equilibrium output occurs where $MC = MR = 28$, $Q = 19$, $P = \$47$, economic profit = \$466 per day.

The profit-maximizing quantity of output occurs where marginal cost equals marginal revenue, at 19 units. The maximum price the firm can charge and still sell 19 units is \$47. This combination of quantity and price yields a total economic profit of \$466, which, as can be seen from the table, is the maximum possible profit.

c The requested diagram appears in Fig. 12.4 Solution.

FIGURE **12.4**   SOLUTION

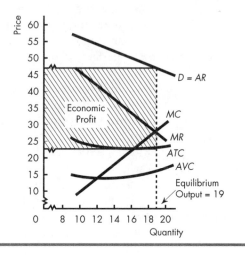

d Completed Table 12.4 is given here as Table 12.4 Solution.

TABLE **12.4**   SOLUTION

Price (P)	Quantity Demanded (Q_D)	Total Revenue (TR)	Marginal Revenue (MR)	Total Cost (TC)	Marginal Cost (MC)	Economic Profit (TR–TC)
24.50	9	220.50		247		−26.50
			... 19.50		... 9	
24.00	10	240.00		256		−16.00
			... 18.50		... 11	
23.50	11	258.50		267		−8.50
			... 17.50		... 13	
23.00	12	276.00		280		−4.00
			... 16.50		... 15	
22.50	13	292.50		295		−2.50
			... 15.50		... 17	
22.00	14	308.00		312		−4.00
			... 14.50		... 19	
21.50	15	322.50		331		−8.50
			... 13.50		... 21	
21.00	16	336.00		352		−16.00
			... 12.50		... 23	
20.50	17	348.50		375		−26.50
			... 11.50		... 25	
20.00	18	360.00		400		−40.00
			... 10.50		... 27	
19.50	19	370.50		427		−56.50
			... 9.50		... 29	
19.00	20	380.00		456		−76.00

Equilibrium output occurs where $MC = MR = 16$, $Q = 13$, $P = \$22.50$, economic profit = −\$2.50.

The profit-maximizing quantity of output occurs where marginal cost equals marginal revenue, now at 13 units. The maximum price the firm can charge and still sell 13 units is $22.50. This combination of quantity and price yields a total economic profit of –$2.50 (an economic loss). As can be seen from the table, this is the minimum possible loss. The firm will continue to produce in the short run because this loss is less than its shutdown loss which would be $112, the amount of its fixed cost.

e   The requested diagram appears in Fig. 12.5 Solution.

FIGURE **12.5**   SOLUTION

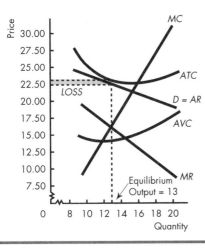

f   The requested diagram appears in Fig. 12.6 Solution. Since the demand curve is everywhere below the *AVC* curve, no matter what quantity of output the firm might produce, price will be less than *AVC*. This means that the firm will lose money on every unit produced in addition to losing its total fixed cost. The monopolist will minimize loss in this case by shutting down and losing just its fixed cost ($112).

FIGURE **12.6**   SOLUTION

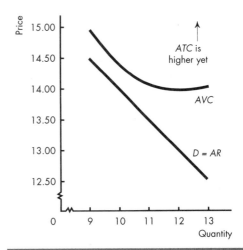

6 a   The monopolist will choose the quantity of output where marginal revenue equals marginal cost. To calculate this quantity, set the equation for marginal revenue equal to the equation for *industry* marginal cost (since the monopolist controls all of the firms).

$$36 - 0.02Q = -12 + 0.02Q$$
$$48 = .04Q$$
$$1,200 = Q$$

To calculate the price that the monopolist will charge, substitute the quantity 1,200 into the demand equation. This is the mathematical equivalent of graphically, after finding the quantity corresponding to the intersection of *MC* and *MR*, moving your eye up to the demand curve to read the price.

$$P = 36 - 0.01Q$$
$$P = 36 - 0.01(1,200)$$
$$P = 36 - 12$$
$$P = 24$$

b   The perfectly competitive industry's short-run equilibrium quantity of output occurs where industry demand intersects industry supply. Set the industry demand equation equal to the industry supply equation, which is the horizontal sum of the marginal cost curves of all the firms in the industry.

$$36 - 0.01Q = -12 + 0.02Q$$
$$48 = 0.03Q$$
$$1,600 = Q$$

To calculate the short-run equilibrium price for the industry, we can substitute the quantity 1,600 into either the industry demand equation or the industry supply equation.

Using the industry demand equation yields

$$P = 36 - 0.01Q$$
$$P = 36 - 0.01(1,600)$$
$$P = 36 - 16$$
$$P = 20$$

Using the industry supply equation yields the same result

$$P = -12 + 0.02Q$$
$$P = -12 + 0.02(1,600)$$
$$P = -12 + 32$$
$$P = 20$$

c If industry output is 1,600 units and there are 100 identical firms, then obviously the output per firm is 1,600 units/100 firms equals 16 units/firm. But the question specifically asks you not to use the information about industry output.

　　The other way to calculate the short-run equilibrium output per firm is to substitute the equilibrium price of 20 into the individual firm's marginal cost curve, which is also its short-run supply curve.

$$P = -12 + 2Q$$
$$20 = -12 + 2Q$$
$$32 = 2Q$$
$$16 = Q$$

d The monopoly price ($24) is higher than the perfect competition price ($20) and the monopoly quantity of output (1,200) is lower than the perfect competition quantity of output (1,600).

7 a The completed table is given in Table 12.5 Solution.

b The profit-maximizing output for stockbrokers occurs when $MC = \$2 = MR_{SB}$. This is at 3 lunches and the price is $5 per lunch to stockbrokers.

c The profit-maximizing output for senior citizens occurs when $MC = \$2 = MR_{SC}$. This occurs at 2 lunches and the price to senior citizens is $4 per lunch.

d Total revenue is $15 from stockbrokers and $8 from senior citizens, or $23. Since average total cost is $2 per lunch, total cost is $2 × 5 lunches = $10. Thus total economic profit is $13.

e If Barney served 1 additional lunch each to stockbrokers and senior citizens, that would make 4 lunches for stockbrokers (at $4 per lunch) and 3 lunches for senior citizens (at $3 per lunch). Since average total cost is $2 per lunch, the total cost is $2 × 7 lunches = $14. Total revenue is $16 from stockbrokers and $9 from senior citizens, or $25. Thus total economic profit is $11, less than the $13 in part d.

TABLE **12.5** SOLUTION

	Stockbrokers				Senior Citizens		
Price (P)	Quantity Demanded (Q_D)	Total Revenue (TR_{SB})	Marginal Revenue (MR_{SB})		Quantity Demanded (Q_D)	Total Revenue (TR_{SC})	Marginal Revenue (MR_{SC})
8	0	0			0	0	
			7				0
7	1	7			0	0	
			5				0
6	2	12			0	0	
			3				5
5	3	15			1	5	
			1				3
4	4	16			2	8	
			−1				1
3	5	15			3	9	
			−3				−1
2	6	12			4	8	
			−5				−3
1	7	7			5	5	
			−7				−5
0	8	0			6	0	

If Barney served 1 less lunch each to stockbrokers and senior citizens, that would make 2 lunches for stockbrokers (at $6 per lunch) and 1 lunch for senior citizens (at $5 per lunch). Since average total cost is $2 per lunch, the total cost is $2 × 3 lunches = $6. Total revenue is $12 from stockbrokers and $5 from senior citizens, or $17. Thus total economic profit is $11, less than the $13 in part **d**.

f The consumer surplus of stockbrokers is

$$($7 - $5) + ($6 - $5) + ($5 - $5) = $3.$$

The consumer surplus of senior citizens is

$$($5 - $4) + ($4 - $4) = $1.$$

The consumer surplus of all customers is

$$$3 + $1 = $4.$$

☉ 8 a The requested table is given as Table 12.6 Solution.

TABLE **12.6** SOLUTION

Price (P)	Quantity Demanded (Q_D)	Total Revenue (TR)	Marginal Revenue (MR)
8	0	0	
			········ 7
7	1	7	
			········ 5
6	2	12	
			········ 4
5	4	20	
			········ 2
4	6	24	
			········ 0
3	8	24	
			········ −2
2	10	20	
			········ −4
1	12	12	
			········ −6
0	14	0	

b The profit-maximizing output occurs when MC = $2 = MR$. This occurs halfway between a combination of 4 lunches at $5 per lunch, and 6 lunches at $4 per lunch. Either combination yields the same economic profit. Let's look at the combination of 6 lunches at $4 per lunch.

c Total revenue is $4 per lunch × 6 lunches = $24. Average total cost is $2 per lunch. Total cost is $2 × 6 lunches = $12. Thus total economic profit is $12.

Barney's economic profits as a single-price monopolist ($12) are less than his economic profits as a price-discriminating monopolist ($13).

d From the demand curves we can tell that there is 1 customer (stockbroker) who values lunch at $7, 1 customer (stockbroker) who values lunch at $6, 2 customers (stockbroker and senior) who value lunch at $5, and 2 customers (stockbroker and senior) who value lunch at $4. The consumer surplus for all customers is

$$1($7 - $4) + 1($6 - $4) + 2($5 - $4)$$
$$+ 2($4 - $4) = $7.$$

This consumer surplus without price discrimination ($7) is greater than consumer surplus with price discrimination ($4).

9 a Under perfect competition, price equals marginal cost. The amount of consumer surplus is given by the area under the demand curve but above the price (P_0) while the amount of producer surplus is given by the area above the MC curve but below the price; see Fig. 12.7 Solution (a).

b If the industry is a single-price monopoly, price will be greater than MC and output will be less than under competition. Consumer surplus is still given by the area under the demand curve but above the price (P_2), while producer surplus is given by the area above the MC curve but below the price up to the monopoly level of output. The remaining part of the large triangle is a deadweight loss since it is the amount of surplus under competition that is lost under a single-price monopoly; see Fig. 12.7 Solution (b).

c Similar reasoning allows us to establish regions in Fig. 12.7 Solution (c) corresponding to consumer surplus, producer surplus, and deadweight loss.

d Under perfect price discrimination, all of the potential surplus is captured by the producer and there is no deadweight loss (or consumer surplus). See Fig. 12.7 Solution (d).

FIGURE **12.7** SOLUTION

(a)

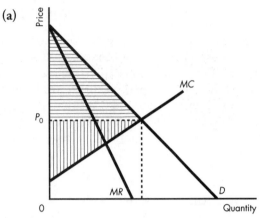

(b)

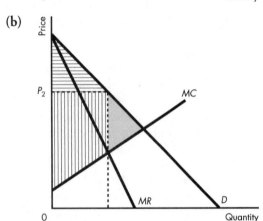

(c)

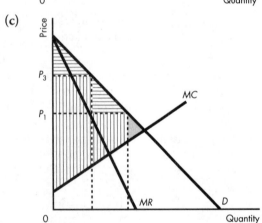

(d)

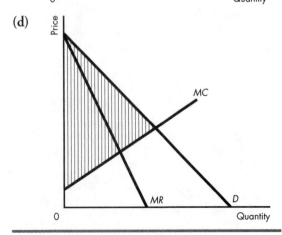

10 a NBC had a legal monopoly, based on a public franchise—an exclusive right granted to a firm to supply a good or service.

  b The requested diagram is shown in Fig. 12.9 Solution. The quantity of commercial spots sold is Q_{CS} and the price is P_{CS}.

FIGURE **12.9** SOLUTION

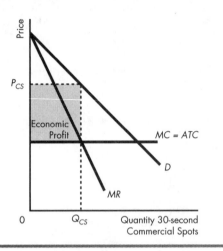

  c The shaded rectangle above ATC and below P_{CS} in Fig. 12.9 Solution represents economic profit. That profit, which is based on costs that exclude the US$456 payment to the IOC, will be US$456 if the analysts are correct.

  d NBC fails to make an economic profit because of the costs of rent seeking. NBC had to compete for the monopoly rights to televise the Olympics. It makes sense for bidders to continue to offer a higher price for those rights up to the point where the price of the rights equals the value of the economic profit to be earned from owning them.

Monopolistic Competition and Oligopoly

KEY CONCEPTS

Varieties of Market Structure

Market structure of most industries lies between extremes of perfect competition and monopoly.

◆ To evaluate competitiveness of a market, economists use two measures of industrial concentration:

- **Four-firm concentration ratio**—percentage of industry sales made by largest four firms.
- **Herfindahl–Hirschman Index (HHI)**—sum of squared market shares of 50 largest firms in industry.

◆ High concentration ratios usually → low degree competition.

◆ Problems with concentration ratios:
- national, but many industries local/international.
- no indication entry barriers.
- firms operate in other industries.

Monopolistic Competition

Monopolistic competition is market structure where many firms compete through **product differentiation**—making similar but slightly different products. This gives firms an element of monopoly power. There is free entry and exit.

◆ Implications
- Firm faces downward-sloping demand curve.
- Marginal revenue curve ≠ demand curve.
- Firm can choose price and output.

◆ Outcomes
- Profit maximization: choose Q where $MC = MR$, charge highest price (on demand curve).

- Short-run economic profits possible, attract entry → leftward shift demand curve facing each firm.
- Long-run economic profits = 0, $P = ATC$, ATC not minimum (*excess capacity*).
- Losses of ↓ allocative efficiency and high advertising expenditure must be weighed against gains of ↑ product variety, ↑ product innovation, and ↑ information to consumers.

Oligopoly

Oligopoly is market structure where few firms compete and *strategically interact*. Firm considers effects of its actions on behaviour of others and actions of others on its own profit.

◆ *Kinked demand curve model* assumes if firm ↑ price, no firms follow, and if firm ↓ price, all firms follow. Result is each firm faces kinked demand curve, with kink at current P, Q.

- Predictions: sticky prices—kink causes break in MR curve so MC curve can vary within break without affecting price or quantity.
- Problems: no indication how current P determined or how firms react if discover beliefs about demand curve incorrect.

◆ *Dominant firm oligopoly model* assumes one large firm with major cost advantage, many small firms.

- Predictions: large firm acts like monopoly, sets profit-maximizing price. Small firms take price, act like perfect competitors.
- Problems: no indication why large firm has cost advantage or what happens if small firms acquire low-cost technology.

Game Theory

Game theory analyses strategic behaviour. Games have

◆ Rules—specify permissible actions by players.

◆ **Strategies**—actions such as raising or lowering price, output, advertising, or product quality.

◆ Payoffs—profits and losses of players. **Payoff matrix** relates payoffs and strategies.

A "prisoners' dilemma" is a one-time, two-person game. Each player has a dominant strategy of cheating, that is, confessing. Concepts include

◆ *Dominant strategy*—unique best strategy independent of other player's action.

◆ **Dominant strategy equilibrium**—occurs when there is a dominant strategy for each player.

◆ **Nash equilibrium**—A takes best possible action given action B, and B takes best possible action given action A.

Oligopoly Game

Duopoly is a market structure with two firms.

◆ In a duopoly game, each firm can *comply* with a **collusive agreement** to restrict output and ↑ price, or it can *cheat*.

◆ A **cartel** is a group of firms in a collusive agreement.

◆ In a one-time game, a "prisoners' dilemma" solution occurs—each firm has the dominant strategy of cheating, even though both firms would be better off if they could trust each other and comply.

◆ In a repeated game, other strategies can create a **cooperative equilibrium** where each firm complies with the collusive agreement.

- A *tit-for-tat strategy* is taking the same action the other player took last period.
- A *trigger strategy* is cooperating until the other player cheats, and then cheating forever.

Game theory can be used to analyse other choices facing firms—how much to spend on research and development or on advertising, whether to enter or exit an industry, etc.

In a **contestable market** there are few firms but free entry and exit so existing firms face perfect competition from *potential* entrants. Existing firms may use strategies of

◆ An entry-deterrence game—set a competitive price and earn normal profit to keep out a potential competitor.

◆ **Limit pricing**—compared to monopoly outcome, ↓ price and ↑ quantity in order to deter entry.

HELPFUL HINTS

1 Most industries are neither perfectly competitive nor pure monopolies; they lie somewhere between these two extremes. This does not mean that the last two chapters have been wasted. By examining firms under these extreme market structures, we are now able to discuss the wide range of industries between them in just a single chapter.

  The intermediate forms of market structure share many of the characteristics of perfect competition and/or monopoly. Consider the profit-maximizing rule of choosing the output where $MC = MR$. The rule applies not only in perfect competition and monopoly, but also in monopolistic competition, kinked demand curve, and dominant firm oligopoly models. Free entry leads to zero long-run economic profits both in perfect competition and monopolistic competition. The downward-sloping demand and marginal revenue curves of monopoly also apply to monopolistic competition, kinked demand curve, and dominant firm oligopoly models.

  The extreme and unrealistic assumptions of models of perfect competition and monopoly allow us to isolate the impact of important forces like profit maximization and important constraints like competition and market demand. These forces and constraints also operate in more realistic market structures. But it was necessary to isolate these forces and constraints beforehand rather than attempt to immediately analyse "realistic" market structures like monopolistic competition and oligopoly, which would have been a confusing jumble of details and possible outcomes. It would have been like driving in a strange, large city without a road map.

2 In graphing a monopolistically competitive firm in long-run equilibrium, be sure that the ATC curve is tangent to the demand curve at the same level of output at which the MC and MR curves intersect. Also be sure that the MC curve intersects the ATC curve at the minimum point on the ATC curve.

3 This chapter uses elementary game theory to explain oligopoly. The prisoners' dilemma game illustrates the most important game theory concepts (rules, strategies, payoffs), which are then used in more complex game theory models like those of repeated games.

It is important to learn how to find the equilibrium of a prisoners' dilemma-type game. Take the example of players *A* and *B*, where each player has to choose between two strategies—confess or deny. First set up the payoff matrix. Then look at the payoff matrix from *A*'s point of view. *A* does not know if *B* is going to confess or deny, so *A* asks two questions: (1) Assuming that *B* confesses, do I get a better payoff if I confess or deny? (2) Assuming that *B* denies, do I get a better payoff if I confess or deny?

If *A*'s best strategy is to confess, regardless of whether *B* confesses or denies, confessing is *A*'s dominant strategy. Next, look at the payoff matrix from *B*'s point of view. Let *B* ask the equivalent two questions, and find *B*'s dominant strategy. The combination of *A*'s dominant strategy and *B*'s dominant strategy comprises the equilibrium outcome of the game.

4 The key insight of the prisoners' dilemma game is the *tension* between the equilibrium outcome (where both players' best strategy is to confess because they can't trust each other) and the fact that both players could make themselves better off if only they would cooperate. All of the equilibrium situations we have examined up until now have been stable outcomes where all agents' self-interests (utility and profit) have been maximized. Remember, equilibrium is defined as a situation where there is no tendency to change. The equilibrium of the prisoner's dilemma is different. Even though both players confess, their individual self-interests are *not* maximized. It is the additional possibility of *strategic interaction* (to trust or not trust the other player) that creates the instability of outcomes.

The instability of outcomes in this simple game helps us to understand more complex market phenomena such as gasoline price-wars. When gasoline station owners trust each other, prices remain relatively high and profits are maximized. But there is always an incentive to cheat on a collusive agreement. Once cheating begins, trust breaks down and the owners are driven to the equilibrium outcome where all owners cheat, prices fall, and profits are reduced. Eventually, the reduced profits lead the owners to take a chance on trusting each other again, since they figure it couldn't be worse than the existing low prices and profits. All stations raise their prices, and the cycle begins again. This instability of price and profit outcomes stems from the cycle of trust and not-trust. In other words, the instability arises from strategic interaction between station owners.

S E L F - T E S T

True/False/Uncertain and Explain

1 A high concentration ratio indicates a low degree of competition.

2 Product differentiation gives a monopolistically competitive firm some monopoly power.

3 Free entry is the key characteristic of monopolistic competition that produces excess capacity.

4 The kinked demand curve model predicts that price and quantity will be sensitive to small cost changes.

5 When a monopolistically competitive industry is in long-run equilibrium, economic profits are zero and price equals minimum average total cost.

6 Advertising by monopolistic competitors is allocatively inefficient.

7 An oligopolist will consider the reaction of other firms before it decides to cut its price.

8 A Nash equilibrium occurs when *A* takes the best possible action given the action of *B*, and *B* takes the best possible action given the action of *A*.

9 If duopolists agree to collude, they can (jointly) make as much profit as a single monopoly.

10 In the case of colluding duopolists, the dominant strategy equilibrium is for both firms to cheat.

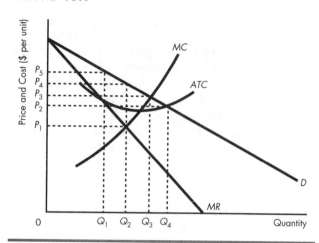

FIGURE **13.1**

Multiple-Choice

1 The four-firm concentration ratio measures the share of the largest four firms in total industry

a profits.
b sales.
c cost.
d capital.
e none of the above.

2 For a monopolistically competitive firm in long-run equilibrium,

a $P = MC$.
b $MC = ATC$.
c $AR = ATC$, but $P > MC$.
d $MC = AR$, but $ATC > AR$.
e none of the above is true.

3 Figure 13.1 represents a monopolistically competitive firm in short-run equilibrium. What is the firm's level of output?

a Q_1
b Q_2
c Q_3
d Q_4
e zero

4 Figure 13.1 represents a monopolistically competitive firm in short-run equilibrium. What is the firm's economic profit *per unit*?

a $P_4 - P_2$
b $P_4 - P_1$
c P_4
d P_3
e none of the above

5 Figure 13.1 represents a monopolistically competitive firm in short-run equilibrium. In the long run,

a new firms will enter, and each existing firm's demand shifts leftward.
b new firms will enter, and each existing firm's demand shifts rightward.
c existing firms will leave, and each remaining firm's demand shifts leftward.
d existing firms will leave, and each remaining firm's demand shifts rightward.
e there will be no change from the short run.

6 In the dominant firm model of oligopoly, the smaller firms act like

a oligopolists.
b monopolists.
c monopolistic competitors.
d perfect competitors.
e a cartel.

7 Which of the following is *not* an aspect common to all games?

a rules
b collusion
c strategies
d payoffs
e the analysis of strategic interaction

8 In the prisoners' dilemma with players Art and Bob, each prisoner would be best off if

a both prisoners confess.
b both prisoners deny.
c Art denies and Bob confesses.
d Bob denies and Art confesses.
e none of the above is done.

9 Limit pricing refers to

a the highest price a monopolist can set.
b a firm lowering its monopoly price to deter entry.
c a strategy used by entering firms in contestable markets.
d the price determined in a kinked demand curve model.
e none of the above.

10 Which of the following is *not* a problem with concentration ratios as a measure of industry competitiveness?

a Concentration ratios are national measures, but firms in some industries operate in regional markets.
b Concentration ratios are national measures, but firms in some industries operate in international markets.
c Concentration ratios tell us nothing about the severity of barriers to entry in the industry.
d Concentration ratios tell us nothing about how cost varies among firms in the industry.
e Concentration ratios have difficulty classifying multiproduct firms by industry.

11 Under monopolistic competition, long-run economic profits tend towards zero *because of*

a product differentiation.
b the lack of barriers to entry.
c excess capacity.
d inefficiency.
e the downward-sloping demand curve each firm faces.

12 Each of the following is a characteristic of monopolistic competition. Which is *not* a characteristic of oligopoly?

a Each firm faces a downward-sloping demand curve.
b Firms are profit-maximizers.
c The sales of one firm will not have a significant effect on other firms.
d There is more than one firm in the industry.
e Firms set prices.

13 If a duopoly with collusion maximizes profit,

a each firm must produce the same amount.
b each firm must produce its maximum output possible.
c industry marginal revenue must equal industry marginal cost at the level of total output.
d industry demand must equal industry marginal cost at the level of total output.
e total output will be greater than without collusion.

14 In the long run, a monopolistically competitive firm will earn the same economic profits as

a a monopolistically competitive firm in the short run.
b a member of a cartel.
c a pure price-discriminating monopolist.
d a perfectly competitive firm.
e none of the above.

15 The firms Trick and Gear form a cartel to collude to maximize profit. If this game is nonrepeated, the dominant strategy equilibrium is

a both firms cheat on the agreement.
b both firms comply with the agreement.
c Trick cheats, while Gear complies with the agreement.
d Gear cheats, while Trick complies with the agreement.
e indeterminate.

16 Consider the same cartel consisting of Trick and Gear. Now, however, the game is repeated indefinitely and each firm employs a tit-for-tat strategy. The equilibrium is

a both firms cheat on the agreement.
b both firms comply with the agreement.
c Trick cheats, while Gear complies with the agreement.
d Gear cheats, while Trick complies with the agreement.
e indeterminate.

17 The equilibrium in Question **16** is called a

a credible strategy equilibrium.
b dominant player equilibrium.
c duopoly equilibrium.
d trigger strategy equilibrium.
e cooperative equilibrium.

18 Which of the following is true for perfect competition, monopolistic competition, and single-price monopoly?

a   homogeneous product
b   zero long-run economic profits
c   short-run profit-maximizing quantity where $MC = MR$
d   easy entry and exit
e   none of the above

19 Which of the following statements about the sections of kinked demand curve in Fig. 13.2 is *correct*?

a   *AB* assumes new firms will enter the industry, while *BC* assumes no new firms will enter.
b   *AB* assumes no new firms will enter the industry, while *BC* assumes new firms will enter.
c   The kink between sections reflects market imperfections.
d   *AB* assumes other firms will match a price increase, while *BC* assumes other firms will not match a price decrease.
e   *AB* assumes other firms will not match a price increase, while *BC* assumes other firms will match a price decrease.

FIGURE **13.2**

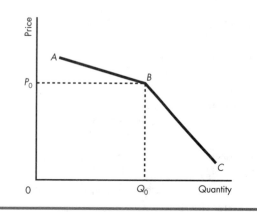

20 In the long run, the firm in monopolistic competition will

a   face a perfectly elastic demand curve.
b   produce more than the quantity that minimizes *ATC*.
c   produce less than the quantity that minimizes *ATC*.
d   produce the quantity that minimizes *ATC*.
e   earn economic profits.

21 Table 13.1 gives the payoff matrix in terms of profit for firms *A* and *B*, when there are two strategies facing each firm: (1) charge a low price or (2) charge a high price. The equilibrium in this game (played once) is a dominant strategy equilibrium since

a   firm *B* will reduce profit by more than *A* if both charge a lower price.
b   firm *B* is the dominant firm.
c   the best strategy for each firm does not depend on the strategy chosen by the other.
d   there is no credible threat by either firm to punish the other if it breaks the agreement.
e   all of the above are true.

TABLE **13.1**

		Firm B			
		Low Price		High Price	
	Low Price	A:	$2	A:	$20
		B:	$5	B:	−$15
Firm A					
	High Price	A:	−$10	A:	$10
		B:	$25	B:	$20

22 Refer to the nonrepeated game in Table 13.1. In equilibrium, what are firm *A*'s profits?

a   −$10
b $2
c $10
d $20
e   indeterminate.

23 Refer to the nonrepeated game in Table 13.1. If both firms could agree to collude, what would be firm *A*'s profits?

a   −$10
b $2
c $10
d $20
e   indeterminate.

24 In the long run, a monopolistically competitive firm will produce the output at which price equals

a   marginal cost.
b   marginal revenue.
c   average variable cost.
d   average total cost.
e   b and d.

25 Which of the following characteristics is *not* shared by single-price monopoly and monopolistic competition?

a firms face a downward-sloping demand curve
b profit-maximizing quantity where $MC = MR$
c equilibrium ATC above minimum ATC
d positive long-run economic profits
e positive long-run normal profits

Short Answer Problems

1 Considering the geographical scope of markets, how might a concentration ratio *understate* the degree of competitiveness in an industry? How might it *overstate* the degree of competitiveness?

2 Compare the advantages and disadvantages of perfect competition and monopolistic competition in terms of allocative efficiency.

3 Consider the case of two colluding duopolists in a nonrepeated game. In equilibrium, will the firms comply or cheat on the agreement? Explain why.

4 How can a price war that eliminates profits be explained using game theory?

5 Consider a single firm in a monopolistically competitive industry in the short run. Using axes like those shown in Fig. 13.3, draw a new graph for each of the following situations.

FIGURE **13.3**

a The firm is making an economic profit.
b The firm is making a loss that will cause shutdown.
c The firm is making a loss, but is still producing.
d Starting from the situation in part **c**, explain what will happen in this industry and how your graph in part **c** will be affected? (No new graph required.)
e The firm is in long-run equilibrium.

6 Consider a monopolistically competitive industry in long-run equilibrium. Firm *A* in this industry attempts to increase profits by advertising.

a On the graph in Fig. 13.4, show what will happen in the short run as a result of the decision to advertise. Briefly explain your graph.

FIGURE **13.4**

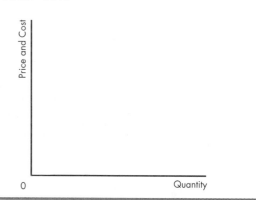

b If the firm is successful in raising profits in the short run, what will happen in the long run?

7 A small prairie town has two bakeries—Always Fresh and Never Stale. Transportation costs are high relative to the price of bread, so the bakeries do not get any out-of-town competition; the local bread industry is a duopoly. Always Fresh and Never Stale have the same cost curves, and each currently makes an annual profit of $2,000.

　Suppose that a new advertising service, Philomena's Flyers, starts up. If one bakery advertises in Philomena's Flyers, its annual profits will increase to $5,000, while the other bakery will lose $2,000. If both advertise, each will make a zero profit. If neither advertises, each bakery will continue to make an annual profit of $2,000.

a Represent this duopoly as a game by identifying the players, strategies, and possible outcomes.
b Construct the payoff matrix.
c What is the equilibrium outcome? Explain.

8 Figure 13.5(a) gives the identical average total cost (*ATC*) curve for Always Fresh and Never Stale. Figure 13.5(b) gives the town's market demand curve for bread and the firms' joint marginal cost curve. Suppose that the two bakeries collude to maximize profit and agree to divide output equally for a single year.

a How much will each bakery produce and what price per loaf will they charge?
b What is each bakery's average total cost and profit?

FIGURE **13.5**

(a) *ATC* Curve for Each Bakery

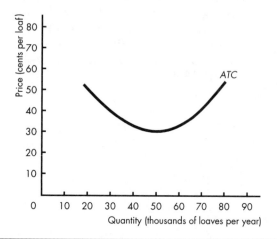

(b) Market Demand for Bread and Firm's Joint *MC* Curve

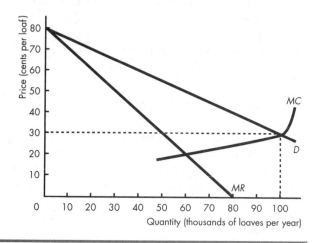

9 Now suppose that Never Stale convinces Always Fresh that demand has decreased and they must reduce their price by 10 cents per loaf in order to sell their agreed upon quantity. Of course, demand has *not* decreased, but Always Fresh produces its agreed amount and charges 10 cents less per loaf. Never Stale, the cheater, also charges 10 cents less than before, but increases output sufficiently to satisfy the rest of demand at this price.

a How many loaves of bread does Never Stale produce?

b What is Always Fresh's average total cost and profit?

c What is Never Stale's average total cost and profit?

10 Return to the initial situation. The firms are preparing to enter into a *long-term* collusive agreement. Always Fresh credibly assures Never Stale that if Never Stale cheats, Always Fresh will undercut Never Stale's price as soon as the cheating is discovered. Would Never Stale want to cheat on the agreement now? Why or why not?

ANSWERS

True/False/Uncertain and Explain

1 U Often true, but depends on geographical scope market, barriers to entry, and multimarket firms. (286–289)

2 T Creates downward-sloping demand curve. (290–291)

3 F Product differentiation → downward-sloping demand. (291–292)

4 F Insensitive to small cost changes. (293–294)

5 F Zero profits, but *P* > minimum *ATC*. (290–292)

6 U Depends on information content advertising and gains from ↑ product variety. (292–293)

7 T Oligopoly involves strategic behaviour. (293, 296)

8 T Definition. (297–298)

9 T With collusion, they act exactly like monopoly. (300–301)

10 U True for nonrepeated game but may be false for repeated game. (303–305)

Multiple-Choice

1 b Definition. (286–287)

2 c Demand curve (*AR* = *P*) tangent to *ATC* and above *MC*. (290–291)

3 b Where *MC* = *MR*. (290–291)

4 a At Q_2, *AR* – *ATC*. (290–291)

5 a With new entrants, industry demand divided among more firms so each firm's demand curve shifts left. (290–291)

6 d Dominant firm sets price, smaller firms take that price as given. (294–295)

7 b No collusion in prisoners' dilemma. (296–298)

8 b But doesn't happen because players cannot trust each other enough to collude. (296–298)

9 b Definition. **c** would be true for *existing* firms. (308–309)

10 d Concentration ratios do not attempt to measure cost. (286–289)

11 b **a** and **e** → possibility profits, **c** and **d** are outcomes, not forces → zero profits. (290–292)

12 c Oligopoly involves interdependence between firms. (290–293)

13 c See Text Fig.13.6(b). (298–301)

14 d Zero economic profits. (290–292)

15 a Similar to prisoners' dilemma outcome. (302–304)

16 b Cooperative equilibrium; each player responds rationally to credible threat of other. (304–305)

17 e Definition. (304–305)

18 c **b** and **d** false for monopoly. **a** false for monopolistic competition. (290–293)

19 e *AB* more elastic than *BC* because price changes unmatched. (293–294)

20 c Excess capacity at *Q* where demand tangent to downward slope *ATC*. (290–292)

21 c Definition of dominant strategy equilibrium. (302–304)

22 b Both firms charge low price. (302–304)

23 c Both firms charge high price. (302–304)

24 d Where demand curve tangent to *ATC*. (290–291)

25 d Zero long-run economic profits for monopolistic competition. (290–293)

Short Answer Problems

1 Concentration ratios are calculated from a national geographical perspective. If the actual scope of the market is not national, the concentration ratio will likely misstate the degree of competitiveness in an industry. If the actual market is global, the concentration ratio will understate the degree of competitiveness. A firm may have a concentration ratio of 100 as the only producer in the nation, but may face a great deal of international competition. When the scope of the market is regional, the concentration ratio will overstate the degree of competitiveness. The concentration ratio includes firms elsewhere in the nation that are not real competitors in the region.

2 The advantage of perfect competition is that it leads to production at minimum average total cost, while monopolistic competition leads to a higher average total cost due to reduced output and high advertising expenditures.

The advantage of monopolistic competition is that it leads to greater product variety, which consumers value, while in a perfectly competitive

industry there is a single, identical product produced by all firms. Monopolistic competition also leads to greater product innovation and, as a positive by-product of greater advertising, valuable information to consumers. Thus the loss in allocative efficiency and greater advertising costs (higher *ATC*) that occur in monopolistic competition have to be weighed against the gains of greater product variety, greater product innovation, and more valuable information provided to consumers.

3 Each firm's best strategy is to cheat regardless of the strategy of the other firm. Call the firms *A* and *B*. Firm *A* knows that if firm *B* follows the collusive agreement, *A* can increase its profit by cheating. If firm *B* cheats, then firm *A* knows that it must also cheat to minimize its loss of profit. Thus cheating is the dominant strategy for firm *A*. Accordingly, it is also the dominant strategy for firm *B*.

4 Game theory explains price wars as the consequence of firms in a colluding industry responding to the cheating of a firm. If one firm cheats by cutting its price, then all other firms will cut their prices, and a price war will ensue. Once the price has fallen sufficiently (perhaps to the zero profit level), the firms will again have a strong incentive to rebuild their collusion.

5 a Figure 13.3 Solution (a) illustrates a monopolistically competitive firm making an economic profit in the short run. The important feature of the graph is that at the profit-maximizing output, price is greater than average total cost. The economic profit is indicated by the shaded area.

FIGURE **13.3** SOLUTION (a)

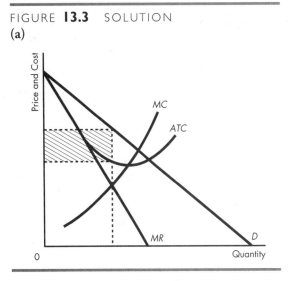

b Figure 13.3 Solution (b) illustrates a firm that will shut down in the short run since price is less than average variable cost at the profit-maximizing (loss-minimizing) level of output.

FIGURE **13.3** SOLUTION
(b)

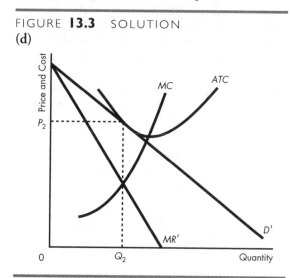

c Figure 13.3 Solution (c) illustrates a firm making a loss but continuing to produce. The loss is indicated by the shaded area. Note that, at the profit-maximizing output, price is less than ATC but greater than AVC.

FIGURE **13.3** SOLUTION
(c)

d Since firms are typically experiencing a loss, firms will leave the industry. This means that the demand curves facing each of the remaining firms will begin to shift rightward as they each attract some of the customers of the departing firms. As the firms' demand curves shift rightward, losses are reduced. Firms will continue to have an incentive to leave until losses have been eliminated. Thus firms' demand curves will continue to shift until they are tangent to the ATC curve.

e Figure 13.3 Solution (d) illustrates a typical monopolistically competitive firm in long-run equilibrium. The key feature is that the demand curve facing the firm is tangent to the ATC curve at the profit-maximizing output. Thus the firm is making a zero economic profit.

FIGURE **13.3** SOLUTION
(d)

6 a Advertising will increase firm A's cost, but also increase demand (it hopes). If the increase in demand (revenue) is greater than the increase in cost, then firm A will have increased its profit. Figure 13.4 Solution illustrates this situation. The initial curves are given by D_0, ATC_0, and MR_0.

  Initially the firm is producing Q_0 and selling at price P_0 and making zero economic profit. Advertising, which is a fixed cost, raises the ATC curve to ATC_1 (MC does not shift), but also increases the demand and marginal revenue curves to D_1 and MR_1, respectively. The shift in the demand curve is sufficiently great that there is now a positive economic profit at the new profit-maximizing level of output (Q_1). The economic profit is indicated by the shaded area.

FIGURE **13.4**   SOLUTION

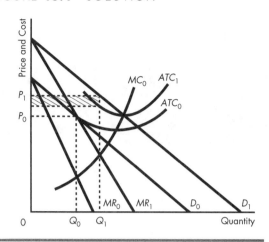

b No doubt other firms will also begin to advertise in an attempt to increase their profit (or recover lost profit). As all other firms advertise, the demand curve for our firm will shift back to the left as it loses some of the customers it has gained. In the long run, once again, all firms will be making zero profit even after advertising.

7 a The players are Always Fresh and Never Stale. Each firm has two strategies: to advertise or not to advertise. There are four possible outcomes: (1) both firms advertise, (2) Always Fresh advertises but Never Stale does not, (3) Never Stale advertises but Always Fresh does not, and (4) neither firm advertises.

b The payoff matrix is given in Table 13.2. The entries give the profit earned by Always Fresh (*AF*) and Never Stale (*NS*) under each of the four possible outcomes.

TABLE **13.2**

		Never Stale	
		Advertise	Not Advertise
Always Fresh	Advertise	*AF*: 0 *NS*: 0	*AF*: $5,000 *NS*: −$2,000
	Not Advertise	*AF*: −$2,000 *NS*: $5,000	*AF*: $2,000 *NS*: −$2,000

c First, consider how Always Fresh decides which strategy to pursue. If Never Stale advertises, Always Fresh can advertise and make zero profit or not advertise and make a $2,000 loss. Thus Always Fresh will want to advertise if Never Stale does.

 If Never Stale does not advertise, Always Fresh can advertise and make a $5,000 profit or not advertise and make a $2,000 profit.

Therefore Always Fresh will want to advertise whether Never Stale advertises or not. Never Stale will come to the same conclusion. The dominant strategy equilibrium is that both firms advertise.

8 a The firms will agree to produce 30,000 loaves each and sell at a price of 50 cents per loaf. We determine this by noticing (Fig. 13.5b) that the profit-maximizing (monopoly) output is 60,000 loaves for the industry ($MR = MC$ at 60,000) and the industry price is 50 cents per loaf. Since the firms have agreed to divide output equally, each will produce 30,000 loaves.

b From Fig. 13.5(a) we determine that, at 30,000 loaves, each firm's average total cost is 40 cents per loaf. Since price is 50 cents per loaf, profit will be $3,000 for each firm.

9 a At the new price of 40 cents per loaf, the total quantity demanded is 80,000 loaves. Since Always Fresh continues to produce 30,000 loaves, this means that Never Stale will produce the remaining 50,000 loaves demanded.

b Since Always Fresh continues to produce 30,000 loaves, its average total cost continues to be 40 cents per loaf. With the new price also at 40 cents, Always Fresh will make a zero economic profit.

c Never Stale has increased output to 50,000 loaves, which implies average total cost of 30 cents per loaf. Thus, given a price of 40 cents, Never Stale's economic profit will be $5,000.

10 Given that the agreement is long term, Never Stale would almost surely not cheat. The reason is that, while Never Stale could increase short-term profit by cheating, it would lose much more future profit if Always Fresh retaliates.

 The key point is that Never Stale's behaviour changes, not because cost or demand have changed, but rather because Always Fresh's behaviour has changed. In duopoly and oligopoly, the best strategy for any firm depends on the behaviour of other firms.

PROBLEM

FIGURE **P2.1**

(a) Industry

(b) Firm

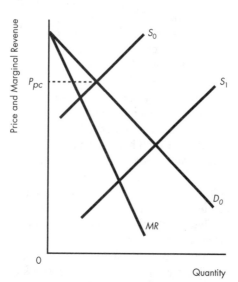

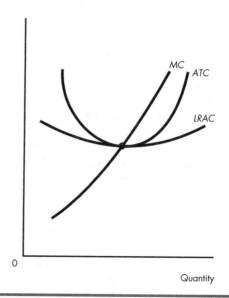

Despite significant differences between perfect competition, monopoly, and monopolistic competition, all of these market structures can be analysed using the diagrams in Fig. P2.1.

Figure P2.1(a) shows an industry in short-run equilibrium at the intersection of the demand (D_0) and supply (S_0) curves. Ignore for the moment the other supply curve (S_1) and the marginal revenue curve (MR). Long-run market demand is the same as short-run market demand. There are no external economies or diseconomies. Figure P2.1(b) shows the cost curves of one of the many identical firms in the industry.

Let's first suppose this is a perfectly competitive (pc) industry.

a   Describe the demand curve facing an individual firm; describe the marginal revenue curve.

b   On Fig. P2.1, identify and label the industry short-run equilibrium price (P_{pc}) [this is a giveaway!], output (Q_{pc}), and individual firm output (q_{pc}). Is each individual firm making a profit or loss? Explain.

c   What happens in the long run? On Fig. P2.1, identify and label the industry long-run equilibrium price (P^{LR}_{pc}), output (Q^{LR}_{pc}), and individual firm ouput (q^{LR}_{pc}).

Now suppose that the market in Fig. P2.1(a) is supplied by a single-price monopolist (*m*) with a legal monopoly. S_1 is the monopolist's marginal cost curve. Ignore S_0 and part (b) of the figure.

d Describe the demand curve facing the monopolist; describe the supply curve of the monopolist.
e On Fig. P2.1(a), identify and label the industry short-run equilibrium price (P_m) and output (Q_m).
f At Q_m, if the monopolist's average total cost is less than P_m, explain what happens in the long run. On Fig. P2.1(a), identify and label the industry long-run equilibrium price (P^{LR}_m) and output (Q^{LR}_m).
g Compare the long-run allocative efficiency of this industry under monopoly versus under perfect competition. Identify any deadweight loss on the appropriate figure.

Finally, suppose that the industry in Fig. P2.1(a) is supplied by many monopolistically competitive (*mc*) firms. The industry supply curve is S_0, and at price P_{pc} each firm is in long-run equilibrium. Ignore S_1 and *MR*. Each firm has the cost curves in Fig. P2.1(b), but produces a slightly differentiated product.

h Describe the demand curve facing an individual firm and draw it on Fig. P2.1(b).
i On Fig. P2.1(b), identify and label the long-run output (q_{mc}) for an individual monopolistically competitive firm. Describe one point that you can identify precisely on the marginal revenue curve facing an individual firm. Explain why this is a long-run equilibrium.
j Compare the long-run allocative efficiency of this industry under monopolistic competition versus under perfect competition. What consideration must be taken into account that is not taken into account for a monopoly?

MIDTERM EXAMINATION

You should allocate 56 minutes for this examination (28 questions, 2 minutes per question). For each question, choose the one *best* answer.

1 Marginal utility equals
a total utility divided by price.
b total utility divided by the total number of units consumed.
c the slope of the total utility curve.
d the inverse of total utility.
e the area below the demand curve but above market price.

2 A consumer maximizes his utility by purchasing 2 units of good *X* at $5/unit and 3 units of good *Y* at $7/unit. What is the ratio of the marginal utility of *X* to the marginal utility of *Y*?
a 5/7
b 7/5
c 2/3
d 3/2
e 10/21

3 The supply curve for a single-price monopoly is
a its marginal cost curve.
b its marginal cost curve above minimum average variable cost.
c its average variable cost curve.
d its marginal revenue curve.
e none of the above.

4 A successful price-discriminating firm must be able to
a prevent consumer resale.
b differentiate consumers with high price elasticity of demand and charge them low prices.
c differentiate consumers with low price elasticity of demand and charge them high prices.
d do all of the above.
e do none of the above.

5 The marginal cost curve slopes upward because of
a diminishing marginal utility.
b diminishing marginal returns.
c technological inefficiency.
d economic inefficiency.
e none of the above.

6 In economics, the long run is a time period in which
a one year or more elapses.
b all inputs are variable.
c all inputs are fixed.
d there is at least one fixed input and at least one variable input.
e all inputs are variable but plant size is fixed.

7 Suppose good X is measured on the horizontal axis and good Y on the vertical axis. The marginal rate of substitution is best defined as the

a relative price of good X in terms of good Y.
b relative price of good Y in terms of good X.
c rate at which a consumer will give up good Y in order to obtain more of good X and remain indifferent.
d rate at which a consumer will give up good X in order to obtain more of good Y and remain indifferent.
e slope of the budget line.

8 When the price of a good changes, the change in consumption that leaves the consumer indifferent is called the

a utility effect.
b substitution effect.
c income effect.
d price effect.
e inferior effect.

9 Figure P2.2 represents a monopolistically competitive firm in short-run equilibrium. What is the firm's price?

a P_1
b P_2
c P_3
d P_4
e P_5

FIGURE **P2.2**

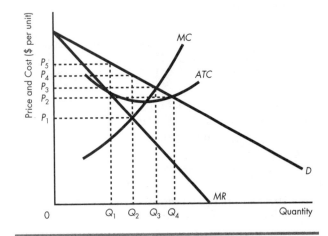

10 Figure P2.2 represents a monopolistically competitive firm in short-run equilibrium. In the long run, what is the firm's economic profit *per unit*?

a $P_4 - P_2$
b $P_4 - P_1$
c P_3
d P_2
e none of the above

11 For a single-price monopolist, which of the following statements is *false*?

a There is no unique one-to-one relationship between price and quantity supplied.
b For any output greater than zero, $MR < AR$.
c The industry demand curve is the monopolist's demand curve.
d The intersection of MR and MC provides all information necessary for identifying the profit-maximizing quantity and price.
e Total revenue is at a maximum where $MR = 0$.

12 A single-price monopoly never operates

a on an elastic portion of the demand curve.
b on a portion of the demand curve that is unit elastic.
c on an inelastic portion of the demand curve.
d at a quantity where marginal revenue is positive since total revenue is not at a maximum.
e under any of the above conditions.

13 Shelley is maximizing her utility in her consumption of mink coats and Porsches. If the marginal utility of her last purchased mink coat is twice the marginal utility of her last purchased Porsche, then we know with certainty that

a Shelley buys twice as many mink coats as Porsches.
b Shelley buys twice as many Porsches as mink coats.
c Shelley buys more Porsches than mink coats, but we do not know how many more.
d the price of a mink coat is twice the price of a Porsche.
e the price of a Porsche is twice the price of a mink coat.

14 The difference between the value of a good and its price is known as

a excess demand.
b excess supply.
c consumer surplus.
d consumer excess.
e marginal utility.

15 If the present value of 100 received one year from now is $80, what is the annual interest rate?

a   50 percent
b   10 percent
c   20 percent
d   25 percent
e   8 percent

16 A firm has $200 in explicit costs and sells the resulting output for $250. The normal rate of profit is 10 percent. Which of the following statements is *true?*

a   Implicit costs are $25.
b   Economic profits are $20.
c   Economic profits are $50.
d   Economic profits exceed accounting profits.
e   Explicit costs exceed implicit costs.

17 In a perfectly competitive industry of 100 firms, the demand curve facing the individual firm

a   has unitary elasticity.
b   is identical to the industry demand curve.
c   is 1/100 of the industry demand curve.
d   is one where $AR = MR$.
e   is none of the above.

18 If economic profits are being made by firms in a competitive industry, new firms will enter. This will shift

a   the industry demand curve to the left, causing market price to fall.
b   the industry demand curve to the right, causing market price to rise.
c   the industry supply curve to the left, causing market price to rise.
d   the industry supply curve to the right, causing market price to fall.
e   none of the above curves.

19 A change in income changes which aspect(s) of the budget equation?

a   slope and *y*-intercept
b   slope and *x*-intercept
c   *x*- and *y*-intercepts but not slope
d   slope only
e   none of the above

20 When the price of a normal good rises, the income effect

a   increases consumption of the good and the substitution effect decreases consumption.
b   decreases consumption of the good and the substitution effect increases consumption.
c   and the substitution effect both increase consumption of the good.
d   and the substitution effect both decrease consumption of the good.
e   is always larger than the substitution effect.

21 If *AFC* is falling then *MC* must be

a   rising.
b   falling.
c   above *AFC.*
d   below *AFC.*
e   none of the above.

22 If all inputs are increased by 10 percent and output increases by more than 10 percent, it must be the case that

a   average total cost is decreasing.
b   average total cost is increasing.
c   the *LRAC* curve is positively sloped.
d   there are increasing returns to scale.
e   there are decreasing returns to scale.

23 In Table P2.1, which method(s) of making a medical hologram is/are technologically efficient?

a   1
b   2
c   3
d   all of the above
e   1 and 3 only

TABLE **P2.1**   THREE METHODS OF MAKING ONE MEDICAL HOLOGRAM

	Quantities of Inputs	
Method	Labour	Capital
1	5	10
2	10	15
3	15	5

24 Refer to Table P2.1. If the price of labour is $20 per unit and the price of capital is $10 per unit, which method(s) is/are economically efficient?

a   1
b   2
c   3
d   2 and 3 only
e   1 and 3 only

25 The kinked demand curve model

a suggests that price will remain constant even with fluctuations in demand.

b suggests how the current price is determined.

c assumes that marginal revenue sometimes increases with output.

d assumes that competitors will match price cuts and ignore price increases.

e suggests none of the above.

26 In the prisoners' dilemma with players Art and Bob, the dominant strategy equilibrium is

a both prisoners confess.

b both prisoners deny.

c Art denies and Bob confesses.

d Bob denies and Art confesses.

e indeterminate.

27 In a perfectly competitive industry, the market price is $5. An individual firm is producing the level of output at which marginal cost is $5 and is increasing, and average total cost is $25. What should the firm do to maximize its short-run profits?

a shut down

b expand output

c contract output

d leave output unchanged

e insufficient information to answer

28 The long-run competitive industry supply curve will be positively sloped if there are

a external economies.

b external diseconomies.

c no external economies or diseconomies.

d external costs.

e external benefits.

ANSWERS

Problem

a The individual firm's demand curve and marginal revenue curve is a horizontal line at P_{pc}.

b See Fig. P2.1(b) Solution. Each firm is making economic profits because at output q_{pc}, price (P_{pc} = average revenue) is greater than average total cost.

c See Fig. P2.1 Solution. In response to economic profits, new firms enter the industry, causing the industry supply curve to shift rightward until it reaches S_1. When the price has fallen to P^{LR}_{pc}, economic profits have been eliminated and each firm is earning normal profits only.

d The monopolist's demand curve is the industry demand curve D_0. The monopolist does not have a supply curve since she can choose a combination of price and quantity.

e See Fig. P2.1(a) Solution.

FIGURE **P2.1** SOLUTION

(a) Industry

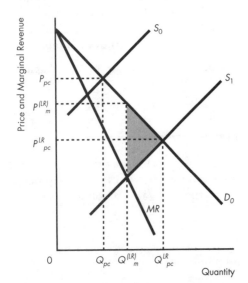

(b) Firm

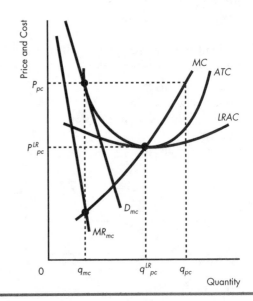

f Even though the monopolist is earning economic profits, nothing happens in the long run because legal barriers prevent new entry. Long-run equilibrium price and output are the same as short-run price (P_m) and output (Q_m).

g Monopoly is less efficient than perfect competition, by the shaded area of deadweight loss indicated on Fig. P2.1(a) Solution.

h See Fig. P2.1(b) Solution. Since the firm is in long-run equilibrium, the downward-sloping demand curve must be tangent to the ATC curve at the equilibrium price P_{pc}.

i See Fig. P2.1 Solution. A profit-maximizing firm chooses the output (q_{mc}) where MC intersects MR. Hence the MR curve must intersect MC at q_{mc}. This is a long-run equilibrium because the firm is earning zero economic profits, so there is no incentive for entry or exit.

j Under monopolistic competition, ATC is higher (P_{pc}) than under perfect competition (P^{LR}_{pc}), implying less efficiency. However, the loss in allocative efficiency of monopolistic competition must be weighed against the gain in increased product variety.

Midterm Examination

1 c $MU = \Delta$ total utility/Δ quantity. (150–151)

2 a Quantities irrelevant. Ratios MUs must be = ratio prices. (152–154)

3 e Monopoly has no supply curve. (265–266)

4 d See text discussion. (271)

5 b $\downarrow$ marginal returns = $\downarrow MP \rightarrow \uparrow MC$. (216–219)

6 b Definition. All inputs and plant size variable. (211)

7 c Definition. **a** and **b** relate to slope budget line. MRS = **e** only at best affordable point. (173–179)

8 b Definition. (179–181)

9 d Highest possible price to sell Q_2. (290–292)

10 e Long-run economic profit per unit = zero. (290–292)

◑11 d Need demand curve to identify price. (265–266)

12 c If demand is inelastic $\rightarrow MR < 0$. But MR must always be > 0 to intersect (positive) MC. (263–264)

13 d From maximum condition of equal MU/P. No necessary relation between MU and quantity. (152–154)

14 c Definition. (160–161)

15 d $\$80 = \$100/(1 + r)$. Solve for r. (194–196)

16 e Implicit costs = .10 ($\$200$) = $\$20$; economic profits = $\$25$; accounting profits = $\$50$. (196–198)

17 d Horizontal at market price. Infinite elasticity. (234–235)

18 d Economic profits/losses signal for supply shifts. Profits $\rightarrow$ entry new firms. (243–244)

◑19 c See Chapter 8 Helpful Hint **2**. Δ income (y) does not change slope (P_m/P_p) but does Δ intercepts (y/P_m) and (y/P_p). (170–171)

20 d Both work in same direction. $\uparrow P \rightarrow \downarrow$ consumption. (179–181)

21 e AFC always $\downarrow$; no necessary relation to MC. See Text Fig. 10.5(b). (216–219)

22 d Definition. Since all inputs variable, **a** and **b** irrelevant. (222–225)

23 e 2 uses more labour and more capital than 1. (200–201)

24 a 1 costs $\$200$ while 2 and 3 cost $\$350$. (200–201)

25 d **a** true if fluctuation in MC. MR always $\downarrow$ with $\uparrow Q$ so **c** false. (293–294)

26 a Outcome of game. (296–298)

◑27 e Firm at Q where $P = MC$, but losing $ since $AR < ATC$. Need AVC information to determine if **a** or **d** correct. (238–239)

28 b $\uparrow$ costs as industry $Q \uparrow$ (247–248).

Chapter 14

Pricing and Allocating Factors of Production

Factor Prices and Incomes

Firms hire the *services* of factors of production (labour, capital, land, entrepreneurship) to produce output.

◆ Demand and supply in factor markets for labour, capital, and land determine those factor prices (PF) (wages, interest, rent) and quantities (QF).

 • Factor income = ($PF \times QF$).
 • The factor price for entrepreneurship is normal profit. Economic profit/loss is a residual income going to a firm's owners.

◆ ↑ demand for factor → ↑ PF, ↑ QF, and ↑ income.
 ↓ demand for factor → ↓ PF, ↓ QF, and ↓ income.

◆ ↑ supply of factor → ↓ PF, ↑ QF, and ↑ income if $\eta_D > 1$; ↓ income if $\eta_D < 1$.

◆ ↓ supply of factor → ↑ PF, ↓ QF, and ↓ income if $\eta_D > 1$; ↑ income if $\eta_D < 1$.

Demand for Factors

Demand for factors is a **derived demand**, stemming from firms' profit-maximizing objective and technology and market constraints.

◆ **Marginal revenue product** (*MRP*) is extra revenue from employing one more unit of factor.

 • $MRP = MP \times MR$
 • For a perfectly competitive firm, $MR = P$ output. So $MRP = MP$ (additional output produced by employing additional unit of a factor) $\times P$ output.

◆ Profit-maximizing firm hires additional units of factor up to point where $MRP = PF$. For labour (L), this is where MRP_L = wage rate.

◆ Firm's demand curve for factor is identical to the marginal revenue product curve of the factor.

◆ Firm's demand curve for labour shifts right if

 • ↑ P output.
 • ↑ price other inputs.
 • technological change ↑ MP labour.

◆ Market demand curve for labour—sum of quantities of labour demanded by all firms at each wage rate.

$$\text{Elasticity of demand for labour} = \left| \frac{\% \, \Delta \text{ quantity labour demanded}}{\% \, \Delta \text{ wage rate}} \right|$$

Demand for labour will be *more elastic*

◆ when production is more labour-intensive (wages a greater percentage of total cost)

◆ the slower the MP labour diminishes

◆ the greater the elasticity of demand for the final product

◆ the greater the substitutability of capital for labour in the long run

Supply of Factors

Supply of labour determined by households' decisions of allocating time between **market activity** (work) and **nonmarket activity** (leisure, nonmarket production).

◆ At wage rates above household's **reservation wage**, household supplies labour.

◆ *Substitution effect* from ↑ wage → ↑ quantity labour supplied.

◆ *Income effect* from ↑ wage → ↓ quantity labour supplied.

◆ When wage ↑, quantity labour supplied ↑ when substitution effect > income effect.

♦ Individual household labour supply curve bends backward when income effect > substitution effect.

♦ Market supply of labour curve is horizontal sum of all household supply curves. Upward sloping on normal range of wage rates.

Supply of capital determined by households' saving decisions. Households supply *financial capital* that firms use to buy physical capital goods.

♦ Quantity of financial capital supplied ↑ when

  • current income > expected future income.
  • interest rates ↑.

♦ Market supply of capital curve is horizontal sum of all household supply curves. Short-run supply is inelastic. Long-run supply is more elastic.

♦ To an individual firm, short-run supply of capital is fixed. Long-run supply is perfectly elastic.

Supply of land is fixed and perfectly inelastic. But to an individual firm, supply of land is elastic.

Incomes, Economic Rent, and Transfer Earnings

Economic rent is income received by factor owner *above* amount required to induce supply. Income required to induce supply is **transfer earnings**. Transfer earnings are the opportunity cost of using a factor.

♦ Income consists of transfer earnings (area under supply curve) and economic rent (area above supply curve but below factor price).

♦ The more inelastic the supply of a factor, the greater the proportion of its income that is economic rent.

♦ Distinction between *rent* (price paid to factor of production, land) and *economic rent* (component of income of almost every factor production).

HELPFUL HINTS

1 This chapter gives a broad overview of the characteristics that are common to all markets for factors of production. For example, the assumption that firms are profit-maximizers implies that they will hire each factor of production up to the point where marginal revenue product is equal to the marginal cost of the factor, regardless of whether the factor of production is labour, land, or capital.

2 Distinguish carefully between the marginal revenue product of a factor of production and the marginal revenue of a unit of output. As noted in the text, the marginal revenue product of a factor of production can be calculated by multiplying marginal revenue and marginal product ($MRP = MR \times MP$). We can think of this intuitively as follows: marginal product tells us how much more output we receive from using more of a factor, and marginal revenue tells us how much more revenue we receive from selling each unit of that additional output. Therefore MP times MR tells us how much more revenue we receive from using more of the factor (the MRP).

3 The most important graph in this chapter appears in Text Fig. 14.4, reproduced here as Fig. 14.1. Using the example of Max's Wash 'n' Wax, the figure demonstrates that a firm's demand for labour curve is the same as its marginal revenue product curve of labour.

FIGURE **14.1**

(a)

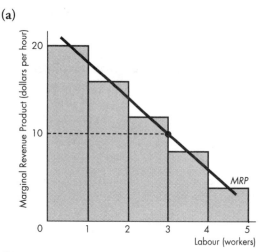

(b)

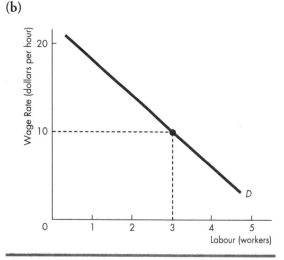

Part (a) of the figure shows the marginal revenue product curve (*MRP*) that is based on the numbers in Text Table 14.1 on page 324. Notice that the values for *MRP* are plotted midway between the labour inputs used in their calculation. For example, the *MRP* of moving from 0 to 1 labourer is 20, so the value of 20 on the *MRP* curve is plotted midway between 0 and 1 labourers.

Part (b) constructs Max's demand for labour by asking how much labour Max would be willing to hire at alternative wage rates. Since Max is a profit-maximizer, he will want to hire labour up to the point where the marginal revenue product of labour is equal to the wage rate. For example, if the wage rate is $10 per hour, Max will hire 3 workers since marginal revenue product is $10 when 3 workers are hired. Other points on the labour demand curve can be obtained in similar fashion. The result is that the labour demand curve is the same as the *MRP* curve.

S E L F - T E S T

True/False/Uncertain and Explain

1 Economic profit is the factor price of entrepreneurship.

2 If the production of good *A* is labour-intensive, the demand for labour used in the production of good *A* tends to be inelastic.

3 An increase in the supply of labour increases labour income.

4 A household supplies no labour at wage rates below its reservation wage.

5 A backward-bending supply curve for labour will arise if the substitution effect dominates the income effect.

6 If a household's current income is low compared with its expected future income, it will save very little.

7 The supply curve of capital is highly elastic.

8 The market supply of a particular piece of land is perfectly elastic.

9 If the supply of a factor of production is perfectly inelastic, its entire income is transfer earnings.

10 If Lloyd Robertson would be willing to read the news for $100,000 per year, and he is paid $2,100,000 per year to do so, he is earning economic rent of $2,000,000.

Multiple-Choice

1 Factor prices are wages for labour, rent for land,
a normal profit for capital, and interest for money.
b dividends for capital, and interest for money.
c interest for capital, and normal profit for entrepreneurship.
d interest for capital, and economic profit for entrepreneurship.
e economic profit for capital, and normal profit for entrepreneurship.

2 Suppose that the supply of a factor of production is very elastic. An increase in the demand for that factor results in a
a large increase in the quantity supplied of the factor and a small increase in its price.
b small increase in the quantity supplied of the factor and a large increase in its price.
c large increase in the supply of the factor and a small increase in its price.
d small increase in the supply of the factor and a large increase in its price.
e small increase in the supply of the factor and a small increase in its price.

3 An increase in the supply of a factor of production will

a increase the factor's income if the elasticity of factor demand is less than 1.

b decrease the factor's income if the elasticity of factor demand is less than 1.

c increase the factor's income if the elasticity of factor supply is less than 1.

d decrease the factor's income if the elasticity of factor supply is less than 1.

e always decrease the factor's income.

4 When a firm is a price-taker in the labour market, its marginal revenue product of labour curve is also its

a marginal cost curve for labour.

b demand curve for labour.

c supply curve of labour.

d supply curve of output.

e average revenue curve.

5 A profit-maximizing firm will continue to hire units of a variable factor of production until the

a marginal cost of the factor equals its marginal product.

b marginal cost of the factor equals its average revenue product.

c average cost of the factor equals its marginal revenue product.

d marginal cost of the factor equals its marginal revenue product.

e factor's marginal revenue product equals zero.

6 If the wage rate increases, the *substitution* effect will give a household an incentive to

a raise its reservation wage.

b increase its nonmarket activity and decrease its market activity.

c increase its market activity and decrease its nonmarket activity.

d increase both market and nonmarket activity.

e decrease both market and nonmarket activity.

7 If the wage rate increases, the *income* effect will give a household an incentive to

a raise its reservation wage.

b increase its nonmarket activity and decrease its market activity.

c increase its market activity and decrease its nonmarket activity.

d increase both market and nonmarket activity.

e decrease both market and nonmarket activity.

8 If the price of its output falls, a perfectly competitive firm will hire

a less labour, causing the wage to fall.

b less labour, causing the marginal product of labour to rise.

c less labour, causing the marginal product of labour to fall.

d more labour, causing the marginal product of labour to rise.

e more labour, causing the marginal product of labour to fall.

9 A technological change that causes an increase in the marginal product of labour will shift

a the labour demand curve leftward.

b the labour demand curve rightward.

c the labour supply curve leftward.

d the labour supply curve rightward.

e **b** and **d**.

10 In the short run, a firm faces a supply of capital that is

a perfectly elastic.

b perfectly inelastic.

c positively sloped.

d negatively sloped.

e backward bending.

11 If the desire for leisure increased, the wage rate would

a rise and the quantity of labour hired would fall.

b rise and the quantity of labour hired would rise.

c fall and the quantity of labour hired would fall.

d fall and the quantity of labour hired would rise.

e fall and the quantity of labour demanded would rise.

12 As the wage rate rises, a household will have a backward-bending supply of labour curve if

a the income effect is in the same direction as the substitution effect.

b the wage rate rises above the reservation wage.

c the substitution effect dominates the income effect.

d the income effect dominates the substitution effect.

e leisure is an inferior good.

13 An example of derived demand is the demand for

a sweaters derived by an economics student.

b sweaters produced by labour and capital.

c labour used in the production of sweaters.

d sweater brushes.

e none of the above.

14 The change in total revenue resulting from employing an additional unit of capital is the

a marginal product of capital.
b marginal revenue of capital.
c marginal revenue cost of capital.
d marginal revenue product of capital.
e average revenue product of capital.

15 Other things remaining the same, the larger the proportion of total cost coming from labour, the

a more elastic is the demand for labour.
b less elastic is the demand for labour.
c more elastic is the supply of labour.
d less elastic is the supply of labour.
e lower is the demand for labour.

16 Which of the following statements about the short-run demand for labour, *ceteris paribus*, is *true*?

a The larger the elasticity of demand is for the product, the less elastic is the demand for labour.
b The higher the labour intensity of the production process is, the less elastic is the demand for labour.
c The more rapidly the marginal product of labour curve diminishes, the less elastic is the demand for labour.
d All of the above are true.
e None of the above is true.

17 Consider the supply schedule of a factor of production given in Table 14.1. If 4 units of the factor are supplied at a price of $8 per unit, what are the transfer earnings?

a $8
b $12
c $20
d $32
e none of the above

TABLE **14.1**

Price of Factor ($)	Quantity of Factor Supplied
2	1
4	2
6	3
8	4
10	5

18 Consider the supply schedule of a factor of production given in Table 14.1. If 4 units of the factor are supplied at a price of $8 per unit, what is the economic rent?

a $8
b $12
c $20
d $32
e none of the above

19 Whether a household's current income is high or low *compared with expected future income* is influenced by

a the stage of the life cycle the household is in.
b whether the household is rich or poor.
c whether interest rates are high or low.
d whether saving is high or low.
e all of the above.

20 Economic rent is the

a price paid for the use of a hectare of land.
b price paid for the use of a unit of capital.
c income required to induce a given quantity of a factor of production to be supplied.
d income received above the amount required to induce a given quantity of a factor of production to be supplied.
e transfer earnings of a factor of production.

21 The supply curve of labour facing the individual firm in a perfectly competitive labour market is

a upward sloping.
b backward bending.
c first upward sloping and then backward bending as the wage increases.
d vertical.
e horizontal.

22 The income effect of a higher wage is

a the increased income workers must be paid to be willing to work more.
b the increased prices of consumer goods that result from increased worker incomes.
c the increased demand for leisure that results from increased worker incomes.
d the increased workers' purchasing power that results from increased worker incomes.
e all of the above.

23 Which of the following will *not* be true in a profit-maximizing equilibrium?

a marginal revenue equals marginal product
b marginal revenue equals marginal cost
c marginal revenue times marginal product of a factor equals marginal factor cost
d marginal revenue product of a factor equals marginal factor cost
e marginal revenue product of a factor divided by marginal factor cost equals marginal product of a factor

24 The income of a factor in relatively inelastic supply will consist of

a transfer earnings only.
b economic rent only.
c more transfer earnings than economic rent.
d more economic rent than transfer earnings.
e equal amounts of transfer earnings and economic rent.

25 A factor that affects *only* the long-run elasticity of demand for labour is

a the labour intensity of the production process.
b the substitutability of capital for labour.
c the elasticity of demand for the product.
d how rapidly the marginal product of labour curve diminishes.
e none of the above.

Short Answer Problems

1 Why isn't the factor price for capital the price of the specific pieces of capital equipment that the firm buys?

2 Discuss the substitution and income effects on the quantity of labour supplied if the wage rate *decreases*.

3 Why do younger households tend to save less than older households?

4 Are prices of retail goods in Toronto's trendy Yorkville district high because rents are high, or are rents high because prices are high? Explain.

5 Table 14.2 gives the total and marginal product schedules for a firm that sells its output and buys labour in competitive markets. Initially the price at which the firm can sell any level of output is $5 per unit and the wage rate at which it can purchase any quantity of labour is $15 per unit.

TABLE **14.2**

Quantity Labour (L)	Output (Q)	Marginal Product (MP$_L$)	P = $5 Total Revenue (TR)	P = $5 Marginal Revenue Product (MRP$_L$)	P = $3 Total Revenue (TR)	P = $3 Marginal Revenue Product (MRP$_L$)
0	0					
		... 12				
1	12					
		... 10				
2	22					
		... 8				
3	30					
		... 6				
4	36					
		... 4				
5	40					
		... 2				
6	42					

a Complete the first two blank columns in Table 14.2 by computing the *TR* and *MRP$_L$* corresponding to a price of output = $5.
b The marginal revenue product of labour (*MRP$_L$*) can be computed by either of the following formulas:

$$MRP_L = \Delta TR/\Delta L$$
$$MRP_L = MR \times MP_L$$

where ΔTR = the change in total revenue, ΔL = the change in labour, MR = marginal revenue, and MP_L = marginal product of labour. Show that these two formulas are equivalent for the case when the quantity of labour changes from 1 to 2 units.
c If the firm maximizes profit, what quantity of labour will it hire? How much output will it produce?
d If total fixed cost is $125, what is the amount of profit?
e What is its profit if the firm hires one more unit of labour than the profit-maximizing quantity? one less unit of labour than the profit-maximizing quantity?
f Draw a graph of the demand for labour and the supply of labour and illustrate labour market equilibrium.

6 Now, suppose that the market demand for the output of the firm in Short Answer Problem 5 decreases, causing the price of output to decrease to $3 per unit. The total and marginal product schedules remain unchanged.
  a Complete the last two blank columns in Table 14.2 by computing the TR and MRP_L corresponding to price of output = $3.
  b If the wage remains at $15 per unit of labour, what is the profit-maximizing quantity of labour that the firm will hire? How much output will it produce?
  c Total fixed cost continues to be $125. What is the amount of profit?
  d Will the firm shut down in the short run? Explain.
  e Draw a new graph of the new labour market equilibrium.

7 The price of output for the firm in Short Answer Problem **6** remains at $3, but the wage now rises to $21 per unit of labour. The total and marginal product schedules remain unchanged.
  a What happens to the demand curve for labour (the MRP of labour curve)?
  b Under these circumstances, what is the profit-maximizing quantity of labour that the firm will hire? How much output will it produce?
  c Total fixed cost continues to be $125. What is the amount of profit?
  d Draw a graph of the labour market equilibrium.

8 A perfectly competitive firm in long-run equilibrium produces flubits using only two factors of production—labour and capital. Each factor is sold in a perfectly competitive factor market. Labour costs $30 per unit and capital costs $50 per unit.
  a Assuming the firm has hired the profit-maximizing quantity of capital in part **b** of this question, the marginal revenue product of labour curve is

$$MRP_L = 110 - 8/5\ Q_L$$

where MRP_L is the marginal revenue product of labour and Q_L is the quantity (in units) of labour hired. How many units of labour does the firm hire?
  b Assuming the firm has hired the profit-maximizing quantity of labour in part **a** of this question, the marginal revenue product of capital curve is

$$MRP_K = 125 - 75/40\ Q_K$$

where MRP_K is the marginal revenue product of capital and Q_K is the quantity (in units) of capital hired. How many units of capital does the firm hire?
  c The price of a flubit is $10.
    i How many flubits is the firm producing? [*Hint*: Remember that the firm is in long-run equilibrium.]
    ii What is the marginal (physical) product of the 25th unit of labour hired?

9 Table 14.3 gives the market labour demand and supply schedules.

TABLE **14.3**

Wage Rate (dollars per hour)	Quantity of Labour Supplied (hours)	Quantity of Labour Demanded (hours)
0	0	240
1	20	200
2	40	160
3	60	120
4	80	80
5	100	40
6	120	0

  a What is the equilibrium wage rate and the quantity of labour hired?
  b What is the total amount of income received by labour in this market?
  c Represent the market graphically. Identify the equilibrium wage and quantity of labour.
  d Based on your graph from part **c**, how much of labour income is transfer earnings? How much is economic rent?
  e Now suppose that the demand for labour increases by 60 hours at each wage rate.
    i What are the new equilibrium wage rate and quantity of labour?
    ii What is the new total amount of labour income?
    iii How much of this income is transfer earnings? How much is economic rent?

10 A constant cost perfectly competitive industry is initially in long-run equilibrium at P_0 and Q_0 in Fig. 14.2. Each firm in the industry faces the marginal revenue product (MRP^0_L) and wage curves in Fig. 14.3, and initially hires QL_0 units of labour.

FIGURE **14.2** INDUSTRY

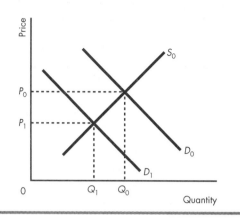

FIGURE **14.3** FIRM

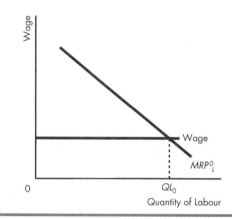

a A decrease in preferences causes industry demand to shift to D_1. As a result of decrease in demand, draw the appropriate new curves (if any) on Fig. 14.3 and explain any shifts. What happens to the short-run quantity of labour hired by the individual firm?

b There are no further shifts in demand. Explain what will happen in the long run and why. Draw any necessary additional curve(s) on Figs. 14.2 and 14.3 showing the final long-run equilibrium.

ANSWERS

True/False/Uncertain and Explain

1 F Normal profit. Economic profit is residual income to firm's owners, who may include the entrepreneur. (320)

2 F Tends to be elastic. (328)

3 U True if elasticity demand for labour > 1; false if < 1. (321–322)

4 T Reservation wage minimum for labour supply. (329–330)

5 F Income effect dominates substitution effect. (329–330)

6 T Saving for greater future consumption not sensible if expect to be better off in future anyway. (331–332)

⏱ **7** U True for long run, false for short run. (331–332)

8 F Perfectly inelastic. (332–333)

9 F Entire income is economic rent. (334–335)

10 T Excess of income over transfer earnings. (334–335)

Multiple-Choice

1 c Definition. (320)

2 a Movement up along flat supply curve. (321–322)

3 b $\uparrow PF$ with inelastic demand $\rightarrow \uparrow (PF \times QF)$. (321–322)

4 b Shows quantity labour hired at each wage rate. (325)

5 d Where supply curve of factor to firm (MC) intersects demand curve for factor (MRP). (325–326)

6 c Substitute work for leisure. (329–330)

7 b Consume more normal goods, including leisure, which entails working less. (329–330)

⏱ **8** b Labour demand curve shifts left. Supply horizontal. Because of diminishing MP, $\downarrow L \rightarrow \uparrow MP$. (326–327)

9 b See text discussion. (326–327)

10 b Fixed in specific capital equipment. (331–332)

11 a Labour supply would shift left. (329–330)

12 d Income and substitution effects opposite for labour. (329–330)

13 c Factor of production used as input. (323–324)

14 d Revenue from selling marginal product of capital. (323–324)

15 a $\uparrow$ wage $\rightarrow$ greater $\uparrow$ total costs and $\uparrow$ product $P \rightarrow$ greater $\downarrow$ sales and $\downarrow$ labour hired. (328)

⏱ **16** c Reverse of **a, b** true. (328)

17 c $\$2 + \$4 + \$6 + \$8$. (334–335)

⏱ **18** b Total income ($\$32 = 4 \times \$8$) minus transfer earnings ($\$20$). (334–335)

⏱ **19** a Younger households have relatively low current income, older households relatively high current income. (331–332)

20 d Definition. Price paid for land use is rent. (334–335)

21 e Because firm small part of labour market, can buy as much labour as desired at market wage. (329–330)

22 **c** ↑ wage → ↑ income → ↑ demand for normal goods, including leisure. (329–330)

⊘ **23** **a** *MR* measured in $, *MP* measured in physical units. Other answers definitions or profit-maximizing conditions. (325–326)

24 **d** Draw graph with steep supply and compare areas above and below supply curve at equilibrium *PF* and *QF*. (334–335)

25 **b** **a, c, d** affect both short and long run. (327–328)

Short Answer Problems

I In general, factor prices represent the *opportunity cost* to the firm of *using* that factor of production. Wages are the cost of using labour and rent is the cost of using land. The cost of using a piece of capital equipment bought by the firm is the interest that must be paid (explicitly or implicitly) on the funds tied up in the purchase of the equipment. Capital equipment lasts for a long period of time. The cost of capital during any one period is not the purchase price of the equipment, it is the cost of the funds tied up in the equipment over the period.

2 If the wage rate decreases, the opportunity cost of leisure decreases and households will have a tendency to shift from work to leisure (the substitution effect), thereby reducing the quantity of labour supplied. The lower wage also decreases the household's income and, thus causes the household to reduce its demand for leisure and other normal goods (the income effect) thereby increasing the quantity of labour supplied.

3 Households will tend to save less when current income is low relative to expected future income and save more when current income is high relative to expected future income. Younger households are largely in this first situation, while older households are largely in the second.

4 Rents are high because prices are high. Land in Yorkville has a perfectly inelastic supply, so the price of land (its rent) is determined entirely by demand for the land.

Demand is high because merchants know that the prime retail location will allow them to charge higher prices and potentially earn higher profits than in other locations.

5 a The completed columns for *TR* and MRP_L corresponding to a price of output = $5 are shown in Table 14.2 Solution. The values for *TR* are obtained by multiplying the quantity of

output by the price of output ($5). The values for MRP_L between any two quantities of labour are obtained by dividing the change in *TR* by the change in quantity of labour, or by multiplying *MR* ($5) by MP_L.

TABLE **14.2** SOLUTION

			P = $5		P = $3	
Quantity Labour (L)	Output (Q)	Marginal Product (MP_L)	Total Revenue (TR)	Marginal Revenue Product (MRP_L)	Total Revenue (TR)	Marginal Revenue Product (MRP_L)
0	0		0		0	
		··· 12		··· 60		··· 36
1	12		60		36	
		··· 10		··· 50		··· 30
2	22		110		66	
		··· 8		··· 40		··· 24
3	30		150		90	
		··· 6		··· 30		··· 18
4	36		180		108	
		··· 4		··· 20		··· 12
5	40		200		120	
		··· 2		··· 10		··· 6
6	42		210		126	

---

b From part **a**, the formula $MRP_L = \Delta TR/\Delta L$, yields a marginal revenue product of labour of 50 when the quantity of labour changes from 1 to 2 units. To confirm that the second formula ($MRP_L = MR \times MP_L$) gives the same answer when the quantity of labour changes from 1 to 2 units, substitute in the values for *MR* ($5, the price of an additional unit of output) and MP_L (10 units of output). This yields the same marginal revenue product of labour as above; $5 × 10 units = $50.

c The firm maximizes profit by hiring labour up to the point where the *MRP* of labour is equal to the marginal cost of labour (the wage rate). That point occurs at 5 units of labour. The *MRP* of moving from 4 to 5 units of labour is 20, and the *MRP* of moving from 5 to 6 units of labour is 10. Thus by interpolation, the *MRP* at exactly 5 units of labour is 15 (midway between 20 and 10). So when 5 units of labour are hired, the *MRP* of labour is equal to the wage rate ($15). Given that 5 units of labour are hired, the profit-maximizing output will be 40 units (from Table 14.2 Solution).

d To calculate profit, we must first calculate total revenue and then subtract total cost. Total revenue is $200 (40 units of output × $5 per unit) and total cost is also $200—the sum of total variable (labour) cost of $75 (5 units of labour × $15 per unit) and total fixed cost of $125. Thus profit is zero.

e If the firm hires one more unit of labour (6 units), total revenue will be $210 (42 units of output × the $5 price). Total cost will be the $125 fixed cost plus $90 in total variable cost (6 units of labour × the $15 wage rate) or $215. Thus profit will be a negative $5 (a $5 loss).

If the firm hires one less unit of labour (4 units), total revenue will be $180 (36 units of output × the $5 price). Total cost will be the $125 fixed cost plus $60 in total variable cost (4 units of labour × the $15 wage rate) or $185. Thus profit will be a negative $5 (a $5 loss).

f The graph of labour market equilibrium appears in Fig. 14.4. The demand for labour is given by the firm's MRP_L curve which is labelled D_0 (D_1 will be discussed in Short Answer Problem 6).

Notice that the values for MRP are plotted midway between the corresponding quantities of labour. For example, MRP of 60 is plotted midway between 0 and 1 units of labour.

Since the firm purchases labour in a perfectly competitive labour market, the supply of labour to the firm is perfectly elastic at the market wage rate. The labour supply curve is labelled $W = 15. The equilibrium is at the intersection of these curves, and corresponds to a wage rate of $15 and a quantity of labour hired of 5 units.

FIGURE **14.4**

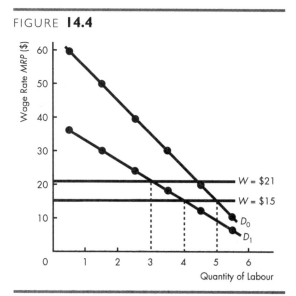

6 a The completed columns for TR and MRP_L corresponding to price of output = $3 are shown in Table 14.2 Solution. The values for TR are obtained by multiplying the quantity of output by the price of output ($3). The values for MRP_L between any two quantities of labour are obtained by dividing the change in TR by the change in quantity of labour, or by multiplying MR ($3) by MP_L.

b If the wage rate remains at $15, the profit-maximizing quantity of labour will fall to 4 units since MRP_L equals the wage rate at 4 units of labour. The MRP of moving from 3 to 4 units of labour is 18, and the MRP of moving from 4 to 5 units of labour is 12. Thus, by interpolation, the MRP at exactly 4 units of labour is 15 (midway between 18 and 12). Given that 4 units of labour are employed, the profit-maximizing output will be 36 units (from Table 14.2 Solution).

c Profit equals total revenue minus total cost. Total revenue is $108 (36 units of output × $3 per unit) and total cost is $185—the sum of total variable (labour) cost of $60 (4 units of labour × $15 per unit) and total fixed cost of $125. Thus profit is −$77, or a loss of $77.

d The firm will not shut down since total revenue ($108) is enough to cover total variable cost ($60) and part of fixed cost. If the firm decided to shut down, it would lose the $125 of fixed cost rather than just $77.

e The graph of labour market equilibrium appears in Fig. 14.4. The new demand for labour is given by the firm's new MRP_L curve, which is labelled D_1. The supply of labour has not changed; it continues to be horizontal at $15, the competitive market wage. The new equilibrium is at the intersection of these curves and corresponds to a wage rate of $15 and a quantity of labour hired of 4 units.

7 a Since marginal revenue and the marginal product of labour are unaffected by a change in the wage rate, the demand curve for labour (the MRP of labour) will remain at D_1.

b If the wage rate rises to $21, the profit-maximizing quantity of labour will fall to 3 units since MRP_L equals the wage rate at 3 units of labour. Given that 3 units of labour are employed, the profit-maximizing output will be 30 units (from Table 14.2 Solution).

c Profit equals total revenue minus total cost. Total revenue is $90 (30 units of output × $3 per unit) and total cost is $188—the sum of total variable (labour) cost of $63 (3 units of labour × $21 per unit) and total fixed cost of $125. Thus profit is −$98, or a loss of $98.

d See Fig. 14.4. The relevant demand for labour curve continues to be D_1, but the labour supply curve reflects the rise in the competitive wage rate; it is now horizontal at a wage rate of $21 (labelled $W = \$21$). The equilibrium is at the intersection of these curves and corresponds to a wage rate of $21 and a quantity of labour hired of 3 units.

⊚◑ 8 a By assuming that the firm has already hired its capital, we know (in principle) fixed costs and can calculate the profit-maximizing quantity of the variable factor (labour) by setting the MRP_L equal to the wage rate ($30).

$$30 = 110 - 8/5 \; Q_L$$
$$8/5 \; Q_L = 80$$
$$Q_L = 50$$

b By assuming that the firm has already hired its labour, we can treat labour as the fixed cost and treat capital as the variable factor of production. Calculate the profit-maximizing quantity of the capital hired by setting the MRP_K equal to the cost of a unit of capital ($50).

$$50 = 125 - 75/40 \; Q_K$$
$$75/40 \; Q_K = 75$$
$$Q_K = 40$$

c i The fact that the firm is in long-run equilibrium provides the key to calculating the quantity of flubits produced. In long-run equilibrium, the firm earns zero economic profit, so total revenue is exactly equal to total cost.

We can calculate total cost by adding the costs of the (only) two factors of production. Labour cost is 50 units of labour × $30 per unit or $1,500. Capital cost is 40 units of capital × $50 per unit or $2,000. Total cost is, therefore, $3,500.

Total revenue must also be equal to $3,500. Since total revenue (TR) is just the price of output (P) times quantity sold (Q), we can calculate Q by substituting in the values we have for TR ($3,500) and P ($10).

$$TR = P \times Q$$
$$\$3,500 = \$10 \times Q$$
$$Q = 350$$

ii To calculate the marginal product of the 25th unit of labour, we begin by calculating the marginal *revenue* product of the 25th unit of labour. Substituting $Q_L = 25$ into the equation for MRP_L yields

$$MRP_L = 110 - 8/5 \; (25)$$
$$= 110 - 40$$
$$= 70$$

One definition of the marginal revenue product of labour is the marginal product of labour (MP_L) times marginal revenue (MR) or $MRP_L = MP_L \times MR$. Rearranging to solve for MP_L yields

$$MP_L = MRP_L / MR$$

Substituting in the values for the marginal revenue product of the 25th unit of labour (70) and for MR (the price of output $10) yields

$$MP_L = 70/10$$
$$MP_L = 7$$

9 a The equilibrium wage rate is $4 per hour and the quantity of labour hired is 80 hours.

b Total income is $320 ($4 per hour × 80 hours).

c The supply and demand curves for labour are given in Fig. 14.5. The supply of labour is given by S_0 and the initial demand for labour is represented by D_0. The equilibrium occurs at the intersection of these two curves. You can see that the equilibrium wage is $4 per hour and the quantity of labour is 80 hours.

FIGURE **14.5**

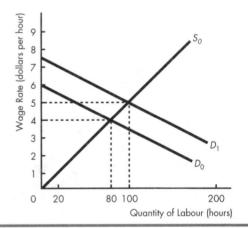

d Given that the supply of labour curve is a 45-degree line starting at the origin, half of income is transfer earnings (the area below the supply curve) and the other half is economic rent (the area above the supply curve). Since income is $320, each of these is $160.

e i Each entry in the last column of Table 14.3 will increase by 60 units. The new equilibrium wage rate is $5 per hour and the new equilibrium quantity of labour is 100 hours. The new labour demand curve appears in Fig. 14.5 as D_1.

ii Total income is now $500 ($5 per hour × 100 hours).

iii Once again the slope of the labour supply curve (which has not changed) implies that income is split evenly between transfer earnings and economic rent. Each will be equal to $250.

↻ 10 a See Fig.14.2 Solution and Fig.14.3 Solution. The decrease in demand causes the industry price of output to fall to P_1, which causes each firm's marginal revenue product of labour curve to shift leftward. There is no change in the wage, so the quantity of labour hired by the individual firm decreases to QL_1.

b The key to understanding what will happen in the long run is the fact that this is a constant cost industry initially in long-run equilibrium. At P_0 and Q_0, firms earn zero economic profits. When price falls to P_1, firms make economic losses. This leads some firms to exit the industry, causing the industry supply curve to shift leftward. Because this is a constant cost industry, we know that the new long-run equilibrium, even at reduced levels of output, must occur at the same price as the initial equilibrium. Thus the industry supply curve shifts to S_1. The final long-run equilibrium for the industry is back at the original price P_0 and new quantity Q_2.

As the price of output returns to P_0, the marginal revenue product of labour curve for each remaining firm shifts back to the right, ending up at its original position. The quantity of labour hired by each remaining firm increases from QL_1 to QL_0.

When firms exit, industry supply decreases, price increases, and the quantity supplied by each remaining firm increases. In Chapter 10, we saw that this means each remaining firm moves up its marginal cost curve. Here, we can see why. Each remaining firm increases its hiring of the variable factor of production, labour. Because of diminishing returns, the marginal (physical) product of labour falls. With a fixed wage, marginal cost ($MC = W/MP_L$) increases.

FIGURE **14.2** SOLUTION INDUSTRY

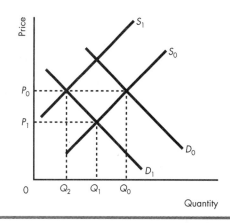

FIGURE **14.3** SOLUTION FIRM

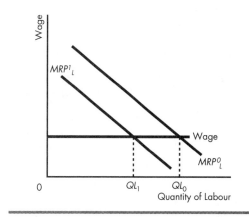

KEY CONCEPTS

Skill Differentials

Skill differentials arise because of difference in

♦ Demand—skilled labour has higher marginal revenue product (*MRP*) than unskilled labour. Higher $MRP \rightarrow$ higher demand.

♦ Supply—skills costly to acquire. **Human capital** is accumulated skill and knowledge human beings. Costs of acquiring skill → supply curve skilled labour above supply curve unskilled labour.

Union-Nonunion Wage Differentials

Labour unions are organized groups of workers.

♦ **Craft union**—group of workers with similar range of skills working for different firms/industries.

♦ **Industrial union**—group of workers with variety of skills and job types working for same firm/industry.

♦ **Rand formula** requires all workers in a *closed shop* to contribute to the union whether or not they belong.

♦ **Collective bargaining**—process of negotiation between unions and employers.

Labour unions' objectives are increasing compensation, improving working conditions, and expanding job opportunities. Methods of achieving objectives include

♦ Restricting supply of labour.

♦ ↑ demand for union labour or making demand more inelastic by encouraging import restrictions, supporting minimum wage laws and immigration restrictions, ↑ product demand, ↑ marginal product union members.

Monopsony—market structure in which there is a single buyer. Firm that is only employer in town is monopsonist in the labour market.

♦ To hire more labour, monopsonist must pay a higher wage. Marginal cost of labour curve (*MCL*) for monopsonist is upward sloping and above and steeper than the market supply curve of labour.

♦ Profit-maximizing rule for monopsonist is to hire quantity of labour where *MCL* curve intersects *MRP* curve, then offer lowest wage for which labour will work (on supply curve).

♦ For monopsonist, employment and wage are lower than for competitive labour market. More elastic supply of labour → ↓ *opportunity* for monopsony to ↓ wages, to ↓ employment or to ↑ economic profit.

♦ Adding union to a monopsony labour market can → **bilateral monopoly**, where wage determined by relative bargaining strength firm and union. Highest possible wage where *MCL* intersects *MRP*. Lowest possible wage is pure monopsony wage.

♦ Adding a minimum wage law to a monopsony labour market can → ↑ wage and ↑ employment.

Wage Differentials Between the Sexes

Wage differentials between men and women because of

♦ Job types—men and women doing different jobs; men's jobs often better paid than women's jobs.

♦ Discrimination—results in lower wages and employment for those discriminated against.

♦ Differences in human capital—differences in schooling (mostly eliminated), work experience, and job interruptions (lessened recently).

◆ Differences in degree of specialization—because of social conventions men have specialized in market activities, while women have divided their time between market activities and nonmarket activities.

  • *Household production* creates goods and services consumed within household rather than supplied to market.
  • Market specialization → ↑ productivity and ↑ wages.

Pay Equity Laws

Pay equity laws determine wages by assessing value of jobs on objective characteristics rather than on what the market will pay.

◆ *Pay equity*—paying same wage for different jobs judged objectively to be comparable.

◆ Pay equity laws can → ↑ equity where discrimination exists.

◆ Pay equity laws can → unintended consequences of ↑ unemployment for women where existing market wage differentials are productivity-based.

HELPFUL HINTS

1 This chapter introduces the concept of a monopsonist, a firm that is the only buyer in a market, such as labour. The monopsonist faces an upward-sloping supply curve of labour. As a result, its marginal cost of labour curve (*MCL*) is different from the labour supply curve.

There is a close parallel between (a) the relationship between the labour supply curve and the *MCL* curve for the monopsonist and (b) the already familiar relationship (Chapter 12) between the demand curve and the marginal revenue curve (*MR*) for the monopolist. Both sets of relationships stem from the assumption of a single price for labour or output in the relevant market.

The monopolist, as the only seller in an output market, faces a downward-sloping demand curve. The marginal revenue from the sale of an additional unit of output is *less* than the selling price because the monopolist must *lower* the price on all previous units as well. Thus the *MR* curve lies *below* the demand curve for the single-price monopolist.

For the monopsonist in a labour market, the marginal cost of hiring an additional unit of labour is *higher* than the wage because the

monopsonist must *raise* the wage on all previous units of labour as well. Thus the *MCL* curve lies *above* the supply of labour curve for the monopsonist.

SELF-TEST

True/False/Uncertain and Explain

1 The marginal revenue product of unskilled workers is lower than that of skilled workers.

2 The vertical distance between the labour supply curves for skilled and unskilled workers is the marginal revenue product of the skill.

3 The larger the marginal revenue product of the skill and the more costly it is to acquire, the smaller is the wage differential between skilled and unskilled workers.

4 Unions support minimum wage laws in part because they increase the cost of unskilled labour, a substitute for skilled union labour.

5 For a firm that is a monopsonist in the labour market, the supply curve of labour is the marginal cost of labour curve.

6 The more elastic is labour supply, the less opportunity a monopsonist has to make an economic profit.

7 The introduction of a minimum wage that is above the current wage will raise the wage but reduce employment.

8 In the case of bilateral monopoly in a labour market, the wage depends on the bargaining strength of the two traders.

9 Economic theory tells us that discrimination in employment will result in wage differentials.

10 If males on average earn more than females, there is discrimination.

Multiple-Choice

1 Which of the following is *not* a reason why the wage of skilled workers exceeds the wage of unskilled workers?

a The market for skilled workers is more competitive than the market for unskilled workers.

b The marginal revenue product of skilled workers is greater than that of unskilled workers.

c The cost of training skilled workers is greater than the cost of training unskilled workers.

d Skilled workers have acquired more human capital than unskilled workers.

e The demand curve for skilled workers lies to the right of the demand curve for unskilled workers.

2 Other things remaining the same, if education costs rise substantially, we would expect to see a(n)

a decrease in the marginal revenue product of skilled workers.

b decrease in the demand for skilled workers.

c increase in the supply of skilled workers.

d increase in the wage of skilled workers.

e increase in the number of skilled workers employed.

3 A union that organizes workers with a similar skill regardless of the firm or industry that employs them is a(n)

a industrial union.

b craft union.

c local union.

d national union.

e public sector union.

4 Figure 15.1 illustrates a monopsonist in the labour market (*MCL* = marginal cost of labour). The profit-maximizing wage rate and quantity of labour hired will be

a $4 per hour and 800 hours of labour.

b $4 per hour and 400 hours of labour.

c $7 per hour and 600 hours of labour.

d $9 per hour and 400 hours of labour.

e none of the above.

FIGURE **15.1**

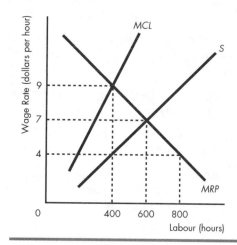

5 If the labour market illustrated in Fig. 15.1 became competitive, the equilibrium wage rate and quantity of labour hired would be

a $4 per hour and 800 hours of labour.

b $4 per hour and 400 hours of labour.

c $7 per hour and 600 hours of labour.

d $9 per hour and 400 hours of labour.

e none of the above.

6 If a union forms to face the monopsonist in Fig. 15.1, the situation is one of

a binding arbitration.

b derived demand.

c duopoly.

d collusive oligopoly.

e bilateral monopoly.

7 If a union and the monopsonist in Fig. 15.1 agree to collective bargaining, the outcome will be an hourly wage

a of $7.

b between $4 and $7.

c between $4 and $9.

d between $7 and $9.

e that is indeterminate without additional information.

8 Wage differentials between males and females can be explained by

a occupational differences.
b human capital differences.
c degree of specialization differences.
d discrimination.
e all of the above.

9 If discrimination takes the form of restricting a group's access to education and training, the effect on this group of workers will be to shift the

a *MRP* curve rightward and increase the wage.
b *MRP* curve leftward and decrease the wage.
c *MRP* curve rightward and decrease the wage.
d supply of labour curve up and decrease the wage.
e supply of labour curve down and decrease the wage.

10 The Rand formula made

a collective bargaining compulsory.
b it compulsory for all workers in a partially unionized plant to contribute to the union.
c binding arbitration legal.
d strikes and lockouts illegal under some circumstances.
e none of the above.

11 Pay equity is an attempt to pay women and men the same wage

a for doing the same job.
b for household production as for market activity.
c for different jobs that are judged to be comparable.
d regardless of their jobs.
e regardless of gender.

12 Refer to Fig. 15.2. For any given quantity of labour employed,

a the elasticity of demand for skilled workers is less than the elasticity of demand for unskilled workers.
b skilled workers will receive a lower wage than unskilled workers.
c skilled workers will receive a higher wage than unskilled workers.
d the vertical distance between the curves is the compensation for the cost of acquiring skill.
e the vertical distance between the curves is the present value of human capital.

FIGURE **15.2**

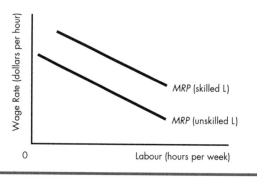

13 The vertical distance between the two supply curves in Fig. 15.3

a is the compensation for the cost of acquiring skill.
b is the *MRP* of skill.
c is the result of discrimination against unskilled workers.
d will disappear if there is free entry in the skill market.
e will disappear with equal pay for work of equal value.

FIGURE **15.3**

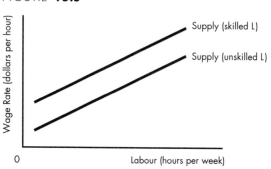

14 Refer only to the information in Fig. 15.3. For any given wage rate, more hours of

a unskilled labour will be demanded than skilled labour.
b skilled labour will be demanded than unskilled labour.
c unskilled labour will be supplied than skilled labour.
d skilled labour will be supplied than unskilled labour.
e unskilled labour will be supplied if the *MRP* of skill increases.

15 If a strike or lockout occurs in a bilateral monopoly situation, it is usually because the

a demand for labour is relatively inelastic.
b demand for labour is relatively elastic.
c supply of labour is relatively inelastic.
d supply of labour is relatively elastic.
e union or firm has misjudged the bargaining situation.

16 Which of the following would unions be *least* likely to support?

a increasing the legal minimum wage
b restricting immigration
c encouraging imports
d increasing demand for the goods their workers produce
e increasing the marginal product of union labour

17 Productivity differences in competitive labour markets cause the wage paid to secretaries to be substantially higher than the wage paid to cleaners. A new pay equity law judges secretaries and cleaners to be comparable. To equalize wages, the wage rate for cleaners is forced up and the wage rate for secretaries is forced down. Employment of secretaries

a will rise, while employment of cleaners will fall.
b will fall, while employment of cleaners will rise.
c and cleaners will rise.
d and cleaners will fall.
e and cleaners will remain unchanged.

18 Refer again to the situation in Question 17. As a result of the pay equity law, *unemployment* of

a secretaries will rise.
b cleaners will rise.
c secretaries and cleaners will rise.
d secretaries and cleaners will fall.
e secretaries and cleaners will remain unchanged.

19 Which of the following statements is *false*? Human capital

a is the accumulated skill and knowledge of human beings.
b is costly to acquire.
c increases from on-the-job training.
d increases from higher wages.
e increases from education.

20 When compared with a competitive labour market with the same marginal revenue product and labour supply curves, a monopsonist labour market has a(n)

a lower wage and lower employment.
b lower wage and higher employment.
c higher wage and lower employment.
d higher wage and higher employment.
e indeterminate outcome.

21 A union is formed to restrict labour supply in a previously perfectly competitive labour market. If the union succeeds in raising the wage,

a employment will fall.
b employment will rise.
c employment will not change.
d the total wage bill will rise.
e the total wage bill will fall.

22 Pay equity laws

a cannot achieve their objective if wage differentials are discrimination-based.
b can achieve their objective if wage differentials are productivity-based.
c can achieve their objective if wage differentials are discrimination-based.
d analyse job characteristics and determine their worth on market grounds.
e compare the market value of objective job characteristics.

23 For the monopsonist employer illustrated in Fig. 15.4, the profit-maximizing wage rate and quantity of labour hired will be

a $9 per hour and 300 hours of labour.
b $8 per hour and 350 hours of labour.
c $8 per hour and 500 hours of labour.
d $7 per hour and 400 hours of labour.
e $6 per hour and 300 hours of labour.

FIGURE **15.4**

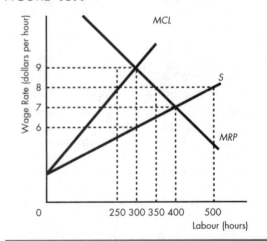

24 Suppose the government passes a minimum wage law that prohibits anyone from hiring labour at less than $8 per hour. In Fig. 15.4, the marginal cost of labour (*MCL*) for the monopsonist

a is not affected.
b equals $8 only from 0 to 250 hours of labour.
c equals $8 only from 0 to 350 hours of labour.
d equals $8 only from 0 to 500 hours of labour.
e shifts up by a vertical distance of $8.

25 A working arrangement in which all workers must be members of the union before they can be hired by the firm is called a(n)

a open shop.
b closed shop.
c union shop.
d craft shop.
e professional association.

Short Answer Problems

1 Members of labour unions earn wages well above the minimum wage. Even so, why is it in the interest of a union to support increases in the legal minimum wage?

2 Bob and Sue form a household. They have decided that Sue will fully specialize in market activity and Bob will pursue activities both in the job market and in the household. If most households are like Bob and Sue, why would the result be a difference between the earnings of men and women, even if there is no discrimination?

3 Suppose the labour market for investment advisors is exactly as shown in Text Fig. 15.8 on page 356, where there is discrimination against female advisors and discrimination for male advisors. Explain the effects of introducing a scheme of pay equity that equalizes wage rates at $40,000 per year.

4 In what situations can laws enforcing pay equity achieve their objective of greater equity? In what situations can such laws not achieve their objectives?

5 Figure 15.5 shows the demand and supply of unskilled and skilled labour. S_U and S_S are the supply curves for unskilled and skilled workers, respectively, and D_U and D_S are the demand curves for unskilled and skilled workers, respectively.

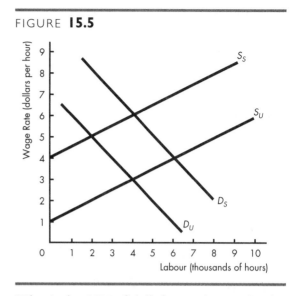

FIGURE **15.5**

a What is the *MRP* of skill if 5,000 hours of each kind of labour are hired?
b What amount of extra compensation per hour is required to induce the acquisition of skill at the same level of hiring?
c What are the equilibrium wage and quantity of labour in the market for skilled labour?
d What are the equilibrium wage and quantity of labour in the market for unskilled labour?

6 Yuri has an opportunity to increase his human capital by taking a training course that will raise his income by $100 every year for the rest of his life. Assume that there are no other benefits of the course. The cost of the course is $1,200 and Yuri's best alternative investment pays an interest rate of 10 percent per year for the rest of his life. Should Yuri pay the $1,200 and take the course? Explain.

7 Initially we observe an industry facing a competitive labour market in which the supply of labour comes from two sources: domestic workers and foreign workers. All workers have similar skills. Also assume that the output of the industry competes with imported goods.
a In Fig. 15.6, graphically represent the initial competitive labour market. Draw the labour demand and supply curves and identify the equilibrium wage rate and level of employment.

FIGURE **15.6**

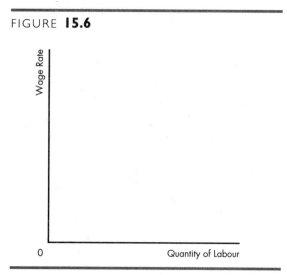

b Now suppose a union consisting of domestic workers is formed. Through its support a law is passed that prohibits firms from hiring foreign workers. What effect will this have on employment and the wage rate? Illustrate graphically using the graph in part **a**.

c Finally, the industry and union support the passage of a law that legally restricts imports that compete with industry output. Using the same graph, show the consequences for the wage rate and employment.

8 Pollutionless Paper is a pulp and paper mill that employs almost all of the labour in a small town in New Brunswick. The town's labour market, which approximates a monopsony, is illustrated in Fig. 15.7, where S is the supply curve of labour, and MRP and MCL are Pollutionless Paper's marginal revenue product of labour and marginal cost of labour curves, respectively.

FIGURE **15.7**

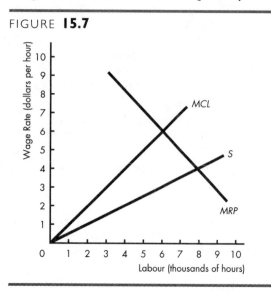

a If Pollutionless Paper is a profit-maximizing monopsonist, what wage rate will it pay and how much labour will it employ? What is the value of labour's MRP at this level of employment?

b If the town had a competitive labour market with the same MRP curve, what would the equilibrium wage rate and the level of employment be? Compare these outcomes with the monopsony outcomes in part **a**.

9 Consider the following alternatives for the labour market in Fig. 15.7.

a Suppose the government imposes a minimum wage of $4 per hour. What wage rate will Pollutionless Paper pay and how much labour will it employ? Compare these outcomes with the monopsony outcomes in Short Answer Problem **8a**.

b Suppose there is no legal minimum wage, but the workers form a union. If the union tries to negotiate a higher wage rate while maintaining employment at the monopsony level, what is the maximum wage rate that Pollutionless Paper will be willing to pay? What is the minimum wage rate that the union will accept?

10 Consider the negotiations between Pollutionless Paper and the union in Short Answer Problem **9b**.

a What determines the wage rate that will actually be paid?

b If Pollutionless Paper and the union are equally strong and realize it, what will the wage rate likely be?

c If Pollutionless Paper and the union are equally strong, but the union mistakenly believes it is stronger, what is the likely outcome of negotiations?

d If Pollutionless Paper and the union are equally strong, but Pollutionless Paper mistakenly believes it is stronger, what is the likely outcome of negotiations?

ANSWERS

True/False/Uncertain and Explain

1 **T** Consequences → demand unskilled workers to left of demand skilled workers. (346–347)

2 **F** Vertical distance compensation for cost of acquiring skill. (346–347)

3 **F** The larger the wage differential. (346–347)

4 T ↑ price substitute → ↑ demand union labour. (351–352)

5 F *MCL* curve above supply curve of labour. (352–353)

⌀ 6 T ↑ η labour supply → ↓ differences between *MCL* and wage. (352–353)

⌀ 7 U True for competitive labour market, false for monopsonistic labour market (where ↑ wage and ↑ employment). (354)

8 T See text discussion. (352–353)

9 T ↓ wages for discriminated against and ↑ wages for discriminated for. (355–357)

10 U Differences may be due to job type differences, discrimination, human capital differences, and/or specialization differences. (356–358)

Multiple-Choice

1 a Wage differences not due to competitive differences. In any case, ↑ competitiveness would → ↓ skilled wages. (346–347)

2 d ↑ cost acquiring skill → upward shift supply curve skilled workers. (346–347)

3 b Definition. (348–349)

4 b *QL* where *MCL* intersects *MRP*. Then lowest wage required for labour to supply that *QL* (on supply curve). (352–353)

5 c Where *S* intersects *MRP*. (352–353)

6 e See text discussion. (352–353)

7 c Between minimum firm can achieve ($4) and maximum union can achieve ($9). (352–353)

8 e All can contribute to differentials. (355–358)

9 e Education and training would ↑ human capital and shift supply curve labour up. (356–357)

10 b See text discussion. (348–349)

11 c See text discussion. (358–359)

⌀ 12 c Reverse **a** true. **d** applies to supply. **e** nonsense. (346–347)

13 a See Text Fig. 15.1. (346–347)

14 c No demand curves on figure. ↑ *MRP* skill shifts demand, not supply. (346–347)

15 e **a – d** may affect relative bargaining strength but do not cause strikes or lockouts. (352–353)

16 c ↑ imports → ↓ domestically produced goods → ↓ demand for domestic, union labour. (351–352)

17 d But ↓ employment secretaries due to shortages and ↓ employment cleaners due to unemployment. (358–359)

18 b Labour market for secretaries experiences shortage, not unemployment. (358–359)

19 d ↑ wages are often an effect, but not a cause, of ↑ human capital. (346–347)

20 a See Text Fig. 15.5. (352–353)

21 a Leftward shift supply → ↓ employment. Impact on wage bill depends on elasticity of demand for labour. (350–351)

22 c Reverse **a**, **b** true. Assess job characteristics on objective grounds, not market value. (358–359)

23 e *QL* where *MCL* intersects *MRP*. Then lowest wage required for labour to supply that *QL* (on supply curve). (352–353)

⌀ 24 d *MCL* horizontal at minimum wage until intersects *S*. Firm must then ↑ wage to get ↑ quantity supplied labour. (354)

25 b Definition. (348–349)

Short Answer Problems

1 An increase in the minimum wage will increase the cost of hiring unskilled labour, which will tend to increase the demand for skilled labour which is a substitute.

2 If Sue specializes in market activity while Bob is diversified, it is likely that Sue's earning ability will exceed Bob's because of the gains from her specialization. If most households followed this pattern of specialization, the income of women would exceed that of men even without discrimination.

3 The wages of female investment advisors will increase from $20,000 to $40,000 per year and employment will increase from 1,000 to 2,000. The wages of male investment advisors will decrease from $60,000 to $40,000 per year and employment will decrease from 3,000 to 2,000. The effects of the scheme will be to produce the competitive outcome that would have prevailed without discrimination. There is no excess demand or supply of either female or male advisors.

4 Laws enforcing pay equity can achieve their objective of greater equity in situations where discrimination is the source of wage differentials. The wages of the lower paid group that is discriminated against can be raised to reflect their true productivity without increasing their unemployment.

Such laws cannot achieve their objectives in situations where wage differentials arise from differences in productivity. If productivity differences exist, pay equity laws can have the unintended consequence of increasing unemployment among the lower paid group of workers.

5 a The *MRP* of skill is the difference between the *MRP* of skilled versus unskilled labour; the vertical distance between the demand curves for skilled and unskilled labour. In Fig. 15.5, the *MRP* of skill is $3 per hour when 5,000 hours of each kind of labour are employed.

b Since labour supply curves give the minimum compensation workers are willing to accept in return for supplying a given quantity of labour, the extra compensation for skill is the vertical distance between the supply curves of skilled and unskilled labour. At 5,000 hours of employment for both kinds of labour, this is $3 per hour.

c In equilibrium in the market for skilled labour, the wage rate will be $6 per hour and employment will be 4,000 hours of labour. This occurs at the intersection of the D_S and S_S curves.

d In equilibrium in the market for unskilled labour, the wage rate will be $3 per hour and employment will be 4,000 hours of labour. This occurs at the intersection of the D_U and S_U curves.

6 Yuri should take the course only if the value of the course exceeds the cost of the course. The cost of the course is $1,200 while the value of the course is the present value of the extra $100 in income Yuri can expect to receive each year for the rest of his life. The present value of this income stream is the amount of money which, if invested today at 10 percent (Yuri's best alternative return), would yield an equivalent stream of income. Thus the present value of the extra income is $1,000. Since this is less than the cost of the training course, Yuri should *not* take it.

7 a The initial competitive demand for labour and supply of labour curves are given by D_C and S_C respectively, in Fig. 15.6 Solution (ignore the other curves for now). The equilibrium wage rate is W_C and the competitive equilibrium level of employment is QL_C

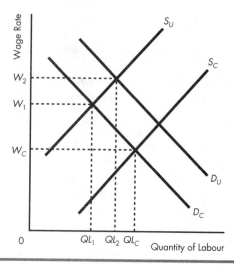

FIGURE **15.6**   SOLUTION

b If a law is passed prohibiting firms from hiring foreign workers, the labour supply curve (now under a union) will shift leftward (to S_U in Fig. 15.6 Solution). This will have the effect of raising the wage rate to W_1 and decreasing the quantity of labour employed to QL_1.

c Restrictions on imports will increase the demand for the product produced in the industry and thus increase the derived demand (*MRP*) of labour in the industry. In Fig. 15.6 Solution this is illustrated by a shift from D_C to D_U. The result will be a further increase in the wage rate to W_2 and an increase in employment to QL_2. Whether the quantity of labour hired now exceeds the initial competitive quantity depends on the magnitude of the shift in the labour demand curve.

8 a A profit-maximizing monopsonist will hire additional labour up to the point where *MCL* equals *MRP*. Referring to Fig. 15.7, this means that Pollutionless Paper will hire 6,000 hours of labour. To hire that quantity of labour, the labour supply curve *S* tells us that the wage rate must be $3 per hour. This is less than the $6 per hour marginal revenue product of labour.

b In a competitive labour market, the wage rate would be $4 per hour and 8,000 hours of labour would be employed. The competitive labour market results in a higher wage rate and a higher level of employment than the monopsony outcomes.

9 a If the government establishes a minimum wage at $4 per hour, the marginal cost of labour to Pollutionless Paper becomes constant at $4 per hour (up to 8,000 hours of labour). Thus equating the marginal cost of labour and the marginal revenue product of labour leads to a wage rate of $4 and 8,000 hours of labour employed. The addition of a minimum wage to the monopsony labour market results in a higher wage rate and a higher level of employment.

b The maximum wage rate Pollutionless Paper is willing to pay for 6,000 hours of labour is $6 per hour (the *MRP* of that amount of labour). The minimum wage rate that the union will accept for 6,000 hours of labour is $3 per hour (the supply price of that amount of labour).

10 a The wage rate that will actually be paid as the outcome of bargaining depends on the relative bargaining strengths of the firm and the union. Bargaining strength depends on the costs (from lockouts and strikes) that each side can inflict on the other if there is a failure to agree.

b Pollutionless Paper and the union will split the difference between $6 and $3 and agree on a wage rate of $4.50.

c If the union holds out for more than a $4.50 wage rate, Pollutionless Paper will likely lockout the workers.

d If Pollutionless Paper holds out for less than a $4.50 wage rate, the union will likely strike. When lockouts or strikes occur, it is usually because one side has misjudged the situation.

Chapter 16

Capital and Natural Resource Markets

The Structure of Capital Markets

Capital markets link saving decisions households (supply of financial capital) and investment decisions firms (demand for financial capital to buy capital goods).

◆ The price of capital is the interest rate.

◆ **Financial intermediaries** facilitate transactions in the three capital markets.

- **Stock market**—stocks of corporations traded.
- **Bond market**—bonds of corporations and governments traded.
- **Loan market**—households and firm borrow and lend.

The Demand for Capital

Capital is a *stock*.

Net investment = Δ capital stock.
= *Gross investment* (*flow* purchase of new capital) − *Depreciation* (*flow* amount of capital stock that wears out)

Demand for capital determined by firms' profit-maximizing choices.

◆ Profit-maximizing rule for *renting* capital—use additional capital until marginal revenue product equals price of using capital. Price of using capital is the interest rate.

◆ Profit-maximizing rule for *buying* capital—buy additional capital until present value of future flow of marginal revenue products equals purchase price. Or, buy additional capital when **net present value** (*NPV*) is positive.

- *NPV* = present value of future flow of marginal revenue products − purchase price.

Market demand curve for capital is horizontal sum of individual firm demand curves.

◆ $\uparrow r \to \downarrow NPV \to \downarrow$ quantity capital demanded.

◆ Rightward shift demand curve for capital because of

- technological change
- population growth

The Supply of Capital

Supply of capital determined by households' saving decisions.

◆ Saving (income − consumption) is a *flow* addition to household **wealth** (stock of accumulated past saving).

◆ Household's decision how to allocate its wealth across various assets is called *portfolio choice*.

◆ Saving determined by

- income—$\uparrow$ income $\to \uparrow$ saving.
- expected future income—when current income > expected future income $\to \uparrow$ saving.
- interest rate—substitution effect from $\uparrow r \to \uparrow$ saving. Income effect from $\uparrow r \to \uparrow$ saving for net lender and $\downarrow$ saving for net borrower.

Market supply curve of capital curve is horizontal sum of all household supply curves. Short-run supply is inelastic. Long-run supply is more elastic.

◆ $\uparrow r \to \uparrow$ quantity capital supplied.

◆ Rightward shift supply curve for capital because of

- $\uparrow$ income or $\uparrow$ population.
- more unequal distribution income or more middle-aged distribution of population.

Interest Rates and Stock Prices

Interest rates and asset prices adjust to achieve equality between quantity capital demanded and supplied. Interest rate on a stock is the *stock yield* (stock dividend/stock price). Interest rate on a bond is the *bond yield* (coupon payment/bond price).

◆ Price of stock ↑ if

- expected future dividend ↑.
- interest rate ↓.

◆ *Price-earnings ratio*—ratio of current price of stock share to current profit per share.

- If expected future profit > current profit → ↑ price-earnings ratio.
- Volume trading ↑ with divergent expectations future profits.

◆ **Takeover** when stock market value firm < present value expected future profits from operating firm.

◆ **Merger** when two firms believe that combining assets → ↑ combined stock market values.

Natural Resource Markets

Natural resources are nonproduced factors of production. **Exhaustible natural resource** can only be used once and cannot be replaced. **Nonexhaustible natural resource** can be used repeatedly (with careful management) and not be depleted.

◆ For a natural resource; the stock is the total amount that exists; the flow is the rate of use.

◆ Demand for stock of a natural resource determined by expected interest rate from holding the stock. Expected interest rate on stock of a natural resource = rate of economic profit from using the resource + expected rate of price appreciation.

Stock equilibrium for a natural resource occurs when expected interest rate on owning natural resource stock equals the interest rate on assets of comparable risk.

◆ **Hotelling Principle**—price natural resource will grow at rate = interest rate on other assets.

◆ **Choke price**—price at which use of the natural resource (the flow demand) is zero.

◆ The price of a natural resource is such that its future price is expected to rise at a rate equal to the interest rate, and to reach the choke price at the moment the resource is exhausted. Price and rate of use depend on

- Interest rate—↑ r → ↓ current price and ↑ current use.
- Demand for flow—↑ demand → ↑ current price and ↑ current use.
- Stock resource remaining—↑ current stock → ↓ current price and ↑ current use.

HELPFUL HINTS

1 A profit-maximizing firm will hire an additional factor as long as the factor's use adds more to revenue than to cost; in other words, as long as its marginal revenue product (*MRP*) is greater than its marginal cost (*MC*). The profit-maximizing quantity will be the quantity at which the marginal revenue product of a factor is just equal to its marginal cost. Since, in a competitive market, the marginal cost is the price of the factor (*PF*), this profit-maximizing condition becomes *MRP* = *PF* in a competitive factor market. This implies that the demand curve for a factor is given by its *MRP* curve.

2 The profit-maximizing condition given in Helpful Hint **1** generally applies to all competitive factor markets. However, in the case of capital markets, the condition must be adapted depending on whether the firm rents or buys capital.

The profit-maximizing firm will **rent** *capital equipment up to the point at which the marginal revenue product per rental period is equal to the rent per period.* This is the "flow version" of the profit-maximizing condition for the firm's capital input.

If, however, a firm considers buying capital rather than renting it, we must adapt the profit-maximizing condition. The reason is that capital is generally operated over more than one period and will generate marginal revenue products that are distributed over time. The purchase price, however, must be paid now. In order to compare the purchase price (*PF*) with the stream of marginal revenue products, we must compute the present value of that stream.

In the case of capital equipment that will be used over more than one period, the profit-maximizing condition becomes: buy an additional unit of capital until the present value of the stream of marginal revenue products is equal to the price of the unit of capital. Since the net present value (*NPV*) of an investment is defined as the present value of the stream of marginal revenue products minus the price of the unit of capital, an equivalent condition is: **buy** *capital equipment until the net present value* *of investment is zero*. This is the "stock version" of the profit-maximizing condition for the firm's capital input. (If you need to review the concept of present value, return to Chapter 9.)

3 You may have wondered why financial analysts equate a *rise* in bond prices with a *fall* in interest rates. This chapter explains why interest rates and all asset prices (including bond prices) are inversely related.

The interest rate or yield on an asset is equal to the income from the asset divided by the price of the asset.

$$\text{interest rate} = \frac{\text{fixed income}}{\text{price of asset}}$$

Given a *fixed* annual income from the asset, the higher the price of the asset, the lower is the interest rate or yield. For example, if a Northern Telecom bonds pays a fixed annual income of $10, and the price of a Northern Telecom bond is $100, the interest rate or yield on the bond is $10/$100 = 0.1 or 10 percent. A fall in the price of the bond to $91 will cause the yield on the bond to rise to $10/91 = 0.11 or 11 percent. Thus a fall in bond prices is equivalent to a rise in the interest rate on bonds, and vice versa.

4 The inverse relationship between the interest rate and assets prices also applies to prices of shares of stock. The relationship is slightly more complicated because the annual income from a stock—its dividend—is *variable* instead of *fixed*. Nonetheless, *ceteris paribus*, a rise in interest rates will cause a fall in stock prices, and vice versa.

S E L F - T E S T

True/False/Uncertain and Explain

1 Natural resources can be used only once and cannot be replaced.

2 If the price of a unit of capital exceeds the present value of its marginal revenue product, a profit-maximizing firm should buy it.

3 A new machine that is expected to last one year and, at the end of the year, to increase firm revenue by $1,050, sells at a price of $1,000. The firm should buy the machine if the interest rate is 6 percent.

4 If a household has negative net financial assets, a decrease in the interest rate will increase its saving.

5 The Hotelling Principle states that equilibrium occurs in the market for hotel stocks when the stock price is expected to rise at the rate of interest.

6 To say that the price of a bond has risen is the same as saying that the yield on the bond has declined.

7 A takeover of firm *A* by firm *B* would occur if firm *B* believes that the stock market value of firm *A* is greater than the present value of expected future profits from operating firm *A*.

8 While markets may efficiently allocate goods that can be replaced or reproduced, they cannot allocate exhaustible natural resources efficiently.

9 If a cheap substitute for oil is developed, we would expect to see the choke price for oil decline.

10 The economic model of exhaustible natural resources implies that the market will provide an automatic incentive to conserve as the resource gets closer to being depleted.

Multiple-Choice

1 Which of the following is physical capital?

a   a shovel
b   IBM stock
c   money
d   a General Motors bond
e   all of the above

2 Which of the following is an example of a stock?

a   investment
b   depreciation
c   capital
d   income
e   none of the above

3 The decline in the value of capital resulting from its use over time is given by

a   the level of saving.
b   investment.
c   net investment.
d   gross investment minus net investment.
e   net present value.

4 A firm is expected to pay an $8 dividend per share of stock each year indefinitely. If the market rate of interest is 8 percent, what will be the price of a share of stock in this firm?

a $8
b $8.64
c $64
d $80
e $100

5 The yield on a stock will rise when

a   either the dividend increases or the share price of the stock increases.
b   either the dividend increases or the share price of the stock decreases.
c   either the dividend decreases or the share price of the stock increases.
d   either the dividend decreases or the share price of the stock decreases.
e   none of the above occurs.

6 Bond *A* is more risky than bond *B*. Then, in equilibrium,

a   the interest rate on *A* must be higher than that on *B*.
b   the interest rate on *A* must be lower than that on *B*.
c   the interest rate on *A* must be equal to the interest rate on *B*.
d   no one will want to buy bond *A*.
e   only those who prefer risk will buy bond *A*.

7 Which of the following is an exhaustible natural resource?

a   coal
b   land
c   water
d   trees
e   none of the above

8 The yield on a stock of a natural resource is the

a   rate of interest on the loan used to buy the resource.
b   marginal revenue product of the resource.
c   marginal revenue product of the resource divided by its price.
d   marginal revenue product of the resource multiplied by the market interest rate.
e   rate of change in the price of the resource.

9 In Table 16.1, which company has the highest price-earnings ratio?

a   Company A
b   Company B
c   Company C
d   All have the same ratio.
e   Insufficient information to calculate.

TABLE **16.1**

Data	Company A	Company B	Company C
Last year's profits per share	$8	$10	$5
Dividend per share	$4	$2	$5
Value of stock per share	$80	$20	$25
Outstanding shares	1,000	10,000	3,000
Present value of expected profit	$200,000	$200,000	$50,000

10 In Table 16.1, which company has the highest yield?

a   Company A
b   Company B
c   Company C
d   All have the same yield.
e   Insufficient information to calculate.

11 In Table 16.1, which company is the most likely target of a takeover?

a Company A
b Company B
c Company C
d All are equally likely targets.
e Insufficient information to calculate.

12 The higher the rate of interest, the

a higher the net present value of an investment.
b lower the present value of the flow of marginal revenue products of an investment.
c greater the quantity of capital demanded.
d greater the marginal revenue product of capital.
e lower the marginal revenue product of capital.

13 If the interest rate increases, the

a substitution effect encourages more saving only if the household is a net borrower.
b substitution effect encourages more saving only if the household is a net lender.
c income effect encourages more saving only if the household is a net borrower.
d income effect encourages more saving only if the household is a net lender.
e statements in **b** and **d** are true.

14 Household determination of how much to hold in various assets and how much to owe in various liabilities is called

a investment.
b balance sheet decision making.
c portfolio choice.
d the price-earnings problem.
e the net present value problem.

15 If the market for a stock of a natural resource is in equilibrium, then the price of the resource is

a expected to rise at a rate equal to the rate of interest.
b expected to fall at a rate equal to the rate of interest.
c equal to the choke price of the resource.
d equal to the marginal revenue product of the resource.
e equal to the Hotelling price of the resource.

16 The current price of a natural resource is higher when

a its marginal revenue product is lower.
b the stock of the resource remaining is larger.
c the interest rate is lower.
d the choke price is lower.
e none of the above is true.

17 A bond has a redemption value of $100 and pays $10 interest each year. If you paid $100 for the bond and its price today is $98, what is its current yield?

a 2 percent
b 8.2 percent
c 10 percent
d 10.2 percent
e 12.2 percent

18 The price of a share of XYZ Corporation's stock is $80, and the current dividend payment is $4. What is the stock yield?

a 3.2 percent
b 4 percent
c 5 percent
d 8 percent
e 20 percent

19 An event occurs which almost everyone agrees will cause a decline in the future profit of the XYZ Corporation. Immediately after the event becomes known, the price of XYZ stock will

a fluctuate up and down with a high volume of trading.
b fluctuate up and down with a low volume of trading.
c fall gradually with a high volume of trading.
d fall quickly with a low volume of trading.
e fall quickly with a high volume of trading.

20 A *takeover* of a firm is likely to occur when

a the stock market value of the firm is higher than the present value of expected future profit from operating the firm.
b the stock market value of the firm is lower than the present value of expected future profit from operating the firm.
c current firm profit is higher than the present value of expected future profit from operating the firm.
d current firm profit is lower than the present value of expected future profit from operating the firm.
e interest rates are high.

21 Institutions that are primarily engaged in taking deposits, making loans, and buying securities are called

a brokers.
b financial intermediaries.
c insurance companies.
d monopsonists.
e pension funds.

22 A profit-maximizing firm will choose to buy an extra unit of capital whenever

a the present value of the flow of marginal revenue product is greater than zero.
b the cost of capital exceeds the present value of the flow of marginal revenue product.
c the cost of capital equals the present value of the flow of marginal revenue product.
d net present value is greater than zero.
e none of the above occurs.

23 Firms will invest as long as net present value

a exceeds the rate of interest.
b equals the rate of interest.
c is less than the rate of interest.
d is positive.
e is zero.

24 Which of the following would cause the supply of capital curve to shift rightward?

a an increase in the proportion of young households in the population
b an increase in the interest rate
c a decrease in the interest rate
d an increase in average household income
e an increase in the marginal revenue product of capital

25 A machine that costs $2,000 will generate marginal revenue product of $1,100 at the end of one year and the same amount at the end of two years. What is the net present value of the machine if the rate of interest is 10 percent?

a −$90.91
b −$49.90
c $0
d $90.91
e $1,909.09

Short Answer Problems

1 Why does the quantity of capital demanded increase when the interest rate falls?

2 Suppose firms A and B earned the same amount of profit per share in the most recent year but that the price of a share of stock in firm A is higher than for firm B. What does this imply about the two firms' price-earnings ratios? What does this reflect about expected future profits of the two firms?

3 Exxoff Oil Co. experiences a large and potentially very costly oil spill Sunday night. What can we infer about the degree of consensus among stock market participants' beliefs if on Monday: the price of Exxoff stock declines significantly at the opening of the stock market and remains there? the price of Exxoff stock fluctuates narrowly all day with a large volume of trade?

4 Why does a higher interest rate imply a lower current price of an exhaustible resource?

5 Larry's Lawn Care began the year with a stock of capital equal to $100,000. The capital stock depreciated by 12 percent during the year. Larry also bought $10,000 worth of new lawn care equipment during the year. What was Larry's gross investment during the year? net investment?

◐ 6 Larry's Lawn Care is considering the purchase of additional lawn mowers. These lawn mowers have a life of two years and cost $120 each. Marginal revenue products for each year are given in Table 16.2.

TABLE **16.2**

Number of Lawn Mowers	MRP in First Year	MRP in Second Year	NPV (r = 0.05)	NPV (r = 0.10)	NPV (r = 0.15)
1st	100	80			
2nd	80	64			
3rd	72	62			

a Complete Table 16.2 by computing net present values (NPV) if the interest rate is 5 percent (r = 0.05), 10 percent (r = 0.10), or 15 percent (r = 0.15).
b How many lawn mowers will Larry's Lawn Care purchase if the interest rate is 15 percent? 10 percent? 5 percent?
c Construct an approximate lawn mower demand curve for Larry's Lawn Care by graphically representing the three points identified in part **b** and drawing a curve through them.

7 The present value of expected future profits for Larry's Lawn Care is $400,000. There are 8,000 outstanding shares of stock in Larry's Lawn Care. The dividend paid in the current year was $7.50 a share.

a What is the market price of a share of Larry's Lawn Care stock?

b What is the stock yield?

8 The city of Metropolis (in which Larry's Lawn Care operates) initiates a "Yard Beautiful" award with a cash prize. As a result, the present value of expected future profits for Larry's Lawn Care increases to $600,000.

a If the market price of a share of Larry's Lawn Care stock does not change, will there be a takeover? If so, what is the highest price someone would pay for a share of stock?

b If the share price now changes to the market price and the dividend remains at $7.50 a share, what is the stock yield?

9 Gunk is an exhaustible natural resource which is running out. Only 1,215 barrels of gunk remain. Table 16.3 gives the marginal revenue product schedule for gunk.

TABLE **16.3**

Barrels of Gunk per Year	Marginal Revenue Product ($)
0	14.64
133	13.31
254	12.10
364	11.00
464	10.00
555	9.09

a Draw a graph of the demand curve for gunk (as a flow).

b What is the choke price of gunk?

10 You remain mired in the gunk problem. Suppose that the interest rate is 10 percent.

a What is the current equilibrium price of a barrel of gunk? How did you determine this?

b If the current year is year 1, complete Table 16.4 for each year until the stock of gunk is exhausted.

TABLE **16.4**

Year	Price	Initial Stock of Gunk	Final Stock of Gunk
1		1,215	
2			
3			
4			
5			

ANSWERS

True/False/Uncertain and Explain

1 U True for exhaustible, false for nonexhaustible natural resources. (377–378)

2 F Reverse is true. (369–370)

3 F $PV = \$1,050/(1 + .06) = \$990.56$. $NPV = \$990.56 - \$1,000 = -\$9.44$. Since NPV negative, don't buy. (369–370)

4 U Depends on relative strength income effect ($\uparrow$ savings) and substitution effect ($\downarrow$ savings). (372–373)

5 F True for market for natural resources. (378)

6 T Bond yield = (fixed earnings)/(price of bond). (374–375)

7 F Reverse true—if value firm *A less than* ... (376–377)

8 F Markets can be efficient if no externalities. As resource used up, price $\uparrow \rightarrow \downarrow$ quantity demanded and $\uparrow$ use substitutes. (381)

9 T Less demand for oil so people would stop using it at a lower price. (378–379)

10 T Because price will $\uparrow$. (380–381)

Multiple-Choice

1 a Others are financial capital. (368–369)

2 c Others are flows. (368–369)

3 d Equals depreciation. (368–369)

4 e r = dividend/share price. .08 = $8/share price. Share price = $8/.08. (375–376)

5 b Yield = dividend/share price. (374–376)

6 a Higher return necessary to compensate for higher risk if investor willing to hold bond. (374–375)

7 a Others are nonexhaustible natural resources. (377)

8 e See text discussion. (378–379)

9 a Current share price/most recent profit per share = $80/$8. (375–376)

10 c Dividend/share price = $5/$25. (375–376)

☉ **11 a** Stock market value company ($80/share × 1,000 shares = $80,000) < present value expected profit ($200,000). (376–377)

12 b Reverse **a**, **c** true. r does not affect MRP capital. (369–370)

13 d Because ↑ household income from lending. Substitution effect always → ↑ savings. (372–373)

14 c Definition. (372–373)

15 a This is the Hotelling Principle. (378–379)

☉ **16 c** Reverse **a**, **b** true. No direct relation current and choke prices. (378–380)

17 d Yield = yearly earnings/price bond. (374–375)

18 c Yield = dividend/share price. (375–376)

19 d ↓ expected future profit → ↓ price. Agreement → low volume. (376–377)

20 b Cost of buying < value of firm. (376–377)

21 b Definition. **c** is example of financial intermediary. (367–368)

22 d When present value flow marginal product > cost of capital. (369–370)

23 d **a**, **b**, and **c** are nonsense comparisons. (369–370)

24 d **a** → leftward shift. **b** and **c** → movement along supply curve. **e** shifts demand curve. (373–374)

☉ **25 a** $NPV = [\$1,100/(1.1) + \$1,100/(1.1)^2] - \$2,000$. (369–370)

Short Answer Problems

1 Profit-maximizing firms will demand capital as long as the present value of the stream of future marginal revenue product from the new capital exceeds the price of the new capital; in other words, as long as its net present value is positive. Since a lower interest rate implies that the present value of any given future stream of marginal revenue product will be larger, the net present value will be positive for a *larger* number of additional capital goods and thus more capital will be purchased. Therefore, the quantity of capital demanded increases as the interest rate falls.

2 The price-earnings ratio is the current price of a share of stock divided by the most recent profits per share. Thus, the price-earnings ratio of firm A's stock is greater than the price-earnings ratio of firm B's stock. This implies that, although the recent profits (per share) of the two firms may be the same, future profits (per share) for firm A are expected to be higher than for firm B.

The price of a share of stock represents the present value of *expected* future profits, so a higher price implies higher expected future profits.

3 A significant decline in the price of Exxoff stock with little volume of trade implies that there is wide consensus that the oil spill means a significant reduction in the present value of future Exxoff profits.

If, on the other hand, there is a large volume of trade in Exxoff stock with little net price movement, it implies that there is little consensus about the implications of the oil spill for the future profitability of Exxoff.

4 In equilibrium, the current price of the resource will be the price which, if the price continues to increase at a rate equal to the interest rate, the choke price will be reached at the same time that the resource is depleted. A higher interest rate means that the price is expected to rise at a faster rate. Therefore if it is to reach the choke price at the right time, it must start from a lower current price.

Another answer from a portfolio choice perspective is: the higher interest rate raises the relative attractiveness of financial assets, lowering the demand for resource assets and therefore lowering the price of a resource.

5 Gross investment is $10,000, the amount of the purchase of new capital. Net investment is –$2,000, the amount of gross investment minus depreciation of $12,000.

☉ **6 a** Completed Table 16.2 appears here as Table 16.2 Solution. NPV is calculated as the present value of the stream of marginal revenue products resulting from an investment minus the cost of the investment. For lawn mowers with a two-year life, the NPV is calculated using the following equation:

$$NPV = \frac{MRP_1}{1 + r} + \frac{MRP_2}{(1 + r)^2} - P_L$$

In this equation, MRP_1 and MRP_2 are the marginal revenue products in the first and second years, respectively, and P_L is the price of a lawn mower. The values of MRP_1 and MRP_2 are given in Table 16.2 for the first, second, and third lawn mowers and P_L is given as $120. The values for NPV given in Table 16.2 Solution are obtained by substituting these values into the above equation and evaluating the expression for the alternative values of r, the interest rate.

TABLE **16.2** SOLUTION

Number of Lawn Mowers	MRP in First Year	MRP in Second Year	NPV ($r = 0.05$)	NPV ($r = 0.10$)	NPV ($r = 0.15$)
1st	100	80	47.80	37.02	27.45
2nd	80	64	14.24	5.62	−2.04
3rd	72	62	4.81	−3.31	−10.51

b If the interest rate is 15 percent, only one additional lawn mower will be purchased since the second lawn mower has negative net present value. If the interest rate is 10 percent, two lawn mowers will be purchased, and if the interest rate is 5 percent, three lawn mowers will be purchased.

c The approximate lawn mower demand curve is illustrated in Fig. 16.1. The curve indicates that, at an interest rate of 15 percent, one lawn mower will be demanded. At an interest rate of 10 percent, two lawn mowers will be demanded and, at an interest rate of 5 percent, three lawn mowers will be demanded.

FIGURE **16.1**

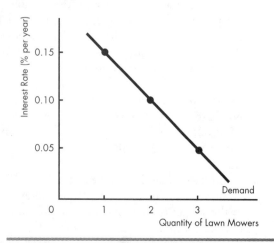

7 a The market price of a share of Larry's Lawn Care stock will be the present value of expected future profits for the firm divided by the number of shares outstanding: $50.

b The stock yield is 15 percent. This is the dividend ($7.50) as a percentage of the price of a share of stock ($50).

8 a Yes, there will be a takeover because the stock market value ($400,000) is less than the present value of expected future profits ($600,000). The highest price someone would pay for a share of stock is $75, the present value of expected future profits divided by the number of shares ($600,000/8,000).

b The stock yield will now be 10 percent. This is the dividend ($7.50) as a percentage of the new market price of a share of stock ($75).

9 a The demand curve for gunk is given by the marginal revenue product curve. It is illustrated in Fig. 16.2.

FIGURE **16.2**

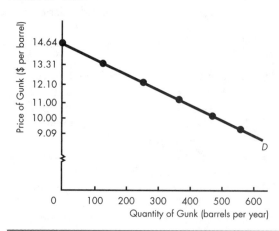

b The choke price for gunk is $14.64. This is the price that is high enough that the resource will not be used at all.

10 a If the interest rate is 10 percent, the current price of a barrel of gunk is $10. We know that the current (equilibrium) price must be such that if the price of gunk is increasing at a rate of 10 percent per year (equal to the rate of interest), the stock will be depleted just as the choke price is achieved. We can find the current price by noting that (1) the choke price is $14.64 and (2) the remaining stock is 1,215 barrels, and then working backward.

Since the price of gunk is growing at the rate of 10 percent per year, the price in the year before the choke price is reached must be $14.64 (the choke price) divided by 1.10 (1 + the 10% growth rate of price) or $13.31. From Table 16.3 (and recognizing that gunk is just depleted as the $14.64 price is reached) we can infer that 133 barrels of gunk would be purchased in that year. Proceeding in a similar manner, working backward until all 1,215 barrels of gunk have been purchased, we discover that the current equilibrium price must be $10.

b Using the procedure outlined in part **a**, Table 16.4 can be completed as shown in Table 16.4 Solution.

TABLE **16.4** SOLUTION

Year	Price	Initial Stock of Gunk	Final Stock of Gunk
1	10.00	1,215	751
2	11.00	751	387
3	12.10	387	133
4	13.31	133	0
5	14.64	0	

KEY CONCEPTS

Uncertainty and Risk

Uncertainty—more than one event may occur, but we don't know which one. Related concepts are

- *Probability*—number between 0 and 1 measuring the chance of an event occurring.

- **Risk**—can estimate the probability of uncertain events.

Facing uncertainty, individuals maximize **expected utility**—average utility from all possible events. Expected utility may differ from *actual* utility (utility the individual actually gets when an event actually occurs).

- **Utility of wealth**—utility an individual gets from wealth. ↑ wealth → ↑ utility, but *marginal utility of wealth* ↓. Utility of wealth curve measures cost of risk.

- Cost of risk = amount expected wealth must ↑ to → same expected utility as no-risk situation.

- The more *risk averse* (prefer less risk), the more rapidly marginal utility wealth ↓ (the more curved is utility of wealth curve) and the greater the cost of risk.

- For a *risk-neutral* individual, risk is costless and her utility of wealth curve is linear.

Insurance

People buy insurance to reduce risk.

- Insurance works by pooling a large number of risks so that the total number of adverse outcomes is relatively certain. Insurance companies collect premiums from everyone to cover total cost of accidents, but payout benefits only to those suffering losses.

- Insurance is profitable because people are risk averse and will pay to ↓ risk. People pay a small premium to insure that they will not suffer a large loss.

Information

Economic information reduces uncertainty, but gathering information has an opportunity cost—**information cost**. Because information is costly, people economize on its use.

- Buyers searching for lowest price use *optimal-search rule*:
  - search until expected marginal benefit search = marginal cost search, then buy; or
  - search until a price ≤ **reservation price** (highest price buyer willing to pay) is found, then buy.

Sellers advertise to persuade and inform.

- Quality of *experience goods* can only be assessed after they are bought → advertising for *experience goods* usually persuades.

- Quality of *search goods* can be assessed before they are bought → advertising for *search goods* usually informs.

Advertising → ↑ costs, ↑ competition, and possibly → ↓ costs if allow economies of scale.

Private Information

Private information is available to one person but too costly for others to obtain → two problems.

- **Moral hazard**—post-agreement incentive to ↑ personal benefits at expense of uniformed party.

◆ **Adverse selection**—tendency for people to accept contracts with private information that can be used to their own advantage and to disadvantage of uninformed.

Information problems can be overcome through **signals**—actions conveying information that can be used by market. Examples are warranties on used cars; credit information and loan limits in the loan market; driving record and deductibles in car insurance.

Asymmetric Information in Labour Markets

Asymmetric information in labour markets → difficulty for employer to monitor efforts employee.

◆ Employers use compensation schemes (sales commissions, **rank-tournament compensation schemes**, profit shares) to spur employees to unmonitored actions that maximize profit.

Managing Risk in Financial Markets

Risk in financial markets can be lowered through diversifying asset holdings (don't put all eggs in same basket).

In an **efficient market**, if something can be anticipated, it will be, and the anticipation will affect the current price.

◆ Actual price = expected future price and embodies all available information.

◆ No forecastable profit opportunities available.

The stock market is an efficient market. Stock prices fluctuate when new information becomes available.

H E L P F U L   H I N T S

1   Uncertainty plays a part in almost every economic decision. Yet in previous chapters we have ignored uncertainty in analysing consumers' and firms' choices. Why? To keep the analysis simple and because uncertainty usually does not negate important economic rules. For example, the key rule for understanding profit maximization is for the firm to choose the level of output where $MC = MR$. The firm may be uncertain about both its MC and MR, but it still tries to find the level of output where they are equal. If we had incorporated uncertainty into the analysis from the start, the profit-maximizing rule would have been more complicated, and it

would have been harder to see the $MC = MR$ rule.

A correct model-building strategy initially leaves out the complication of uncertainty. Remember from Chapter 1 that models are highly simplified representations of the real world that attempt to focus on essential forces (like profit maximization) while abstracting from some less important real-world detail (like uncertainty). Before drawing final conclusions about the real world from simple models, it is important to consider whether, when we reinsert real-world complexities like uncertainty, the outcomes will be the same. This chapter on uncertainty provides some basic tools that can be used, in more advanced courses, to "complicate" or enrich the simple models of consumers' and firms' choices.

2   The existence of risk and uncertainty is an objective feature of reality. How decision makers cope with uncertainty, however, depends on their *attitudes* towards risk. Some people are more risk averse than others.

A person's *utility of wealth* schedule reflects her degree of risk aversion. Economists believe that most people's utility of wealth schedules exhibit diminishing marginal utility as wealth increases. However, for two people, for example, Alexis and Madeleine, Alexis's marginal utility of wealth may decrease at a faster rate than Madeleine's. Alexis would be more risk averse than Madeleine and less likely to undertake risky ventures that offer the possibility of a high return at the cost of a greater probability of loss. *Ceteris paribus*, Alexis would be less likely to undertake risky ventures because she will attach a relatively greater utility weight to the probable decrease of wealth from a loss than to the probable increase in wealth from a success. Because of these relative weights, a risk averse person is also more likely to take out insurance against loss.

There are many markets besides that for insurance (e.g., the stock market) that exist, in part, to allow risk averse people to offload risk to those who are less risk averse.

3   Two important concepts for analysing choice under uncertainty are *expected wealth* and *expected utility*. Expected wealth (sometimes called expected value) is the average wealth arising from all possible outcomes. It is computed as the weighted average of the wealth associated with each possible outcome, where the weights are the probabilities of each outcome.

For example, if there are three possible outcomes yielding wealth of W_1, W_2, and W_3, and the probabilities associated with these outcomes are p_1, p_2, and p_3, respectively, then expected wealth equals

$$(W_1 \times p_1) + (W_2 \times p_2) + (W_3 \times p_3).$$

Expected utility is the average utility arising from all possible outcomes. It is calculated in the same way. If the utilities associated with each possible wealth outcome are U_1, U_2, and U_3, respectively, then expected utility equals

$$(U_1 \times p_1) + (U_2 \times p_2) + (U_3 \times p_3).$$

In analysing choice under uncertainty, we must first calculate expected wealth. But a decision is ultimately based on the expected utility associated with that expected wealth.

S E L F - T E S T

True/False/Uncertain and Explain

1 Risk is a state in which more than one event may occur, but we don't know which one.

2 The more rapidly your marginal utility of wealth diminishes, the less risk averse you are.

3 A risk-neutral person has a constant marginal utility of wealth.

4 If Petro-Canada drills in an uncharted region of the Northwest Territories without any idea of the likelihood of striking oil, Petro-Canada faces uncertainty rather than risk.

5 Advertising for search goods is designed mainly to inform rather than persuade.

6 If you are careless with matches because you know you have fire insurance, an adverse selection problem exists.

7 An efficient compensation scheme maximizes both profits for the firm and compensation for the employee.

8 Diversified investment portfolios are preferable to undiversified portfolios.

9 In an efficient market, the actual price is rarely equal to the expected future price.

10 If prices in an efficient market are volatile, expectations about future prices must be volatile.

Multiple-Choice

1 The more rapidly a person's marginal utility of wealth diminishes, the

a more risk inclined the person is.
b more risk-neutral the person is.
c more risk averse the person is.
d more likely it is that the person has a moral hazard problem.
e less likely the person is to take out insurance.

2 The expected value of a game that gives a 50 percent chance of winning $60 and a 50 percent chance of winning nothing is

a $10.
b $20.
c $30.
d $60.
e none of the above.

3 On a normal utility of wealth curve diagram with wealth on the horizontal axis and utility on the vertical axis, the marginal utility of wealth is

a a point on the horizontal axis.
b a point on the vertical axis.
c an area under the utility of wealth curve.
d the slope of a ray from the origin to a point on the utility of wealth curve.
e the slope of the utility of wealth curve.

4 Goods whose quality can be assessed only after they are bought are called

a private information goods.
b search goods.
c experience goods.
d inferior goods.
e lemons.

5 The buyer's reservation price is

a the lowest price that the buyer is willing to pay.
b the highest price that the buyer is willing to pay.
c the price equating the expected marginal benefit and marginal cost of searching.
d a and c.
e b and c.

6 Warranties will distinguish good cars from lemons only if

a warranties cost the dealer nothing.
b car prices are not affected by whether or not the dealer gives a warranty.
c providing warranties is worthwhile for dealers of good cars and too costly for dealers of lemons.
d providing warranties is worthwhile for both dealers of good cars and lemons.
e a and b.

7 According to the utility of wealth schedules in Table 17.1,

a Chloe is more risk averse than Esther.
b Esther is more risk averse than Chloe.
c Chloe is risk-neutral, while Esther is risk averse.
d Esther is risk-neutral, while Chloe is risk averse.
e it is impossible to calculate risk aversion and risk neutrality.

TABLE **17.1** UTILITY OF WEALTH

| Wealth ($) | Utility (units) | |
	Chloe	Esther
0	0	0
20	45	60
40	80	90
60	110	100
80	130	105

8 Chloe's expected *wealth* from an investment opportunity that will pay either $40 or $80 with equal probability is

a $60.
b $105.
c $120.
d $210.
e none of the above.

9 Refer to Table 17.1 and Fact 17.1. If Esther has no sickness insurance, her expected *wealth* is

a $30.
b $48.
c $60.
d $80.
e $100.

FACT **17.1**

Esther earns $60 if she stays healthy and works, but earns zero if she gets sick and cannot work. Esther has an 80 percent chance of staying healthy and a 20 percent chance of getting sick.

10 Refer to Table 17.1 and Fact 17.1. If Esther has no sickness insurance, her expected *utility* is

a 0.
b 50.
c 80.
d 100.
e none of the above.

11 Refer to Table 17.1 and Fact 17.1. Esther pays $20 for sickness insurance that pays out $60 if she is sick and nothing if she is healthy. Esther's expected *wealth* is now

a $36.
b $40.
c $56.
d $100.
e none of the above.

12 Refer to Table 17.1 and Fact 17.1. Esther pays $20 for sickness insurance that pays out $60 if she is sick and nothing if she is healthy. Esther's expected *utility* is now

a 40.
b 90.
c 92.
d 100.
e none of the above.

13 Which compensation scheme is most likely to be efficient in the case of a chief executive officer of a corporation?

a commission on sales
b share of total firm profits
c salary based on years of employment
d tournament-like prize
e b and d

14 Which compensation scheme is most likely to be efficient in the case of a salesperson?

a hourly wage rate
b commission on sales
c share of total firm profits
d salary based on years of employment
e none of the above

15 Mira must choose Option *A* or Option *B*. Option *A* guarantees her $10,000. Option *B* gives her $5,000 with probability 0.5 and $15,000 with probability 0.5. Having a normal utility of wealth curve, Mira will

a prefer and choose *A*.
b prefer and choose *B*.
c prefer *A* but choose *B*.
d prefer *B* but choose *A*.
e be indifferent between *A* and *B*.

16 If there are three possible events and each has a probability of occurrence of one-third, then

a neither uncertainty nor risk exists.
b uncertainty exists, but not risk.
c risk exists, but not uncertainty.
d both uncertainty and risk exist.
e there is not enough information to distinguish between uncertainty and risk.

17 In an efficient market, which of the following statements is *false*?

a The current price is equal to the expected future price.
b The current price embodies all available information.
c No forecastable profit opportunities exist.
d Prices are stable.
e Expectations are subject to fluctuations.

18 An efficient compensation scheme

a cannot incorporate the effects of luck.
b will not be accepted by the employee.
c splits revenues equally between the employee and employer.
d maximizes the employee's expected income.
e maximizes the employer's expected profit.

19 Optimizing buyers will devote additional resources searching for information when

a expected marginal benefit is positive.
b expected marginal benefit is less than the marginal cost of searching.
c expected marginal benefit equals the marginal cost of searching.
d marginal cost of searching is positive.
e none of the above.

20 If buyers cannot assess the quality of used cars and there are no warranties,

a only bad used cars will be sold.
b only good used cars will be sold.
c good cars will be sold at a higher price than bad cars.
d there is a moral hazard problem.
e there is no adverse selection problem.

21 An increase in Robin's wealth from $3,000 to $6,000 raises her utility from 80 units to 100. If she has a normal utility of wealth curve, with wealth of $9,000 her utility might be

a 100 units.
b 115 units.
c 120 units.
d 125 units.
e 180 units.

22 The cost of risk is the amount by which expected wealth must increase to give the same

a marginal utility as a no-risk situation.
b expected utility as a no-risk situation.
c expected wealth as a no-risk situation.
d probability as a no-risk situation.
e insurance as a no-risk situation.

23 After purchasing theft insurance, you decide to spend less on home security devices. Your behaviour is an example of

a adverse selection.
b free riding.
c insurance market signalling.
d asymmetric information.
e moral hazard.

24 Advertising

a for search goods is designed to persuade.
b for experience goods is designed to inform.
c that is persuasive increases competition.
d is costly.
e is all of the above.

25 Stock market prices are volatile because

a expectations are irrational.
b expectations change frequently due to new information.
c stock markets are inefficient markets.
d stockholders do not behave like inventory holders.
e all of the above statements are true.

Short Answer Problems

1 If you agree to pay the first $200 worth of damage ($200 deductible), your car insurance premium might be $1,000 per year. But if you agree to a $500 deductible, your insurance premium might be $800 per year. Why do insurance companies charge premiums that are related inversely to the total loss that the customer agrees to bear?

2 Why do banks often lend more readily to people who have credit cards and have previously borrowed from the bank than to people who have always paid in cash and never borrowed?

3 Many large firms are owned by a group of stockholders who hire managers to run the firm. Why is profit sharing a good compensation scheme for top management in such a firm?

4 What is meant by an efficient market? Explain why the current market price will always be equal to the expected future price in an efficient market.

5 Figure 17.1 presents Katherine's utility of wealth curve. She is considering an investment that will pay either W_1 with a 50 percent probability or W_2 with a 50 percent probability.
  a Label as U_1 Katherine's utility if she receives W_1. Label as U_2 Katherine's utility if she receives W_2. Label Katherine's expected wealth EW and her expected utility U. What does her expected wealth equal?
  b What is Katherine's cost of risk? Explain.

FIGURE **17.1**

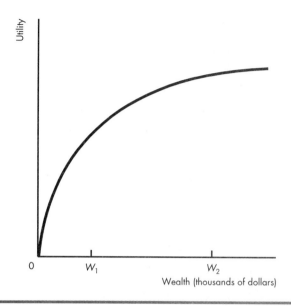

6 Table 17.2 presents the utility of wealth schedules for Ren and Stimpy. Who is more risk averse, Ren or Stimpy? Explain.

TABLE **17.2** UTILITY OF WEALTH

Wealth ($)	Utility (units)	
	Ren	**Stimpy**
0	0	0
20	100	60
40	150	110
60	175	150
80	187	180
100	193	200

7 Suppose that Ren and Stimpy initially have $40 each. They are offered a chance to play a game that costs $20 to play. There is a 50 percent chance of winning $60 and a 50 percent chance of winning nothing.
  a What is the expected value (*expected wealth*) of the game?
  b What is the *expected utility* of the game for Ren? for Stimpy?
  c If Ren and Stimpy are optimizers, who will be willing to play the game and who will prefer not to play and hold on to the initial $40? Explain.

8 Table 17.3 presents Leonard's utility of wealth schedule. Leonard is considering an investment project that will pay either zero or $20,000 with equal probability.

TABLE **17.3** LEONARD'S UTILITY OF WEALTH

Wealth (000 $)	Utility (units)
0	0
4	52
5	60
8	79
10	87
15	98
20	104

a What is Leonard's expected wealth from the project?
b What is Leonard's expected utility?
c What is Leonard's cost of risk?
d Is Leonard willing to undertake the project if it costs him $5,000?

9 Suppose that there are many investment projects identical to the one in Short Answer Problem **8**, and many individuals with the same utility of wealth schedule as Leonard. Leonard wants to buy insurance against the failure of the project (the zero payment outcome).

a What is the most that Leonard would be willing to pay for an insurance policy that pays him $20,000 if the project fails? [*Hint*: You do not need to consider the cost of the project.]
b What is the least an insurance company would charge if its operating cost (above money paid out in claims) is $1,000 per policy?
c Is there a market opportunity for insurance?

10 Dylan owns some land on which he usually grows vegetables. This year he has accepted a job as a bartender and will not be able to tend the vegetable patch. Dylan is thinking of hiring Thomas, who has some gardening experience, to grow vegetables for him.

Thomas has been milking cows for a dairy farmer, and working very hard for $30 per day. From conversations with Thomas, Dylan gathers that Thomas places a value of $10 on relaxation —Thomas prefers to relax rather than to work, but a day of working for $10 or a day of relaxing are equally acceptable.

Dylan knows that income from growing vegetables depends on how hard the cultivator works and on weather conditions. Table 17.4 gives the alternative total incomes from the possible combinations of work effort and weather conditions. There is a 50 – 50 chance of good or bad weather.

TABLE **17.4** INCOME FROM VEGETABLE GROWING ($ PER DAY)

| Weather | Worker's Effort | |
	Works Hard	Relaxes
Good	$160	$80
Bad	$80	$80

Dylan is considering two alternative compensation schemes.

Scheme 1 Dylan pays Thomas $31 per day.
Scheme 2 Dylan pays Thomas $10 per day plus 26 percent of the income from vegetable growing.

Using this information, work out which compensation scheme Dylan should adopt. [*Remember*: An efficient compensation scheme has two features. It must maximize profit for the principal and be acceptable to the agent (make the agent at least as well off as in the best alternative job).]

A N S W E R S

True/False/Uncertain and Explain

1 **F** Definition uncertainty. (389)
2 **F** More risk averse. (389–391)
3 **T** See text discussion. Linear marginal utility of wealth curve. (391)
4 **T** Risk means probabilities could be estimated. (389)
5 **T** Quality can be assessed before buying. (394)
6 **F** Moral hazard problem. (395, 397–398)
7 **F** Maximize profit and be acceptable to employee. (398)
8 **U** True if investor risk averse, but may be false otherwise. (402–403)
9 **F** Actual price = expected future price. (403)
10 **T** See text discussion. (403)

Multiple-Choice

 1 c Moral hazard irrelevant. More likely to insure. (389–391)
 2 c ($60 × 0.5) + ($0 × 0.5). (389–391)
 3 e Δ utility/Δ wealth. (389–390)
 5 e See text discussion. (393–394)
 6 c Buyers believe warranty signal because cost of false signal high. (395–396)
 7 b Marginal utility of wealth diminishes more rapidly. (389–391)
 8 a ($40 × 0.5) + ($80 × 0.5). (389–391)
 9 b ($60 × 0.8) + ($0 × 0.2). (390–392)
10 c (100 × 0.8) + (0 × 0.2). (389–392)
11 b (($60 − $20) × 0.8) + (($60 − $20) × 0.2). (389–392)
12 b Wealth in either case = $40 ($60 − $20). Expected utility = (90 × 0.8) + (90 × 0.2). (389–392)
13 e Strong connection effort/competition and profit. (398–401)
14 b Directly links unmonitored effort to outcome. (398–400)
15 a Expected value A and B equal, but A less risky, so preferable. (389–391)
16 d Definitions. Risk is subset of uncertainty. (389)
17 d Prices fluctuate with changes in expectations. (403)
18 e Designed by principal and must be acceptable to agent. (398)
19 e When expected marginal benefit > marginal cost. (393–394)
20 a Opposite **d**, **e** true. (395–396)
21 b With diminishing marginal utility of wealth, must be < 120. (389–391)
22 b See text discussion. (391)
23 e See text discussion. (395)
24 d **a**, **b**, **c** true if reverse persuade and inform. (394)
25 b Only source of change in efficient market. (403)

Short Answer Problems

1 By allowing customers to pay lower premiums if they agree to bear a higher share of total damages, insurance companies alleviate the adverse selection problem. High-risk drivers know that they are accident prone and are willing to pay higher premiums for nearly full coverage, while low-risk drivers know that they seldom have accidents and will choose lower premiums with lower coverage. With deductibles, the adverse-selection problem of high-risk people driving low-risk people out of the market is less likely to occur. The insurance company can charge differential premiums that reflect the different risks that it is insuring.

2 Banks have more information about the ability and willingness to pay of people who have previously borrowed from them or from other financial institutions. A good loan repayment record is evidence (a signal) that the customer is a low-risk borrower. If a customer has never borrowed before, the bank must find other ways to assess whether the customer is a high-risk or a low-risk borrower.

3 Neither the effort nor the output of the managers can be monitored easily by the stockholders. But since the decisions of managers have a direct and significant bearing on the profit of the firm, their incentive is to make decisions that maximize stockholder profit if they share in any increase in profit through a profit-sharing compensation scheme.

4 An efficient market is one in which the actual price embodies all available relevant information. The price will thus be equal to the expected future price and there will be no forecastable profit opportunities. The current market price will always be equal to the expected future price in an efficient market because any deviation would be eliminated immediately since it provides an expected profit opportunity.

5 a Figure 17.1 Solution illustrates Katherine's utilities if she receives W_1 and W_2. Her expected wealth (EW) equals the probability of receiving W_1 multiplied by W_1, plus the probability of receiving W_2 multiplied by W_2. Because each probability equals 0.5, EW is simply the average of (halfway between) W_1 and W_2. In a similar calculation, expected utility (U) is the weighted average of (halfway between) U_1 and U_2.
  b The cost of risk is the amount expected wealth must increase to give the same expected utility as a no-risk situation. If Katherine receives wealth W with no-risk, that gives the same level of utility as does EW. Katherine's expected wealth (EW) needs to be greater than the no-risk wealth (W) by the amount ($EW − W$) in order for her to be indifferent between the two outcomes. Therefore, ($EW − W$) is the cost of risk.

FIGURE **17.1** SOLUTION

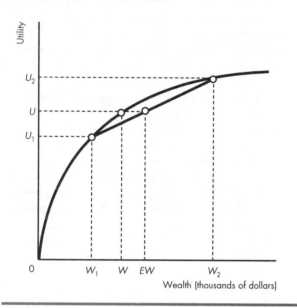

6   To find out who is more risk averse, we must determine whose marginal utility of wealth decreases faster as wealth increases. Table 17.6 presents the total and marginal utility of wealth for Ren and Stimpy. Since Ren's marginal utility of wealth decreases faster than Stimpy's, Ren is the more risk averse.

TABLE **17.6**   TOTAL/MARGINAL UTILITY OF WEALTH

	Ren		Stimpy	
	Total	Marginal	Total	Marginal
	Utility	Utility	Utility	Utility
Wealth ($)	(units)	(units)	(units)	(units)
0	0		0	
		 100		 60
20	100		60	
		 50		 50
40	150		110	
		 25		 40
60	175		150	
		 12		 30
80	187		180	
		 6		 20
100	193		200	

7 a   The expected value of the game, or the *expected wealth* from playing the game, can be calculated using the method in Helpful Hint **3**. Multiply each possible wealth outcome by its probability of occurrence and sum the results. Winning the game yields a wealth of $80 ($40 to start − $20

to play + $60 prize). Losing yields a wealth of $20 ($40 to start − $20 to play). The expected value or expected wealth of the game is ($80 × 0.5) + ($20 × 0.5) = $50.

   b   The *expected utility* of the game can also be calculated using the method in Helpful Hint **3**. Multiply the utility of each possible wealth outcome by its probability of occurrence and sum the results.
      For Ren, expected utility is (187 × 0.5) + (100 × 0.5) = 143.5 units. For Stimpy, expected utility is (180 × 0.5) + (60 × 0.5) = 120 units.

   c   To decide whether or not to play the game, each player compares the expected utility of the outcome of the game with the expected utility of not playing the game and keeping $40.
      For Ren, the expected utility of the game is 143.5 units, which is less than the 150 units of utility of keeping the $40 wealth. Ren will not play the game. For Stimpy, the expected utility of the game is 120 units, which is more than the 110 units of utility of keeping the $40 wealth. Stimpy will play the game. These results are not surprising, since Ren is more risk averse than Stimpy and, *ceteris paribus*, is less likely to play a game of chance and more likely to hold on to a sure $40.

8 a   Leonard's expected wealth is ($0 × 0.5) + ($20,000 × 0.5) = $10,000.

   b   Leonard's expected utility is (0 × 0.5) + (104 × 0.5) = 52 units.

   c   Uncertain wealth of $0 or $20,000 yields expected wealth of $10,000 and expected utility of 52 units. From Table 17.3, we can see that certain (no-risk) wealth of $4,000 also yields utility of 52 units. The cost of risk is $6,000, the amount by which expected wealth must be increased beyond no-risk wealth to give the same utility as the no-risk situation ($10,000 − $4,000).

   d   For Leonard, the forgone utility of the $5,000 cost of investing in the project (60 units) is greater than the expected utility of the risky project (52 units). Leonard is not willing to undertake the project.

9 a   Leonard is willing to buy insurance as long as the utility from the certain outcome after buying insurance yields at least as much expected utility as the risky project. Since the expected utility of the project (52 units) is the same as the expected utility of a certain outcome of $4,000, Leonard would be willing to pay up to $16,000 for an insurance policy that pays him $20,000 if the project fails. With insurance, Leonard will receive $20,000 whether the project succeeds or

fails. Subtracting an insurance premium of $16,000 leaves him with a certain net income of $4,000. Leonard would be indifferent between purchasing insurance and taking the risk on the project. At any premium less than $16,000, Leonard would be better off with insurance. He would have a certain net income greater than $4,000 and a utility of greater than 52 units.

b A profit-maximizing insurance company would charge at least enough to cover its expected costs per project—the expected payout plus operating costs. Since half of the projects fail, the expected payout is $10,000 per project ($20,000 × 0.5). With operating costs of $1,000 per project, the least an insurance company would charge is $11,000 ($10,000 + $1,000).

c Since individuals are willing to pay $16,000, which is more than the minimum price insurance companies must charge to make a profit ($11,000), there is a market for insurance. Compared with a situation with no insurance, individuals and insurers will both be better off at any premium between $11,000 and $16,000.

10 Income depends on whether Thomas works hard or relaxes and whether there is good or bad weather. The probability of good or bad weather is 0.5.

If Thomas works hard, expected total income is ($160 × 0.5) + ($80 × 0.5) = $120.

If Thomas relaxes, expected total income is ($80 × 0.5) + ($80 × 0.5) = $80.

To see which compensation scheme is efficient, calculate the outcome of each scheme for the principal and the agent.

Scheme 1: Dylan (principal) pays Thomas (agent) $31 per day. Will Thomas work hard or relax? If Thomas relaxes, he receives $31. Since he does not have to exert himself, the value of relaxing is also $31. If Thomas works hard, he also receives $31, but since he has to exert himself, the value of working hard is $31 − $10 = $21. Thomas will choose to relax. Expected income will be $80 per day, with $31 going to Thomas and $49 going to Dylan.

Scheme 2: Dylan (principal) pays Thomas (agent) $10 plus 26 percent of the income from vegetable growing. If Thomas relaxes, he receives $10 + (0.26 × $80) = $30.80. Since he does not have to exert himself, the value of relaxing is also $30.80. If Thomas works hard, he receives $10 + (0.26 × $120) = $41.20. Since he has to exert himself, the value of working hard is $41.20 − $10 = $31.20. Thomas will choose to work hard. Expected income will be $120 per day, with $41.20 going to Thomas and $78.80 going to Dylan.

Both Dylan and Thomas are better off under compensation scheme 2.

But is Thomas better off growing vegetables under compensation scheme 2 than he would be milking cows? If Thomas milks cows, he earns $30, but since he has to work hard, the value to him is $30 − $10 = $20. This is lower than the value he receives working hard growing vegetables under scheme 2. Therefore, compensation scheme 2 is more efficient.

P R O B L E M

FIGURE **P3.1**   LABOUR MARKETS FOR PROGRAMMERS

(a) Left-Handed

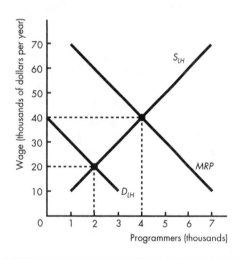

(b) Right-Handed

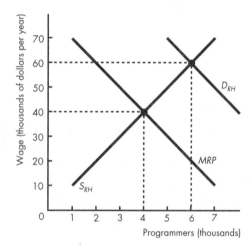

Suppose the computer software industry uses only two inputs—programmers (labour) and computers (capital). All programmers, whether left-handed or right-handed, have computer science degrees, are equally skilled and productive, and have the marginal revenue product (*MRP*) curve in Fig. P3.1(a) and (b).

Software firms (run mostly by right-handers) discriminate against left-handed programmers, believing (wrongly) that left-handers are less productive than right-handers. Figure P3.1(a) shows the supply curve of left-handed programmers and firms' demand curve for left-handed programmers.

Software firms also discriminate in favour of right-handed programmers, believing (wrongly) that right-handers are more productive than left-handers. Figure P3.1(b) shows the supply curve

of right-handed programmers and firms' demand curve for right-handed programmers.

a   What is the relationship between the wage and the marginal revenue product for left-handed programmers? for right-handed programmers?

b   Explain the competitive forces that would tend to eliminate this form of discrimination, even without government legislation.

c   If owners of firms are so strongly prejudiced against left-handers that they are willing to accept lower profits rather than employ left-handers, will competitive forces eliminate this discrimination?

d   The government introduces pay equity legislation, designed to equalize wages between left-handers and right-handers. The legislation includes an educational program to inform firms of the true and equal productivity of all programmers, regardless of their "handedness." If the program is successful, what will be the wage of programmers? the employment of left-handed programmers? the employment of right-handed programmers?

e   With equalized programmer wages, what is now the relationship between the wage and the marginal revenue product for left-handed programmers? for right-handed programmers? What other meaning does *pay equity* have besides paying different groups equal wages?

f   As a result of the pay equity legislation, what has happened to the *average* wage of programmers? Assuming programmers and capital are substitute inputs, use a diagram to explain the impact on each firm's demand for capital. What will happen to the price and employment of capital in the software industry in the short run? in the long run?

g   As a result of the pay equity legislation, what has happened to the average wage of *left-handed* programmers? Explain the impact on the decisions of left-handers to invest in human capital.

MIDTERM EXAMINATION

You should allocate 32 minutes for this examination (16 questions, 2 minutes per question). For each question, choose the one *best* answer.

I   Refer to Fig. P3.2. If demand for a factor of production increases from D_0 to D_1, the *change* in transfer earnings is

a   area *ihfc*.
b   area *jcfk*.
c   area *Ofk*.
d   area *Ofh*.
e   none of the above

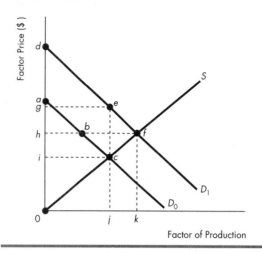

2   Household savings are larger when either current income is

a   low compared with expected future income or interest rates are high.
b   low compared with expected future income or interest rates are low.
c   high compared with expected future income or interest rates are high.
d   high compared with expected future income or interest rates are low.
e   above or below the reservation wage.

3   An increase in Katherine's wealth from $3,000 to $6,000 raises her utility from 80 units to 100. If she is risk-neutral, with wealth of $9,000, her utility might be

a   100 units.
b   115 units.
c   120 units.
d   125 units.
e   180 units.

4   A department store that pays clerks a fixed wage that does not depend on sales is likely to have problems of

a   moral hazard.
b   adverse selection.
c   private information.
d   creating work incentives.
e   all of the above.

5 XYZ Corporation is expected to pay a dividend of $5 a share every year. If the annual interest rate is 5 percent, what is the market price of a share of XYZ stock?

a $50.00
b $5.00
c $5.25
d $4.76
e $100.00

6 The choke price of a natural resource is the price at which

a the resource will begin to be used.
b no one uses the resource.
c the resource will be used as a substitute for other scarce resources.
d the resource will begin to be conserved.
e economists check into the Heartbreak Hotelling.

7 The demand curve for a factor of production will shift rightward as a result of a(n)

a decrease in the price of the factor.
b increase in the price of the factor.
c decrease in the price of a substitute factor.
d increase in the price of a substitute factor.
e decrease in the price of output.

8 Suppose a profit-maximizing firm hires labour in a competitive labour market. If the marginal revenue product of labour is greater than the wage, the firm should

a increase the wage rate.
b decrease the wage rate.
c increase the quantity of labour it hires.
d decrease the quantity of labour it hires.
e shift to a more labour-intensive production process.

9 A group of union workers with a variety of skills who work for the same firm or industry is a(n)

a industrial union.
b craft union.
c local union.
d national union.
e public sector union.

10 Refer to Fig. P3.3. For any given wage,

a the elasticity of demand for skilled workers is greater than the elasticity of demand for unskilled workers.
b more skilled workers will be hired than unskilled workers.
c more unskilled workers will be hired than skilled workers.
d the horizontal distance between the curves is the compensation for the cost of acquiring skill.
e the horizontal distance between the curves is the *MRP* of skill.

FIGURE **P3.3**

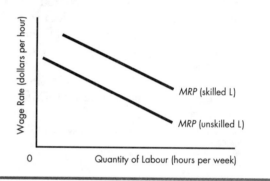

11 A high price-earnings ratio means

a current share price is higher than the expected future share price.
b investors will want to sell the stock to realize profits.
c future profits are expected to be high relative to current profits.
d future profits are expected to be low relative to current profits.
e none of the above.

12 If the net present value of a new machine is positive then

a the firm should not buy the machine.
b the present value of the machine's stream of marginal revenue products is greater than the purchase price.
c the present value of the machine's stream of marginal revenue products is less than the purchase price.
d a and b.
e a and c.

13 Which of the following statements is/are *true*?
1 Quality of search goods can only be assessed after they are bought.
2 Quality of search goods can be assessed before they are bought.
3 Advertising for experience goods usually persuades.
4 Advertising for experience goods usually informs.

a 1 and 3
b 1 and 4
c 2 and 3
d 2 and 4
e none of the above

14 Insurance is most likely to be purchased by someone whose

a total utility of wealth diminishes rapidly.
b total utility of wealth diminishes slowly.
c marginal utility of wealth diminishes rapidly.
d marginal utility of wealth diminishes slowly.
e marginal utility of wealth is constant.

15 For a monopsonist facing an upward-sloping supply curve of labour (*S*), the marginal cost of labour (*MCL*) curve

a intersects the *MRP* curve of labour at the equilibrium wage.
b is below and parallel to *S*.
c is identical to *S*.
d is above and parallel to *S*.
e is none of the above.

16 Suppose the government passes a minimum wage law that prohibits anyone from hiring labour at less than $8 per hour. In Fig. P3.4, the monopsonist will hire

a 250 hours of labour.
b 300 hours of labour.
c 350 hours of labour.
d 400 hours of labour.
e 500 hours of labour.

FIGURE **P3.4**

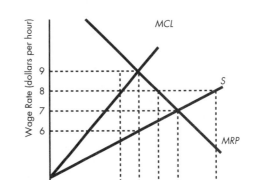

ANSWERS

Problem

a For the 2,000 left-handed programmers employed, the wage ($20,000 per year) is much less than the marginal revenue product of $60,000 per year. For the 6,000 right-handed programmers employed, the wage ($60,000 per year) is much more than the marginal revenue product of $20,000 per year.

b A nondiscriminating firm could earn higher profits by employing more left-handed programmers as long as their marginal revenue product exceeds the wage. Similarly, profits will increase by employing fewer right-handed programmers as long as their wage exceeds their marginal revenue product. The competitive outcome would be a wage of $40,000 per year for every programmer, and employment of 4,000 left-handed and 4,000 right-handed programmers.

c No. Firms can continue to discriminate if they "pay" for the discrimination in the form of lower profits.

d A successful education program alter's firms' beliefs about left-handed and right-handed programmers and moves the demand curves to the true *MRP* curves. The outcome will be the same as the competitive outcome—a wage of $40,000 per year for every programmer, and employment of 4,000 left-handed and 4,000 right-handed programmers.

e The wage is equal to the marginal revenue product for every programmer. Pay equity also means each labourer being paid an amount *equal* to the value of his or her marginal revenue product.

f Before legislation, the average yearly wage of programmers was a weighted (by employment) average of the wages of left-handers and right-handers.

$$\frac{(\$20,000 \times 2,000) + (\$60,000 \times 6,000)}{8,000} = \$50,000$$

After legislation, the average yearly wage has fallen to $40,000. The decrease in wages causes a decrease in the demand for capital, as firms try to economize on the now relatively more expensive capital input (see Fig. P3.5).

FIGURE **P3.5**   CAPITAL MARKET FOR
                 COMPUTERS

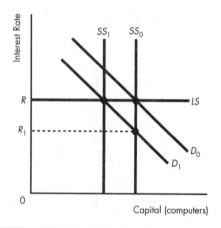

In the short run, the supply of capital (SS_0) is perfectly inelastic. The decrease in demand from D_0 to D_1 causes the price of capital to fall to R_1, while the quantity employed remains constant. In the long run, the supply curve of capital to the industry (LS) is perfectly elastic at the economy-wide interest rate R. The fall in price eventually shifts capital resources out of this industry into other industries where the rate of interest is higher. The short-run supply curve shifts to SS_1, the price of capital returns to R, and the quantity of capital employed decreases.

g The average yearly wage of left-handed programmers has increased from $20,000 to $40,000. This creates an incentive for more left-handers to invest in the necessary human capital (computer science degrees) to become a programmer, increasing the quantity supplied of left-handed programmers.

Midterm Examination

 1 b ↑ in area under supply curve. (334–335)
 2 c See text discussion. (331–332)
 3 c Risk-neutral → constant marginal utility wealth. Marginal utility of extra $3,000 is 20 units utility. (389–391)
 4 e All are problems created by private information. (395, 398–400)
 5 e For indefinite future, PV = yearly amount paid/r = $5/0.05. (375–376)
 6 b Definition. (378–379)
 7 d Firm demands more of this now relatively cheaper factor at every price for factor. **a** and **b** move along curve, **e** shifts curve left. (327)
 8 c Hiring ↑ labour → ↑ profit since $MRP > MC$. Firm can't change wage. (325–326)
 9 a Definition. (348–349)
⌾10 b Reverse **a** true. **d** true for vertical distance between supply. **e** true for vertical distance. (346–347)
⌾11 c Reverse of **a**, **b** true. (375–376)
 12 b Definition. Firm should buy machine. (369–370)
 13 c Definition for search goods. Experience goods cannot be judged in advance so advertising for information purposes is useless. (394)
 14 c More rapidly marginal utility wealth ↓, the more risk averse the person. Total utility wealth always ↑. (391–392)
⌾15 e MCL is above, but not parallel to S. MCL intersects S at equilibrium QL, not wage. (352–354)
⌾16 c New MCL flat at $8 until it hits S curve → QL where new MCL intersects MRP. (352–354)

The Government Sector

Total spending by all levels of government (federal, provincial, local) in Canada is 46 percent of total income. Eleven percent of the Canadian labour force is employed by government. Government expenditure peaked in 1992 at 50 percent of total income and has since declined.

The Economic Theory of Government

Government economic activity stems from attempts to correct

- **Market failure**—inability of unregulated market to achieve allocative efficiency. There are three cases:
  - **Public goods**—goods and services that can be consumed simultaneously by everyone and from which no one can be excluded.
  - *Monopoly*—output restriction by monopolies and cartels and rent seeking prevent efficient allocation resources.
  - **Externalities**—production of goods and services creates *external costs* or *external benefits* that fall on people not involved in the transaction.
- Economic inequality—an unregulated market economy produces what most people regard as an inequitable distribution of income.

Public Choice and the Political Marketplace

Public choice theory analyses government as a political marketplace analogous to the economic marketplace. Actors are

- Voters—consumers of the outcomes of the political process. They express their demand by voting, lobbying, and making campaign contributions.
- Politicians—officials elected by voters. Objective is to get and stay elected.
- Bureaucrats—officials hired by politicians who work in government. Objective is to maximize budget of their agency.

Political equilibrium is situation where choices of voters, politicians, and bureaucrats are compatible, and no group will be better off with a different choice.

Public Goods

Pure public goods can be consumed by everyone, no one can be excluded. They have two features:

- **Nonrivalry**—one person's consumption does not ↓ amount available for another.
  - Opposite is **rival good**—one person's consumption ↓ amount available for another (e.g., a hot dog).
- **Nonexcludability**—no one can be excluded from consuming.
  - Opposite is **excludable good**—can exclude others from consuming (e.g., cable television).

Public goods → **free rider** (someone who consumes without paying) and *free-rider problem*—tendency for too little of public good to be provided if produced and sold privately.

- Efficient scale of provision of public good occurs where net benefit is maximized or where marginal benefit equals marginal cost of public good.
  - *Total benefit* is total $ value placed on public good.

- *Net benefit* is total benefit – total cost.
- **Marginal benefit** is ↑ total benefit from a unit ↑ public good.

◆ Private provision of a public good creates a free-rider problem and provides less than the efficient quantity of the good.

◆ Government provision can provide an efficient quantity of a public good, where politicians compete for votes of well-informed voters.

The quantity of government provision of a public good generally depends on the political marketplace and the actions of voters, politicians, and bureaucrats.

◆ Politicians tend to follow **principle of minimum differentiation**—tendency for competitors to make themselves identical to appeal to maximum number voters/clients.

◆ Voters may be **rationally ignorant**—deciding not to acquire information because cost of acquisition > expected benefit. Then politicians, influenced by bureaucrats and special-interest lobbyists, may allow inefficient overprovision of a public good.

Taxes

Income taxes generate large percentage of government revenues.

◆ High-income voters prefer lower tax rates and fewer government benefits.

◆ Low-income voters prefer higher tax rates and greater benefits.

◆ Tax policy is outcome of **median voter theorem**—political parties pursue policies maximizing net benefit of median voter.

Excise tax is tax on sale of particular good.

◆ Tax on good → supply curve shifts upward, ↑ equilibrium P, ↓ equilibrium Q, and ↑ *deadweight loss.*

◆ Size of deadweight loss depends on elasticity of demand. To minimize deadweight loss, governments place highest tax rates on goods with lowest elasticities of demand.

HELPFUL HINTS

I   The criterion economists use to judge the success of the market (or any other institution for that matter) is allocative efficiency. Allocative efficiency means that the economy is producing

all goods and services up to the point at which the marginal cost is equal to the marginal benefit. In such a state, no one can be made better off without making someone else worse off.

When the market fails to achieve this "ideal" state of efficiency, we call it *market failure*. The market can fail by producing too little if the marginal benefit of the last unit exceeds the marginal cost. On the other hand, the market can fail by producing too much if the marginal cost of the last unit exceeds the marginal benefit.

In this chapter (and in Chapter 20), we learn that governments can correct market failures, but can also fail to achieve allocative efficiency. Since both markets and governments can fail, the relevant economic question in each case is: Which fails less?

2   Public choice theory provides a theory of the political marketplace that parallels the economic theory of markets for goods and services. It is useful to draw analogies between the operation of political markets and ordinary markets.

In political markets, the demanders are voters, whereas in ordinary markets, the demanders are consumers. In both cases, demanders are concerned about their costs and benefits.

The suppliers in political markets are politicians and bureaucrats, whereas in ordinary markets, the suppliers of goods and services are firms.

In political markets, voters express their demands by means of votes, political contributions, and lobbying. This occurs because the suppliers (politicians) in this market are motivated by a desire to retain political office. In ordinary markets, consumers express their demands by means of dollars, since suppliers are motivated by a desire to maximize profit.

In both markets, equilibrium is a state of rest. In equilibrium there is no tendency to change because participants cannot become better off by making a different choice or by engaging in an additional transaction.

3   Understand the logic behind the median voter theorem. Politicians want to be elected and then remain in office. To do so they must receive a majority of votes; they must win at least one more than 50 percent of the votes. Since all politicians realize this, the median voter, the "middle" voter, becomes the key voter. A politician who offers a platform that deviates from the preferences of the median voter will lose to a politician who offers a platform closer to those preferences.

4 Well-informed special interest groups are able to induce the government to conduct programs that do not maximize net benefits because most voters are *rationally* ignorant. For most voters, it does not pay to be well informed about any particular issue. As a result, a small, well-informed interest group will be able to have an influence on government programs that greatly exceeds its size relative to all voters.

5 All goods provided by the government are not necessarily public goods. A public good is defined by the characteristics of nonrivalry and nonexcludability, not by whether or not it is publicly provided. For example, many cities and communities provide swimming pools and residential garbage pickup. Neither of these is a pure public good in spite of the fact that each may be provided by the government. Indeed, in many other communities, the same services are provided by the private market.

6 It is important to understand why the properties of nonrivalry and nonexcludability associated with pure public goods imply that we obtain the marginal benefit curve for the economy as a whole differently than for private goods.

A private good is a rival in consumption. Therefore to obtain the demand curve for the whole economy, we sum the individual marginal benefit (demand) curves *horizontally*. However, the economy's marginal benefit curve for a public good is obtained by summing the individual marginal benefit curves *vertically*. This is the relevant marginal benefit curve for evaluating the efficient provision level of the public good.

S E L F - T E S T

True/False/Uncertain and Explain

1 Restriction of output by monopolies is an example of market failure.

2 According to public choice theory, not only is there possibility of market failure, but there is also the possibility of "government failure."

3 The existence of public goods gives rise to the free-rider problem.

4 The economy's marginal benefit curve for a public good is obtained by adding the marginal benefits of each individual at each quantity of provision.

5 The private market will produce much less than the efficient quantity of pure public goods.

6 Net benefit is zero when the allocatively efficient level of output is obtained.

7 The public choice theory of government behaviour assumes that politicians and bureaucrats are motivated primarily by concern for the public interest.

8 Political parties will tend to propose fundamentally different policies in order to give voters a clearer choice.

9 If politicians respond to voters, government policies will maximize net benefit.

10 It is irrational for voters to be uninformed about an issue as important as national defence.

Multiple-Choice

1 The market demand curve for a *private* good is obtained by

a summing the individual marginal cost curves horizontally.

b summing the individual marginal cost curves vertically.

c summing the individual marginal benefit curves horizontally.

d summing the individual marginal benefit curves vertically.

e none of the above methods.

2 The economy's total demand curve for a *public* good is obtained by

a summing the individual marginal cost curves horizontally.

b summing the individual marginal cost curves vertically.

c summing the individual marginal benefit curves horizontally.

d summing the individual marginal benefit curves vertically.

e none of the above methods.

3 The efficient scale of provision of a public good occurs where

a net benefit is at a maximum.

b marginal benefit is at a maximum.

c marginal benefit minus marginal cost equals zero.

d marginal cost is at a minimum.

e a and c are true.

4 When a city street is not congested, it is like a(n)

a external good.

b internal good.

c rival good.

d private good.

e public good.

5 Governments provide pure public goods like national defence because

a governments are more efficient than private firms at producing such goods.

b of the free-rider problems that result in underproduction by private markets.

c people do not value national defence very highly.

d of the potential that private firms will make excess profits.

e of external costs.

6 Which of the following goods has the nonexcludability feature?

a city bus

b toll bridge

c lighthouse

d art museum

e all of the above

7 The quantity of public goods produced by an unregulated market tends to be

a less than the allocatively efficient quantity.

b equal to the allocatively efficient quantity.

c greater than the allocatively efficient quantity.

d that which maximizes total public benefit.

e that which maximizes net public benefit.

8 Public choice theory

a argues that government has a tendency to conduct policies that help the economy towards allocative efficiency.

b argues that politicians and bureaucrats tend to be more concerned about the public interest than individuals in the private sector.

c argues that the public choices of government maximize net benefits.

d applies economic tools used to analyse markets to the analysis of government behaviour.

e applies the tools of political analysis to the analysis of economic markets.

9 According to public choice theory, a voter will favour a candidate whose political program is

a perceived to offer the greatest personal benefit to the voter.

b best for the majority of the people.

c closest to allocative efficiency.

d favoured by the median voter.

e all of the above.

10 In general, a tax of $3 per unit of good *A* will shift the supply curve of *A* up by

a $3 and increase the price of *A* by $3.

b $3 and increase the price of *A* by less than $3.

c $3 and increase the price of *A* by more than $3.

d more than $3 and increase the price of *A* by $3.

e less than $3 and increase the price of *A* by $3.

11 The deadweight loss due to a price increase resulting from a tax is the loss of

a   consumer surplus.
b   producer surplus.
c   consumer surplus plus the loss of producer surplus.
d   consumer surplus minus the loss of producer surplus.
e   tax revenue from the decreased equilibrium quantity.

12 Figure18.1 gives the demand and supply for imported cheese. If the government imposes a $3 tax per kilogram of imported cheese, price will increase by

a $3 to $7.
b $3 to $6.
c $2 to $6.
d $2 to $5.
e   none of the above.

FIGURE **18.1**

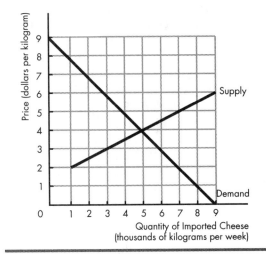

13 Competitors who make themselves identical to appeal to the maximum number of voters illustrate the

a   principle of maximum differentiation.
b   principle of minimum differentiation.
c   principle of rational ignorance.
d   principle of nonrivalry.
e   Niskanen theory of bureaucratic behaviour.

14 Refer to Fig. 18.2 which shows the total cost and total benefit of proposals for building four different-sized high schools. The proposal with the largest net benefit is

a   A.
b   B.
c   C.
d   D.
e   impossible to identify without additional information.

FIGURE **18.2**

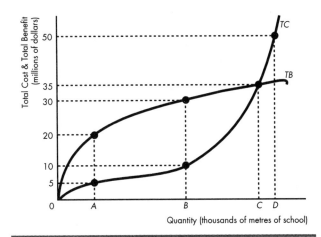

15 Refer to Fig. 18.2 which shows the total cost and total benefit of proposals for building four different-sized high schools. The proposal most likely to appeal to voters in an election is

a   A.
b   B.
c   C.
d   D.
e   impossible to identify without additional information.

16 Refer to Fig. 18.2 which shows the total cost and total benefit of proposals for building four different-sized high schools. The proposal that best meets the goals of the school district's bureaucrats is

a   A.
b   B.
c   C.
d   D.
e   impossible to identify without additional information.

17 If voters have similar views and are well informed, the quantity of national defence provided by the government will tend to be

a greater than the allocatively efficient quantity.
b less than the allocatively efficient quantity.
c the least costly quantity.
d the quantity that maximizes net benefit.
e the quantity that maximizes the Ministry of Defence budget.

18 Competition between two political parties will cause those parties to propose policies

a that are quite different.
b that are quite similar.
c of rational ignorance.
d that reduce the well-being of middle-income families and increase the well-being of the rich and the poor.
e that equate total costs and total benefits.

19 Rational ignorance

a results when the cost of information exceeds the benefits of having the information.
b allows special interest groups to exert political influence.
c combined with special interest groups can yield allocative inefficiency in the provision of public goods.
d results in all of the above.
e results in none of the above.

20 Refer to Fig. 18.3. Pre-tax consumer surplus is equal to triangle

a *gmc.*
b *gkc.*
c *mkc.*
d *dac.*
e *dbc.*

21 Refer to Fig. 18.3. Pre-tax producer surplus is equal to triangle

a *gmc.*
b *gkc.*
c *mkc.*
d *dac.*
e *abc.*

22 Refer to Fig. 18.3. Deadweight loss from the tax is equal to triangle

a *abc.*
b *dbc.*
c *dac.*
d *edc.*
e *gdj.*

23 According to public choice theory, a voter will tend to be well informed if the issue in question

a is complicated and difficult to understand.
b affects everyone a little.
c is of special interest to a small group to which the voter does not belong.
d has a large direct effect on the voter.
e is important even if it does not directly affect the voter.

24 The budget of a government bureau is likely to increase beyond the quantity that maximizes net benefit of the economy if

a voters are well informed.
b there is rational voter ignorance combined with special interest lobbying.
c it is allocatively efficient to do so.
d bureaucrats are rationally ignorant.
e there are negative externalities.

25 On any given spending issue subject to a vote, the median voter is the one who favours

a the least spending.
b the most spending.
c the efficient level of spending.
d the average level of spending.
e spending more than the level favoured by half the voters and less than the level favoured by half the voters.

Short Answer Problems

1 Explain the *nonrivalry* and *nonexcludability* features of a pure public good.

2 What is the free-rider problem?

FIGURE **18.3**

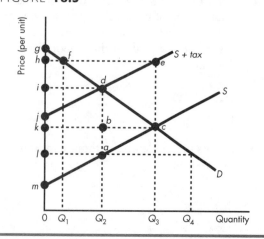

3 Briefly compare an equilibrium in a political market with an equilibrium in a market for goods and services.

4 Explain why it may be rational for voters to be ignorant.

5 Why does the imposition of an excise tax cause the supply curve of the taxed good to shift upward?

6 Heritage Apartments has 100 residents who are concerned about security. Table 18.1 gives the total cost of hiring a 24-hour security guard service as well as the marginal benefit to each of the residents.

TABLE **18.1**

Number of Guards	Total Cost per Day ($)	Marginal Benefit per Resident ($)	Marginal Benefit to All Residents ($)
1	300	10	
2	600	4	
3	900	2	
4	1,200	1	

a Why is a security guard a public good for the residents of Heritage Apartments?
b Why will zero guards be hired if each of the residents must act individually?
c Complete the last column of Table 18.1 by computing the marginal benefit of security guards to all of the residents together.

⊘ 7 Now suppose that the residents form an Apartment Council that acts as a governing body to address the security issue.
a What is the optimal (allocatively efficient) number of guards? What is the net benefit at the optimal number of guards?
b Show that net benefit is less for either one less guard or for one more guard than the net benefit for the optimal number of guards.
c How might the Apartment Council pay for the optimal number of guards?

8 Two candidates are competing in an election for president of the Economics Club. The only issue dividing them is how much will be spent on the annual Economics Club party. It is well known that the seven voting members of the club (*A* through *G*) have preferences as shown in Table 18.2. These are strongly held preferences regarding exactly how much should be spent on the party.

TABLE **18.2**

Voting Member	Proposed Amount ($)
A	10
B	20
C	30
D	40
E	50
F	60
G	70

a How much will each candidate propose to spend?
b To demonstrate that your answer to part **a** is correct, consider the outcome of the following two contests.
  i Candidate 1 proposes the amount you gave in part **a** and candidate 2 proposes $1 less. Which candidate will win? Why?
  ii Candidate 1 proposes the amount you gave in part **a** and candidate 2 proposes $1 more. Which candidate will win? Why?
c Suppose that the Sociology Club is also electing a president and that the same single issue prevails. It is well known that the seven voting members of the Sociology Club have the following strongly held preferences regarding exactly how much should be spent on their party (see Table 18.3).

TABLE **18.3**

Voting Member	Proposed Amount ($)
T	0
U	0
V	0
W	40
X	41
Y	42
Z	43

How much will each of the two candidates propose in this case?

9 Table 18.4 gives three alternative income distributions for five individuals, *A* through *E*. Currently income is distributed according to distribution 1 (given in the first column of the table). Consider alternative proposed distributions 2 and 3 one at a time.

TABLE **18.4**

Individual	Distribution 1 ($)	Distribution 2 ($)	Distribution 3 ($)
A	0	200	150
B	200	300	250
C	400	350	450
D	700	600	600
E	1,000	850	850

a If distribution 2 is proposed as an alternative to distribution 1, will it have majority support? Why or why not?

b If distribution 3 is proposed as an alternative to distribution 1, will it have majority support? Why or why not?

10 Figure 18.4 gives the supply and demand for movie tickets in Ourtown. The market is initially in equilibrium (point *a*) with a price of $5 per ticket and 5,000 tickets sold per week. Suppose that the town government establishes a new tax of $2 per movie ticket.

FIGURE **18.4**

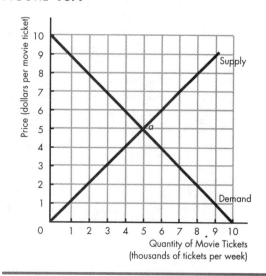

a Illustrate the effect of the new tax graphically. What will the new equilibrium price and quantity be?

b How much of the $2 tax is paid by consumers in the form of a higher price and how much is paid by movie ticket sellers in the form of reduced revenue per ticket?

c How much tax revenue will be collected each week?

d How much consumer surplus will be lost due to the tax? How much producer surplus will be lost? What is the deadweight loss of the tax?

ANSWERS

True/False/Uncertain and Explain

1 **T** Allocatively inefficient output. (416–417)
2 **T** Believe government agents act in own interest, not necessarily public interest. (418–419)
3 **T** Nonexcludability → no incentive to pay. (416–417)
4 **T** See text discussion. (420–422)
5 **T** Because no accounting for external benefits. (420–422)
6 **F** Net benefit is maximized. (420–422)
7 **F** Concern for own self-interest. (418–419)
8 **F** Propose similar policies as vote-maximizing strategy appealing to median voter. (422–424)
9 **U** True if voters well informed, false if voters rationally ignorant. (424–425)
10 **F** May pay to be rationally ignorant. (424–425)

Multiple-Choice

1 **c** See text discussion. (420–422)
2 **d** See Text Fig. 18.4. (420–422)
3 **e** Equivalent conditions. (420–422)
4 **e** Features nonrivalry and nonexcludability. Congestion → rivalry. (416–417)
5 **b** Would not be profitable for private firms. (419–423)
6 **c** Can't prevent ships from seeing the light. (416–417)
7 **a** Private production unprofitable because of free-rider problem. (422–423)
8 **d** Political marketplace. (418–419)
9 **a** Voter assumed concerned only with own self-interest. (418–419)
10 **b** Draw graph. **a** true only for perfectly elastic supply. Other answers always false. (427–429)
11 **c** See text discussion. (427–428)

12 c Draw graph. Shift supply upward by $3. (427–429)

13 b Definition. (423–424)

14 b Largest $TB - TC$. (420–423)

15 b Maximizes net benefit. (420–423)

16 d Public choice theory assumes bureaucrats maximize budget (TC). (424–425)

17 d Government will respond to demands of voters. (424–425)

18 b Vote maximizing by principle minimum differentiation. (422–424)

19 d a definition, b, c outcomes of rational ignorance. (424–425)

20 b Area below demand, above market price. (249–250)

21 c Area above supply, below market price. (249–250)

22 c Lost consumer + producer surplus. (427–429)

23 d Information acquired only if value > cost acquisition. (424–425)

24 b Bureaucratic overprovision. (424–425)

25 e Median = exactly halfway between. (426–427)

Short Answer Problems

1 A good has the nonrivalry feature if its consumption by one person does not reduce the amount available for others. The nonexcludability feature means that if the good is produced and consumed by one person, others cannot be excluded from consuming it as well.

2 The free-rider problem is the problem of unregulated markets producing too little of a pure public good because there is little incentive for individuals to pay for the good. The reason is that the person's payment will likely have no perceptible effect on the amount the person will be able to consume.

3 In both cases, the equilibrium is a state of rest in the sense that no group has an incentive to change their choices. In the case of equilibrium in an ordinary market for goods and services, neither demanders nor suppliers are able to make an exchange that will make them better off. Similarly, when a political market is in equilibrium, neither demanders (voters) nor suppliers (politicians and bureaucrats) are able to make an alternative choice that will make them better off.

4 Most issues have only a small and indirect effect on most voters. In such cases it would be irrational for a voter to spend much time and effort to become well informed because the

additional cost would quickly exceed any additional benefit. Only if the voter is significantly and directly affected by an issue will it pay to become well informed. As a result, most voters will be rationally ignorant regarding any given issue.

5 When an excise tax is imposed on a supplier, it raises the minimum price the supplier must receive in order to be willing to offer any given quantity for sale. This is nothing more than an upward shift in the supply curve. It is useful to think of a new excise tax as an increase in the cost of production.

6 a A security guard is a public good because, in this case, it has the features of nonrivalry and nonexcludability. It has nonrivalry because one resident's *consumption* of the security provided by a guard does not reduce the security of anyone else. The nonexcludability property is evidenced by the fact that once a security guard is in place, all residents enjoy the increased security; none can be excluded.

b If each resident must act individually in hiring a security guard none will be hired because each resident receives only $10 in benefit from the first guard, which costs $300 per day.

c The entries in the last column of Table 18.1 Solution are obtained by multiplying the marginal benefit per resident by the number of residents, 100. This multiplication is the numerical equivalent of summing the individual marginal benefit curves vertically for each quantity of guards.

TABLE **18.1** SOLUTION

Number of Guards	Total Cost per Day ($)	Marginal Benefit per Resident ($)	Marginal Benefit to All Residents ($)
1	300	10	1,000
2	600	4	400
3	900	2	200
4	1,200	1	100

7 a If the Apartment Council hires each guard for whom the marginal benefit exceeds the marginal cost, they will hire the optimal number of guards. The marginal cost of each additional guard is $300. The marginal benefit of the first guard is $1,000, so he will be hired. Similarly, the marginal benefit of the second guard is $400, and she will be hired.

The marginal benefit of the third guard, however, is only $200, which is less than marginal cost. Therefore we conclude that the allocatively efficient (optimal) number of guards is two. For two guards, the net benefit is $800: total benefit ($1,400) minus total cost ($600).

b For one guard, the net benefit is $700: total benefit ($1,000) minus total cost ($300). For three guards, the net benefit is also $700: total benefit ($1,600) minus total cost ($900). Thus the net benefit of $800 is greatest for two guards.

c The Apartment Council might pay for the optimal number of guards by collecting a security fee of $6 per day from each of the 100 residents in order to hire two security guards.

8 a Each candidate will propose spending $40 since that is the preference of the median voter (voter *D*).

b i Candidate 1 will win because *D*, *E*, *F*, and *G* will vote for that candidate because $40 comes closer to matching their preferences than the $39 proposed by candidate 2. Only *A*, *B*, and *C* will vote for candidate 2.
ii Candidate 1 will win because *A*, *B*, *C*, and *D* will vote for that candidate while only *E*, *F*, and *G* will vote for candidate 2.

c Once again, the candidates will both propose spending $40 on the party since that is the preference of the median voter. Note that in this case, the median voter's view is not "average."

9 a Only *A* and *B* are better off under distribution 2. Distribution 2 will receive the support of only *A* and *B* with *C*, *D*, and *E* opposed. Note particularly that the median voter (*C*) is worse off under distribution 2.

b Distribution 3 will receive majority support since it makes the median voter better off. It will be supported by *A*, *B*, and *C* and opposed by *D* and *E*.

10 a The new tax shifts the supply curve for movie tickets up by $2, the amount of the tax. In Fig. 18.4 Solution, the new curve is labelled S_1. The new equilibrium (point *b*) price and quantity are $6 per ticket and 4,000 tickets per week, respectively.

FIGURE **18.4**   SOLUTION

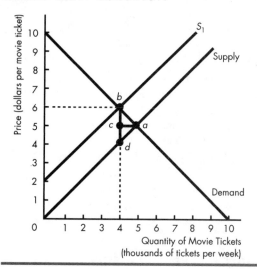

b Of the $2 tax, $1 is paid by consumers since the price of a ticket rises from $5 to $6, and $1 is paid by sellers, since the revenue per ticket they receive falls from $5 to $4.

c Total tax revenue will be $8,000 per week: $2 per ticket times 4,000 tickets sold.

d The loss of consumer surplus is given by the area of triangle *abc* in Fig. 18.4 Solution and is equal to $500 (from the formula for the area of a right-angled triangle—area = 1/2 × base (*ac*) × height (*bc*) = 1/2 × 1,000 × $1). Similarly, the loss of producer surplus is given by the area of triangle *adc*, and is equal to $500. Thus the deadweight loss is $1,000, the sum of consumer and producer surplus.

Chapter 19

Inequality and Redistribution

Economic Inequality in Canada

There is a great deal of inequality of income and wealth. The degree of inequality is measured by the Lorenz curve.

◆ The **Lorenz curve** for income (wealth) graphs the cumulative percentage of income (wealth) against the cumulative percentage of families.

◆ The 45° "line of equality" represents a hypothetically equal distribution of income (wealth).

◆ The farther the Lorenz curve is from the line of equality, the more unequal the distribution.

◆ The distribution of wealth in Canada is even more unequal than the distribution of income.

Poverty exists when families cannot buy adequate food, shelter, and clothing.

◆ **Low-income cutoff** (families spending 54.7 percent or more of their income on food, shelter, and clothing) is used to measure poverty. In Canada, 13.5 percent of families have incomes below the low-income cutoff.

◆ Most important factors influencing poverty are source of income, family type, and age of household head.

Comparing Like with Like

Wealth is the *stock* of assets owned by an individual. Wealth includes *human capital* as well as *tangible assets*. *Income* is the *flow* of earning received by an individual from his or her stock of wealth.

◆ Data used to construct wealth distributions do not include human capital and therefore overstate wealth inequalities.

◆ Distributions of annual income and wealth are more unequal than distributions of lifetime income and wealth.

◆ Even correcting for these factors, there are significant inequalities in distributions of income and wealth in Canada.

Factor Prices, Endowments, and Choices

The unequal distribution of income arises from unequal wage rates, unequal distribution of endowments, and personal choices.

◆ Inequalities can be bequeathed to the next generation through *bequests* (gifts to next generation) and *assortative mating* (marrying within one's own socioeconomic class).

Income Redistribution

Income is redistributed by governments through income taxes, income maintenance programs, and provision of goods and services below cost.

◆ **Income taxes** can be
  • **Progressive**—marginal tax rate ↑ with ↑ level income.
  • **Regressive**—marginal tax rate ↓ with ↑ level income.
  • **Proportional** (*flat-rate tax*)—marginal tax rate constant at all levels income.

◆ Income maintenance programs include social security, unemployment compensation, and welfare.

◆ Provision of education and health-care services below cost (often for free) reduces inequality.

Income redistribution creates a **big tradeoff** between inequality and efficiency. Redistribution uses scarce resources and weakens incentives, so a more equally shared pie results in a smaller pie. The "big tradeoff" problem can be approached with

◆ Piecemeal reforms → limited response to most pressing current problems.

◆ Radical reforms including a **negative income tax**— give every family *guaranteed annual income* and decrease family benefits at specified *benefit-loss rate* as market income ↑. Negative income tax avoids most problems of existing programs, but is costly.

Ideas About Fairness (see website)

A theory of distributive justice is a set of principles for testing the fairness of the distribution of economic well-being. Two classes of such theories are the

◆ End-state theory of distributive justice—focus on fairness of *outcomes* or *ends* (equality of outcome).

  • *Utilitarian* theory—outcome must maximize the sum of the utilities of all individuals. Redistribute income until marginal utility of last dollar spent by each individual is equal. Complete equality of income → maximum total utility.
  • *Maximin* theory—outcome must yield maximum possible utility (income) for the person with the minimum utility (income). Fairest distribution is not complete equality but redistribution only until least well-off person can gain no more.

◆ Process theory of distributive justice—focus on fairness of *process* or *means* by which outcomes achieved (equality of opportunity). Classical liberalism emphasizes equality of opportunity and voluntary exchange, and any outcome resulting from this process is fair.

HELPFUL HINTS

I Statistics used to construct Lorenz curves do not always give an accurate picture of inequality. It is important to understand why inaccurate pictures might arise. For example, you should understand why a distribution of wealth that excludes the value of human capital will give a distorted picture relative to the distribution of income.

You should also understand why the distribution of annual (static) income will give a distorted picture relative to the distribution of lifetime (dynamic) income. Finally, you should understand why the distribution of before-tax, before-transfer income will give a distorted picture relative to the distribution of after-tax, after-transfer income.

2 The issue of fairness discussed in this chapter is a normative issue. Note, however, that the tradeoff between equity and economic efficiency (the so-called big tradeoff) is a positive issue.

SELF-TEST

True/False/Uncertain and Explain

I In Canada, income is more unequally distributed than wealth.

2 The farther the Lorenz curve is from the 45° line, the more equal the distribution of income.

3 Under a proportional income tax, total taxes rise as income rises.

4 The marginal tax rate does not change as income rises.

5 A regressive income tax redistributes income from the rich to the poor.

6 Compared with the market distribution of income, government benefits and taxes reduce the inequality of income distribution.

7 The financial wealth distribution ignores the distribution of human capital and thus *overstates* inequality among individuals.

8 If debts could be bequeathed, the distribution of wealth would become more equal over time.

9 A negative income tax creates a welfare trap by discouraging employment.

10 In general, reducing income inequality by redistributing income from the rich to the poor will lead to greater production of goods and services.

Multiple-Choice

1 Differences in the wage rates received by different individuals reflect differences in

a marginal product of labour.
b natural ability.
c human capital.
d all of the above.
e none of the above.

2 A bequest is a(n)

a mistake.
b tax on inherited wealth.
c gift from one generation to another.
d incentive for one generation to work harder.
e conditional inheritance.

3 Assortative mating means that

a poor women tend to marry rich men.
b rich women tend to marry rich men.
c rich women tend to marry poor men.
d same sex marriages occur because "like attracts like."
e same sex marriages are prohibited.

4 Consider the Lorenz curves in Fig. 19.1. Which Lorenz curve corresponds to the greatest income *inequality*?

a *A*
b *B*
c *C*
d *D*
e impossible to tell without additional information

FIGURE **19.1**

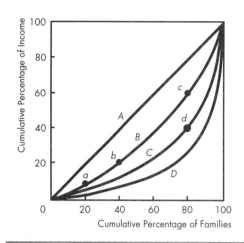

5 In Fig. 19.1, what is curve *A* (a straight line) called?

a market distribution line
b line of equality
c fairness line
d Okun tradeoff curve
e none of the above

6 Which point in Fig. 19.1 indicates that the richest 20 percent of families earn 40 percent of the income?

a *a*
b *b*
c *c*
d *d*
e none of the above

7 Even if the distribution of wages is symmetric, the distribution of income will be skewed because

a abilities are distributed symmetrically.
b abilities are distributed asymmetrically.
c individuals tend to supply more labour at higher wages.
d individuals tend to supply less labour at higher wages.
e **b** and **d** are true.

8 Which of the following *reduces* the inequality of income or wealth relative to the market distribution?

a government payments to the poor
b a regressive income tax
c large bequests
d assortative mating
e all of the above

9 A theory of distributive justice that emphasizes the mechanism by which distribution takes place is a(n)

a utilitarian theory.
b end-state theory.
c maximin theory.
d process theory.
e outcomes theory.

10 Wealth differs from income in that

a income is a stock, wealth is a flow.
b wealth is derived from income.
c income is what you earn, wealth is what you own.
d income is what you own, wealth is what you earn.
e wealth is preferable to income.

11 In Table 19.1, which tax plan is proportional?

a Plan *A*
b Plan *B*
c Plan *C*
d Plan *D*
e impossible to calculate without additional information

TABLE **19.1**

Current Gross Income	Tax Payment Plan A	Tax Payment Plan B	Tax Payment Plan C	Tax Payment Plan D
0	0	0	0	200
1,000	100	100	200	200
2,000	200	400	200	200
4,000	400	1,600	200	200

12 In Table 19.1, which tax plan is progressive?

a Plan *A*
b Plan *B*
c Plan *C*
d Plan *D*
e c and d

13 The distribution of *annual income*

a understates the degree of inequality because it does not take into account the family's stage in its life cycle.
b understates the degree of inequality because it does not take into account the distribution of human capital.
c overstates the degree of inequality because it does not take into account the family's stage in its life cycle.
d overstates the degree of inequality because it does not take into account the distribution of human capital.
e is an accurate measure of the degree of inequality.

14 The distribution of *wealth*

a understates the degree of inequality because it does not take into account the family's stage in its life cycle.
b understates the degree of inequality because it does not take into account the distribution of human capital.
c overstates the degree of inequality because it does not take into account the family's stage in its life cycle.
d overstates the degree of inequality because it does not take into account the distribution of human capital.
e is an accurate measure of the degree of inequality.

15 According to the maximin theory, income should be redistributed if the

a average person can be made better off.
b poorest person can be made better off.
c richest person can be made worse off.
d wage rate is greater than the marginal product of labour.
e wage rate is less than the marginal product of labour.

16 Which of the following is an example of an end-state theory of distributive justice?

a marginal product theory
b classical liberalism theory
c utilitarian theory
d process theory
e none of the above

17 In Fig. 19.2, the richest 20 percent of all families receive what share of all income?

a 10 percent
b 20 percent
c 30 percent
d 40 percent
e none of the above

FIGURE **19.2**

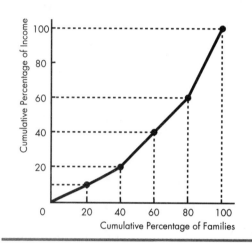

18 In Fig. 19.2, the poorest 20 percent of all families receive what share of income?

a 10 percent
b 20 percent
c 30 percent
d 40 percent
e none of the above

19 In Fig. 19.2, the middle 20 percent of all families receive what share of income?

a 10 percent
b 20 percent
c 30 percent
d 40 percent
e none of the above

20 The curve in Fig. 19.2 represents the
a line of market income distribution.
b line of perfect equality.
c Okun tradeoff curve.
d Nozick curve.
e Lorenz curve.

21 Suppose that if a family earns zero income, it receives a monthly transfer payment of $1,000 from the government. If the family earns $400 in a month, the government payment drops to $700. What is the marginal tax rate in this case?

a 0 percent
b 10 percent
c 40 percent
d 50 percent
e 75 percent

22 The most important factor influencing the incidence of low income is
a source of income.
b sex of household head.
c age of household head.
d family type.
e geographical region.

23 If the marginal tax rate increases as income increases, the income tax is defined as
a progressive.
b proportional.
c negative.
d regressive.
e excessive.

24 Redistribution of income from the rich to the poor will lead to a reduction in total output. This is known as the
a market distribution.
b process theory of distributive justice.
c end-state theory of distributive justice.
d big tradeoff.
e capitalist dilemma.

25 Which diagram is used by economists to illustrate the distribution of income or wealth?
a Lorenz curve
b normal distribution
c Rawls curve
d Okun tradeoff curve
e none of the above

Short Answer Problems

1 Explain the differences and connections between the concepts of wealth and income.

2 What are the two factors that determine a person's income? To what extent are these factors the result of forces beyond the control of the individual and to what extent are they the result of individual choice?

3 The two classes of theories of distributive justice are process theories and end-state theories. What is the principal characteristic of a process theory of distributive justice? Why is the utilitarian theory an end-state theory of distributive justice?

4 Why is there a "big tradeoff" between fairness and efficiency?

5 Table 19.2 gives information regarding the distribution of income in an economy which generates $100 billion in total annual income.

TABLE **19.2**   TOTAL FAMILY INCOME

Percentage of Families	Total Income (billions of $)	Income Share (%)	Cumulative Percentage of Families	Cumulative Percentage of Income
Poorest 20%	5			
Second 20%	10			
Third 20%	15			
Fourth 20%	20			
Richest 20%	50			

a Complete Table 19.2 by computing the entries in the last three columns.
b Draw the Lorenz curve for income in this economy and label it *A*.

6 Now suppose that a progressive income tax is levied on the economy. The distribution of after-tax income is given in Table 19.3. We have assumed that none of the revenue is redistributed to families in the economy. Note that total after-tax income is $71 billion.

TABLE **19.3**   AFTER-TAX FAMILY INCOME

Percentage of Families	After-Tax Income (billions of $)	After-Tax Income Share (%)	Cumulative Percentage of Families	Cumulative Percentage of After-Tax Income
Poorest 20%	5			
Second 20%	9			
Third 20%	12			
Fourth 20%	15			
Richest 20%	30			

a Complete Table 19.3.
b Draw the Lorenz curve for after-tax income on the same graph you used for Short Answer Problem 5b and label it *B*.
c What effect has the progressive income tax had on inequality?

7 Finally, suppose that, in addition, the government redistributes all of the tax revenue so that the after-transfer (after-tax) income distribution is that given in Table 19.4. For example, those in the poorest group receive transfer income in the amount of $10 billion so that their after-transfer income becomes $15 billion.

TABLE **19.4**   AFTER-TRANSFER FAMILY INCOME

Percentage of Families	After-Transfer Income Share (billions of $)	After-Transfer Income Share (%)	Cumulative Percentage of Families	Cumulative Percentage of After-Transfer Income
Poorest 20%	15			
Second 20%	16			
Third 20%	18			
Fourth 20%	20			
Richest 20%	31			

a Complete Table 19.4.
b Draw the Lorenz curve for after-transfer income on the same graph you used for Short Answer Problems 5b and 6b and label it *C*.
c What effect has income redistribution through transfer payments had on inequality?

8 Consider an economy consisting of 100 individuals who are identical in every way. Each lives to be 80 years of age and no older. Between birth and the age of 20 years they earn zero income; between the ages of 21 and 35 each earns an annual income of $30,000; between the ages of 36 and 50 each earns an annual income of $40,000; between the ages of 51 and 65 each receives an annual income of $60,000; and between the ages of 66 and 80 each receives an annual income of $20,000. At any given time there are 20 individuals in each of the 5 age groups. For simplicity we assume that there are no bequests. This information is summarized in Table 19.5.

TABLE **19.5** LIFETIME INCOME PATTERNS

Age Group (years)	Number in Age Group	Individual Annual Income ($)
0–20	20	0
21–35	20	30,000
36–50	20	40,000
51–65	20	60,000
66–80	20	20,000

a Draw the Lorenz curve for lifetime income in this economy and label it *A*.

b Draw the Lorenz curve for annual income in this economy and label it *B*.

c Which of these is a better measure of the inequality among individuals in this economy? Why?

9 Consider the worlds of Vulcan and Klingon. The Vulcan Lorenz curve is given in Fig. 19.3, and the Klingon income distribution data are given in Table 19.6.

FIGURE **19.3**

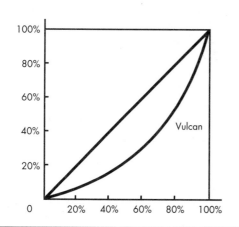

TABLE **19.6** KLINGON INCOME DISTRIBUTION

Family Income Rank	Percentage Share Total Income
Lowest 20%	10%
Second 20%	10%
Middle 20%	20%
Fourth 20%	30%
Highest 20%	30%

a Label the axes of Fig. 19.3 and explain what the diagonal line represents.

b Using the data from Table 19.6, draw the Klingon Lorenz curve on Fig. 19.3.

⊜ 10 There are two major theories of distributive justice.

a State and define one theory.

b State and define the other theory.

c Using *only* the information in Short Answer Problem 9, which theory(s) of distributive justice can be used to judge Vulcan and Klingon? Which world is more just according to the theory(s)?

ANSWERS

True/False/Uncertain and Explain

1 **F** See Text Fig. 19.1. (437–438)
2 **F** More unequal. (437–438)
3 **T** Marginal tax rate constant, but total taxes ↑. (443–444)
4 **U** Depends if tax regressive (**F**), proportional (**T**), or progressive (**F**). (443–444)
5 **F** From poor to rich. (443–444)
6 **T** See Text Fig. 19.5. (444–445)
7 **T** Human capital wealth more equally distributed than financial wealth. (440)
8 **T** Only assets can be bequeathed. (442–443)
9 **F** Removes welfare trap and encourages employment. (446–447)
10 **F** Lower production due to the big tradeoff. (445–446)

Multiple-Choice

1 **d** All affect marginal revenue product of labour. (441–443)
2 **c** Definition. (442–443)
3 **b** Marriage within socioeconomic class. (443)
4 **d** Curve farthest from 45° line. (437–438)
5 **b** Definition. (437–438)
6 **c** Moving from 80 percent to 100 percent of families (richest 20 percent) moves income from 60 percent to 100 percent of total (40 percent). (437–438)
7 **c** Higher wages associated with even higher incomes (wage × quantity labour). (441–442)
8 **a** Others increase inequality. (443–445)
⊜ 9 **d** Definition. (See website.)
10 **c** Wealth is a stock, income a flow derived from wealth. (437–438)
11 **a** Taxes always 10 percent of income. (443–444)
12 **b** With ↑ income, tax rate ↑ from 0 percent, to 10 percent, to 20 percent, to 40 percent. (443–444)

❻13 c Human capital affects distribution of wealth, not income. (440)

❻14 d Life cycle biases distribution income, not wealth. (440)

ⓔ15 b Definition. (See website.)

ⓔ16 c Maximize sum of utilities (end-states) of individuals. (See website.)

17 d 100 percent – 60 percent of cumulative income. (437–438)

18 a 10 percent – 0 percent of cumulative income. (437–438)

19 b 40 percent – 20 percent of cumulative income. (437–438)

20 e Definition. (437–438)

❻21 e $\Delta T/\Delta Y = \$300/\$400$. (446–447)

22 a See Text Fig. 19.3 notes. (438–439)

23 a Definition. (443–444)

24 d See text discussion. (445–446)

25 a Definition. (437–438)

Short Answer Problems

1 Wealth is the *stock* of assets owned by an individual, while income is the *flow* of earnings received by an individual. The concepts are connected in that an individual's income is the earnings that flow from her stock of wealth.

2 A person's income is determined by the market prices for productive resource services and the quantity of resource services the person is able and willing to sell at those prices. These two factors depend on a number of things, some of which are (at least partially) under the control of the individual and some of which are not.

　　The price of labour services, the wage rate, is determined in the market for labour. But, as we learned in Chapters 14 and 15, the wage rate will depend on the marginal product of labour, which is affected by individual choices about training and education as well as personal inherent ability.

　　The quantity of labour services supplied will also depend on personal choices about how to spend one's time. The quantity of other resource services supplied will also depend on personal choices as well as the individual's endowment of the factor.

ⓔ3 A process theory of distributive justice focuses on the fairness of the process or mechanisms by which results are achieved instead of focusing on the results themselves. The utilitarian theory suggests that the fairest system is one in which the sum of the utilities in the society is a maximum. Since the theory focuses on the outcome or the ends, it is an end-state theory of distributive justice.

4 If greater fairness means increasing the equality of income, it can only be achieved by income redistribution; the income of some must be taxed in order to make transfer payments to others. However, there are incentive effects that reduce the total amount of income available to be distributed.

　　If productive activities such as work are taxed, there will be a tendency to reduce time spent in those activities. Furthermore, any redistribution program would require the use of resources to administer it and thus leave fewer resources for other productive activities. Thus we arrive at the insight: A more equally shared pie results in a smaller pie.

5 a Table 19.2 is completed as Table 19.2 Solution. The income share for each group of families is the total income of that group as a percent of total income in the economy ($100 billion). The cumulative percentage of income (last column) is obtained by adding the percentage income share of the group (from the third column) to the total percentage income share of all poorer groups of families.

TABLE **19.2** SOLUTION
TOTAL FAMILY INCOME

Percentage of Families	Total Income (billions of $)	Income Share (%)	Cumulative Percentage of Families	Cumulative Percentage of Income
Poorest 20%	5	5	20	5
Second 20%	10	10	40	15
Third 20%	15	15	60	30
Fourth 20%	20	20	80	50
Richest 20%	50	50	100	100

b The curve labelled *A* in Fig. 19.4 is the Lorenz curve for total family income. This simply plots the values in the last two columns of Table 19.2 Solution.

FIGURE **19.4**

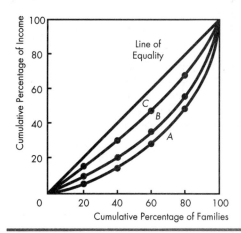

6 a Table 19.3 is completed as Table 19.3 Solution.

TABLE **19.3** SOLUTION
AFTER-TAX FAMILY INCOME

Percentage of Families	After-Tax Income (billions of $)	After-Tax Income Share (%)	Cumulative Percentage of Families	Cumulative Percentage of After-Tax Income
Poorest 20%	5	7	20	7
Second 20%	9	13	40	20
Third 20%	12	17	60	37
Fourth 20%	15	21	80	58
Richest 20%	30	42	100	100

b The curve labelled *B* in Fig. 19.4 is the Lorenz curve for after-tax family income.

c The progressive income tax has reduced inequality by taking a larger percentage of income from higher income groups.

7 a Table 19.4 is completed as Table 19.4 Solution.

TABLE **19.4** SOLUTION
AFTER-TRANSFER FAMILY INCOME

Percentage of Families	After-Transfer Income Share (billions of $)	After-Transfer Income Share (%)	Cumulative Percentage of Families	Cumulative Percentage of After-Transfer Income
Poorest 20%	15	15	20	15
Second 20%	16	16	40	31
Third 20%	18	18	60	49
Fourth 20%	20	20	80	69
Richest 20%	31	31	100	100

b The curve labelled *C* in Fig. 19.4 is the Lorenz curve for after-tax, after-transfer family income.

c Income redistribution through transfer payments has reduced inequality.

8 a Since each individual in the economy earns exactly the same lifetime income, the Lorenz curve for lifetime income coincides with the line of equality and is labelled *A* in Fig. 19.5.

FIGURE **19.5**

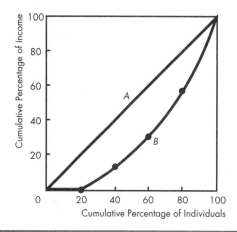

b The Lorenz curve for annual income is labelled *B* in Fig. 19.5. It reflects the fact that the poorest 20 percent of the individuals (0–20 years) receive 0 percent of the annual income; the second poorest 20 percent, those 60–80 years, receive 13 percent of the annual income; the third poorest 20 percent, those 21–35 years, receive 20 percent of the annual income; the fourth poorest 20 percent, those 36–50 years, receive 27 percent of the annual income; and the richest 20 percent, those 51–65 years, receive 40 percent of the annual income.

c The distribution of lifetime income is a better measure of the degree of inequality. In this imaginary economy all individuals are identical (equal), a fact that is reflected by equal lifetime incomes. The only reason annual income distribution in this economy is not equal is because the individuals are at different stages of identical life cycles.

9 a See Fig. 19.3 Solution. The diagonal line
 represents hypothetical income equality.
 b See Fig. 19.3 Solution.

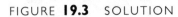

FIGURE **19.3** SOLUTION

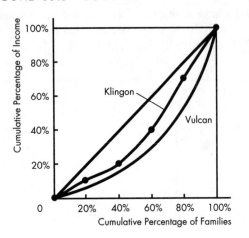

Cumulative Percentage of Income

Klingon

Vulcan

Cumulative Percentage of Families

10 a An end-state theory of distributive justice
 focuses on the fairness of *outcomes* (equality of
 outcomes).
 b A process theory of distributive justice focuses
 on the fairness of the *process* by which outcomes
 are achieved (equality of opportunity).
 c Since we have information only on income
 outcomes and not on the process by which they
 are achieved, only the end-state theory of
 distributive justice can be used to judge Vulcan
 and Klingon. Since the Klingon Lorenz curve is
 closer to the line of equality, the Klingon world
 is more just according to the end-state theory.

Competition Policy

Market Intervention

Forms of government intervention in monopolistic and oligopolistic markets:

◆ Regulation—rules determining prices, product standards, and entry conditions. *Deregulation*—removing rules.

◆ Public ownership—publicly owned firms are **Crown corporations. Privatization**—selling publicly owned corporation to private shareholders.

◆ **Anti-combine law**—makes some market behaviour (monopolistic practices) illegal.

Government intervention designed to influence surpluses. **Total surplus** represents the combined gains from trade to consumers and producers; sum of *consumer surplus* and *producer surplus*.

◆ *Consumer surplus*—value of goods to consumers – price paid = area below demand curve and above market price.

◆ *Producer surplus*—total revenue – opportunity cost = area below market price and above supply curve.

Total surplus maximized under competition when *deadweight loss* = 0.

◆ Under monopoly, ↑ producer surplus, ↓ consumer surplus and creation *deadweight loss.*

◆ Monopolistic practices create a tension between consumer interests and producer interests. This tension is the key to the economic theory of regulation.

Economic Theory of Regulation

Economic theory of regulation part of broader theory of public choice (Chapter 18), but emphasizing government regulation.

◆ Demand for regulation ↑ with ↑

  • consumer surplus per buyer.
  • number buyers.
  • producer surplus per firm.
  • number firms.

◆ Supply of regulation ↑ with ↑

  • consumer surplus per buyer.
  • producer surplus per firm.
  • number people affected.

In political equilibrium, no interest group presses for changes in existing regulation, and no politicians plan to offer different regulations. There are two theories of political equilibrium.

◆ **Public interest theory**—predicts regulations supplied to maximize total surplus and eliminate deadweight loss. Government will act in the public interest to eliminate waste and achieve allocative efficiency.

◆ **Capture theory**—predicts regulations supplied to maximize producer surplus and economic profit. Government "captured" by interests of producers.

Regulation and Deregulation

Government regulatory agencies set rules for prices, quantities, and market access.

Natural monopoly (because of economies of scale, one firm can supply the market at lower *ATC* than multiple firms can) can be regulated with the following rules.

◆ **Marginal cost pricing rule**—set price equal to marginal cost. Maximizes total surplus, but not viable because firm makes economic loss.

◆ **Average cost pricing rule**—set price equal to average total cost. May be most efficient even though deadweight loss.

◆ **Rate of return regulation**—set price to achieve specified target rate of return on capital.

   • Ideally, yields normal profit only; same outcome as average-cost pricing rule.
   • But there is a problem of incentive for firm to inflate cost (of capital) to yield economic profits.

◆ Evidence mixed, but regulated natural monopolies seem to earn profits equal to or greater than average, supporting more of predictions of capture theory than public interest theory.

Cartel (collusive agreement among firms in an oligopoly to restrict output and ↑ price) can be regulated with the following rules.

◆ Set price and quantity at competitive levels (intersection of industry demand and *MC* curves). Public interest theory outcome.

◆ Set price and quantity to maximize profit (highest price associated with quantity at intersection of industry *MC* and *MR* curves). Capture theory outcome.

◆ Evidence mixed, but regulated cartels seem to earn profits equal to or greater than average, supporting more of predictions of capture theory than public interest theory.

Public Ownership

Publicly owned corporations can be operated with the following objectives:

◆ **Allocative efficiency**—set price equal to marginal cost and subsidize the economic loss. Maximizes consumer surplus.

◆ **Budget maximization with marginal cost pricing**—set price equal to marginal cost but pad production costs to maximum. Allocatively efficient, but maximizes producer benefits.

◆ **Budget maximization at zero price**—↑ output until price falls to zero. Inefficient (deadweight loss), results in overproduction and maximizes producer benefits.

◆ Evidence suggests publicly owned firms will overproduce and be less efficient than a private firm. Recent tendency to privatize publicly owned firms.

Anti-Combine Law

Competition Act of 1986 distinguishes between

◆ Criminal actions (conspiracy to fix prices, bid-rigging, false advertising) dealt with by courts.

◆ Noncriminal actions (mergers, abuse of market position, exclusive dealing) dealt with by Competition Tribunal.

Evidence suggests anti-combine laws have served the public interest.

HELPFUL HINTS

I Figure 20.1 depicts revenue and marginal cost curves for an industry. Use this figure to think of regulation as determining the division of the potential total surplus (the area of triangle *abc*) among consumer surplus, producer surplus, and deadweight loss.

FIGURE **20.1**

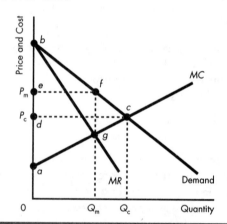

If the industry is perfectly competitive, then output will be Q_c and the market price will be P_c. Total surplus is maximized and is given by the area of triangle *abc*. Total surplus is equal to the sum of consumer surplus (triangle *dbc*) and producer surplus (triangle *adc*). There is no deadweight loss.

If the industry is a profit-maximizing monopoly, output will be Q_m and the price will be P_m. In this case, total surplus is represented by the area of trapezoid *abfg*. Because of monopoly restriction of output, total surplus under monopoly is less than under competition. The difference is the deadweight loss from monopoly, the amount of total surplus that is lost when we go from competition to monopoly. The deadweight loss is given by the area of triangle *gfc*. Total surplus can be divided into consumer surplus (triangle *ebf*) and producer surplus (trapezoid *aefg*). Consumer surplus is quite small, but producer surplus is at a maximum.

Actual output is likely to be between these bounds. As output moves from Q_c to Q_m, consumer surplus decreases, while producer surplus and the deadweight loss both increase. If this industry is regulated, the public interest theory of intervention predicts that the result will be a level of output close to Q_c, while the capture theory of intervention predicts a level of output closer to Q_m.

SELF-TEST

True/False/Uncertain and Explain

1 In a monopoly industry, producer surplus is maximized at the profit-maximizing level of output.

2 In a monopoly industry, total surplus is maximized at the profit-maximizing level of output.

3 Evidence of higher-than-normal rates of return for regulated natural monopolies matches the predictions of the capture theory.

4 The evidence that producers are strongly supporting deregulation matches the predictions of the capture theory.

5 Government intervention will move the economy closer to allocative efficiency.

6 According to the capture theory, government regulatory agencies eventually capture the profits of the industries they regulate.

7 In practice, rate of return regulation is equivalent to marginal cost pricing.

8 Under rate of return regulation, firms can get closer to maximizing producer surplus if they inflate their costs.

9 If industry prices and profits fall after *deregulation*, the regulation was likely serving the interest of consumers.

10 Anti-combine laws have generally been directed towards achieving allocative efficiency and serving the public interest.

Multiple-Choice

1 Which of the following is *not* a federal regulatory agency?
a Atomic Energy Control Board
b Canadian Radio-television and Telecommunications Commission
c Petro-Canada
d Canadian Transport Commission
e National Farm Products

2 The difference between the maximum amount consumers are willing to pay and the amount they actually do pay for a given quantity of a good is called
a government surplus.
b consumer surplus.
c producer surplus.
d total surplus.
e deadweight surplus.

3 Which of the following is *least* likely to be a *natural monopoly*?
a subway service
b electric utilities
c water and sewer service
d taxi cab service
e cable TV service

4 The supply of economic regulation originates with

a monopolists.
b labour unions.
c fair trade associations.
d voters.
e politicians and bureaucrats.

5 Total surplus is maximized when

a marginal cost equals marginal revenue.
b marginal cost equals average total cost.
c price equals marginal cost.
d price equals average total cost.
e price equals average variable cost.

6 In a monopoly industry, producer surplus is maximized when

a marginal cost equals marginal revenue.
b marginal cost equals average total cost.
c price equals marginal cost.
d price equals average total cost.
e price equals average variable cost.

7 A large demand for intervention by *producers* will result when there is a

a small consumer surplus per buyer.
b large consumer surplus per buyer.
c large number of buyers.
d small producer surplus per firm.
e large producer surplus per firm.

8 The supply of intervention increases with

a smaller consumer surplus per buyer.
b larger producer surplus per firm.
c smaller number of people affected.
d all of the above.
e none of the above.

9 The total number of Crown corporations in Canada is about

a 25.
b 35.
c 90.
d 125.
e 1,000.

10 Figure 20.2 gives the revenue and cost curves for an industry. This industry will become a natural monopoly because

a one firm can supply the entire market at a lower price than can two or more firms.
b there are decreasing returns to scale over the entire range of demand.
c there are diseconomies of scale over the entire range of demand.
d even a single firm will be unable to earn a positive profit in this industry.
e all of the above are true.

FIGURE **20.2**

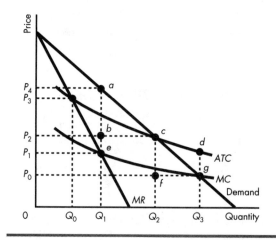

11 Consider the natural monopoly in Fig. 20.2. If the firm is unregulated and operates as a private profit-maximizer, what output will it produce?

a 0, because the firm suffers economic losses when $P = MC$
b Q_0
c Q_1
d Q_2
e Q_3

12 Consider the natural monopoly in Fig. 20.2. If a regulatory agency sets a price just sufficient for the firm to earn normal profits, what output will it produce?

a 0, because the firm suffers economic losses when $P = MC$
b Q_0
c Q_1
d Q_2
e Q_3

13 Consider the natural monopoly in Fig. 20.2. Total surplus is a maximum when quantity is

a Q_0 and price is P_3.
b Q_1 and price is P_1.
c Q_1 and price is P_4.
d Q_2 and price is P_2.
e Q_3 and price is P_0.

14 Consider the natural monopoly in Fig. 20.2. If a regulator uses a marginal cost pricing rule, what line segment gives the amount of subsidy (per unit of output) required to assure that the monopolist remains in business?

a *ba*
b *ea*
c *fc*
d *gd*
e *eb*

15 Consider the natural monopoly in Fig. 20.2. What region in the graph represents the deadweight loss arising from an average cost pricing rule?

a *abc*
b *cdg*
c *cfg*
d *aeg*
e none of the above

16 A monopolist under rate of return regulation has an incentive to

a pad costs.
b produce more than the efficient quantity of output.
c charge a price equal to marginal cost.
d maximize consumer surplus.
e do **a** and **b**.

17 Which of the following is consistent with the public interest theory of regulation?

a regulation of a natural monopoly by setting price equal to marginal cost
b regulation of a competitive industry in order to increase output
c regulation of the airline industry by establishing minimum airfares
d regulation of agriculture by establishing barriers to exit from the industry
e none of the above

18 Which of the following is consistent with the capture theory of regulation?

a regulation of a natural monopoly by setting price equal to marginal cost
b regulation of a competitive industry in order to increase output
c regulation of the airline industry by establishing minimum airfares
d regulation of agriculture by establishing barriers to exit from the industry
e none of the above

19 In a political equilibrium,

a allocative efficiency must be achieved.
b no one wants to change his or her proposal.
c firms will be making zero economic profit.
d all parties will agree that the appropriate level of regulation has been achieved.
e all of the above are true.

20 Anti-combine laws attempt to

a support prices.
b establish Crown corporations.
c prevent monopoly practices.
d establish fair trade laws.
e regulate monopolies.

21 A Crown corporation that maximizes its budget together with marginal cost pricing will

a produce the efficient level of output.
b produce more than the efficient level of output.
c maximize consumer surplus.
d maximize producer surplus.
e do **a** and **d**.

22 The public interest theory of intervention predicts that government regulation will

a promote the interests of public officials.
b attempt to maximize total surplus.
c attempt to maximize producer surplus.
d attempt to minimize producer surplus.
e attempt to maximize consumer surplus.

23 Allocative efficiency is achieved when

a consumer surplus is maximized.
b producer surplus is minimized.
c total surplus is maximized.
d total surplus is minimized.
e none of the above.

24 Regulation refers to

a the discipline of the marketplace.
b rules administered by a government agency.
c selling a publicly owned corporation to private shareholders.
d cartelization of a competitive industry.
e the formation of monopolies.

25 A natural monopoly is likely to have

a low fixed cost and low marginal cost.
b low fixed cost and high marginal cost.
c high fixed cost and low marginal cost.
d high fixed cost and high marginal cost.
e high fixed cost and increasing marginal cost.

Short Answer Problems

1 Regulation of monopoly is necessary because of the tension between the public interest and the producer's interest. Explain.

2 In the regulation of a natural monopoly, when would an average cost pricing rule be better than a marginal cost pricing rule?

3 Why is rate of return regulation equivalent to average cost pricing?

4 Explain the problem that the recent deregulation process poses for the capture theory of intervention.

5 Suppose the government tried to eliminate monopoly profit by taxing each unit of monopoly output.

a What effect would such a policy have on the quantity a monopolist produces and the price it charges?
b What is the effect on economic efficiency?

ⓔⓓ**6** The demand for Aerodisks, a disk made from a unique material that flies a considerable distance when thrown, is given by the equation

$$P = 10 - 0.01 Q_D.$$

The corresponding marginal revenue (*MR*) equation is

$$MR = 10 - 0.02 Q.$$

The Aerodisk Company is a natural monopoly. The firm's total fixed cost is $700 and the marginal cost is constant at $2 per disk. [*Note*: This implies that average variable cost is also constant at $2 per disk.] Suppose that the Aerodisk Company is *not* regulated.

a What will be the quantity sold and the price of an Aerodisk?
b How much is economic profit or loss?
c How much is producer surplus?
d How much is consumer surplus?
e How much is total surplus?

ⓔⓓ**7** Now suppose that the Aerodisk Company becomes regulated and that the regulator uses a marginal cost pricing rule.

a What will be the quantity sold and the price of an Aerodisk?
b How much is economic profit or loss?
c How much is producer surplus?
d How much is consumer surplus?
e How much is total surplus?

8 Suppose that the regulator of the Aerodisk Company uses an average cost pricing rule.

a What will be the price of an Aerodisk and how many will be sold?
b How much is economic profit or loss?
c How much is producer surplus?
d How much is consumer surplus?
e How much is total surplus?

9 Since the Aerodisk Company will make a loss under marginal cost pricing, the government must subsidize the production of Aerodisks in order for the firm to be willing to produce.

a What is the total subsidy necessary under a marginal cost pricing rule to leave the firm with a zero economic profit?
b What is the amount of the deadweight loss associated with an average cost pricing rule?
c In order to pay the necessary subsidy under the marginal cost rule, the government must raise tax revenue in the amount of the subsidy. If the deadweight loss associated with the tax is $100, which pricing rule is superior?

10 Figure 20.3 illustrates the industry demand, marginal revenue (*MR*) and marginal cost (*MC*) curves in an oligopoly industry. The industry is regulated.

a What price and quantity will be predicted by the public interest theory of regulation? Why?
b What price and quantity will be predicted by the capture theory of regulation? Why?
c Can you explain why the firms in this industry might be demanders of regulation?

FIGURE **20.3**

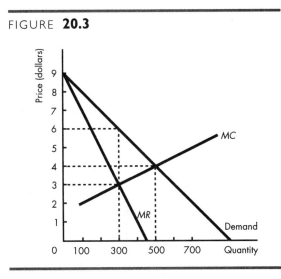

ANSWERS

True/False/Uncertain and Explain

1 T See text discussion. (455–456)
2 F True for competition. (455–456)
3 T Regulators act in interest of monopoly. (462–463)
4 F Matches public interest theory. (462–465)
5 U True according to public interest theory, false according to capture theory. (457–458)
6 F Industry captures more of total surplus. (457–458)
7 F More like average cost pricing. (460–462)
8 T ↑ costs → ↑profits. (462–463)
9 F Serving producers. (463–465)
10 T See text discussion. (468–469)

Multiple-Choice

1 c Crown corporation. (458–459)
2 b Definition. (455–456)
3 d No major economies of scale. (459–460)
4 e Create legislation. (456–457)
5 c Pricing rule for allocative efficiency. (455–456)
6 a Pricing rule of monopoly profit maximization. (455–456)
7 e **b, c** → ↑ demand by buyers. (456–457)
8 b Reverse **a, c** true. (456–457)
9 d See Text Table 20.2. (465–466)
10 a Definition natural monopoly. (459–460)
11 c Where $MC = MR$. (459–461)
12 d Where $P = ATC$. (459–461)
13 e Where $P = MC$. (459–461)
14 d To cover loss per unit of output. (460–461)

15 c See Text Fig. 20.3. (459–461)
16 a To increase profits. (461–462)
17 a Only option → ↑ efficiency. (457–458)
18 c Helps airline firms, not consumers. (457–458)
19 b See text discussion. (457–458)
20 c See text discussion. (455)
⌖21 e See Text Fig. 20.7(b). (465–467)
22 b Attempt to achieve allocative efficiency. (457–458)
23 c See text discussion. (455–456)
24 b See text discussion. (455)
25 c Yielding always downward sloping ATC. (459–460)

Short Answer Problems

1 It is in the public interest to achieve allocative efficiency; that is, to expand output to the level that maximizes total surplus. On the other hand, it is in the interest of the monopoly producer to restrict output in order to maximize producer surplus and thus monopoly profit.

  Since these interests are not the same, monopoly must be regulated in order to achieve allocative efficiency. The public interest theory of regulation suggests that this is the principle that guides regulation of monopoly industries.

2 An average cost pricing rule will create a deadweight loss but so will a marginal cost pricing rule, through the need to impose a tax.

  Since, for a natural monopoly, marginal cost is less than average total cost, regulation by use of a marginal cost pricing rule requires the government to pay a subsidy in order for the firm to be willing to produce at all.

  In order to pay that subsidy the government must levy a tax that will impose a deadweight loss on the economy. If the deadweight loss associated with the tax (for example, the deadweight loss of the marginal cost pricing rule with its attendant subsidy) is greater than the deadweight loss of an average cost pricing rule, the average cost pricing rule is superior.

3 The key here is to recall that economic cost includes a normal rate of return. Thus because rate of return regulation sets a price that allows the firm to achieve a normal rate of return, it is setting the price equal to average total cost.

4 The capture theory predicts that producers will capture the regulatory process and use it to maximize producer surplus. But if the producer lobby was strong enough to achieve regulation, why have producers been unable to stop

deregulation? A further question is why do many producers *favour* deregulation? The capture theory has no good answers to these questions.

5 a Imposing a tax on each unit sold by a monopolist will increase marginal cost. As a consequence the profit-maximizing monopolist will raise the price and reduce the quantity produced.

  b The tax will certainly reduce the profit of the monopolist and may even eliminate it, but the consequence will be to make the inefficiency due to monopoly even worse. This is illustrated in Fig. 20.4. The curve *MC* is the marginal cost curve before the tax. An unregulated monopolist will produce amount Q_2, while the economically efficient output is Q_3. The tax, however, causes the monopolist to reduce output from Q_2 to Q_1, which moves the market outcome farther away from efficiency.

FIGURE **20.4**

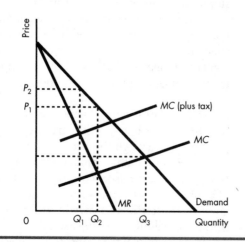

@ⓓ 6 Figure 20.5 will be helpful in answering questions about the Aerodisk market. It gives the relevant revenue and cost curves for the Aerodisk Company.

FIGURE **20.5**

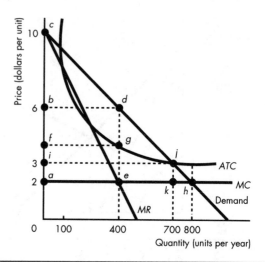

a In an unregulated market, the Aerodisk Company will choose output so as to maximize profit, where *MR = MC.* To calculate this output, set *MR = MC =* 2 and solve for *Q:*

$$10 - 0.02Q = 2$$
$$8 = 0.02Q$$
$$400 = Q$$

To calculate price, substitute $Q = 400$ into the demand equation:

$$P = 10 - 0.01Q_D$$
$$= 10 - 0.01\,(400)$$
$$= 10 - 4$$
$$= 6$$

400 Aerodisks will be produced and sold at a price of $6 each.

b To determine economic profit we first determine average total cost (*ATC*) when output (*Q*) is 400 units.

$$ATC = AFC + AVC$$
$$= (TFC/Q) + AVC$$
$$= (700/400) + 2$$
$$= 3.75$$

Therefore economic profit is the difference between price (average revenue) and *ATC* times the quantity sold. This is equal to $900 and is represented in Fig. 20.5 by region *fbdg*.

c Producer surplus is the difference between the producer's revenue and the opportunity cost of production. Total revenue is $2,400 ($6 × 400 units) and total opportunity cost is $800 ($2 × 400 units). Thus producer surplus is $1,600. Graphically, producer surplus is the area of rectangle *abde* in Fig. 20.5.

d Consumer surplus is readily obtained graphically as the area in triangle *bcd* in Fig. 20.5. The area of that triangle is $800.

e Total surplus is $2,400, the sum of producer and consumer surplus.

◎◑ **7 a** Under a marginal cost pricing rule, the price of an Aerodisk will be equal to marginal cost or $2. To calculate the quantity sold, substitute the price into the demand equation:

$$P = 10 - 0.01 Q_D$$
$$2 = 10 - 0.01 Q_D$$
$$0.01 Q_D = 8$$
$$Q_D = 800.$$

b To determine the amount of economic profit or loss, we must first determine *ATC* when output is 800. Using the procedure in the previous problem we find that at $Q = 800$, *ATC* is $2.875, which is greater than price by $0.875 (87.5¢). Therefore the Aerodisk Company will make a loss in the amount of $700 ($0.875 × 800). Alternatively, since *MC* is constant, if the price is set equal to *MC* which is equal to *AVC*, the total loss will be just *TFC* or $700.

c Producer surplus is zero.

d Consumer surplus is given by the area of triangle *ach* in Fig. 20.5, which is $3,200.

e Total surplus is $3,200 (a maximum).

8 a Computation of *ATC* at various levels of output allows us to determine that the *ATC* curve crosses the demand curve when $Q = 700$ and $ATC = \$3$. Thus under an average cost pricing rule, the price of an Aerodisk will be $3 and 700 units will be sold.

b Since price is equal to average total cost, economic profit is zero.

c Producer surplus is $700, area *aijh* in Fig. 20.5.

d Consumer surplus is $2,450, the area of triangle *ijc* in Fig. 20.5.

e Total surplus is $3,150.

9 a The total subsidy is equal to the loss under marginal cost pricing. In Short Answer Problem **7b** we computed this to be $700.

b The deadweight loss associated with the average cost pricing rule is the loss of total surplus relative to the marginal cost pricing rule. We have computed the total surplus under marginal cost pricing ($3,200) in Short Answer Problem **7e** and the total surplus under average cost pricing ($3,150) in Short Answer Problem **8e**. The deadweight loss is the difference: $50.

c The average cost pricing rule is superior because it has the smaller deadweight loss.

10 a The public interest theory predicts that regulators will set price and quantity so as to maximize total surplus. This means that they will choose quantity (and price) where *MC* is equal to demand. This corresponds to a quantity of 500 units and a price of $4 per unit.

b The capture theory predicts that the regulator will choose quantity and price so as to maximize the profit of the industry. This is the quantity that would be chosen by a profit-maximizing monopolist, 300 units, where $MC = MR$. The highest price that could be charged and still sell that quantity can be read from the demand curve: $6 per unit.

c Firms in the industry would be demanders of regulation if the regulation had the effect of increasing profit to the industry. As we discovered in Chapter 13, cartels are unstable because there is always an incentive to cheat on output restriction agreements and it is very difficult to enforce the agreements. If, however, the firms in an industry can get the government, through regulation, to enforce a cartel agreement, they will want to do it.

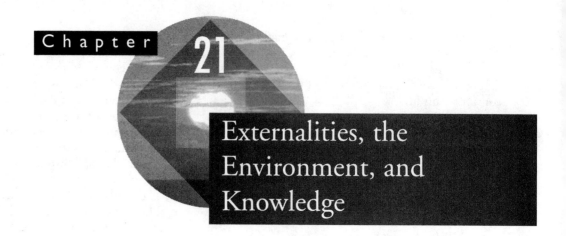

Chapter **21**

Externalities, the Environment, and Knowledge

KEY CONCEPTS

Externalities

Externality is cost or benefit from production or consumption activities that affects people who are not part of the original activity. Externalities may be negative (from pollution) or positive (from education).

- *External cost* (negative externality)—cost of producing a good/service not borne by consumers but by others.

- *External benefit* (positive externality)—benefit from consuming a good/service going not to consumers but to others.

Externalities create market failure (allocative *in*efficiency). Markets overproduce goods/services with external costs and underproduce goods/services with external benefits.

Economics of the Environment

Many people assume that all environmental damage must be stopped. Economic analysis of the environment, however, evaluates the costs and benefits of actions in order to identify efficient amounts of pollution or environmental damage.

- Demand ↑ over time for a cleaner environment due to ↑ incomes (high-quality environment is a normal good) and ↑ knowledge about environmental problems. Environmental problems include air pollution, water pollution, and land pollution.

Externalities arise because of an *absence* of property rights.

- **Property rights** are social arrangements governing ownership, use, and disposal of factors of production and goods and services. In Canada, property rights are legally established titles enforceable in court.

- Without property rights, for example in a river, the marginal cost (*MC*) of polluting the river is zero. Firms will pollute as long as a marginal benefit (*MB*) of polluting is greater than zero. Negative externalities like pollution can often be corrected by establishing property rights.

- **Coase theorem**—if property rights are established and transactions costs are low, there will be no externalities and private transactions will be efficient. How property rights are assigned will *not* affect the efficiency of the outcome, but will affect the distribution of costs and benefits.

Where property rights cannot be established or transactions costs are high, other policies can be used by government regulators to achieve efficiency even with externalities.

- To achieve efficiency, policies must yield a quantity of output where marginal social cost = marginal social benefit.

  - **Marginal social cost** (*MSC*) equals marginal private cost directly incurred by producer *plus* marginal cost imposed as externality on others.
  - **Marginal social benefit** (*MSB*) equals marginal private benefit directly received by consumer *plus* marginal benefit received as externality by others.

- Emission charges—policy of setting a price per unit of pollution so that *MSC* = *MSB*. In practice,

  - difficult to determine marginal benefit of pollution
  - polluters have incentive to mislead regulators about benefit.

◆ Marketable permits—quantitative limits on emissions that overcome the need for the regulator to know firms' marginal benefits of pollution. Each firm given a pollution limit (permit) that can be bought and sold.

- Firms reducing their pollution below their limit can sell the "excess" reduction to other firms who then can pollute more.
- In a competitive market for permits, price of permits will yield efficient outcome where $MSC = MSB$.

◆ Taxes—to control a negative externality, regulator can impose a tax equal to external marginal cost.

- This makes the MSC curve the relevant MC curve for the polluting producer's decision → output where $MSC = MSB$.

A carbon-fuel tax would limit carbon emissions and potentially limit global warming of the atmosphere.

◆ There is no such tax because there is scientific uncertainty about carbon dioxide's contribution to global warming and uncertainty about the costs of global warming; costs would be borne now while uncertain benefits would accrue only in the future; and there are problems of international cooperation.

◆ Industrial and developing countries are in a prisoners' dilemma game where no one cuts back carbon dioxide emissions because it is in every country's interest to let others carry the costs of environmental policies.

The Economics of Knowledge

Knowledge creates significant external benefits, so that the marginal social benefit (MSB) exceeds the marginal private benefit (MPB). Market outcomes that result from choosing quantities where $MPB = MSC$ yield less than the efficient quantity of knowledge; there is *market failure*.

To achieve efficiency, policies must yield a quantity of knowledge output where $MSB = MSC$.

◆ **Subsidies**—payment by government to producers of knowledge-based goods/services.

- To encourage production of goods/services with a positive externality, pay subsidy to producers equal to external marginal benefit.
- This makes the MSB curve the relevant MB curve for the knowledge producer's decision → output where $MSB = MSC$.

◆ Below-cost provisions—government provides the good/service (public education) and charges a price (often zero) below cost.

◆ **Patents** and **copyrights**—provide creators of knowledge with **intellectual property rights** in their discoveries, and help insure that the creator will profit.

- Because knowledge does not seem to have *diminishing marginal productivity*, incentives must be created to encourage an efficient level of development of new ideas.
- Patents and copyrights encourage development of new knowledge, but create a temporary monopoly, so gains from ↑ knowledge must be balanced against loss from monopoly.

HELPFUL HINTS

1 A competitive market will result in the quantity of output at which the marginal private cost is equal to the marginal private benefit. The efficient quantity is the quantity at which marginal social cost is equal to marginal social benefit.

The difference between *marginal social cost* and *marginal private cost* is external cost, and the difference between *marginal social benefit* and *marginal private benefit* is external benefit.

In most economic activities, people who are not part of the original activity are not affected, so there are no external costs or benefits. This means that private and social costs and benefits coincide and competitive markets will be efficient. However, when third parties are affected, there are external costs or benefits and competitive markets will *not* be efficient. Markets overproduce goods/services with external costs and underproduce goods/services with external benefits.

2 Competitive markets with externalities are not efficient because some of the costs or benefits are *external*. If those costs or benefits could be *internalized* somehow, then the market would be efficient. There are two main approaches to internalizing externalities that are discussed in this chapter.

The first is to clearly define and strictly enforce property rights. Then costs imposed on people who are not part of the original activity can be recovered through the legal process and will thus be paid by those involved in the activity: the costs will become internal (private).

The second approach to internalizing externalities is to tax activities that generate external costs and subsidize activities that generate external benefits. By charging a tax equal to the external cost, the entire cost becomes internal. Similarly, by paying a subsidy in the amount of external benefits, the entire benefit becomes internal.

3 If the production of a good or service produces external costs, a competitive market will result in a quantity that exceeds the allocatively efficient level. Text Fig. 21.7, reproduced as Fig. 21.1, illustrates that taxing the production of that good or service can induce the allocatively efficient quantity. The example is of transportation services, which produce external costs of pollution and congestion.

FIGURE **21.1**

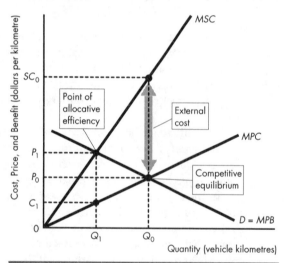

The demand curve for transportation services is the same as the marginal benefit curve. The marginal private cost (MPC) and marginal social cost (MSC) curves are *not* the same, however. The MPC curve reflects the costs that directly accrue to the producer of transportation services. There are, however, other costs in the form of pollution and congestion that are imposed on others. The MSC curve reflects both the marginal cost incurred by the producer and these external costs.

The allocatively efficient quantity of transportation services occurs at Q_1, the intersection of the $D = MB$ curve and the MSC curve. A competitive market, however, will result in the quantity at which the D and MPC curves intersect since producers only take private costs into account; market price will be P_0 and

quantity will be Q_0, which is greater than the allocatively efficient quantity.

If, however, a tax is levied on producers in the amount of the external costs, the MSC curve becomes the new relevant marginal cost curve for producers. As a result, the market price will rise to P_1 and the quantity will fall to Q_1, and allocative efficiency is achieved. Note that the efficient quantity of output is not zero, which means that there will be some pollution and congestion. The efficient (optimal) level of pollution/congestion is not zero.

Generally, the costs saved by reducing pollution to zero are less than the benefits lost (benefits from consuming goods whose production created pollution as a by-product).

S E L F - T E S T

True/False/Uncertain and Explain

1 If negative externalities exist, marginal social cost and external cost are equivalent.

2 If the production of a good involves no external cost, then marginal social cost is equal to marginal private cost.

3 Externalities often arise from the absence of private property rights.

4 The existence of external benefits means that marginal social cost is less than marginal private cost.

5 When external costs are present, the private market will tend to produce more than the allocatively efficient level of output.

6 Assigning property rights solves the problem of a negative externality.

7 The allocatively efficient quantity of pollution is always zero.

8 Patents encourage invention and innovation.

9 Marketable pollution permits require regulators to know firms' marginal benefit schedules.

10 The outcome of a global warming dilemma game is that industrial countries control pollution and developing countries pollute.

Multiple-Choice

1 An externality is a cost or benefit arising from an economic activity that falls on

a consumers but not producers.
b producers but not consumers.
c free riders.
d rivals.
e none of the above.

2 Figure 21.2 depicts the demand for good *A* as well as the marginal private cost (*MPC*) and marginal social cost (*MSC*) associated with the production of good *A*. Production of the sixth unit of output generates an *external*

a cost of $1.50.
b cost of $3.
c cost of $6.
d benefit of $3.
e benefit of $6.

FIGURE **21.2**

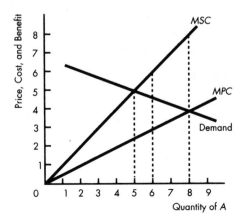

3 In Fig. 21.2, how many units of good *A* will be produced in an unregulated market?

a 0 units
b 5 units
c 6 units
d 8 units
e impossible to calculate without additional information

4 In Fig. 21.2, what is the allocatively efficient quantity of good *A*?

a 0 units
b 5 units
c 6 units
d 8 units
e impossible to calculate without additional information

5 At the current level of production of buckyballs, marginal social benefit is less than marginal social cost. To achieve allocative efficiency,

a buckyballs should be taxed.
b buckyballs should not be produced.
c output of buckyballs should increase.
d output of buckyballs should decrease.
e property rights in buckyballs should be established.

6 Which of the following illustrates the concept of external cost?

a Bad weather reduces the size of the wheat crop.
b A reduction in the size of the wheat crop causes the income of wheat farmers to fall.
c Smoking harms the health of the smoker.
d Smoking harms the health of nearby nonsmokers.
e Public health services reduce the transmission of disease.

7 The production of too many goods with negative externalities is an example of

a redistribution.
b consumer sovereignty.
c producer sovereignty.
d public failure.
e market failure.

8 Figure 21.3 depicts the demand curve for good *B*, the marginal social benefit (*MSB*) curve, and marginal private and social cost (*MPC* = *MSC*) curve. How many units of good *B* will be produced and consumed in an unregulated market?

a 0 units
b 3 units
c 5 units
d 6 units
e 9 units

FIGURE **21.3**

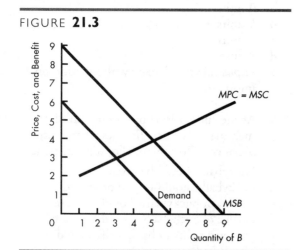

9 In Fig. 21.3, what is the allocatively efficient quantity of good *B*?

a 0 units
b 3 units
c 5 units
d 6 units
e 9 units

10 In Fig. 21.3, which of the following government policies would induce the market to achieve allocative efficiency?

a Tax the production of *B* at $3 per unit.
b Tax the production of *B* at $4 per unit.
c Subsidize the consumption of *B* at $1 per unit.
d Subsidize the consumption of *B* at $3 per unit.
e Subsidize the consumption of *B* at $4 per unit.

11 When market failure occurs, the government will act to reduce the level of inefficiency. This is a prediction of a(n)

a end-state theory of government behaviour.
b process theory of government behaviour.
c public interest theory of government behaviour.
d public choice theory of government behaviour.
e rent-seeking theory of government behaviour.

12 An externality is

a the amount by which price exceeds marginal private cost.
b the amount by which price exceeds marginal social cost.
c the effect of government regulation on market price and output.
d someone who consumes a good without paying for it.
e a cost or benefit that arises from a decision but is not borne by the decision maker.

13 The marginal private cost curve (*MPC*) is a positively sloped straight line starting at the origin. If external costs per unit of output are constant, then the marginal *social* cost curve is a positively sloped straight line

a parallel to and above *MPC*.
b parallel to and below *MPC*.
c starting at the origin and above *MPC*.
d starting at the origin and below *MPC*.
e identical to *MPC*.

14 A market economy tends to _____ goods with negative externalities and _____ goods with positive externalities.

a overproduce; overproduce
b overproduce; underproduce
c underproduce; overproduce
d underproduce; underproduce
e produce; consume

15 Policies for correcting problems of negative externalities include all of the following *except*

a emission charges.
b patents.
c quantitative limits.
d taxes.
e marketable permits.

16 Policies to achieve allocative efficiency when there are external benefits include

a intellectual property rights.
b subsidies.
c below-cost provision.
d all of the above.
e none of the above.

17 A battery acid producer pollutes the water upstream from the nude swimmers belonging to the Polar Bear Club. If transactions costs are low, the quantity of pollution will be efficient

a only if Ronald Coase is a member of the Polar Bear Club.

b only if the distribution of costs and benefits is equal.

c only if water property rights are assigned to the producer.

d only if water property rights are assigned to the Polar Bear Club.

e if water property rights are assigned either to the producer or the Polar Bear Club.

18 Knowledge, as a factor of production,

a displays diminishing marginal productivity.

b creates external costs.

c has costs totalling those paid to the patent holder.

d is encouraged by intellectual property rights.

e is all of the above.

19 The income elasticity of demand for a better environment is

a negative.

b zero.

c positive.

d trendy.

e impossible to know without additional information.

20 The production of too few goods with positive externalities is an example of

a market failure.

b government failure.

c producer sovereignty.

d consumer sovereignty.

e external costs.

21 Polluters are best informed about the marginal benefits of pollution and have an incentive to mislead regulators about those benefits. An emission charge set by the regulators will likely be too

a high, resulting in excessive pollution.

b high, resulting in excessive cleanup.

c low, resulting in excessive pollution.

d low, resulting in excessive cleanup.

e good to be true.

22 Refer to Table 21.1. If the fertilizer market is perfectly competitive and unregulated, output is

a 1.

b 2.

c 3.

d 4.

e 5,

TABLE **21.1**   CHEMICAL FERTILIZER MARKET

Output (tonnes)	Marginal Private Benefit ($)	Marginal Social Benefit ($)	Marginal Private Cost ($)	Marginal Social Cost ($)
1	140	140	50	80
2	120	120	60	90
3	100	100	70	100
4	80	80	80	110
5	60	60	90	120

23 Refer to Table 21.1. Fertilizer has a marginal external

a cost of $100.

b benefit of $100.

c cost of $30.

d benefit of $30.

e cost of $0.

24 Refer to Table 21.1. The allocatively efficient output of fertilizer is

a 1.

b 2.

c 3.

d 4.

e 5.

25 In the past, the levels of chlorofluorocarbons (CFCs) in refrigerators and aerosols have been

a less than socially optimal due to external costs.

b less than socially optimal due to external benefits.

c more than socially optimal due to external costs.

d more than socially optimal due to external benefits.

e decreasing the earth's average temperature.

Short Answer Problems

1 Governments provide education for free, or at least at a price (tuition) much less than cost. What is the economic argument that supports this policy?

2 Explain how a tax can be used to achieve efficiency in the face of external costs.

3 The production of steel also produces pollution and thus generates an external cost. Suppose the government attempts to solve the problem by imposing a tax on steel producers (who also produce pollution). At the after-tax level of output, we observe that the original marginal social cost curve is below the demand curve. Is the after-tax level of output efficient? If it is not, should steel production, and therefore pollution production, be increased or decreased?

4 Your roommate is an environmentalist who is appalled at the economic concept of an "efficient" level of pollution. She argues that since everyone agrees that pollution is "bad," society must work towards eliminating all pollution. How would you, as an economics major, convince her that it is not in society's best interests to eliminate all pollution?

5 What are the benefits and costs of creating intellectual property rights for the creation of new knowledge?

6 Two prairie pioneers, Jethro and Hortense, have adjacent fields. Because they get along so well and always work out any problems that arise, they have not bothered to put up a fence. Then one day Jethro buys a new pig, Babe. Babe sometimes wanders into Hortense's field and eats her corn. If Babe would only stay on Jethro's farm, he would eat valueless garbage. Suppose that Babe eats $500 worth of Hortense's corn per year (a negative externality imposed on Hortense) and that to build a fence between the farms costs $300. No property rights to keep animals off the fields have been established yet.

a If the property right is given to Jethro so Babe can continue to wander, will Hortense build a fence? Explain.

b If, instead, the property right is given to Hortense, so that she can charge Jethro for the corn Babe eats, will Jethro build a fence? Explain.

c Explain how this example illustrates the Coase theorem.

7 The first two columns of Table 21.2 give the demand schedule for education in Hicksville, while the third column gives the marginal private cost. In Hicksville, unlike the textbook example of education, marginal cost increases with the quantity of students. Since education generates external benefits, marginal social benefit given in the last column is greater than marginal private benefit.

TABLE **21.2**

Quantity (number of students)	Marginal Private Benefit ($)	Marginal Private Cost ($)	Marginal Social Benefit ($)
100	500	200	800
200	400	250	700
300	300	300	600
400	200	350	500
500	100	400	400
600	0	450	300

a Represent the data in Table 21.2 graphically.

b What equilibrium price and quantity would result if the market for education is unregulated?

c What is the allocatively efficient quantity of students in Hicksville?

8 In an attempt to address the inefficient level of education in Hicksville, the town council has decided to subsidize schooling. The council offers $200 to each student who buys a year of education.

a Draw the new marginal private benefit curve, which includes the subsidy, on your graph and label it MPB_1.

b What are the approximate new equilibrium price and quantity?

9 The Hicksville town council increases the subsidy to $400.

a Draw another marginal private benefit curve, which includes the subsidy, on your graph and label it MPB_2.

b What are the approximate corresponding equilibrium price and quantity?

c What level of subsidy will achieve the efficient quantity of education?

10 Lever Sisters Company produces Flatulost, a popular room deodorizer. Unfortunately, the production process releases sulfur dioxide into the atmosphere. The marginal private cost (MPC) to Lever Sisters of producing Flatulost is

$$MPC = 1Q_S.$$

The marginal social cost (MSC) is

$$MSC = 3/2 Q_S.$$

The demand curve for Flatulost (there are no external benefits) is

$$P = 12 - 1/2 Q_D.$$

Q_S is the quantity of Flatulost supplied, P is the price of Flatulost in dollars, and Q_D is the quantity demanded.

a In an unregulated market, what is the equilibrium quantity of Flatulost? the equilibrium price?

b To achieve allocative efficiency, what should be the equilibrium quantity of Flatulost? the equilibrium price?

c Compare the unregulated market quantity and price with the allocatively efficient quantity and price.

d The government wants to impose a tax on Flatulost to achieve the allocatively efficient quantity of output. What should the tax be?

ANSWERS

True/False/Uncertain and Explain

1 F $MSC = MPC +$ externality. (485–486)
2 T $MSC = MPC +$ externality. (485–486)
3 T Property rights would allow recovery of (external) costs. (480–482)
⊘ 4 F External benefits affect MSB, not MSC. (489–490)
5 T Where MPC (instead of MSC) intersects demand. (477–478)
6 U True if transactions costs are low; false otherwise. (482–483)
7 F Quantity where $MSB = MSC$ of pollution. (485–487)
8 T Intellectual property rights overcome positive externality problem of knowledge. (490–491)
9 F Permits overcome the need for regulators to know. (484–485)
10 F All countries have dominant strategy of polluting. (487–488)

Multiple-Choice

1 e Falls on third party. (477)
⊘ 2 b Vertical distance between MSC and MPC at $Q = 6$. (485–486)
3 d Where MPC intersects demand. (485–486)
4 b Where MSC intersects demand. (485–486)
5 d Draw graph. Don't know if positive, negative, or any externality. (489–490)
6 d Cost falls on third party. (477)
7 e Failure to achieve allocative efficiency. (477–478)
8 b Where MC intersects demand. (489–490)
9 c Where MC intersects MSB. (489–490)

⊘ 10 d Shift MC down by vertical distance between MSB and demand. (489–490)
11 c Public interest to achieve allocative efficiency. (418–419, 457)
12 e Definition. (477)
⊘ 13 a MPC shifts up by vertical distance equal to external cost per unit. (485–486)
14 b Outcomes of market failure. (477–478)
15 b Patents correct problems of positive externalities. (483–487)
16 d All move output to where $MSB = MSC$. (489–491)
17 e This is the Coase theorem. (480–483)
18 d No ↓ marginal productivity; creates external benefits; patent monopoly → loss from restricted use. (488–491)
19 c Better environment is normal good so $\eta_y > 0$. (478–479)
20 a Markets fail to produce the allocatively efficient quantity of goods with positive externalities. (477–478)
21 c True MB greater than that reported, so true MB curve above reported curve. (483–485)
22 d Where $MPB = MPC = 80$. (485–486)
23 c $MSC - MPC$ is constant in this example. (485–486)
24 c Where $MSB = MSC$. (485–486)
25 c Market overproduction of good with external costs. (485–486)

Short Answer Problems

1 Government subsidizes education heavily. The economic argument is that education generates external benefits. In particular, when individuals are educated, society at large receives benefits beyond the private benefits that accrue to those choosing how much education to obtain.

2 The existence of external costs means that producers do not take into account all costs when deciding how much to produce. If a tax is levied that is exactly the amount of the external cost, the cost will no longer be external. As a result, the producer will take it into account and thus be induced to produce the efficient quantity.

3 Since the marginal social cost curve is below the demand curve at the after-tax output, marginal social cost is less than marginal benefit. This means that the tax has been set too high; it has been set at a level in excess of the external cost. As a result, the after-tax level of steel production will be less than the efficient level. The level of steel production and pollution production

should be increased by decreasing the amount of the tax.

4 We all want to eliminate pollution, *ceteris paribus*, but every action, including reducing pollution, has a cost. Once again, the key concept underlying the economic argument is opportunity cost. What is the opportunity cost of reducing pollution, or, what does society have to give up to achieve a pollution-free environment?

Small reductions in pollution are relatively inexpensive—eliminating lead from gasoline and paint, conserving energy to reduce output from coal-fired electrical plants, etc. But to eliminate all pollution would mean eliminating all cars and airplanes, outlawing all power except solar and hydroelectric power, shutting down most factories, etc. The cost of eliminating *all* pollution is enormous, and that additional cost is far greater than the additional benefits from further reductions in pollution. Therefore some level of pollution is efficient. Pollution is part of the opportunity cost of the benefits we receive from driving or flying instead of walking, from enjoying the comfort of air conditioning in hot weather, and from enjoying goods produced in factories. The efficient level of pollution balances the marginal social cost of the pollution against the marginal social benefit of the production and consumption associated with that level of pollution.

5 Intellectual property rights create incentives for individuals to create new knowledge by granting the inventor a limited monopoly to benefit from the application of her idea. Without the property right, anyone could freely use the idea and there would be little profit to the inventor. The limited monopoly, although necessary as an incentive to produce knowledge, has a social cost—the restriction of knowledge-based output below the efficient, competitive quantity.

6 a Hortense will build a fence. Although the fence costs $300 per year, it saves her the $500 in lost corn that Babe would otherwise eat.
b Jethro will build a fence. The $300 per year is less than the $500 per year he would now have to pay Hortense for Babe's wanderings.
c The Coase theorem states that if transactions costs are low and property rights are established, there are no externalities and an efficient outcome occurs regardless of who is assigned the property right. Because Jethro and Hortense can work out their problems amicably, transactions

costs are low. The outcome of building a fence eliminates the negative externality of the wandering pig and occurs regardless of which pioneer is assigned the property right. The outcome is efficient because, for this one decision, the $300 cost to society of the fence is less than the $500 cost of consumed corn.

7 a Figure 21.4 is a graphical representation of the data in Table 21.2. The demand for education is given by the marginal private benefit curve (labelled *MPB*), the marginal private cost curve is labelled *MPC* and the marginal social benefit curve is labelled *MSB*. Ignore the other curves for now.

FIGURE **21.4**

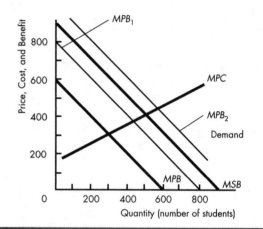

b In an unregulated market, equilibrium price and quantity are determined by the intersection of the *MPB* and *MPC* curves. Thus the equilibrium price would be $300 and the equilibrium quantity is 300 students.
c Since there are no external costs, the efficient quantity is determined by the intersection of the *MPC* and *MSB* curves. This implies that allocative efficiency is attained at a quantity of 500 students.

8 a The subsidy increases the marginal private benefit to each student by the amount of the subsidy, $200. The new *MPB* curve, labelled MPB_1, is included in Fig. 21.4.
b The new equilibrium after the $200 subsidy is at the intersection of the *MPC* and MPB_1 curves. The price of a unit of education will be approximately $370 and there will be approximately 430 students.

9 a With a subsidy of $400 per student, the MPB curve will shift to MPB_2 in Fig. 21.4.

b With this subsidy the equilibrium will be at the intersection of the MPC and MPB_2 curves. The corresponding price of a unit of education will be approximately $430 and the number of students will be approximately 570.

c In order to achieve an efficient outcome, the subsidy must make the MPB curve coincide with the MSB curve. This requires a subsidy of $300 per student.

©◑ **10 a** In an unregulated market, the equilibrium quantity would be determined by the intersection of the supply (MPC) and demand curves. In equilibrium, $Q_S = Q_D = Q^*$. Setting the MPC equation equal to the demand equation yields

$$1Q^* = 12 - 1/2Q^*$$
$$3/2Q^* = 12$$
$$Q^* = 8$$

To solve for the equilibrium price (P^*), substitute Q^* into the demand (or into the MPC) equation.

$$P^* = 12 - 1/2Q^*$$
$$P^* = 12 - 1/2\,(8)$$
$$P^* = 8$$

b In order to achieve allocative efficiency, MSC must equal marginal social benefit (MSB). Since there are no external benefits, the demand curve is also the MSB curve. In equilibrium, $Q_S = Q_D = Q^*$. To find the equilibrium quantity, set the MSC equation equal to the demand equation.

$$3/2Q^* = 12 - 1/2Q^*$$
$$2Q^* = 12$$
$$Q^* = 6$$

To solve for the equilibrium price (P^*), substitute Q^* into the demand (or into the MSC) equation.

$$P^* = 12 - 1/2Q^*$$
$$P^* = 12 - 1/2\,(6)$$
$$P^* = 9$$

c Compared with the allocatively efficient outcomes, the unregulated market produces too much Flatulost (8 units versus 6) and the product sells at too low a price ($8 versus $9).

d The tax should be equal to the cost differential ($MSC - MPC$) at the optimum output of 6 units. Since the MSC curve = $1.5 \times MPC$ curve, the tax should be 50 percent.

4

PROBLEM

The Canadian Radio-television and Telecommunications Commission (CRTC) is holding public hearings on renewing the licence of Cretin's Choice Cable TV Company. You have been hired to help the CRTC evaluate the contradictory claims made by different interest groups in testimony to the commission. Figure P4.1 shows the best available information about costs and revenues for Cretin's Choice.

FIGURE **P4.1**

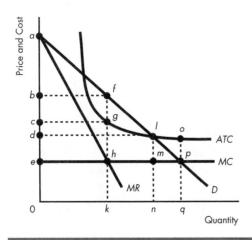

a   On the basis of Fig. P4.1, explain why there is market failure and a potential role for government regulation.

b   Cretin's Choice would like to maximize its profits. Identify the firm's profit-maximizing rule and explain the outcome (price, quantity, economic profit, consumer's surplus, deadweight loss) on Fig. P4.1.

c   Consumer groups are pushing for a regulatory rule that maximizes consumer surplus. Identify the rule and explain the outcome (price, quantity, economic profit, consumer's surplus) on Fig. P4.1. If the CRTC adopts the rule, what options might you suggest that would keep the cable company in business?

d   Any CRTC regulation rule has to appear to meet the public interest goal of maximum allocative efficiency. Identify the rule (other than marginal cost pricing) that comes closest to achieving this goal and explain the outcome (price, quantity, economic profit, consumer's surplus, deadweight loss) on Fig. P4.1.

e   While Cretin's Choice wants maximum profits, it recognizes the CRTC's need to *appear* to use the regulatory rule in part **d**. What argument can you expect to hear from Cretin's Choice? Use Fig. P4.1 to explain.

f   If, despite your advice to the contrary, the CRTC accepts the industry argument in part **e**, what theory of regulation is supported?

g   After years of the type of regulation in part **f**, the CRTC deregulates Cretin's Choice's market. If rates of return increase, what theory of regulation is supported?

MIDTERM EXAMINATION

You should allocate 32 minutes for this examination (16 questions, 2 minutes per question). For each question, choose the one *best* answer.

1 Refer to Fig. P4.2. Producer surplus lost from the tax (not including tax paid) is equal to triangle

a   *abc.*
b   *dbc.*
c   *dac.*
d   *dij.*
e   *gdi.*

FIGURE **P4.2**

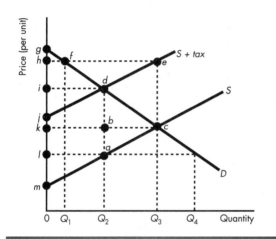

2 Refer to Fig. P4.2. Consumer surplus lost from the tax (not including tax paid) is equal to triangle

a   *abc.*
b   *dbc.*
c   *dac.*
d   *dij.*
e   *gdi.*

3 Total surplus is given by the sum of

a   the gain from trade accruing to consumers and the gain from trade accruing to producers.
b   the gain from regulation and the gain from anti-combine laws.
c   revenues received by firms and government subsidies.
d   consumer payments and producer profit.
e   none of the above.

4 Consider the natural monopoly in Fig. P4.3. Producer surplus is a maximum when quantity is

a Q_0 and price is P_3.
b Q_1 and price is P_1.
c Q_1 and price is P_4.
d Q_2 and price is P_2.
e Q_3 and price is P_0.

FIGURE **P4.3**

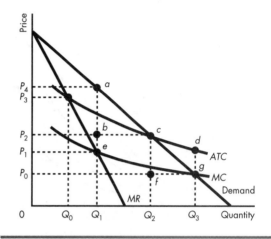

5 The inequality in the distribution of wealth is

a   less than the inequality in the distribution of income.
b   decreased by the existence of assortative mating.
c   a better measure of the inequality in the distribution of economic resources than is the inequality in the distribution of income.
d   even greater if we look at the distribution of wealth among the richest 1 percent of all families.
e   all of the above.

6 The demand for government intervention in a market depends on

a   consumer surplus per buyer.
b   number of buyers.
c   producer surplus per firm.
d   number of firms.
e   all of the above.

7 Consider the Lorenz curves in Fig. P4.4. Which point indicates that the richest 20 percent of families earn 60 percent of the income?

a   *a*
b   *b*
c   *c*
d   *d*
e   none of the above

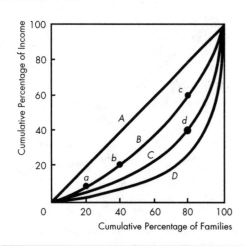

8 Refer to Fig. P4.5. The unregulated outcome in the paper market is

a   quantity = 40, price = 11.
b   quantity = 40, price = 13.
c   quantity = 50, price = 12.
d   quantity = 50, price = 14.
e   quantity = 60, price = 13.

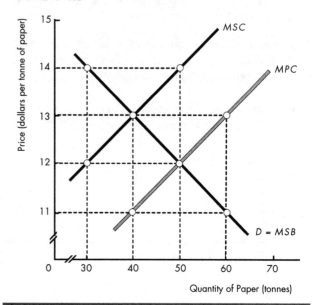

9 Refer to Fig. P4.5. A tax of _____ per tonne is necessary to achieve the efficient output of _____ tonnes of paper.

a $14; 50
b $14; 30
c $13; 40
d $2; 50
e $2; 40

10 The public interest theory predicts that the political process seeks to minimize

a   producer surplus.
b   consumer surplus.
c   total surplus.
d   deadweight loss.
e   allocative efficiency.

11 The factor of production least likely to display diminishing marginal productivity is

a   land.
b   labour.
c   capital.
d   entrepreneurship.
e   knowledge.

12 According to the Coase theorem, if transactions costs are low and property rights exist,

a negative externalities cause deadweight losses.

b positive externalities cause deadweight losses.

c private transactions are efficient.

d public transactions are efficient.

e the efficient level of pollution will be zero.

13 If the marginal tax rate decreases as income increases, the income tax is defined as

a progressive.

b proportional.

c negative.

d regressive.

e redistributive.

14 Which of the following is *not* part of an individual's true wealth?

a stock of assets

b flow of earnings

c human capital

d physical assets

e financial assets

15 The *total benefit* of a given level of provision of a public good can be obtained by

a adding the marginal benefit of each level of provision up to the given level.

b adding the marginal benefit of each level of provision and then subtracting the marginal cost of each level of provision.

c adding the net benefit of each level of provision up to the given level.

d multiplying net benefit by the quantity of the public good provided.

e none of the above methods.

16 Voters are asked to vote for either proposition *A* or proposition *B*. Proposition *A* will win if it

a is closer to allocative efficiency.

b is supported by bureaucrats.

c is preferred by the median voter.

d generates greater social benefits than social costs.

e generates the fewest negative externalities.

ANSWERS

Problem

a Market failure is the inability of an unregulated market to achieve allocative efficiency. Cretin's Choice is a natural monopoly with economies of scale. While only a monopoly can achieve the economies of scale, in the absence of regulation, it will restrict output, increase price, and create a deadweight efficiency loss.

b The profit-maximizing rule is to choose the quantity of output where $MC = MR$ and charge the highest possible price. On Fig. P4.1, price is *b*, quantity is *k*, economic profit is *bcgf*, consumer's surplus is *abf*, and deadweight loss is *fhp*.

c The marginal cost pricing rule (set price equal to MC) maximizes consumer surplus. On Fig. P4.1, price is *e*, quantity is *q*, loss per unit is *op*, and consumer's surplus is *aep*. The firm is making a loss and will not voluntarily stay in business. You could suggest that the company be allowed to price discriminate or that it receive a government subsidy (financed by taxes that would create a deadweight loss elsewhere).

d An average cost pricing rule sets price equal to ATC. On Fig. P4.1, price is *d*, quantity is *n*, economic profit is zero, consumer's surplus is *adl*, and deadweight loss is *lmp*. If this deadweight loss is less than the deadweight loss associated with subsidizing the marginal cost pricing rule in part **c**, then the average cost price rule comes closest to achieving allocative efficiency.

e Cretin's Choice will argue that their costs are much higher than those reflected in the ATC curve of Fig. P4.1. The company will inflate its costs and argue that its real ATC curve is higher and just tangent to the demand curve at point *f*. If the CRTC accepts this argument and applies the average cost pricing rule, the regulated price and outcome will be the same as the monopolist's own profit-maximizing rule in part **b**.

f If the CRTC accepts the industry argument in part **e**, the capture theory of regulation is supported.

g If, after deregulation, rates of return increase, the public interest theory of regulation is supported.

Midterm Examination

1	**a**	See text discussion. (427–429)
2	**b**	See text discussion. (427–429)
3	**a**	Consumer surplus plus producer surplus. (455–456)
4	**c**	Private monopoly outcome. (459–462)
5	**d**	Reverse **a, b** true. Wealth distribution does not capture human capital resources so **c** false. (437–438)
6	**e**	See text discussion. (456–457)
7	**d**	Moving from 80 percent to 100 percent of families (richest 20 percent) moves income from 40 percent to 100 percent of total (60 percent). (437–438)
8	**c**	Where $D = MSB$ intersects MPC. (485–486)
9	**e**	$2 per tonne tax (vertical distance between MPC and MSC) makes firm's MC equal to MSC. Output where $D = MSB$ intersects MSC. (485–486)
10	**d**	Or maximize allocative efficiency. (457–458)
11	**e**	Because of positive externalities. (488–489)
12	**c**	There are no externalities. Level of pollution where $MSB = MSC$. (482–483)
13	**d**	Definition. (443–444)
14	**b**	Flow of earnings is *income* from individual's stock of wealth. (437–438)
15	**a**	**b–d** involve irrelevant costs. (420–422)
16	**c**	50 percent of votes plus 1. (426–427)

Chapter 37

Trading with the World

Patterns and Trends in International Trade

◆ **Imports** are goods and services we buy from other countries, **exports** are what we sell to them.

- **Balance of trade** = value of exports − value of imports.
- If balance of trade > 0 → **net exporter**.
- If balance of trade < 0 → **net importer**.

◆ Canada's major export and import is motor vehicles.

◆ Trade includes trade in services, such as tourism → American vacationing in Banff is Canadian export.

◆ Our major trading partner is the United States.

Opportunity Cost and Comparative Advantage

Countries can produce anywhere on or inside production possibilities frontier (PPF).

◆ Slope of PPF = Δ *y*-axis variable/Δ *x*-axis variable = opportunity cost of one more *x*-axis variable.

◆ A country has **comparative advantage** in production of good for which it has lowest opportunity cost.

Gains from Trade

A country gains from trading by buying goods from other countries with lower opportunity costs and selling to other countries goods for which it has lowest opportunity cost.

◆ The post-trade price is between initial pre-trade opportunity costs of the two countries → buyer gains from price lower than their opportunity cost, seller gains from opportunity cost higher than their opportunity cost.

◆ Countries pay for their imports with their exports → the value of exports = the value of imports (in the absence of international borrowing).

◆ *Both* countries gain by specializing in production of goods in which they have a comparative advantage and trading for other goods → can therefore *consume outside* the PPF.

- Since post-trade prices different than pre-trade opportunity costs, production levels adjust → countries produce more of their exported good, less of imported good.

◆ Country has **absolute advantage** in all goods if it has higher productivity → can produce given output of all goods with less workers.

◆ Even with absolute advantage, if opportunity costs diverge between countries → everyone has comparative advantage in something and can gain from trade.

Gains from Trade in Reality

◆ Most trade can be explained by comparative advantage → but much trade is trade in similar goods, due to

- Diversified tastes → demand for many (similar) products.
- Economies of scale → cheapest way to make many products is specialization and trade.

◆ Increasing our imports benefits us and the exporting nation, but can create *adjustment costs* → lost jobs/wages for those in import-competing industries → leads to government intervention.

Trade Restrictions

Governments restrict trade to protect domestic industries → **protectionism**.

- Two methods of restriction—tariffs and nontariff barriers.

- Canada has always had tariffs, but they have ↓ since 1930s, under **General Agreement on Tariffs and Trade**, an international agreement to limit government trade restriction.

  - North American Free Trade Agreement with the United States and Mexico further ↓ barriers.

- **Tariffs** are taxes on imported goods → ↑ imported price → ↓ imports → ↑ domestic production → net losses to importing country because opportunity cost of domestic production > original import price.

- Tariffs → less imports in home country → exporters in foreign country sell fewer goods → ↓ income → ↓ foreign country imports = home country exports → no change in balance of trade (if there is no international borrowing).

- When tariffs ↑ lots in the 1930s → world trade collapsed.

- **Nontariff barriers** restrict supply of imports.

  - **Quotas** set import quantity restriction, with quota licences distributed by home country.
  - **Voluntary export restraints** (VERs) set export quantity restrictions, with foreign distributors having export licences.

- Quotas/VERs → ↓ import supply → ↑ domestic price → ↑ domestic production.

  - ↑ import prices → owning quotas profitable.
  - Quotas and tariffs have similar effects on price and quantity, difference is who gains profit = selling price – import price.

The Case Against Protection

Trade restrictions are used despite losses of gains from trade for three somewhat credible reasons.

- Protecting strategic industries achieves national security → but hard to identify which industries are strategic.

- Protecting **infant industries** allows them to mature and allows learning-by-doing spillovers. These seem unlikely in reality.

- Foreign companies may **dump** their products on world markets at prices less than cost in order to gain global monopoly.

  - But dumping is very hard to detect since costs are hard to determine.
  - **Countervailing duties** are tariffs imposed to discourage subsidized foreign companies.

- A country may restrict trade for the following less credible reasons:

  - to save jobs in import-competing industries → but free trade creates jobs elsewhere,
  - to compete with cheap foreign labour → but what counts is wages and productivity (comparative advantage),
  - to bring diversity and stability → but economic size provides this,
  - to penalize lax environmental standards → but trade and economic growth work better,
  - to prevent rich countries from exploiting developing countries → but this ignores comparative advantage.

- Major reason for trade restriction is to protect groups/industries that suffer disproportionately under freer trade.

  - Net gains from trade are positive, but there are losers in import-competing industries.
  - Some (incomplete) compensation of losers occurs from unemployment insurance.

The Canada–United States Free Trade Agreement

- Despite protectionism pressures, Canada has free trade agreement with the United States and Mexico, which involves

  - reducing common tariffs to zero in phases,
  - reducing nontariff barriers,
  - freer trade in energy and services,
  - future negotiations on subsidies,
  - a dispute-settling mechanism.

- Total effects of the agreement are unknown at the moment, but they do include

  - large ↑ in total volume of trade.
  - significant changes in some sectors → large adjustment costs.

H E L P F U L   H I N T S

1 This chapter applies the fundamental concepts of opportunity cost and comparative advantage discussed in Chapter 3 to the problem of trade between nations. The basic principles are the same for trade between individuals in the same country and between individuals in different countries.

   Many people involved in debates about trade seem confused by the concept of comparative advantage, partially because they implicitly consider *absolute advantage* as the sole reason for trade. A country has an absolute advantage if it can produce all goods using less inputs than another country. However, such a country can still gain from trade. Consider California and Saskatchewan. California has a better climate and, with widespread irrigation, has an absolute advantage in the production of all agricultural products. Indeed, California frequently has more than one harvest a year! This would seem to imply that California has no need to trade with Saskatchewan. Saskatchewan, however, has a *comparative advantage* in the production of wheat. Therefore California will specialize in fruits and trade them for wheat. California could easily grow its own wheat, but the opportunity cost would be too high—the lost fruit crops. By specializing and trading, both California and Saskatchewan can gain.

2 One of the most crucial results of this chapter is to understand that both countries can gain from trade. This gain occurs because the post-trade price is between the two countries' pre-trade opportunity costs. We can see this illustrated in Text Fig. 37.6, where the equilibrium price of a car is 3 tonnes of grain, between the pre-trade opportunity costs of 1 tonne and 9 tonnes.

   Students are often puzzled by where to put the price when working through these types of examples. How did the authors come up with the value of 3? In a sense, it is an arbitrary value, one they just plucked out of a hat. Given the logic of voluntary trade, it must be between the two pre-trade values of 1 and 9. However, by redrawing the export supply and the import demand curves with different slopes, the authors might have arrived at a value of 6 tonnes. This would have been equally logical, and equally valid.

   In the real world, the strength of the demand for specific products by the consumers of each country will determine the slopes of the export supply and import demand curves, and determine just where the equilibrium price is set. In your examples, you will either be able to pick where you want the price to be (given that it must be between the two pre-trade opportunity costs), or you will be given some specific information telling you where the price is.

3 One of the important things we learn about the economic effects of trade restrictions is that a tariff and a quota are the same. A voluntary export restraint (VER) is also a quota, but it is a quota imposed by the exporting country rather than by the importing country.

   All trade restrictions raise the domestic price of the imported goods and reduce the volume and value of imports. They also reduce the value of exports by the same amount as the reduction in the value of imports. The increase in price that results from each trade restriction produces a gap between the domestic price of the imported good and the foreign supply price of the good.

   The difference between the alternative trade restrictions lies in which party captures this excess. In the case of a tariff, the government receives the tariff revenue. In the case of a quota imposed by the importing country, domestic importers who have been awarded a licence to import capture this excess through increased profit. When a VER is imposed, the excess is captured by foreign exporters who have been awarded licences to export by their government.

4 The major point of this chapter is that gains from free trade can be considerable. Why then do countries have such a strong tendency to impose trade restrictions? The key is that while free trade creates overall benefits to the economy as a whole, there are both winners and losers. The winners gain more in total than the losers lose, but the latter tend to be concentrated in a few industries.

   Given this concentration, free trade will be resisted by some acting on the basis of rational self-interest. Even though only a small minority benefit while the overwhelming majority will be hurt, it is not surprising to see trade restrictions implemented. The cost of a given trade restriction to *each* of the majority will be individually quite small, while the benefit to *each* of the few will be individually large. Thus the minority will have a significant incentive to see that restriction takes place, while the majority will have little incentive to expend time and energy in resisting trade restriction.

5 To understand the source of pressures for trade restrictions, let us summarize those who win and lose from trade restrictions.

Under the three forms of restrictions (tariffs, quotas, and VERs) *consumers* lose, because the price of the imported good rises. *Domestic producers* of the imported good and their factors of production gain from all three, because the price of the imported good rises. *Foreign producers* and their factors of production lose under all three schemes, because their export sales fall. Under quotas and VERs, the *holders of import licences* gain from buying low and selling high (they may be foreign or domestic). *Government* gains tariff revenue under tariffs and, potentially, votes under other schemes.

Given this list, it is hardly surprising that the main supporters of trade restrictions are domestic producers and their factors of production.

S E L F - T E S T

True/False/Uncertain and Explain

1 Elected governments are slow to reduce trade restrictions because there would be many fewer losers than gainers.

2 Japan is dumping steel if it sells it in Japan at a lower price than it sells it in Canada.

3 If a country has an absolute advantage, it will not benefit from trade.

4 Countries may exchange similar goods with each other due to economies of scale in the face of diversified tastes.

5 When governments impose tariffs, they are increasing their country's gain from trade.

6 Trading according to comparative advantage allows all trading countries to consume outside their PPF.

7 If country A must give up 3 units of Y to produce 1 unit of X and B must give up 4 units of Y to produce 1 unit of X, then A has a comparative advantage in the production of X.

8 A tariff on a good will raise its price and reduce the quantity traded.

9 A quota will cause the price of the imported good to fall.

10 When a Canadian citizen stays in a hotel in France, Canada is exporting a service.

Multiple-Choice

1 Consider Table 37.1. Under free trade, the international price of donut holes would be $____ per hundred donut holes, and ____ million holes would be exchanged.
a 0.75; 6
b 1.00; 3
c 1.25; 4
d 1.25; 5
e 1.50; 4

TABLE **37.1** INTERNATIONAL TRADE IN DONUT HOLES

International Price (dollars per 100 holes)	Glazeland's Export Supply of Holes (millions)	Snorfleland's Import Demand for Holes (millions)
0.50	1	10
0.75	2	8
1.00	3	6
1.25	4	4
1.50	5	2
1.75	6	0

2 Consider Table 37.1. Snorfleland's donut hole producers manage to convince their government that there is a need to protect the domestic industry from Glazeland's cheap imports. (They argue that holes are a crucial food group.) In response, Snorfleland's government sets an import quota of 3 million donut holes. The resulting price of a donut hole in Snorfleland will be $_____ per hundred holes, and domestic production of donut holes will _____.

a 0.75; fall
b 0.75; rise
c 1.25; remain unchanged
d 1.38; rise
e 1.38; remain unchanged

3 Consider Table 37.1. Starting from the free-trade equilibrium, Glazeland's donut hole exporters convince their government that making donut holes is a way of life being threatened by the cruel vagaries of the international market and, therefore deserves to be subsidized. Glazeland's government responds by subsidizing donut hole production by $0.25 per hundred holes. The resulting *international price* will be approximately $_____ per hundred holes, and the quantity traded will be _____ million donut holes.

a 1.00; 4
b 1.00; 5
c 1.12; 4
d 1.12; 4.5
e 1.50; 5

4 Consider Table 37.1. Glazeland's government has subsidized donut hole production by $0.25 per hundred holes. Snorfleland's domestic producers have responded by filing a suit with the government that domestic production has been hurt by the unfair subsidy. Snorfleland's government responds by charging a countervailing duty on Glazeland donut holes of $0.25 per hundred holes. The *domestic* price in Snorfleland after the net effects of the subsidy and the countervailing duty will be $_____ per hundred holes, and Snorfleland will import _____ million holes.

a 1.00; 4
b 1.00; 5
c 1.12; 4
d 1.12; 5
e 1.25; 4

5 Refer to Fig. 37.1. The opportunity cost of 1 beer in Partyland is _____, and the opportunity cost of 1 beer in Cowabunga is _____.

a dependent on where on the PPF we measure it; dependent on where on the PPF we measure it
b 100 pizzas; 25 pizzas
c 3 pizzas; 1 pizza
d 1 pizza; 1 pizza
e 1 pizza; 1/3 pizza

FIGURE **37.1** PARTYLAND AND COWABUNGA—PPF FOR BEER AND PIZZA

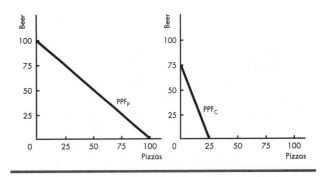

6 Refer to Fig. 37.1. The opportunity cost of 1 pizza in Partyland is _____, and the opportunity cost of 1 pizza in Cowabunga is _____.

a dependent on where on the PPF we measure it; dependent on where on the PPF we measure it
b 100 beers; 25 beers
c 3 beers; 1 beer
d 1 beer; 1 beer
e 1 beer; 3 beers

7 Refer to Fig. 37.1. If trade occurs between Partyland and Cowabunga,

a there will be a lot of drunk turtles.
b Partyland will supply both pizza and beer, because it has a comparative advantage in both.
c Cowabunga will supply both pizza and beer, because it has a comparative advantage in both.
d Partyland will supply pizza, and Cowabunga will supply beer.
e Partyland will supply beer, and Cowabunga will supply pizza.

8 Refer to Fig. 37.1. If trade occurs between Partyland and Cowabunga, the trade price for beer will be

a 1 beer for 1 pizza.
b 1 beer for 1/3 pizza.
c 1 beer for 3 pizzas.
d somewhere between 1 beer for 1 pizza and 1 beer for 3 pizzas.
e somewhere between 1 beer for 1 pizza and 1 beer for 1/3 pizza.

9 If Canada has imposed an import quota of one million pairs of shoes per year, an increase in the domestic demand for shoes will result in

a no change in the domestic prices of shoes, but an increase in the quantity of shoes imported.
b no change in the domestic prices of shoes or in the quantity of shoes imported.
c a rise in the domestic prices of shoes and in the quantity of shoes imported.
d a rise in the domestic prices of shoes and no change in the quantity of shoes imported.
e a rise in the domestic prices of shoes and an uncertain change in the quantity of shoes imported, depending on whether the increase in demand is greater than one million pairs or not.

10 When a *voluntary export restraint* agreement is reached, the gap between the domestic import price and the export price is captured by

a consumers in the importing country.
b the person with the right to import the good.
c the government of the importing country.
d foreign exporters.
e the domestic producers of the good.

11 The implementation of the Canada–United States Free Trade Agreement has revealed that

a Canada has been severely damaged by the agreement.
b Canada has been helped enormously by the agreement.
c free trade does not work.
d all losers from free trade will be compensated.
e there has been a large rise in the volume of international trade, benefiting consumers, but at the cost of a high rate of job destruction in the late 1980s and early 1990s.

12 If we import more than we export, then

a we will be unable to buy as many foreign goods as we desire.
b we will make loans to foreigners to enable them to buy our goods.
c we will have to finance the difference by borrowing from foreigners.
d our patterns of trade, including the direction of exports and imports, will be different than if exports equal imports.
e c and d.

13 If country *A* has an absolute advantage in the production of everything,

a no trade will take place because country *A* will have a comparative advantage in everything.
b no trade will take place because no country will have a comparative advantage in anything.
c trade will probably take place, and all countries will gain.
d trade will probably take place, but country *A* will not gain.
e trade will probably take place, but country *A* will be the only one to gain.

14 Which of the following is *not* an argument for protectionism?

a to protect strategic industries
b to save jobs in import-competing industries
c to gain a comparative advantage
d to allow infant industries to grow
e to prevent rich nations from exploiting poor nations

15 International trade based on comparative advantage allows each country to consume

a more of the goods it exports, but less of the goods it imports than without trade.
b more of the goods it imports, but less of the goods it exports than without trade.
c more of the goods it exports and imports than without trade.
d less of the goods it exports and imports than without trade.
e either a or b, depending on the price of the goods.

16 A tariff on good *X* which is imported by country *A* will cause the

a demand curve for *X* in country *A* to shift upward.

b demand curve for *X* in country *A* to shift downward.

c supply curve of *X* in country *A* to shift upward.

d supply curve of *X* in country *A* to shift downward.

e demand and the supply curve of *X* in country *A* to shift upward.

17 When a *quota* is imposed, the gap between the domestic price and the export price is captured by

a consumers in the importing country.

b the domestic producers of the good.

c the government of the importing country.

d foreign exporters.

e the person with the right to import the good.

18 Which of the following is a Canadian service export?

a A Canadian buys dinner while travelling in Switzerland.

b A Swiss buys a dinner while travelling in Canada.

c A Canadian buys a clock made in Switzerland.

d A Swiss buys a computer made in Canada.

e **a** and **b**.

19 Which of the following statements about international trade is *true*?

a Tariffs will increase jobs in our export industries.

b Quotas are better than tariffs because they do not raise prices.

c Tariffs are needed to allow us to compete with cheap foreign labour.

d No one gains from free trade between a poor country and a rich country.

e VERs raise prices as much as equivalent tariffs do.

20 In country *A*, 1 unit of capital and 1 unit of labour are required to produce 1 unit of *X*, and 2 units of capital and 2 units of labour are required to produce 1 unit of *Y*. What is the opportunity cost of good *X*?

a the price of 1 unit of capital plus the price of 1 unit of labour

b 1 unit of capital and 1 unit of labour

c 2 units of capital and 2 units of labour

d 1/2 unit of *Y*

e 2 units of *Y*

21 When a *tariff* is imposed, the gap between the domestic price and the export price is captured by

a consumers in the importing country.

b the person with the right to import the good.

c the domestic producers of the good.

d foreign exporters.

e the government of the importing country.

22 Country *A* and country *B* are currently engaging in free trade. Country *A* imports good *X* from country *B* and exports *Y* to *B*. If country *A* imposes a *quota* on *X*, country *A*'s *X*-producing industry will

a expand, and its *Y*-producing industry will contract.

b expand, and its *Y*-producing industry will expand.

c contract, and its *Y*-producing industry will contract.

d contract, and its *Y*-producing industry will expand.

e expand, and its *Y*-producing industry will be unchanged.

23 The imposition by country *A* of a tariff on imported goods from country *B* will increase the price consumers pay for imported goods and

a reduce the volume of imports and the volume of exports.

b reduce the volume of imports and increase the volume of exports.

c reduce the volume of imports and leave the volume of exports unchanged.

d will not affect either the volume of imports or the volume of exports.

e increase the volume of imports but decrease the volume of exports.

24 Which of the following is *most* responsible for significant reduction in trade restrictions since World War II?

a the Smoot–Hawley Act

b the voluntary exports restraint agreement between the United States and Japan

c the United Nations

d the General Agreement on Tariffs and Trade

e the Canada–United States Free Trade Agreement

25 Country *A* imports good *X* from country *B* and exports *Y* to *B*. Why would country *A* prefer arranging a voluntary export restraint rather than a quota on *X*?

a to not hurt country *B*'s imports
b to prevent country *B* from retaliating by restricting country *A*'s exports
c to keep the domestic price of *X* low
d to increase government revenue
e to help domestic producers

Short Answer Problems

1 Why can *both* parties involved in trade gain?

2 How does a tariff on a particular imported good affect the domestic price of the good, the export price, the quantity imported, and the quantity of the good produced domestically?

3 How does a tariff on imports affect the exports of the country?

4 It is often argued by union leaders that tariffs are needed to protect domestic jobs. In light of your answers to Short Answer Problems **2** and **3**, evaluate this argument.

5 Consider a simple world in which there are two countries, Atlantis and Beltran, each producing food and cloth. The PPF for each country is given in Table 37.2.
a Assuming a constant opportunity cost in each country, complete the table.
b What is the opportunity cost of food in Atlantis? of cloth?
c What is the opportunity cost of food in Beltran? of cloth?
d Draw the PPFs on separate graphs.

TABLE **37.2** ATLANTIS AND BELTRAN—PPF FOR FOOD AND CLOTH

Atlantis		Beltran	
Food (units)	Cloth (units)	Food (units)	Cloth (units)
0	500	0	800
200	400	100	600
400		200	
600		300	
800		400	
1,000		—	—

6 Suppose that Atlantis and Beltran engage in trade.
a In which good will each country specialize?
b If 1 unit of food trades for 1 unit of cloth, what will happen to the production of each good in each country?
c If 1 unit of food trades for 1 unit of cloth, draw the consumption possibility frontiers for each country on the corresponding graph from Short Answer Problem 5.
d Before trade, if Atlantis consumed 600 units of food, the most cloth it could consume was 200 units. After trade, how many units of cloth can be consumed if 600 units of food are consumed?

7 Continue the analysis of Atlantis and Beltran trading at the rate of 1 unit of food for 1 unit of cloth.
a If Atlantis consumes 600 units of food and 400 units of cloth, how much food and cloth will be consumed by Beltran?
b Given the consumption quantities and the production quantities from Short Answer Problem **6b**, how much food and cloth will Atlantis and Beltran import and export?

8 Figure 37.2 gives the import demand curve for shirts for country *A*, labelled *D*, and the export supply curve of shirts for country *B*, labelled *S*.
a What is the price of a shirt under free trade?
b How many shirts will be imported by country *A*?

FIGURE **37.2**

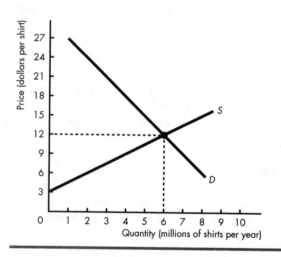

9 Suppose the shirtmakers in country *A* of Short Answer Problem **8** are concerned about foreign competition and, as a result, the government of country *A* imposes a tariff of $9 per shirt.

a What will happen to the price of a shirt in country *A*?

b What is the price the exporter will actually receive?

c How many shirts will be imported by country *A*?

d What is the revenue from the tariff? Who captures it?

10 Suppose that instead of a tariff, country *A* imposes a quota of 4 million shirts per year.

a What will be the price of a shirt in country *A*?

b What price will the exporter actually receive?

c How many shirts will be imported by country *A*?

d What is the difference between the total amount paid by consumers and the total amount received by exporters—the "excess profit"? Who captures it?

A N S W E R S

True/False/Uncertain and Explain

1 F They will be slow because losers' losses are individually much greater than winners' gains. (922)

2 F Dumping would be selling in Canada at lower price than in Japan. (919)

3 U If comparative advantage exists → gains from trade exist. (910)

◑ 4 T Diversified tastes → many products demanded. Economies of scale → cheaper method of production, but requires specialization and trade. (911–912)

5 F Trade restrictions reduce gains from trade → cost of purchasing export < current benefit → lost gains from trade. (914–916)

6 T Countries will specialize and trade to consume outside PPF. (908–909)

◑ 7 T *A* has a lower opportunity cost ($3Y < 4Y$ = lost *Y* per unit of gained *X*. (905–906)

8 T Tariff → shift up in export supply curve → ↑ price and ↓ quantity traded. (914–915)

9 F Quota ↓ supply → ↑ price. (916–917)

10 F Canada is importing (using) a service. (903)

Multiple-Choice

1 c Equilibrium is where export supply = import demand. (914)

2 d Equilibrium is where quota = import demand → ↑ price. Higher domestic price → ↑ domestic production. (916–917)

◑ 3 d Subsidy ↑ Glazeland's export supply by 1 million at each price → new equilibrium where new supply = old demand. (916–917)

◑ 4 e In addition to the change from 3, tariff → ↓ export supply by 1 million, exactly offsetting the subsidy. (914)

5 e Opportunity cost of 1 more beer = lost pizza. For Partyland, going from 0 beer to 25 beers costs 25 pizzas → one for one. Do same calculation for Cowabunga. (905–906)

6 e Same type of calculation as in **5**. (905–906)

7 d Each specializes in where they have comparative advantage (lowest opportunity cost). (906)

◑ 8 e Trade price is between the opportunity costs in each country at the pre-trade equilibrium. (907)

9 d Quota → fixed maximum import quantity. Therefore if ↑ demand → ↑ price. (916–917)

10 d Because they have right to export. (917)

11 e See text discussion. (923–924)

12 c Necessary in order to get foreign exchange. General patterns of trade unchanged, once we have enough dollars. (904)

13 c Absolute advantage in everything → comparative advantage in only some goods. (910)

14 c See text discussion. (918–921)

15 c Consumption possibilities frontier is outside PPF. (908–909)

16 c Tariff → ↑ domestic price = export price + tariff → shift upward of supply curve. (914–915)

17 e Under quota, domestic government allocates the licence to import. (916–917)

18 b a and c → import, d → export of a good. (903)

19 e Tariffs ↓ exports and jobs in export industries, quotas restrict supply → ↑ prices, cheap foreign labour doesn't necessarily hurt us, poor and rich countries can have comparative advantage and gain from trade. VERs restrict supply and raise prices just like tariffs. (914–917)

◑ 20 d Inputs required to make one *X* could make $1/2Y$. (905–906)

21 e They collect tariff revenue = import price − export price. (914–915)

22 a Quota → ↓ imports → ↑ domestic price of X
→ ↑ domestic production. ↓ imports = ↓ B's
exports → ↓ its income → ↓ its imports
→ ↓ A's exports → ↓ Y production in A.
(916–917)

23 a Tariff → ↑ domestic price of imports → ↓
imports → ↑ domestic production. ↓ imports
= ↓ B's exports → ↓ its income → ↓ its
imports → ↓ A's exports → ↓ export
production in A. (914–919)

24 d See text discussion. (912–913)

25 b Under a VER → exporting country gains
excess revenue → less likely to retaliate, since
hurt less. (916–917)

Short Answer Problems

1 For two potential trading partners to be willing
to trade, they must have different comparative
advantages; that is, different opportunity costs.
Then they will trade and both parties will gain.
If the parties do not trade, each will face its own
opportunity costs. A price at which trade takes
place must be somewhere between the
opportunity costs of the two traders. This means
that the party with the lower opportunity cost of
the good in question will gain because it will
receive a price above its opportunity cost.
Similarly, the party with the higher opportunity
cost will gain because it will pay a price below its
opportunity cost.

2 A tariff on an imported good will *raise its price to
domestic consumers* as the export supply curve
shifts upward. The export price is determined by
the original export supply curve. As the domestic
price of the good rises, the quantity of the good
demanded falls, and thus the relevant point on
the original export supply curve is at a lower
quantity and a *lower export price*. This lower
quantity means that the quantity imported falls.
The rise in the domestic price will also lead to
an *increase in the quantity of the good supplied
domestically*.

3 When country A imposes a tariff on its imports
of good X, not only does the volume of imports
shrink, but the volume of exports of Y to
country B will shrink by the same amount. Thus
a balance of trade is maintained. As indicated in
the answer to Short Answer Problem 2, the
export price of good X received by country B
and the quantity exported falls when a tariff is
imposed. This fall in the price and the quantity
exported means that the income of country B
has fallen. This implies that the quantity of Y

(A's export) demanded by country B will fall and
thus A's exports decline.

4 This argument has some partial truth to it. As
Short Answer Problem 2 shows, the tariff will
lead an increase in domestic production of the
protected good, which will lead to an increase in
jobs in that industry. However, as Short Answer
Problem 3 shows, the same tariff will reduce
foreign income, and reduce foreign purchases of
our goods, reducing our exports and our export
production, reducing jobs in the export industry.
The net effect on jobs in unclear, but is
definitely not large.

5 a Completed Table 37.2 is shown here as Table
37.2 Solution. The values in the table are
calculated using the opportunity cost of each
good in each country. See **b** and **c** below.

TABLE **37.2** SOLUTION
ATLANTIS AND BELTRAN—PPF FOR FOOD AND CLOTH

Atlantis		Beltran	
Food (units)	Cloth (units)	Food (units)	Cloth (units)
0	500	0	800
200	400	100	600
400	300	200	400
600	200	300	200
800	100	400	0
1,000	0	—	—

b To increase the output (consumption) of food by
200 units, cloth production (consumption) falls
by 100 units in Atlantis. Thus the opportunity
cost of a unit of food is 1/2 unit of cloth. This
opportunity cost is constant as are all others in
this problem, for simplicity. Similarly, the
opportunity cost of cloth in Atlantis is 2 units of
food.

c In Beltran a 100-unit increase in the production
(consumption) of food requires a reduction in
the output (consumption) of cloth of 200 units.
Thus the opportunity cost of food is 2 units of
cloth. Similarly the opportunity cost of cloth in
Beltran is 1/2 units of food.

d Figure 37.3(a) and (b) illustrate the production possibility frontiers for Atlantis and Beltran, respectively labelled PPF_A and PPF_B. The rest of the diagram is discussed in the solutions to Short Answer Problems 7 and **8**.

FIGURE **37.3**

(a)   **(b)**

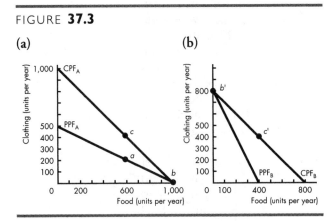

6 a We see from the solution to Short Answer Problems **5b** and **c** that Atlantis has a lower opportunity cost (1/2 unit of cloth) in the production of food. Therefore Atlantis will specialize in the production of food. Beltran, with the lower opportunity cost for cloth (1/2 unit of food), will specialize in cloth.

b Each country will want to produce every unit of the good in which they specialize as long as the amount they receive in trade exceeds their opportunity cost. For Atlantis, the opportunity cost of a unit of food is 1/2 unit of cloth, but it can obtain 1 unit of cloth in trade. Because the opportunity cost is constant, Atlantis will totally specialize by producing all of the food it can: 1,000 units per year, point *b* in Fig. 37.3(a). Similarly, in Beltran, the opportunity cost of a unit of cloth is 1/2 unit of food but a unit of cloth will trade for 1 unit of food. Since the opportunity cost is constant, Beltran will totally specialize in the production of cloth and will produce 800 units per year, point *b'* in Fig. 37.3(b).

c The consumption possibility frontiers for Atlantis and Beltran, labelled CPF_A and CPF_B, are illustrated in Fig. 37.3(a) and (b), respectively. These frontiers are straight lines that indicate all the combinations of food and cloth that can be consumed with trade. The position and slope of the consumption possibility frontier for an economy depend on the terms of trade between the goods (one for one in this example) and the production point of the economy.

The consumption possibility frontier for Atlantis (CPF_A), for example, is obtained by starting at point *b* on PPF_A, the production point, and examining possible trades. For example, if Atlantis traded 400 units of the food it produces for 400 units of cloth, it would be able to consume 600 units of food (1,000 units produced minus 400 units traded) and 400 units of cloth, which is represented by point *c*.

d If Atlantis consumes 600 units of food, trade allows consumption of cloth to be 400 units, 200 units more than possible without trade. The maximum amount of cloth that can be consumed without trade is given by the production possibility frontier. If food consumption is 600 units, this is indicated by point *a* on PPF_A. The maximum amount of cloth consumption for any level of food consumption with trade is given by the consumption possibility frontier. If food consumption is 600 units, this is indicated by point *c* on CPF_A.

7 a Since Atlantis produces 1,000 units of food per year (point *b* on PPF_A), to consume 600 units of food and 400 units of cloth (point *c* on CPF_A) it must trade 400 units of food for 400 units of cloth. This means that Beltran has traded 400 units of cloth for 400 units of food. Since Beltran produces 800 units of cloth, this suggests that Beltran must consume 400 units of food and 400 units of cloth (point *c'* on CPF_B).

b Atlantis exports 400 units of food per year and imports 400 units of cloth. Beltran exports 400 units of cloth per year and imports 400 units of food.

8 a The price of a shirt under free trade will occur at the intersection of country *A*'s import demand curve for shirts and country *B*'s export supply curve for shirts. This occurs at a price of $12 per shirt.

b Country *A* will import 6 million shirts per year.

9 a The effect of the $9 per shirt tariff is to shift the export supply curve (S) upward by $9. This is shown as a shift from S to S' in Fig. 37.2 Solution. The price is now determined by the intersection of the D curve, which is unaffected by the tariff, and the S' curve. The new price of a shirt is $18.

FIGURE **37.2** SOLUTION

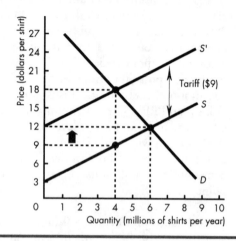

b Of this $18, $9 is the tariff, so the exporter only receives the remaining $9.

c Country A will now import only 4 million shirts per year.

d The tariff revenue is $9 (the tariff per shirt) × 4 million (the number of shirts imported), which is $36 million. This money is received by the government of country A.

10 a The quota restricts the quantity that can be imported to 4 million shirts per year regardless of the price and is represented by a vertical line in Fig. 37.4 (which corresponds to Fig. 37.2). The market for shirts will thus clear at a price of $18 per shirt.

FIGURE **37.4**

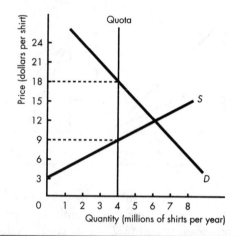

b This $18 price is received by the people who are given the right to import shirts under the quota. The amount received by the exporter is $9, given by the height of the S curve at a quantity of 4 million shirts per year.

c Country A will import 4 million shirts per year, the quota limit.

d The "excess profit" is $9 per shirt (the $18 received by the importer minus the $9 received by the exporter) × 4 million shirts, which is $36 million. This is captured by the importers who have been rewarded by the government of country A because they have been given the right to import under the quota. This is essentially a right to make an "excess profit."